GEORGE T. RUBY

OTHER BOOKS BY CARL H. MONEYHON

Edmund J. Davis: Civil War General, Republican Leader, Reconstruction Governor

Texas after the Civil War: The Struggle of Reconstruction

Portraits of Conflict: A Photographic History of the Civil War in Texas (coauthor)

Arkansas and the New South, 1874–1929

The Impact of the Civil War and Reconstruction on Arkansas, 1850–1874: Persistence in the Midst of Ruin

Republicanism in Reconstruction Texas

GEORGE T. RUBY

Champion of Equal Rights in Reconstruction Texas

CARL H. MONEYHON

THE TEXAS BIOGRAPHY SERIES | NUMBER SIX
A Joint Project of the Center for Texas Studies at TCU
and TCU Press
Fort Worth, Texas

Library of Congress Cataloging-in-Publication Data

Names: Moneyhon, Carl H., 1944-– author.
Title: George T. Ruby : champion of equal rights in reconstruction Texas / Carl H. Moneyhon.
Description: Fort Worth : Center for Texas Studies and TCU Press, [2020] | Series: The Texas biography series ; number 6 | Includes bibliographical references and index. | Summary: "This is the biography of George T. Ruby, an African American statesman who was active in Texas politics and fought for equal rights for black freedmen in Reconstruction Texas"— Provided by publisher.
Identifiers: LCCN 2019045320 (print) | LCCN 2019045321 (ebook) | ISBN 9780875657486 (cloth) | ISBN 9780875657769 (ebook)
Subjects: LCSH: Ruby, George Thompson, 1841–1882. | African American state legislators—Texas—Biography. | African Americans—Texas—Politics and government. | Reconstruction (U.S. history, 1865–1877)—Texas. | African Americans—Texas—History—19th century. | Freedmen—Texas—History. | Texas—Politics and government—1846–1865. | Texas—Politics and government—1865–1950.
Classification: LCC F391.R87 M66 2020 (print) | LCC F391.R87 (ebook) | DDC 976.4/05092 [B]—dc23
LC record available at https://lccn.loc.gov/2019045320
LC ebook record available at https://lccn.loc.gov/2019045321

TCU Press

TCU Box 298300
Fort Worth, Texas 76129
817.257.7822
www.prs.tcu.edu
To order books: 1.800.826.8911

Design by David Timmons

For my devoted wife, Susan Petty Moneyhon

THE TEXAS BIOGRAPHY SERIES

George T. Ruby: Champion of Equal Rights in Reconstruction Texas, by Carl H. Moneyhon

Tejano Tiger: José de los Santos Benavides and the Texas-Mexico Borderlands, 1823–1891, by Jerry Thompson

Adele Briscoe Looscan: Daughter of the Republic, by Laura Lyons McLemore

Fighting Stock: John S. "Rip" Ford of Texas, by Richard B. McCaslin

Edmund J. Davis of Texas: Civil War General, Republican Leader, Reconstruction Governor, by Carl H. Moneyhon

Emily Austin of Texas: 1795–1851, by Light Townsend Cummins

CONTENTS

EDITOR'S FOREWORD

Through its rich and colorful history, Texas has been home to countless fascinating figures. Some of the state's great works of historical literature, such as Eugene C. Barker's biography of Stephen F. Austin and Marquis James's study of Sam Houston, have chronicled the lives of Texas's larger-than-life leaders. Yet there remain many important personalities who have not yet found their biographer, and many more whose stories are in need of fresh examination in a scholarly biography. The Texas Biography Series, jointly published by the TCU Press and the Center for Texas Studies at TCU, offers a venue for telling their stories. From its inception, the series has sought to depart from the traditional "great man" approach—an approach that in Texas too often has really meant "great white men on horseback." Although the series certainly includes biographies of nineteenth-century political and military leaders, it also strives to encourage biographers to examine the full range of historical actors who have shaped the destiny of the Lone Star State, including women, members of racial and ethnic minorities, as well as figures from the worlds of business, the arts, science, religion, and even sports. In doing so, the series aims to keep the field of Texas history vital and relevant in the twenty-first century.

The sixth volume in the series, Carl Moneyhon's biography of George T. Ruby, fulfills several of these goals. Ruby, a New England-born educator and editor, was among the first major African American political leaders of Texas. Elected to the state senate as a Republican in 1869, he fought for political and economic equality of all Texans, including the recently emancipated slaves of his Galveston-based district. Although the bold experiment in racial equality that he helped to lead ultimately failed, Ruby's story brings into sharp relief the complex issues of post-Civil War Texas. Masterfully researched and skillfully written by the leading scholar of Texas Reconstruction, this book serves as a bold corrective to the myths and misconceptions that many Americans still hold about that volatile era. At a time when race continues to occupy a central place in American life, this insightful volume reminds us that African Americans have never been bystanders in our political struggles.

This book and its predecessors in the Texas Biography Series owe their existence to several important institutions. TCU Press and its staff continue to furnish the editorial and production expertise to create books equal to those of the leading national publishing houses. The Center for Texas Studies at TCU is a critical partner in launching, funding, and publicizing the series. And finally, Houston Endowment, the Summerlee Foundation, and the Carl and Florence King Foundation have provided generous grants to underwrite the costs of the series. As editor, I am grateful to all of these partners who continue to make the series a success.

Gregg Cantrell
Erma and Ralph Lowe Chair in Texas History
Texas Christian University

ACKNOWLEDGMENTS

This biography of George T. Ruby grew out of research carried out over almost five decades. As a result I owe a debt to dozens of people who have assisted me over that time. The staffs of the various libraries and archives provided essential help. I am particularly obligated to the staffs at the Briscoe Center for American History at the University of Texas at Austin, where the largest trove of Ruby materials is located in the James P. Newcomb Papers. Staff members at the National Archives in Washington, DC, introduced me to the papers of the Bureau of Refugees, Freedmen, and Abandoned Lands that contained materials essential to understanding Ruby's early career with that agency. I also appreciate the staffs at the National Archives in Fort Worth, Texas, and the University of North Texas, where I was able to reexamine the Bureau records on microfilm long after I had seen them in manuscript. The staff at the Texas State Library and Archives Commission guided me through the many state papers necessary to provide a broader context for Ruby's career. I owe particular thanks to the staff in Special Collections at William & Mary College who helped me locate rare copies of Ruby's Louisiana newspaper.

As usual there are numerous intellectual obligations, sadly to some who are no longer with us. Llerena Friend introduced me to Texas history when I was an undergraduate at the University of Texas. John Hope Franklin broadened that knowledge and focused me on Reconstruction at the University of Chicago. Barry Crouch and James Smallwood were not only intellectual colleagues but also friends. I miss the discussion and argument over Reconstruction issues that often occupied our times together at conferences.

Others remain sources of inspiration and assistance. Donaly Brice, formerly with the Texas State Library and Archives in Austin, has always provided help beyond the call of duty, even temporarily abandoning his retirement in rural Texas to go back to Austin to run down sources for me. His work on the Texas State Police also added to the framework within which I interpreted Ruby. Patrick Williams of the University of Arkansas, Fayetteville, read parts of this manuscript and provided his usual incisive comments. Several of my colleagues at the University of Arkansas at Little Rock also read parts of the manuscript and added to my interpretation of Ruby. Special thanks are owed to Brian Mitchell, whose knowledge of Louisiana steered me through the complex politics of his native state, allowing me to avoid serious misreading of Ruby's life there. Brian also alerted me to the broader framework of Ruby's Masonic connections. Charles Romney helped me place Ruby in a broader context. A general thanks goes to the Works in Progress group at UA Little Rock for their support as this project took shape.

I also want to thank Gregg Cantrell, the editor of TCU Press's Texas Biography Series, for his encouragement and also his considerable editorial assistance in the manuscript's development. I also appreciate the contribution to this manuscript by the press's anonymous reader. Sometimes, readers for a press have their own agendas when reading a manuscript, and their suggestions are not particularly helpful. That was not true here. The reader provided particularly useful suggestions and criticisms that I hope I have dealt with, and I believe the manuscript has greatly benefited from the reader's insights. Let me also thank the staff at TCU Press, particularly Kathy Walton, Molly Spain, and Melinda Esco, for their contribution to the publication of Ruby's story.

I owe a particular obligation to Bob Greene of Portland, Maine. He is a descendant of Sophia Ruby, the sister of George Ruby's father, Reuben. A former journalist, he is now working on his family history, and he provided me with otherwise unobtainable information on George Ruby's family background. He has generously shared that information with me and made sure that I have the early history correct. His suggestions made possible a search for further information that made the first chapter of this book possible.

My wife Susan Petty Moneyhon deserves more than a paragraph of thanks. She cheerfully put up with a husband who disappeared into his office each morning to write, reappearing only about cocktail time. I am not sure she saw that coming in a later-in-life marriage. In addition, I shamelessly took advantage of her editorial experience. To ask a spouse to read a manuscript of this size, mark it up, and make suggestions for its improvement is a risky business. Susan happily undertook the job and brought her considerable skills as an editor to the task. Her insights have, I think, helped make this a better manuscript. I cannot say how much I appreciate her.

George T. Ruby in 1873 (Photo courtesy of DeGolyer Library, Southern Methodist University, Texas: Photographs, Manuscripts, and Imprints).

INTRODUCTION

On June 17, 1870, George Thompson Ruby, an African American senator from Galveston, took the floor in the Texas State Senate to argue in favor of a militia bill backed by Republican Governor Edmund J. Davis. Introduced along with another bill to create a state police force, the governor intended these measures to help suppress the violence against freedmen that had plagued the state since the end of the Civil War, and Ruby strongly supported it. The bill had strong opposition, even among some Republican senators, that threatened its passage. Some opponents charged that it violated the state constitution because it subordinated the civil authority to the military. Ruby would have none of their argument, responding that the governor, head of the civil government, controlled the militia. Even if the bill pushed the limit of the constitution, Ruby saw no alternative. "[W]e are," he began, "the active participants in a great revolution, none greater than which has ever existed in the history of any government the world over." In the midst of revolution men had to sometimes do things revolutionary. Ruby quoted the words of the English parliamentarian and lawyer John Maynard, from Thomas Babington Macaulay's *History of England*, to support his contention. Maynard justified England's Glorious Revolution and the replacement of King James II with William of Orange and supposedly said that years of civil war had taught him that questions of highest interest to the people were "not to be decided by verbal cavils and by scraps of law French and law Latin." "We are," Maynard said in a sentiment Ruby believed appropriate to his own time, "at this moment out of the beaten path. If therefore, we are determined to move only in that path, we cannot move at all. A man in a revolution resolving to do nothing, which is not strictly according to established form, resembles a man who has lost himself in the wilderness, and who stands crying, 'Where is the King's highway? I will walk nowhere but in the King's highway.'" Ruby insisted that in great emergencies the safety of the state and its people was the highest law. Ruby saw "no other course" than to pass the militia bill.[1]

Ruby's remarks clearly identified the revolution taking place during Reconstruction. He saw it in the framework of other revolutions in history. His path to that moment on the senate floor, to the erudition that informed his remarks, and to participation in significant events in state, regional, and even national affairs could not have been predicted only ten years before. A fervent belief in the equality of blacks with whites and a desire to see that equality recognized guided his way. A basic outline of his life shows the stops and starts that journey involved. Born in New York and reared in Maine, Ruby came to Texas after attempting to create a black community in Haiti and working among the freedmen as a teacher in Louisiana. Ruby arrived in Texas in 1867 and worked as a teacher in the schools created by the Bureau of Refugees, Freedmen, and Abandoned Lands. He quickly established himself as a spokesman for the local black community. That role led him to prominence in local Republican politics after 1867, where he helped to organize black voters to support that party. Those voters, in turn, helped elect him to the state's constitutional convention of 1868–1869. In the convention he embraced the Radical faction of the Republican Party and pressured it to support programs that protected and empowered black Texans. While in the convention he gained even greater power when members of the state's Loyal League elected him to be president of the organization's state council, an accomplishment that marked his emergence as a spokesman for blacks across the state. He continued his efforts on behalf of black Texans when elected to the state senate in 1869, championing the creation of a state police force and militia to protect blacks, the forming of a public school system that offered blacks a chance for increased opportunity, and the passage of laws demanding equal treatment before the law and in public accommodations. His last contribution to the state's Republican Party came in 1873, when he chaired the party's state executive committee in the election that year. Ultimately, the refusal of white Democrats to accept a black man as an equal and their appeal to the racism of many white voters led to his political demise and the reversal of many of the causes that he championed. He fought on, moving to Louisiana, where he continued his fight for equality. During his life he offered Texans and Americans a different vision of the future in terms of race relations. Although he died at the relatively young age of forty-two, throughout that life he never retreated from his effort to create a nation that accepted the political and what he thought of as the social equality of his race.

While the outline of Ruby's life is known, little is known about his background, his family, the stands that he took on the issues of his day, or how he gained, maintained, and then lost power. The perspectives of previous historians and the lack of primary sources help to explain the lack of depth in our knowledge of Ruby. The racist views of the first generation of professional historians to write about Reconstruction meant that they largely overlooked him. The first scholar to say anything at all about Ruby was Charles W. Ramsdell. Ramsdell studied with William Archibald Dunning at Columbia University and embraced his mentor's interpretation of blacks in Reconstruction that characterized them as virtually incapable of self-government and his view of Reconstruction as a time in which a rapacious and corrupt group of carpetbaggers and scalawags manipulated black voters to control southern governments in their self-interest. Ramsdell incorporated this point of view into his history of Reconstruction in the state, even though he avoided much of the outright racism of many of his fellow students. Still, Ramsdell saw Reconstruction as a period of "arbitrary rule" by Edmund J. Davis, Republican governor. Davis, according to Ramsdell, surrounded himself with "unprincipled adventurers" who employed methods of government that "aroused resistance and hatred" from his political opponents. For Ramsdell, blacks counted only as a voting base for these unprincipled whites. George Ruby, in this interpretation, deserved little mention other than a reference as "a mulatto carpet-bagger from New England, a man of some ability and fair education, who generally led the negroes [sic] and threw this influence with the white carpet-baggers for the ultra-radical policies." Ramsdell's study carried the story of Reconstruction up to the state's readmission into the Union in 1870, and one of his students, W. C. Nunn, continued coverage up to the end of Reconstruction in 1874. Although published fifty years after Ramsdell's work, Nunn's study embraced Ramsdell's interpretation of Ruby. Like Ramsdell, he found Ruby to be the "most prominent Negro" among the state's black politicians and a "man of some ability," then relegated him to a footnote.[2]

Ruby's reputation changed with the development of a revisionist interpretation of Reconstruction. Almost as soon as the Dunning School studies appeared, African American historians such as Alrutheus Ambush Taylor, David G. Houston, and W. E. B. DuBois challenged the Dunningite conclusions with their own works, which emphasized the agency of the freedmen and the good character of black leaders. By the 1930s white historians joined in with the rehabilitation of black politicians, helping to produce what Howard Rabinowitz called the "Rehabilitation School." These revisionist scholars examined the lives of black politicians and found they hardly looked like the characters described by the Dunning historians. Rabinowitz pointed in particular to Robert Hilliard Woody's study of Jonathan Jasper Wright, an associate justice of the South Carolina supreme court, and the first full-length biography of a black Reconstruction leader, as a "landmark" in the process. Woody's study of White showed the justice to be a competent, capable, moderate politician, thus challenging the Dunningite view. By the 1950s and the development of the civil rights movement, this interpretation of Reconstruction and the role of blacks dominated professional scholarship. In Texas, a reinterpretation of black leadership began with J. Mason Brewer's 1935 study of black legislators, then continued with studies in the Rehabilitation School. This new approach brought a focus on black leaders in Texas and particularly on George Ruby.[3]

Works on Ruby generally fit within the Rehabilitation School and sought to expand the basic details of Ruby's career. Randall B. Woods's 1974 article on Ruby's career in the state legislature was the first serious effort at determining his role in state politics. In that article Woods focused particularly on Ruby's efforts in the state senate from 1870 to 1873 to pursue an agenda favorable to both his black constituency and white business interests in Galveston. He concluded that because he "well and faithfully" represented the white business community, he was allowed latitude in pressing the cause of civil rights. My own 1982 treatment of Ruby again focused primarily on his activity as a legislator. It emphasized his dedication to securing economic opportunity and full civil rights for his black constituency and argued that to obtain those ends he became a consummate politician, shifting alliances throughout his career in ways to best reach his goals. A year later James Smallwood published another article on Ruby, again focusing on his years in the state senate and emphasizing the fact that he did not fit the stereotypical view of a "corrupt carpetbagger" but was throughout his term in office "scrupulously honest." Smallwood noted the difficulty of writing about men like Ruby, observing that little primary evidence existed about their lives, thus making historical assessments of them "difficult."[4]

Use of the manuscript papers of the Bureau of Refugees, Freedmen, and Abandoned Lands in the National Archives made later work on Ruby possible and resulted in two articles by Barry A. Crouch in 1996 and 1997. Since Ruby worked as a teacher and then an agent with the bureau, this massive collection offered insights into parts of his career not previously explored. Crouch's first article investigated Ruby's activities prior to his election to the Texas Constitutional Convention of 1868 and concluded that his work with the bureau in Louisiana and Texas familiarized him with "southern mores and white attitudes" and provided him with a training ground for his later political career. Further, it allowed him to establish ties with the local black community that then gave him a voting constituency once he sought office. A second article that focused on Ruby's work with the bureau in Louisiana drew similar conclusions to those Crouch made in his first article, that Ruby's experiences provided him with the knowledge needed for political success. Even with the records of the bureau, however, Crouch found that questions remained. In particular, he noted that what brought him to the South "remains a mystery, like so many aspects of his life."[5]

Merline Pitre synthesized this previous work in the chapter on Ruby that appeared in her book of essays on black leaders in Texas but raised additional questions about what we know about Ruby. Pitre, like previous scholars, recognized the extent to which Ruby did not fit the stereotype of black political leaders that had been developed by the Dunning School. In her conclusion, however, Pitre saw something not observed in the previous works. Pitre believed, unlike Woods in particular, that Ruby failed to balance out his work in the interest of conservative businessmen with his work supporting black constituents. In her view, he seemed over time to be at odds with important black leaders in Galveston, and once in power he may have forgotten the issues important to black Texans. In fact, Pitre observed, while Ruby fought for the rights of blacks, "it appears that at times he had problems identifying with them." This insight was based largely on one letter complaining that Ruby was not a favorite of Galveston's black community, but Pitre's conclusion brought into question the degree to which Ruby actually represented the men who voted for him.[6]

Revisionist historians reshaped how we think of George Ruby, but, as previously noted, this work consisted of what Rabinowitz called "Rehabilitation History." Such work showed that Ruby was not as the Dunning scholars portrayed him to be, but rather he fit the type characterized by Robert Woody. An additional problem with this work is that all of these studies ultimately had a narrow focus, leaving large parts of Ruby's story untold. As a result of these studies we now know what Ruby did at particular times, but we know little about his origins, what motivated him, his basic views on the issues of his time, or how he secured and exercised power in the many roles that he filled. The limited number of primary sources dealing with Ruby's life helps to account for this lack. Ruby left no personal letters. Those around him who did leave documents provided no real insights.

Crouch noted that even the papers of the Freedmen's Bureau, in the end, left many questions about Ruby unanswered.[7]

The following work seeks to answer many of the unanswered questions about George Ruby in this first full biography of his life. The revolution in the internet and the digitization of newspapers, manuscripts, and previously hard-to-find books has made possible the uncovering of new information on Ruby not used before. Combined with traditional archival materials, these sources opened the way to looking more deeply into Ruby's life. Sadly, for the author, almost all of these sources are written by outsiders who described or tried to explain Ruby. As a result the inner Ruby and particularly his personal relationships remain somewhat of a mystery. Even the few writings of his own, largely formal or professional, provide only glimpses of the man behind the public figure. Still, this work seeks not only to expand the details of his life but also to illuminate the origins of his world view, the development of his political ideas, his relationships with white politicians, and his connection to the black constituents he represented. This book is unquestionably revisionist in its interpretive framework and certainly in its rehabilitation history, yet it seeks to add to our understanding of the complexity of the life of a man who took the floor of the senate on that June 17 and spoke of a world in the midst of a revolution that he hoped would lead to a better life for his race.

CHAPTER I

FAMILY BACKGROUND OF GEORGE RUBY

A young man of fine natural abilities, well educated, and . . . a gentleman in the best sense of the term.—Portland Daily Press, *October 8, 1870, on George Ruby when he graduated from high school*

To understand George Thompson Ruby and the principles and values that guided him through his career, the story must begin with a look at his family. Born in New York City on July 1, 1840, Ruby was the fifth son and the sixth child of Reuben and Rachel Ruby. His father was a well-known African American activist who participated in many of the reform movements of the antebellum era, demanding equal rights for blacks in the North, agitating for abolition, and working to promote black self-help. His mother advocated many of the same movements engaged in by her husband. George's own ideas, particularly those concerning the role of race in the United States, mirrored those of his parents. Born in 1798 in Gray, Maine, George's father Reuben, who was biracial, was a free black. Reuben later moved to Portland, a seaport of about nine thousand people, in the 1820s, where he initially worked as a waiter. In 1821 he married Jennett Pierre in Portland's Second Congregational Church. The Congregational Church provided the religious framework for much of Reuben's subsequent reform activities. Its white minister, Edward Payson, known locally as Praying Payson, was a prominent preacher in the Second Great Awakening and embraced the movement's basic theology. He emphasized the idea that salvation came from a conversion experience and that true conversion could be known only if good works were manifest in the converted. These good works ultimately aimed at purging the world not only of sin in one's own life but also in the world at large. The idea that the saved had the responsibility of fighting sin and removing elements in the everyday world that caused sin, such as liquor, fueled many of the reform movements of the early nineteenth century, and Reuben Ruby's actions indicated that he had fully embraced Payson's theology.[1]

Reuben Ruby came to believe that discrimination against free blacks in the North was one of the sins that had to be confronted, and he devoted much of his life as a young man to achieving that goal. Reuben's son George ultimately embraced this viewpoint. Reuben first acted on this theological concept when he challenged the unequal treatment received by blacks within his own mixed-race church. The Second Congregational Church in Portland welcomed blacks as members but at its services segregated its black congregants, relegating its black members to a balcony. In 1826 Ruby joined with his brother-in-law, Christopher C. Manuel, and three other men in a letter published in the *Eastern Argus* that condemned their church for its segregationist policies. They complained that segregation restricted their ability to improve their lives. The church leadership refused to abandon the practice, however, and Ruby subsequently joined with his brother-in-law and others in applying to the state legislature to incorporate the Abyssinian Religious Society, an all-black church that allowed them to participate more fully in the church's worship. On September 19 they published another letter in which they appealed for support from the community at large in erecting a building for the society. Noting that the "benevolent, the pious, and humane" had done little to provide for the "moral instruction" of their race and in fact had created "circumstances as are calculated to repel rather than unite attendance," they asked for help in building a house of worship that would "improve the character and raise the tone of moral feelings among our people." The society later erected a building, the Abyssinian meetinghouse that became the center of religion and reform movements for the city's black community.[2]

Ruby demonstrated an increasing interest in efforts that focused on the moral self-improvement of his race after his experience with the Abyssinian Society and became involved in numerous national reform movements. His son George also accepted the idea that blacks necessarily had to improve themselves as a part of the fight against the racism that led to discrimination. Reuben evidenced this wider interest in 1827, when he became the agent in Portland for *Freedom's Journal,* the first African American-owned newspaper in the country. *Freedom's Journal* was published by Reverend Peter Williams Jr. of New York City, the second African American Episcopal priest ordained in the United States, and edited by Samuel Cornish, a Presbyterian minister and prominent leader of New York's free black community, and John B. Russwurm, a native of Jamaica who moved to Portland in 1812, graduated from Bowdoin College, and then moved to New York. Its pages contained editorials that attacked slavery but also encouraged free blacks to assert their autonomy, accept the existence of a unique black identity, and push for equal treatment in their communities. Ruby later became active in the antislavery movement, but in 1827 *Freedom's Journal*'s advocacy of black self-help and assertiveness probably interested him more.[3]

Reuben Ruby's personal life changed in the years after 1827. His wife, Jennett, died in October of that year. His and Jennett's three-year-old son, William, died a year later. Sometime after Jennett's death Ruby may have moved to Boston or at least engaged in business activities that took him frequently to that city. Whatever his Boston connection, while there he met Rachel Humphrey of Ingham, Massachusetts, and the two married in Boston on December 29, 1829. They returned to Portland where their first son, Frederick Brindley Ruby, was born the following autumn. On his return to Maine, Ruby began a new line of work. The Portland City Directory of 1831 showed that he had acquired coaches and operated Maine's first hack (or taxi) service out of the Elm Tavern, a tavern and hotel on the city's Federal Street. He continued this enterprise at least until 1837. As the owner of his own business, Ruby became a part of Portland's black middle class of self-employed entrepreneurs, if he had not previously achieved that status.[4]

Ruby became even more active in the various reform movements in Portland following his marriage to Rachel. In particular he began his participation in the antislavery movement, and by 1832 he had become a community leader in this effort. William Lloyd Garrison visited Portland in September of that year, and Reuben's participation in that occasion evidenced his prominence as an advocate of the antislavery movement. Garrison had become an antislavery advocate in the 1820s but had now emerged as a major figure in the movement, beginning in 1831 with his publication of the *Liberator*, a journal he used to support both immediate emancipation and the enfranchisement of the freemen. Garrison had embarked on a tour of New England states in early September to promote the newly created New England Anti-Slavery Society, an organization founded only the previous January, largely through Garrison's efforts. Garrison came to Portland while on a larger trip through Maine, where he hoped to encourage the formation of antislavery societies. He arrived in Portland on Wednesday, September 19, and gave speeches at the Quaker meetinghouse on Friday evening, the twenty-first, and at the Abyssinian meetinghouse on Sunday afternoon, the twenty-third. In his Portland speeches he spoke in favor of immediate emancipation and no compensation and believed that he had convinced his audiences to carry into effect "the measures proposed for their benefit."[5]

Reuben Ruby was in the middle of the activities connected with Garrison's visit and evidenced an ability to associate easily with such a nationally known figure as Garrison. George Ruby, like his father, later showed similar social skills. On the visitor's second day in Portland, Ruby, whom Garrison described as "a colored gentleman held in much esteem in the city," took the reformer on a coach ride, showing him the town and its harbor. On the day after Garrison's speech in the Quaker meetinghouse, Ruby held a reception for him at his home. Ruby brought together twenty other men of color to meet Garrison. Garrison described the men at the reception as "gentlemen of good intelligence and reputable character." The reformer believed that these black leaders appreciated his efforts and concluded that his interview with Ruby and the other men was "a profitable one to myself, and I believe agreeable to all who were present." Ruby emerged from the meeting with Garrison committed to the agenda of the New England Anti-Slavery Society and intent on creating a local branch.[6]

Garrison believed that the people he had met in Portland supported his cause and would act quickly to create an antislavery organization. They may have supported his cause, but the actual formation of the state's antislavery organization did not occur for two more years. Antislavery advocates finally gathered in Augusta, Maine, on October 15, 1834, in response to a call for a meeting of the "friends of immediate abolition." Ruby attended the convention along with three white citizens of Portland. Revealing the standing of the Portland delegation and Ruby's relative position in the community, the other members were prominent local white businessmen and politicians. They included Samuel Fessenden, who had served in the Maine House of Representatives and state senate and would later run for Congress on the Liberty Party ticket; William Coe, a watchmaker; and Isaac Winslow, a businessman involved in the whaling industry and the future inventor of a system for canning corn. Ruby played no active public role in the convention, but he did sign the constitution creating the Maine Anti-Slavery Society with its stated object of working "by moral and religious means, and by no other to secure the Immediate and Entire Emancipation of our enslaved brethren and sisters." Given Ruby's earlier efforts at obtaining equal treatment in his church, a noteworthy addendum to the constitution was a commitment to "promote the intellectual, moral and religious improvement of the free people of color, and by correcting prevailing and wicked prejudices, endeavor to obtain for them, as well as the enslaved, an equality with the whites in civil, intellectual and religious privileges." Denying any intention of attacking slavery with violence, the signers instead stated that they intended working to bring public sentiment on slavery "in harmony with the great principles of God's law."[7]

A significant aspect of the convention for the Ruby family was the presence at the Augusta convention of the prominent English abolitionist and member of Parliament, George Thompson. Thompson had come to Maine specifically for the convention, and on the first evening of the meeting he delivered a speech condemning slavery. His speech so offended some of the white residents of Augusta that the next day they demanded Thompson leave the town, and when he did not, they attacked the home of his host, breaking out the windows of the house. After the August convention he made a further tour of Maine and included Portland on his journey. Reuben Ruby most likely attended the lecture on October 15 to hear Thompson and then probably was present when Thompson spoke at the Abyssinian meetinghouse when he returned to Portland on October 27. In his second speech, Thompson sounded themes that became part of Reuben Ruby's future reform career when he encouraged black people present to exhibit "pure and blameless conduct, both for your sake and for the good of the cause of emancipation, which might be materially advanced or retarded according to the impression made upon the public mind by their public and private demeanor." That Thompson had made an impression on Reuben and Rachel was evident when they named their fifth son George Thompson Ruby.[8]

Ruby's early connection with the Maine Anti-Slavery Society did not last. In 1835 he shifted his alignment to a new movement, the American Association of the Free Persons of Colour. His decision connected him for the first time to the Negro Convention Movement, and he continued that association through the antebellum period. His son George continued that tradition after the Civil War. This movement consisted of numerous conventions held by blacks before and after the war that aimed at a variety of reforms, including abolition and the fight for equal rights. The conventions also allowed the development of a national leadership within the black community. Reuben possibly moved away from the Anti-Slavery Society because he found his role as a leader in the organization co-opted by prominent white abolitionists. After its initial organization and participation by men like Ruby, the leadership of the Maine society came to be dominated by whites. Men like Samuel Fessenden; the Rev. Swan L. Pomeroy, a Congregationalist minister, member of the Board of Overseers at Bowdoin College and an organizer of the American Anti-Slavery Society in 1834; Nathan

Winslow, whose brother Isaac had accompanied Ruby to Augusta; Samuel W. Chase, a future physician studying at Bowdoin; and a number of other ministers and educators emerged as the leaders of the state organization. Not only had they displaced black leaders in the organization, these men were more concerned with slavery than with the condition of free blacks in Maine, and Ruby may have found their emphasis on abolition alone did not coincide with his own interests in changing the lives of free blacks in the North. The reasons for his break with the Maine Anti-Slavery Society cannot be known with any certainty, but the American Association of the Free Persons of Colour provided him with new opportunities for a leadership role and offered an agenda that focused on conditions among free blacks.[9]

The Association of the Free Persons of Colour that attracted Ruby's support in 1835 had been founded in Philadelphia five years earlier, in 1830. On September 20 of that year, forty free blacks from seven states met to consider a suitable response to old laws being enforced or new laws just passed that infringed on the rights of free blacks in the nonslave states. They pointed particularly to Cincinnati, Ohio, where in 1829 officials began enforcing the state's so-called Black Laws of 1804 and 1807. These laws compelled blacks who entered the state to post a $500 bond to guarantee their good behavior, demanded that they produce court papers proving that they were free, and restricted their rights to own guns, marry whites, own real estate, go to public schools, enter certain professions, or exercise many other rights. When the city's authorities announced their intention to apply the laws that required the posting of bonds and presentation of proof of their freedom, they gave blacks thirty days to comply or to leave the city. The initial purpose of the Philadelphia meeting was to consider the suitability of creating a settlement in the province of Upper Canada for those obliged to leave their homes. Resettlement would allow them to live in a land where the organizers believed laws and prejudices would no longer retard their advancement. The delegates to the convention went beyond the Canadian resettlement program, however, to declare their belief that all men were endowed with inalienable rights, as stated in the Declaration of

Independence, and to argue that free blacks had the critical need to "devise and pursue all legal means for the speedy elevation of ourselves and brethren to the scale and standing of men." To further their cause, the delegates called for a national convention to be held in Philadelphia the following June. The organization's emphasis on reform and self-help within the free black community resonated with Ruby's own concerns. It was also an all-black organization.[10]

At the June 1831 meeting in Philadelphia the delegates determined to continue holding conventions to effect the goals they had established, another aspect of the convention movement's concern with the creation of some sort of permanent organization to represent the interests of African Americans. They persisted in their advocacy of a Canadian settlement, but they vigorously attacked the American Colonization Society. That society had been created by whites in 1816 to encourage the emancipation of slaves and the resettlement of them and free blacks to Liberia in Africa. The delegates charged that the African colonization scheme would simply remove free blacks and, in the end, perpetuate slavery. In an address to whites, the delegates declared themselves to be Americans, saying, "Many of our fathers, and some of us, have fought and bled for liberty, independence, and peace which you now enjoy and surely, it would be ungenerous and unfeeling in you to deny us an humble and quiet grave in that country which gave us birth." Relative to the interests of Reuben Ruby, however, the convention also further shifted its agenda towards the improvement of the race and the achievement of self-respect. The delegates stated their mindfulness that ignorance and degraded conditions among many blacks had been used by their enemies to show them as inferior. They condemned any such imputation that their condition, born of denial of educational opportunities, reflected on their inherent intellectual capacity. Nonetheless, to challenge the conclusions of their critics, the delegates urged their brethren to support all efforts at promoting the education of the race and the encouragement of "simplicity, neatness, temperance, and economy in our habits."[11]

Ruby became involved with the Association of the Free Persons of Colour when he attended what the press called "a respectable meeting of colored citizens" held in the vestry of Portland's Abyssinian Church on May 18, 1835. The purpose of the meeting was to nominate delegates to represent them at the Fifth Annual Convention for the Improvement of the Free People of Color to be held the following June. The leadership of the gathering included the town's most prominent black men. It also showed the interconnected character of Portland's black leadership, with many of these men related by blood or marriage. The men present at the meeting elected Christopher C. Manuel, a barber and land speculator and Ruby's brother-in-law, president of the meeting. Franklin G. Pear, probably the brother of Ruby's first wife, Jennett Pierre, was the secretary. Samuel W. Chase, the white Congregational minister of the Abyssinian Church at the time, gave the principal address. At the gathering's close, those who attended elected Ruby and George H. Black, a businessman who owned a clothes-cleaning store, to represent Portland at the meeting in Philadelphia.[12]

Ruby and Black joined forty-four other delegates from around the country when the Convention for the Improvement of the Free People of Colour convened in Philadelphia on June 1, 1835. Among the most widely known of the delegates was William Whipper, a prominent black abolitionist from Philadelphia, but it was apparent that Ruby, even though a relative newcomer, had already achieved a reputation as a leader among the delegates by this time. Ruby clearly knew how to run a formal meeting, a fact that may explain his son George's familiarity with parliamentary rules when he moved into politics. When the Philadelphia convention organized, the committee to nominate officers recommended Ruby for the presidency, and the delegates immediately elected him. The course of the convention and its ultimate Declaration of Sentiment and Address to the American People coincided with Ruby's views on the course that needed to be taken by free blacks in the United States. The delegates firmly rejected all efforts to remove them from the country. Indeed, they asserted, as they had in earlier meetings, that the United States was the land of their nativity and their presence was necessary if for no other reason than to "warn this guilty nation of her injustice and cruelty to the descendants of Africa." The delegates declared their willingness to "terminate our lives as martyrs" to support the principle of freedom for all mankind. More specifically, they dedicated themselves to the promotion of "universal peace and good will" by supporting sound morality through the encouragement of education, temperance, and economy. They believed they were involved in a moral warfare in the ultimate defense of "*liberty, justice*, and *humanity*," and pledged themselves to do all that they could to "hasten the period when *justice and universal liberty shall sway the scepter of nations*."[13]

Ruby was also involved in one of the more significant actions of the convention, the creation of the American Moral Reform Society. In doing this he again showed his belief that blacks must improve themselves in their efforts to end race prejudice, and in doing so further provided an ideological perspective embraced later by his son George. The conventions that had taken place up to this time were connected to no formal organization, but the delegates in Philadelphia concluded that they required a permanent association to achieve their goals. Contending that the United States had descended into moral degeneracy, they proposed an organization committed to the "holy cause" of moral reform. Moral elevation, they contended, would lead to the "extension of righteousness, justice, truth, and evangelical principles throughout the world." They delineated the specific goals of their new society when they declared the dependence of a more moral world on the securing of education, temperance, economy (usually meaning the acquisition of useful skills and knowledge of economics), and universal liberty in the United States. The constitution of the society created at the convention opened membership to all, regardless of race, who pledged themselves to support these principles. The delegates elected James Forten, a black abolitionist from Philadelphia, as the society's first president. The vice presidents included Samuel Cornish, editor of *Freedom's Journal* (the newspaper for which Ruby had served as an agent in Portland); Walter Proctor, pastor of Mother Bethel African Methodist Episcopal Church in Philadelphia; and Jacob C. White, a prominent black Philadelphia businessman. Again, reflecting his reputation by this time, Reuben Ruby also was named as a vice president of the new society. The society, however, got off to a slow start, hindered in part because of inadequate funds. It did not have its first meeting until 1837. In addition, interest in the society had declined since the 1835 Free People of Color Convention, with only thirty-one delegates attending the society meeting in Philadelphia and all but eight of these delegates coming from Pennsylvania. Ruby had shifted his own interests once again. He was not present.[14]

Ruby's association with reform organizations tended to wax and wane, but his concerns with equal rights for his race never seemed to diminish. Through the 1830s he remained an active advocate for that goal and took what action he could to confront prejudice. Reminiscent of his public and personal protest against his church, in 1826 he made a public complaint against the captain of the steamship *Maranough* following the Philadelphia Convention of the Free People of Colour. The captain of that vessel refused access to the steamer's cabin to George Black, another free black who had been in Philadelphia, because of his color. He agreed to take Black aboard only if he consented to remain on deck during the entire passage. Black refused to board, saying that to do so would be to disrespect himself. When Reuben returned home he joined with other blacks in extending thanks to the captain of the steamboat *Lexington* for his treatment of them on their return journey from Philadelphia. Having been treated with dignity, they extended the thanks of the black citizens of Maine to the captain and recommended that all of their "colored friends" who needed to travel to New York patronize the *Lexington*. Contained in their message was the suggestion that their "colored friends" not patronize the *Maronough*. Reuben and his friends, in effect, threatened a boycott to protest their unequal treatment, a tactic that George found useful later in his life. This demand for equal treatment and action to force it came to characterize both Reuben and George's careers in reform.[15]

When the American Moral Reform Society gained no traction, Ruby moved on to participate in other reform efforts. In September 1837, he attended the convention of the New England Temperance Society in Boston. Created only the previous year, the New England Temperance Society, like the Moral Reform Society, attempted to provide an overarching organization to link the numerous local black temperance organizations that had come into being in the Northeast. It also, as in the case of the Moral Reform Society, was an all-black organization. The society's primary purpose was to promote abstinence from alcohol, and Ruby's presence at the convention indicated that he accepted the ideas of sin typically expressed in reform-minded churches such as his, ideas that had also been expressed in the goals of the Moral Reform Society. The temperance organization's members perceived the consumption of alcohol not only to be a sin, but also to be a practice that limited the ability of blacks to move forward financially, one that put "weapons into the hands of our enemies" and retarded the progress of emancipation. Given the impact of drinking, the delegates resolved that securing total abstinence was something that blacks owed to "ourselves, our race, our country, and more than all, to God." Ruby, once again, played a significant leadership role, and at the opening session he was elected to the executive committee. Ruby obviously supported the resolutions tendering support for the promotion of temperance among blacks in New England. As with other organizations that Ruby associated with, the New England Temperance Society held only a few more meetings. Ruby, however, never attended another of its conventions, although he and his family remained committed to the idea of temperance. George embraced the idea of temperance, as he did so many other of his father's notions, in his own career following the Civil War.[16]

Reuben Ruby's reform career received widespread attention, but not much is known of his family life through this period. During the 1830s the Rubys lived in a house on Portland's Preble Street. His family also began to grow. In 1830 Ruby and his wife Rachel had their first son Frederick Brindley Ruby. Frederick was followed in 1832 by their daughter Sarah. The names of two subsequent sons reflected Reuben's increasing interest in the antislavery movement. In 1834 their second son was born and named William Wilberforce Ruby after the prominent English social reformer who had died two years before, had played a major role in the ending of British participation in the slave trade, and became a strong proponent of emancipation throughout the British Empire. The Rubys named their third son, born in 1836, after Arthur Tappan, a New York businessman and abolitionist who had helped to found the American Anti-Slavery Society in 1833. The naming of their sons after these prominent reformers indicated the presence of a family culture strongly committed to reform and centered on the hope that a new era of race relations in which slavery would end and a society created in which blacks would be accepted as equals.[17]

At the same time that Reuben Ruby played a greater role in Portland's reform movements, he also found himself increasingly at odds with some of the members of his local religious community. In 1836 Ruby sued the Abyssinian Society for $900, contending that the society owed him payment for the mortgage that he held on their building and for improvements on it that he had made. Ruby had sold the land and the building already on the property to the society in 1831 on a three-year mortgage. He additionally had finished its interior. He took the property back in 1835 when the society failed to finish payment on the mortgage. The society, in turn, forcibly repossessed the building a month after Ruby acted, resulting in the suit. The suit remained in the court for three years, but a statement by Ruby that he would "not let them have the meeting house for $1,000" indicated that many ties with his associates in the society had frayed.[18]

Ruby also became entangled the following year, 1837, in a lawsuit with Samuel Chase, the pastor of the Abyssinian Church. Chase had embarked on a fundraising tour for the church in 1836, apparently without the endorsement of his congregation. Ruby joined with other men from the church in publishing notices in local papers denying that Chase had authorization to raise money in the name of the church. Ruby and the others also commented on his character in a manner that Chase considered libelous. As a result Chase sued six of the men, including Ruby, for $2,000. The Maine Supreme Court ruled for Chase, finding Ruby and three of the other de-

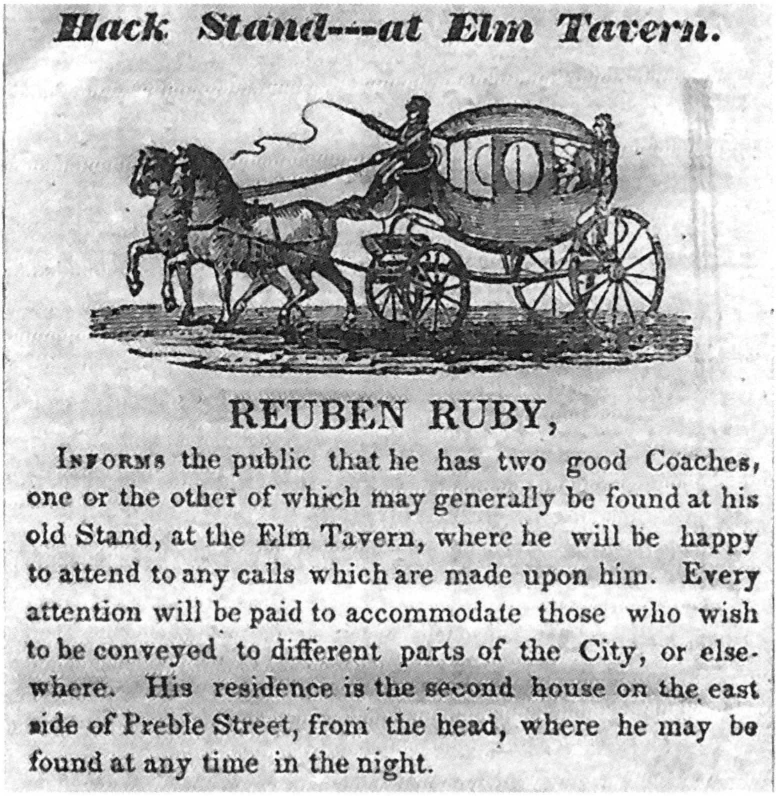

Advertisement for Reuben Ruby's Hack Stand (Portland, Maine, *Daily Argus*).

fendants guilty but limiting the damages to only $150 based on the inability of the parties to pay. The courts seized the property of at least one of the defendants the next year and sold it to satisfy the decision. Whether or not Ruby ever paid his share of the court's award is not known.[19]

Ruby's legal difficulties may explain why he and his family moved to New York City around 1838, although the move may also have been prompted simply by Ruby's desire to find better economic circumstances for his family. Little is known about the family's life in New York, although at one point Reuben owned a restaurant on the corner of Nassau and Beekman streets. As the owner of a business and not a laborer he would have continued to be a part of the black middle class. At his restaurant, Ruby openly exhibited his reform tendencies. An advertisement for his establishment indicated that the bill of fare was "rich and full, embracing the earliest supplies of the market." He also advertised the place as a temperance restaurant, serving breakfast, dinner, and tea, plus "[p]ure spring water at the bar." In New York City, Reuben and Rachel had their fourth son, George, born on July 1, 1840. In keeping with what was now a tradition of naming their sons after prominent abolitionists, the couple named their new baby after George Thompson, the abolitionist who had visited Portland years earlier. The Rubys' fifth son, Horatio, was born in the city in 1843.[20]

In New York, Ruby retained his commitment to reform, and he actively engaged in the reform movements alive in that city at the time. Although George was still quite young during the family's years in New York, his father's activities provided a direct example to him. By the time the Ruby family arrived in New York, black reformers had become divided on their goals. Many blacks, dismayed by the increasing focus of the radical white abolitionists on slavery and decreasing interest in the problems faced by free blacks in the North, moved to separate themselves from the white-dominated organizations. Slavery concerned free blacks, but often as an institution that undermined their own position in society. While opposed to slavery, the problems that racism created in the North—the inequality of opportunities to earn livings and participate on an equal basis in society—became the focus of those who separated. Many of the organizations that Ruby had associated with in Portland had emphasized moral reform among members of their own race as a step towards their recognition as equals. Some black reformers in New York now believed moral reform was no longer the solution, and they contended that the first step to changing society required direct action to improve the lot of black workers. By direct action they meant changing the laws that limited black access to education or discriminated against their entry into trades. In some ways the different tactics, all aimed at securing a better life for blacks, presaged the divisions within the black community that developed between the followers of Booker T. Washington and W. E. B. DuBois later in the century.[21]

In July 1840, Ruby became part of the more activist component of black reformers when he attended the National Reform Convention of the Colored Inhabitants of the United States held in Hartford, Connecticut, a meeting largely encouraged by David Ruggles to resurrect the earlier reform conventions. Ruggles at this time owned a bookstore in New York City, edited the *Mirror of Liberty*, and was a prominent member of the New York Vigilance Committee. That committee had been created in 1835 to help runaway slaves avoid authorities seeking to return them to their masters. Ruggles was one of the more radical black members of the antislavery movement in New York and had broken with many of the city's moral reformers in his abandonment of nonresistance in efforts to protect runaway slaves. He also believed that blacks must undertake their own road to reform and that they should continue to form separate black reform organizations. Ruby was part of a delegation of ten men from New York City who were examples of the city's black middle class. In addition to Ruggles, the committee included Lewis H. Nelson, a barber, and Prince Loveridge, an agent for the city's public schools. In their address to the public, the delegates called for a convention to address the burdens under which their "periled and disfranchised countrymen" groaned. Pointing to a recent law passed in Maryland that encouraged free blacks to consider emigrating to Africa, the delegates condemned what they believed to be an "alarming supineness [sic]" that prevailed within the black community. It was time, they contended, for the "proscribed and down-trodden inhabitants of the United States" to meet to consider their condition. They hoped that, as a result, blacks could form "a bond of union that will secure simultaneous action for reform in the hallowad [sic] cause of HUMAN FREEDOM." As with other conventions of this sort, the delegates ultimately sought to produce some sort of continuity in their efforts, and they called for another convention to meet in New Haven, Connecticut, on September 7.[22]

Three days after the Hartford convention, the New York Reform Society organized in New York City in response to the Hartford convention's call for organization. Four of the men who had been in Hartford were part of this meeting. Ruby, although he would play a role in the development of the Reform Society later and ultimately endorsed the proceedings of the New York meeting, was not there. That meeting endorsed the call for the planned New Haven meeting, agreeing that blacks needed to take action against oppression. The organizers contended that a convention would allow them to concentrate their "energies, intelligence and sympathy." A variety of problems, however, stood in the way of the planned meeting. Lewis Woodson, a black abolitionist from Pittsburgh, wrote a letter addressed to Ruggles, Ruby, and the other men who had called for the New Haven convention. Published in the *Colored American*, the letter provided a list of reasons why he opposed the gathering. His list provided insight into the problems that affected most of the black reform movements at the time. He contended that enough time had not been given for people to respond and that New Haven was "out of the way" and had shown hostility to the antislavery movement. Woodson further maintained that the black community itself did not have enough knowledge of national affairs and would not understand why a convention should be held. Such ignorance, he contended, counseled delay. In addition and perhaps more critically, Woodson pointed out that at this time money was scarce and the price of travel high, and that these factors would prevent many supporters from attending.[23]

The proposed September convention also met opposition at a public meeting of blacks in New Haven. These men criticized the organizers for not having consulted any of the local people about its arrangements. They were more critical, however, of the fact that the convention would be attended exclusively by blacks, a matter that concerned some of the white abolitionists in New Haven. Of course, the whole point of the Reform Society was that it should be an all-black organization that would address not just the concerns of white abolitionists but would consider the plight of free blacks as well. A letter responding to this opposition published in the *Liberator* on August 21 portrayed the New Haven opponents as an example of "the colored man arrayed against himself" and became part of a bitter exchange between rival parties. The September convention assembled nonetheless, but not at the local Quaker meetinghouse. Its doors were barred, allegedly because the supporters of the meeting advocated the equality of women as well of all men. The men who attended, in the end, failed to create the permanent organization that had been desired.[24]

Ruby did not go to New Haven, but he remained engaged in reform efforts, and by the fall of 1840 he became more actively involved in local antislavery efforts. On October 27 of that year he participated in the second meeting of the Manhattan Anti-Slavery Society, an organization that had been formed the previous September as an auxiliary of the American Anti-Slavery Society. While concerned with the impact of slavery on the slaves, the Manhattan Society's constitution reflected the concern of free blacks with the effects of slavery on themselves and certainly aligned with Ruby's own concerns for the improvement of society among free blacks in the North. Ruby's significance as a reformer was again demonstrated when the attending delegates elected him president of the new organization. In the resolutions passed at the meeting, and in the proposed constitution, those who attended the society meeting condemned slavery not only as an evil for the enslaved but also because it "restrains the enterprise, shackles the industry, and destroys the tranquility of 500,000 nominally free people in the North." The society's stated goals included many of those associated with the moral reformers of the black middle class, looking not only to an end of slavery but also to the "improvement of the character and condition of the free people of color, by encouraging their intellectual, moral and religious progress, and by procuring the acknowledgement of their rights as human beings." The Manhattan organization welcomed membership "without respect to sex or color." The new organization, according to the chairman of the organizational committee, consisted of "real 'lap-water' abolitionists." The open membership, insisted the chairman, was needed, "for on no other foundation can genuine anti-slavery rest." The meeting took a radical turn when discussions turned to the proslavery character of the United States Constitution and whether or not abolitionists should advocate an end to all union with slaveholders. Ruby's day-to-day involvement in the organization is unknown after the initial meeting, although he continued his association with David Ruggles, who also helped form the society. Ruby also became connected through his role in the society to Thomas Van Rensselaer, another member of the New York Vigilance Committee.[25]

Two and a half weeks after being elected president of the Manhattan Anti-Slavery Society, Ruby took up another crusade. He came to see having a voice in government as essential to many of the reforms he backed, again creating a model for action embraced by George, and he turned his efforts to securing the franchise for free blacks in the state of New York. On November 16 many black representatives from the city's wards gathered in Philomathean Hall, the home of the Philomathean Literary Society for black men, to organize a drive to circulate petitions and secure the signatures necessary to pressure the New York assembly to extend the vote to blacks. Ruby attended as a delegate from the city's Fourth Ward, and the delegates chose him as chairman of the meeting, a capacity he continued to fill in future meetings. This group's efforts reflected the membership's sophisticated awareness of political organization. The meeting created ward committees to circulate petitions calling for enfranchisement. Ward committee members then turned over the petitions to a county committee that forwarded them to Albany. The petition drive ultimately led to a mass meeting on December 7 where Ruby served as one of the vice presidents. That meeting pushed for a further expansion of the petition drive and publicly called on members of the legislature to recognize "our common humanity and the justice of the cause." All they sought, the members of the meeting said, were the "well earned birthright privileges" that were due to "an injured and oppressed portion of the citizens of this State." Despite their efforts and numerous resolutions introduced in the New York Assembly to grant free blacks suffrage, extension of suffrage would not take place until after the end of the Civil War.[26]

George's mother Rachel also added to the reform-minded culture in the Ruby family. In February 1841, the "anti-slavery women" associated with the Manhattan Anti-Slavery Society announced that they would hold a fair to raise money for the benefit of the American Anti-Slavery Society. Rachel Ruby participated actively with the group, alongside Almira Van Rensselaer, wife of Thomas, and well-known white abolitionists such as Lydia Maria Child, who at this time edited the *National Anti-Slavery Standard,* and Abigail H. Gibbons, a prominent Quaker reformer. Newspaper announcements of the planned fair called for supporters around the nation to provide money or goods, including items of clothing ranging from hats to frocks. They even asked for toys or any other items that would promote "liberal contributions" from the fairgoers. They intended the fair, however, to be more than a simple means for raising funds. In resolutions passed by the men of the Manhattan Society, they not only endorsed the fair but presented it as an opportunity for abolitionists to "hold up their testimony in favor of human freedom, to the light, so that 'he who runs may read,' and that they fail in the duty who hide their light under a bushel and shrink from the just vindication of anti-slavery truth, in the face of the combined forces of prejudice, avarice, and a corrupt public sentiment."[27]

Even while active in the Manhattan Anti-Slavery Society and supporting the effort at securing the franchise, Ruby remained connected with David Ruggles and his efforts at creating some sort of overarching reform organization among free blacks. In the spring of 1841 his connection to Ruggles got him involved in the creation of the American Reform Board of Disfranchised Commissioners. The new organization took its name from the condition of its members, "disfranchised Americans." As has been seen in the various conventions Ruby attended, earlier meetings had provided blacks a forum to express their grievances but resulted in no permanent organization to address these problems. The American Reform Board was an attempt, in the words of its founders, to provide a "nucleus around which we can rally as a depressed and disfranchised people, to exchange views with each other and resolve to 'unite' and 'energize' in the promotion of our suffering cause." In the midst of growing antislavery agitation this effort attempted again to focus reform discussion on the unequal situation free blacks found themselves in throughout the North. Its stated object was to make known the actual condition of free blacks as well as slaves in order to promote the cause of equal human rights, to allow people to "take special cognizance of the oppressive legal or illegal customs under which we groan,—to unite and energize in securing our immediate relief and enfranchisement." It hoped to bring about the mobilization of blacks, "[a]gitating, individually, collectively, and unanimously in State and National Conventions, until equal rights shall crown our labors with success." In a circular distributed on May 1, 1841, Ruby and other members of a committee of the Reform Board asked blacks to attend a convention in New York the following September. Its purpose was to educate the public as to the condition of free blacks, and to effect that end the circular asked delegates to bring to the convention statistics on the state of education for free blacks, their economic opportunities, and the "condition of people generally in relationship to 'the pursuit of happiness.'"[28]

When the convention opened in New York City on September 8, 1841, Ruby, strangely, since he had participated in the efforts at organizing the convention, was absent. In fact, Ruby disappeared for a time from any leadership roles in the various reform movements of the period. This meeting was something of a last gasp for Ruggles's efforts to continue the all-black convention movement. The delegates came largely from New York City, attracting few attendees from other states. Like the previous conventions, this one once again pointed to the relationship between the status of blacks in the North and slavery in the South and the need for free blacks to organize and address that issue. The delegates also resolved to continue the work for reform and called on their white friends to "practise [sic] just principles, and encourage our capable mechanics and youth in their trades and professions, by opening to them their workshops and other avenues of profitable employment." Finally, they condemned the scheme of the American Colonization Society, regarding it "by us in America, as the anaconda is by men and women in Africa." The meeting made a brave statement of the ideas that Ruby had held since his involvement in the movement even though Ruby was not there to affirm its course.[29]

An active reformer, participating in conventions in Maine, Massachusetts, and New York, Ruby suddenly disappeared from public notice following the Reform Board meeting. He did not reappear until 1849. That year Ruby joined thousands of Americans who went to California as a participant in the gold rush set off by the discovery of gold at Sutter's Mill. His pursuit of gold may have reflected problems with his financial situation at the time, the possible need of funds to handle obligations back in Portland, or simply a search for new opportunities. Any of these could have explained his absence from the reform scene in New York. His participation earned newspaper coverage when several northern newspapers reported that a "*free* colored man, Reuben Ruby," had left New York City on February 1, 1849, on the steamer *Falcon* and reached San Francisco on April 1. Reports indicated that he had found a "queer shaped lump [of gold] 11 ounces avoirdupois" and an additional four ounces in various sizes from that of a chestnut to a grain of wheat. An assayer who had seen the gold valued it at $600, and a contemporary newspaper report in Maine placed the value at $3,000, a small fortune at a time when the average worker earned only earned about $300 per year. Ruby returned to New York City that November, having sailed from Chagres in Panama to Kingston, Jamaica, then on to the city. Ruby's family either moved back to Portland at this point or had moved there when he left for California; in any event he rejoined them.[30]

George Ruby was ten years old when the family settled once again in Portland. The 1850 census described his father as a trader. Exactly what that involved is not clear, although it appeared from other information about him that he traded goods between Portland and the markets of New York and Boston. The family took up residence at 9 Hampshire Street, several blocks from the harbor on Portland's east side and just to the north of the new St. Lawrence and Atlantic Railroad station. George grew up in a largely white town with only 395 black residents out of a total population of 20,815. He lived in an integrated neighborhood that consisted of homes and shops whose occupants consisted mainly of whites working as sailors, shipbuilders, and tradesmen of a variety of sorts. Life in a port city tied him to the larger world, with ships leaving and arriving daily in the port carrying everything from foodstuffs such as flour and corn to molasses. Molasses may have been the most important of the goods arriving in the port, for local manufacturers brought it in to be processed into sugar and rum, then shipped the more valuable product elsewhere. Perhaps life in the port gave him a broader outlook on the world that contributed to the search for opportunity outside of Portland he exhibited early in his life.[31]

George was old enough in 1850 to be aware of his parents' concern with the plight of free blacks in the North and the slaves of the South. In 1850 his father Reuben became involved in the Underground Railroad. The Underground Railroad had been in existence for some time, but the Fugitive Slave Act passed by Congress on September 18, 1850, sparked outrage among free blacks and antislavery advocates in the North, which generated renewed interest in helping slaves to escape their masters. The law sought to place further barriers to the escape of runaway slaves by requiring local public officials and law enforcement officers to arrest men suspected of being runaways and return them to their owners. Ruby may have been involved in the Underground Railroad earlier, but it is more likely that he became a conductor, one who helped slaves escape to their freedom, at this time. Traditional stories of the Underground Railroad in Portland indicated that as the network developed, he became its foremost conductor. As a businessman carrying goods from New York and Boston, he may have been able to transport runaways who had managed to reach those cities back to Portland, where they could make their way to Canada and freedom.[32]

On October 10, 1850, Reuben participated in a meeting in Portland held in reaction to the passage of the Fugitive Slave Act. Noting that the new law exposed "every colored man to be kidnapped and carried into slavery," those in attendance concluded that they had no choice but to give shelter and assistance to any fugitive from slavery. They clearly had embraced Charles Sumner's "Higher Law" concept by this time, a view that placed moral authority above legal authority, when they stated that in their action they recognized "no authority higher than the law of God," a view to some degree reflected in his son George's 1870 speech in the Texas Senate. In a concluding resolution those who attended the meeting created a committee of vigilance to "give notice of the approach of danger, to see that every person is provided with the means of defense, and that places of security are selected and to give direction to whatever measures may be necessary for our protection." Reuben Ruby's renewed involvement led him to accept a position on the committee on defense, created as a subsidiary part of the committee of vigilance. This committee's work was similar to that of the New York Vigilance Committee, and Ruby would have been knowledgeable about that organization's operations since he had been associated with David Ruggles while in the city. Unfortunately, the lack of primary sources makes it impossible to determine George's reaction to his father's efforts, although his commitment to similar causes suggests that they made a profound impact.[33]

Reuben and Rachel provided a direct example of activism to their son, but they also helped to develop who he would be in another important way. They sent him to school where he encountered other important role models. George probably attended school in New York. The city had a system of public schools opened to black students, although when and where he may have gone is not known. When the family returned to Portland he continued his education, initially attending a segregated public school, all that was available for black children. This school met in the back rooms of the town's North School, and at the time of the Ruby family's return Rev. Amos N. Freeman, the black pastor of the Abyssinian Church, taught there. It's also possible that Freeman held classes in his home. George received an education in the traditional academic courses under Freeman, but the pastor also emphasized music, and Ruby developed an often-praised singing voice. Freeman included admonitions on the issue of temperance in his curriculum, reinforcing in George the views of his father. In 1853 Peter R. Hall took charge of the school. Hall, only twenty-six years old and the son of a farmer, was still in school himself at the time and working to become an attorney, a goal he ultimately achieved. He was an ambitious young man and showed his students that a black man could achieve any goal if he set out to do so, even entry into the professions. If George's father had not made a strong enough impression on his son's values and hopes, Freeman and Hall added to the development of his character, contributing to the reform orientation learned from his parents and adding lessons of self-reliance that probably contributed to George's belief that blacks must better themselves in order to confront the racism that surrounded them.[34]

In 1856 a lack of students led to North School's discontinuance and the integration of all of the students into previously all-white schools. George went to the high school. Rev. William H. Shailer, pastor of Portland's First Baptist Church and a member of the city's school committee, recalled that Ruby entered the school along with the daughter of Elbridge P. Talbot, another member of Portland's black middle class. Talbot's daughter would have been the first black graduate of Portland High School, but she died before graduation. This unfortunate circumstance made Ruby the first black to graduate from Portland High School, which he did in 1858. He reportedly completed his studies with "high honors," having studied under "Master Libby," Joseph Libby, the first principal of the school. The *Portland Press* later described Ruby at the time of his graduation as "a young man of fine natural abilities, well educated, and . . . a gentleman in the best sense of the term." High school probably offered Ruby his first opportunity to test himself against whites, and the testimony of his teachers suggests that he must have concluded he had survived that test and proven himself an equal.[35]

When he graduated, Ruby was on the verge of adventures that ultimately took him to Haiti, then to Louisiana, to Texas, and back to Louisiana. While the details of his life as a youth are unknown for the most part, and he left no later reminiscences of his feelings about his mother and father, there is no question that growing up in a family and among others who worked to bring an end to the institutional racism that pervaded the North and undergirded slavery throughout the nation helped to shape his character. The idea that a black man was equal to any white man, a view held by his parents, was firmly ingrained in his later thinking. His belief that the removal of barriers created by white society would allow blacks to achieve everything that whites could achieve, another concept associated with his parents and his educators, was ever present in his work. He, perhaps even more than his father, believed that he had a role in producing a new society in which differences of race would disappear. The lessons taught George Ruby by the people who were there in his youth cannot be overestimated.

CHAPTER II

THE HAITIAN ADVENTURE: THE SEARCH FOR RACIAL POSSIBILITIES

He is an adopted citizen of Hayti, and says he could not now endure the prejudices of Americans.—Pine and Palm, *August 28, 1862*

Three years after graduating from Portland's high school, George Ruby moved to Haiti, where he participated in an effort to create a colony of free black Americans. Ruby in his later life embraced most of the basic views of race problems and strategies adopted by his father in Reuben's fight against racism in the United States, but George's decision to leave the country represented a major break with his father. Reuben had endorsed efforts at creating a colony of free blacks in Canada when he joined the Association of the Free Persons of Colour in the 1830s, but afterwards all of the organizations that he joined rejected the idea that free blacks in the United States should leave. Rather than migrate, blacks, in Reuben's view, had to work to secure full rights for themselves as citizens at home. George, however, went to Haiti because he believed that blacks would never achieve his father's goal of an equitable society in the United States. George had concluded that the equality sought by his father could only be realized elsewhere.

How George Ruby became associated with the Haitian colony is not known. He left no evidence of what motivated him. Perhaps he simply concluded from his own experiences that little opportunity existed in the United States for an ambitious, educated black man. His family had achieved a degree of economic success and believed that blacks ultimately could obtain equality in their country. His teachers had provided him with examples of men who had achieved professional status in the ministry and the law. George's own life, however, did not seem to reflect that optimism. Two years after he graduated he lived in the home of his brother William and his brother's wife Madeline in Portland. Instead of having entered a profession, George worked in a restaurant with his brother as a confectioner, baking cakes, cookies, and other sweets. While the bakery may have represented success for his brother William, it must hardly have seemed so for an ambitious young man who had proven, at least in his school experience, his capacity to achieve more. Haiti may have offered him that promise.

Interest in emigration to Haiti had existed among free blacks in the North for some time before George Ruby made his decision to go there. The successful Haitian revolution that ended in 1804 led to the creation of a new republic where blacks held economic, social, and political power. As early as 1824 some Northern blacks came to see the country as a place where they could live free of the prejudices they faced in United States. In that year the New York Colonization Society negotiated an agreement with the then president of Haiti, Jean-Pierre Boyer, for the Haitian government to provide land, support for four months, and passage to the island for any free blacks who desired to go there. Bishop Richard Allen, founder of the African American Episcopal Church and a strong opponent of white-sponsored efforts by the American Colonization Society to send blacks to Liberia in Africa, and James Forten, a black Philadelphia businessman, formed the Haytian Emigration Society of Coloured People to settle free blacks in Haiti and Santo Domingo in response to this agreement. Several thousand free blacks reportedly took advantage of it, although many soon returned to the United States after the Haitian government failed to provide the support that it had promised. Interest in emigration died out as these original settlers returned with tales of the hardships they faced, but as the sectional crisis within the United States intensified in the 1850s, and whites in many states made efforts to restrict the rights of free blacks, the latter looked at

Haiti once again. In 1855 Haitian Emperor Faustin Soulouque and James Theodore Holly, the first black bishop of the Protestant Episcopal Church and a missionary to Haiti, reached an agreement to promote new settlements, although only a few settlers had arrived before Soulouque's abdication in 1859, when Nicholas Fabre Geffrard forced Soulouque out of office and assumed the presidency of the republic.[1]

Geffrard, like previous Haitian leaders, believed that his country would benefit from an influx of black Americans, and his government initiated policies hoping to promote immigration, once again promising gifts of land to and support for blacks who moved to the country. This was the colonial effort that attracted George Ruby. In 1859 and 1860 several hundred free blacks from Louisiana took advantage of the offer, but Geffrard's government wanted even greater numbers to come. To produce this increase they created an agency in the United States to promote immigration and to facilitate the transportation of settlers. They found a partner for this effort in the person of James Redpath, who became a recruiting agent for the Haitian government. Redpath was a native of Berwick upon Tweed, England, who had moved to the United States where he became a journalist, antislavery advocate, and supporter of John Brown's plan for a slave insurrection. Redpath became interested in Haiti after hearing Wendell Phillips, a prominent Massachusetts abolitionist, speak on the Haitian revolution. In January 1859 Redpath went on one of two trips to the country to observe for himself how successful blacks would be in a community where they controlled their own destinies, envisioning the American colonies there as experiments that would show white Americans the capabilities of blacks when freed from discrimination.[2]

As noted, George Ruby never said what initially drew him to immigrate to Haiti, but the publicity used by Geffrard and Redpath to promote the new colonies offers insights into the ideas that probably attracted Ruby. Ruby's writings of his later experiences in Haiti indicated that these ideas unquestionably resonated with him. Both Geffrard and Redpath appealed to a hope that if blacks created their own community free of white prejudice, they could achieve their highest goals. A letter Geffrard wrote in 1860 and published as an invitation for immigrants to come to Haiti to cooperate in restoring the country to its ancient splendor expressed such a viewpoint. Geffrard declared that the nation's constitution recognized all descendants of Africa and inhabitants of the West Indies as being part of the Haitian family and that the country was the "common country of the black race." He called for "negroes and mulattos who, in the vast Continent of America, suffer from the prejudices of caste" to bring their arms and minds to Haiti to effect this goal of regeneration. In his most overt appeal to black pride, he asserted that when Haiti regained her former position as "Queen of the Antilles" that success would put the lie to those "detractors of our race who contest our desire and ability to attain a high degree of civilization."[3]

The message of Redpath in his 1860s *Guide to Haiti* would have been equally appealing to Ruby. Redpath was as optimistic about the political, social, and economic implications of emigration as President Geffrard. He began by declaring, "There is only one country in the Western World where the Black and the man of color are undisputed lords; where the White is indebted for the liberty to live to the race which with us is enslaved." Whites asked what would happen to blacks if slavery was abolished. Redpath answered for them to look to Haiti, "an independent Nationality of immovable stability, and a Government inspired with the spirit of progress" for their answer. For the proscribed people of the United States, Haiti offered "a home and a distinctive Nationality." He not only saw Haiti as a prospective home for free blacks, but like Geffrard he also believed that the Haitian experiment of self-government was a social and political endeavor that free blacks must support. Their settlements would strengthen "a colored nation" and ultimately demonstrate the "capacity of the race for self-government."[4] For a young high school graduate working in a bakery, whose family had fought for equality, the appeal must have been overwhelming.

Redpath also argued that success in Haiti not only would show the world what black men and women could do but that it would ultimately work to bring an end to slavery in the United States. A Haiti producing cotton, sugar, rice, and the other agricultural products that were grown in the American South would be a step towards creating a cordon of freedmen's labor that would surround the slave South. This cordon of labor would make it impossible for the South to move into new territory, and "like a scorpion girded by fire, Slavery must inevitably die." Again, for a young man such as Ruby, such an enterprise offered an opportunity to participate in a work of heroic proportion.[5]

A decree issued by the Haitian government on August 14, 1860, formalized Redpath's part in the emigration plan. The government that authorized him to set up an emigration bureau in Boston named him the director of the Haitian Bureau of Emigration and provided him $20,000 to further his work. Redpath published a guide book to Haiti, appointed agents to recruit prospective emigrants, and in May 1861, began publishing the *Pine and Palm*, a newspaper devoted to the promotion of the emigration scheme. To encourage emigration the Haitian government promised to pay for the emigrants' passage and board and lodging while they sought accommodations. It also assured the migrants that they would have freedom of religion, a matter of considerable concern given that many of the Americans were Protestants; exemption from military service; free schooling; and equal protection under the law. The Haitian authorities did not, however, promise the sale of land to the settlers but instead offered a form of tenantry in which the land remained in the hands of the government. The first group of emigrants left the United States in December, 1860, when sixty-two men, women, and children sailed from Boston on Christmas Day. Ships left irregularly for Haiti thereafter in 1860 and through 1861. The number of people Redpath ultimately managed to send to Haiti is unknown, although probably no more than several thousand individuals emigrated. Redpath himself became disillusioned with the project sometime in the midsummer of 1862. After that little additional emigration took place.[6]

Where Ruby learned of the opportunity of moving to Haiti is unknown. Possibly Dr. J. B. Smith, whom Redpath hired in 1861 to make a recruiting trip through New Hampshire, Vermont, Maine, and the maritime provinces of Canada, encouraged the move. Smith was a Baptist minister in Boston and a member of the African Civilization Society, an organization that also backed the emigration of free blacks to Africa. Smith returned home from his trip with a bleak report of possible emigrants from the area, explaining that relatively few blacks lived in most of the places that he had gone. The ones he encountered showed little interest in moving. He thought this to be true because they believed they were "treated comparatively well." Little overt prejudice existed and they were "treated more as favorites, and rather feel that they are to be more envied than pitied." They, he thought, failed to realize the "true state of their condition" and could not be induced to emigrate. Ruby, certainly aware of the situation his race confronted in the United States, may have been one of the exceptions to the generalization that Smith made.[7]

Ruby sailed for Haiti on March 30, 1861, on the brig *Maria*. He listed his occupation on the ship's passenger manifest as a confectioner. Unlike most of the other emigrants, he did not travel with a group but sailed on his own. The passage to Haiti could take as long as three weeks, and Ruby may have just arrived in Port-au-Prince when he sent a letter to Redpath's *Pine and Palm* dated April 22. In it he provided the first of several accounts of his time in Haiti that not only described the condition of the emigrants who had moved there but also his own perspective of a nation ruled by blacks. These letters provide the first real evidence of both Ruby's skills as a communicator and his thoughts on issues of race. On his arrival, the cosmopolitan character of the inhabitants of the port, where even the people of the lower classes "evince by their action and deportment their perfect freedom and enjoyment," struck him in particular. The mixture of languages reminded him of "Babel." He found the poorer classes to have the characteristics of the French peasantry, although it is unclear how he knew of the French peasants. They were "hospitable, generous, excitable, but not quarrelsome." The upper classes had the manner of the educated French and were "courteous, kind and hospitable."[8]

His literary efforts invariably saw the positive side of the Haitian project, and his first letter revealed that the chance to be among the people of Haiti overawed him. His feelings, he reported, were "indescribable." Being in a country "ruled by a people who have thrown off the galling yoke of oppression" thrilled him. Haitians, he wrote, had freed themselves, fighting "manfully and successfully for liberty." Not only had they succeeded, but "with one gigantic stride" they had achieved a place among the nations of the world. Ruby's sense of racial pride manifested itself strongly when he visited the Custom House. The men who worked there told him of the "nationality of the country" and he found "with surprise and *pleasure*, *black* men filling places he has *always seen white*[s] occupy."[9]

Throughout this earliest letter he manifested great pride in the accomplishment of the Haitians. He had opportunities to visit the homes of some of the residents he considered to be of the higher classes, and he found that their homes, in terms of elegance and style, were "not surpassed by any of our rich friends in America." In this interaction with the city's wealthier residents, he demonstrated an ability to mix with all social classes in the black community that he exhibited throughout the rest of his life. The city of Port-au-Prince, which the opponents of emigration had criticized, he found to be physically appealing with its streets generally paved and its sidewalks above the street level and consisting of brick and sand. The city presented a picture of commercial opportunity and offered numerous jobs and good wages for skilled craftsmen. "Any businessman who comes out here with capital," he observed, "can do well."[10]

A particularly noteworthy discovery that drew Ruby's attention, considering his family's temperance background, were the drinking habits of the Haitians. Those comments came with the observations that he offered on his arrival of how eating practices in Haiti differed from those in the United States. He explained that the Haitians did not eat breakfast until noon, having had only some bread and coffee when they got up in the morning. The breakfast, consisting of meat, vegetables, and fruits, also included "liquors of all kinds." Dinner was served between five and six, this meal consisting of cold meat, rice, and vegetables. Once again, he noted that the Haitians consumed considerable amounts of liquor, although wine was the principal beverage. That the consumption of alcohol did not seem to affect the Haitians like it did Americans surprised him. He found that for the most part, "the people are not drunken nor quarrelsome, and a drunken man is seldom seen about the streets." Still, it may have been the alcohol consumption of the native population that led him to conclude that there was a great need of "missionaries, zealous workers in the Gospel vineyard."[11]

In this first letter Ruby proved himself a remarkable salesman for the Haitian project, offering the *Pine and Palm* detailed and favorable descriptions of what he found in Port-au-Prince. A second letter sent from Port-au-Prince on May 26 continued his in-depth description of the countryside, the people, and the politicians of Haiti. In it he emphasized in particular the economic prospects for those engaged in agriculture, describing the farm goods that had been shown at a national festival held in the city on May 1 in which farmers exhibited their crops. He believed the sugar cane and cotton that had been shown were of particularly high quality, and he concluded that Haiti could produce better yields of these crops than "any part of this continent." He believed that the actual manufacture of sugar had been delayed by the failure of the Soulouque government, "the old tyrant," to invest in machinery, but he found President Geffrard ready to change such conditions. In addition, he noted cooperation between the settlers and the government in the construction of a canal that would bring irrigation waters to their fields. If the picture of conditions was not rosy enough, Ruby also indicated that several settlers had been prospecting for gold and found gold "of the highest quality."[12]

Ruby appeared to be intent on creating support for the Haiti settlement, but his letter at the end of May also indicated that many of the settlers remained interested in what was happening in the United States and especially in war news. Having heard of the attack on Fort Sumter and the call for Union troops, Ruby wrote that everyone in Port-au-Prince was "delighted to find the North united to a man against the rebels." They heard varying stories about the call up, including word that the governors of New

York and Rhode Island had included black troops in their request for regiments. Clearly Ruby still saw events in the United States as important for himself and the Haitian settlers. He, and those he knew in Haiti, hoped that as a result of this "internal agitation" slavery would be brought to an end. Even at this stage, Ruby saw the war as a "contest between freedom and slavery," and he believed all of the other emigrants did as well, reporting that all were united in "praying God to speed the right."[13]

The Haitian emigration project proposed primarily to bring free blacks in from the United States to expand the Haitian labor force and looked to a considerable degree to bring in farmers, but Ruby did not appear in a hurry to go to the countryside. Some two months after he had arrived, Ruby was still in Port-au-Prince. He was there on July 6 to witness an event that proved to be one of the factors in the ultimate failure of Redpath's ability to gain immigrants. At this time Spain had regained control over Santo Domingo (the future Dominican Republic) but still fought a guerilla war against bands of rebels in the countryside. The Haitian government had assisted the rebellion by sending troops across the border into Santo Domingo. On July 6, six Spanish sloops-of-war sailed into the harbor of Port-au-Prince and demanded that the Haitian government pay for damages done to Spanish territory by its troops on the border, that Haiti surrender its claims on land in Santo Domingo and east of the established border, and that the fortifications in the harbor fire a salute in honor of the Spanish queen. The commander of the fleet threatened to destroy the city and others along the Haitian coast unless the government met his demands. Ruby wrote that "rather than yield one inch in any wise dishonoring to the nation, every Haytian declared for war to the death!" By this time Ruby clearly identified with the interests of the Haitians and reported that when called on by the government for service, the immigrants "volunteered their services to a man, determined that ere an invader should land on *their shores* [emphasis added] their bodies should mingle with the dust!" Ultimately, no confrontation took place after President Geffrard agreed to the Spanish demands and withdrew Haitian troops from Santo Domingo. Geffrard's backing down from the Spanish threat may have been wise, but his action hardly lived up to his earlier insistence that Haitians would fight to the death that had so inspired Ruby.[14]

Ruby's letter detailing the Spanish threat to Port-au-Prince also contained evidence that he recognized, despite his steady commitment to the emigration project, a growing discontent among some of his fellow Americans. The *New York Tribune* had published an article based on information provided by the commander of a brig recently arrived from Haiti, a Captain Rice, that a growing tension between government officials and the current immigrants had developed. The commander stated that the government had failed to deliver on many of its promises, and that during the threatened Spanish bombardment the government attempted to press immigrants into the army. Rather than providing adequate support to the immigrants until they could establish themselves, the government gave families only three Haitian dollars per week. As a result, many of them suffered from want and even starvation. Ruby replied to the *Tribune* in a piece written for the *Pine and Palm* and declared all of these assertions to be "*base lies*." He went on to state that "the report is without a shadow of truth." Ruby threatened that if this captain ever returned to Haiti he would "receive such treatment from the hands of the enraged emigrants [sic] whom it has pleased him to malign, that he will ever have a *careful* regard for the truth."[15]

After spending several months in Port-au-Prince, Ruby finally moved on to the St. Mark area approximately ninety miles north of the capital and along the Haitian coast. The town of St. Mark was the center of several American immigrant colonies, including the Lawrence community where Ruby located. He finally was ready to farm, initially partnering with Robert Benjamin Lewis, a friend from Maine who had written the first Afrocentric history of the world, *Truth and Light*. Mr. Lewis had established a farm on the Artibonite River six miles from St. Mark. Ruby informed the editor of the *Pine and Palm* that he intended to "go into cotton planting" and sent them a sample of the local cotton. Ruby probably spent no time growing cotton but instead may have taken up teaching in Lawrence. By August he appeared to have achieved some position of social recognition in the community. On August 1 he participated in a dinner given by the Lawrence Cadets, a military company consisting of the young men of the colony. The occasion, celebrating the British emancipation of slaves in its West Indian territories, included speeches "commemorative of the occasion" and a performance by the Haitian National Guard Band. Ruby attended as an honored guest.[16]

St. Mark and its surrounding American colonies were designed primarily as agricultural communities, and the Haitian government had located the first settlements there in an effort to develop the valley of the Artibonite River. The area offered fair prospects for farming and had been the location of the Louisiana colonization effort in 1859. As a part of the agreement the government had reached with Redpath, each family that immigrated received 15.9 acres of land and each individual 6.7 acres, although the gift was for the use of the land and not a gift of the land itself. Even though Ruby had no known background in farming, his communications with the *Pine and Palm* continued to emphasize the agricultural prospects of Haiti. In a letter sent at the end of August, Ruby declared the area "a perfect garden of Eden." In addition to being beautiful, he believed the soil in the Artibonite Valley to be perfect for growing cotton and reported that Haitians in the area produced this desirable crop. With Americans there, however, he thought that the yield would be increased and that with "American tact and energy, it is presumed that in less than two years, a large business will be carried on, in the exportation of cotton from here to the States, and elsewhere." Ruby remained, even in his expressions of delight at economic prospects of his new country, the antislavery advocate. When cotton from the town of Lawrence supplied the world, he believed the "bugbear King Cotton" would receive a "knock in the head from which he will never recover, unless he comes out on the broad platform of *free labor*." A cotton economy based on slave labor, in his view, could not compete with one based on free labor.[17]

Ruby's positive outlook indicated that by this time he had become a true convert to the idea that blacks from the United States could help establish an independent black republic, and in a world freed from the prejudice of race they could demonstrate the capacities of the race. His youthful enthusiasm allowed him, as it did in his response to the report in the *New York Tribune*, to overlook the many problems that had begun to undermine the effort. Letters from immigrants indicated many problems. Those who attempted to farm faced almost insurmountable problems. The Haitian government only slowly allotted the land promised the colonists and failed to settle land claims effectively. Some of the land in the Artibonite Valley actually needed to be drained, and the government only slowly built the canal it had promised in order to achieve that end. Land allotments often were far from the settlements, forcing farmers to walk miles to their fields. Families could find no clean water for drinking or cooking. Prefabricated cottages that had been sent for their use proved inadequate. In contrast to Ruby's positive assessment of the welcoming character of the Haitians, they even found that the native population not only did not welcome them but also did not hesitate to steal their property. Such information fed the opponents of colonization back in the United States, who spread word in the free black communities of what appeared to be an almost hopeless endeavor.[18]

Ruby recognized many of these problems, although he remained optimistic concerning the long-term possibilities of the American colonies. In an August letter he acknowledged for the first time that a variety of issues concerned the immigrants. He was aware particularly of the impact of disease on the morale of the colonists. In his letter he reported that several residents of Lawrence had died with "acclimating fever." Ruby remained positive about this situation, however, contending that in most cases the fever had only been incident to these deaths, attributing the ultimate causes to "former diseases till existing in the system," or (his temperance background emerging) "intemperance, dissipation, &c." While many had reacted to these deaths by blaming the unhealthiness of the country, Ruby reassured prospective immigrants in the United States that those who had died would have survived had they paid attention to their diet and "more especially in drinking, we are sorry to say it, ardent spirits." Ruby advised any prospective immigrant to "read carefully and attentively Dr. Hawks' Health Hints to

Emigrants [sic]," published in Redpath's guide, assuring them that following Hawks's suggestions would ensure their health. Redpath distributed Dr. J. M. Hawks's "Health Hints" to all of the emigrants departing the United States for Haiti, and Hawks emphasized a good diet as essential to success, contending that most disease in Haiti resulted from imprudence. Unfortunately for many, Hawks counseled drinking water undiluted with the rum or other liquor used by many of the locals. The alcohol might have helped destroy the bacteria that caused the most common problems among the immigrants—diarrhea, cholera, and dysentery.[19]

Ironically, given his assurances that the immigrants had nothing to fear from disease, Ruby contracted one of the fevers that prevailed among the colonists in the winter of 1861–1862. An item in the *Pine and Palm* reported him to be one of the settlers who had died during an epidemic at that time, but the editor suggested that the news was only a rumor and attributed the information to opponents of the colonization plan. Ruby survived his fever and wrote from St. Mark on January 26, 1862, to advise his reader that word of his death was premature. This experience with island disease, however, did not dampen his enthusiasm for Haitian colonization. After admitting that he had been ill, he went on in the same letter to address any complaints that might have reached the United States that the immigration agent in Haiti was inefficient and inactive. Ruby insisted that the agent did as well as any Haitian could do in that capacity. He admitted that a lack of knowledge of how to make a system of immigration work existed in the government. Ruby believed that even to Americans the system was "somewhat complicated, requiring time to understand and fully appreciate," and he advised that appointment of an American agent would reduce friction. Still, even though some friction might exist, Ruby insisted that the colonies were improving and that good things were happening. The canal under construction to bring irrigation waters to the colony's farms neared completion and the government had sent a physician to the community. He ultimately attributed most of the dissatisfaction to the character of individuals who simply were "grumblers." He believed that the majority of immigrants were satisfied with their decision to move to Haiti and thought that nothing would tempt them to leave. As to his whether or not he intended to stay in Haiti, Ruby reported that he thought progress was being made to solve most of the problems, and this fact led him to decide he should stay. After a very short time, Ruby had become an ardent colonist, and he told his readers that he had no intention of returning to the United States.[20]

Ruby had resolved that he would remain in Haiti, but he still had not determined where he would settle permanently after having been in the country for almost a year. After he recovered from his fever, Ruby undertook a journey through Haiti accompanied by friends he had made in the country and examined the prospects for settlement. He continued writing to the *Pine and Palm* and extolling the virtues of the land as he traveled. This trip raises further questions about his exact role in the emigrant movement. His letters at this stage would have been perfectly appropriate for an agent in the employ of Redpath even though no evidence exists that he had such a formal relationship. On March 31 he reached Miragoâne, a coastal community of approximately two thousand inhabitants some seventy miles to the west of Port-au-Prince. Ruby believed that it might be the future port of Haiti since it had a good anchorage and also some protection against storms because of the formation of its bay. He noted that the port already was engaged in considerable trade, with ships that had unloaded in Port-au-Prince taking on their return cargo in Miragoâne. Ruby was particularly enthusiastic in his portrayal of the commerce of the port, reporting that large quantities of coffee and logwood were exported there, while flour, pork, beef, butter, lard, and codfish were among the imports landed there from the United States. Ever the salesman, Ruby addressed one of the greatest concerns of many emigrants when he observed that the town and surrounding area were supposed to be particularly healthy, with cooling breezes from the sea and "gentle winds" from the mountains.[21]

Ruby traveled from Miragoâne to Aquin, on the south side of Haiti's Tiburon Peninsula, on the next stage of his trip. Ruby's writing continued to express his hope for a better future for blacks. When his party left Miragoâne he noted a painting over the gate of the city. It was a picture of Liberty, with the words "Civilization" and "Religion" written on either side. To Ruby, the picture and the words resonated, embodying a "great idea," a view that coincided with the religious ideas of his father. The symbols indicated to him that freedom was a God-given right, but already looking at the world through the eyes of a teacher, he concluded that the symbols also meant that God had given man reason, "which teaches him to rise above the mere level of the brute, and, embracing civilization and religion, become like God, in whose image man was made." He saw this struggle to become more God-like in the history of Haiti. Having gained their independence, the people of Haiti now worked through the "broad light of civilization and religion" to rise above the "degradation, the ignorance" that slavery had imposed. Ruby likened this transition to the growth of an infant, scarcely able to walk, to becoming a "full-grown man—a Nation among Nations." In his understanding of the meaning of words over the gate of Miragoâne, Ruby not only reflected the thoughts of his father but also provided an outline of his own approach to race relations. Blacks had first to improve their own lives. That included accepting the tenets of Christianity. Having done so, they could then demand their place as equals in any society.[22]

Along the way to Aquin, Ruby continued his detailed description of the countryside. As he and his associates moved through the mountains he painted a picture of plenty, a virtual paradise with the trees on the mountains laden with oranges, mangoes, bananas, and plantains. He also found widespread fields with farmers growing both cotton and sugar cane. There was no question in Ruby's mind that the soil was excellent for supporting commercial agriculture. In this letter Ruby also began to use a more florid writing style than he had exhibited previously. He perhaps integrated into his writing his captivation with the beauty of Haiti and the style of the French-speaking Haitians. When a young woman offered him a cup of water as he traveled through the mountains he found himself "refreshed" when he saw "what grace and rustic simplicity the bright-eyed lass" possessed. When the sun set on their way to Aquin, Ruby responded with an outpouring of emotional prose, writing "night came on, and shut out the beautiful sight, hushing pleasant sounds, with which our senses were regaled, leaving only the young moon and the starry heaven to light us on our dark and now rather dubious way." Clearly, Ruby was developing a personal style, even if a bit flamboyant, as a letter writer.[23]

Ruby decided to stay in Aquin, again probably acquiring a teaching position there either as a tutor for the children of the colonists or as a part of the free public school system provided by the Haitian government. From that town he continued to write letters to the *Pine and Palm* providing an optimistic view of colonization, describing the area as one possessed of enormous economic opportunities for any of the free blacks who would come. The town itself, with a population of only fifteen hundred persons, was not as impressive as Miragoâne. There were a few fine mansions, but most of the houses had a "squalid appearance." Still, the place had possibilities. As at Miragoâne, the chief products exported from the port at Aquin were logs and coffee, but Ruby believed greater opportunities existed for the production and export of the latter. The French also had grown sugar and cotton "very easily," and he thought that these crops could be grown again. He portrayed the countryside as languishing because the locals were not working it, thus giving Americans great opportunities. He predicted that "with the influx of a good immigration everything will revive; the 'go ahead' spirit of the immigrants will infuse new life, the land so long left only tilled in part, will again yield its abundant crops as of old."[24]

George Ruby had determined that he was now a Haitian citizen, although he probably meant simply that he intended to remain in the country. He continued to follow events in the United States closely, and his expressions that conditions for his race might change in the United States suggest that his commitment to Haiti may not have been as firm as he made it seem. In his letter from Aquin he indicated that the people in Haiti received regular news from the United States, and the immigrants spent a considerable amount of time discussing the news. That April, 1862, they received news of an action by Lincoln in the *Port-au-Prince Gazette*, probably the announcement of the abolition of slavery in the District of Columbia. It was of particular interest because it provided for the payment of one hundred dollars per person who voluntarily chose to emigrate from the United States. Lincoln signed the bill on April 16, stating his pleasure at having freed the national capital of the institution. Ruby remarked that the message had received "general approbation" among the immigrants, although they waited to see if it would be carried out. He found that there was considerable support in the Haitian government, as well as among the immigrants, that the federal government would now put down the rebellion. In doing so, they hoped that the United States "will crush out and forever, the cause of this dissension." An end to slavery had the potential of bringing a flood of new settlers to Haiti. On the other hand, it might also bring a change to race relations in the United States, thus cutting off the supply of emigrants. Ruby obviously was hopeful that the war would finally bring an end to slavery but was uncertain as to the result for the Haitian colonies.[25]

For all of Ruby's optimism, conditions in Haiti steadily undermined the emigration program. Word of disease and the failure by the Haitian government to readily accommodate the immigrants spread in the United States and discouraged potential migrants. In addition, the outbreak of war and the possibility that it would lead to an end of slavery and a new day in race relations encouraged others to stay in the United States. Whatever the cause, the number of emigrants steadily declined. In the spring of 1862 individuals who had been recruited to join emigrant parties decided to back out and failed to go to Haiti. Redpath, who had remained optimistic about the project through its first year, observed that the efforts undertaken in the spring of 1862 had been a "total failure."[26]

In August 1862, Ruby returned to Maine for what he intended to be a short visit with his family. He alerted the editors of the *Pine and Palm* of his trip and assured them that he would be back, promising to return as early as October. The editor indicated that in the interim Ruby intended to contribute essays and notes to the journal and that he had provided "the most flattering account" of the country, climate, people, and government of his adopted country. After he had spent over a year in Haiti, the *Pine and Palm* reported that Ruby claimed to be "an adopted citizen of Hayti, and says he could not now endure the prejudices of Americans." Ruby had written to the editor that he had become "devoted to the people and country of his adoption, and urges all over whom he has influence to go out with him."[27]

George Ruby submitted what turned out to be his last letter to the *Pine and Palm* for its September 4, 1862, edition. In it he indicated how deeply unhappy he was with his life as a free black in the United States. He provided a scathing review of white policy towards blacks and a renewed plea for free blacks to leave the country. Ruby believed that the war then raging in the United States was proof of God's displeasure with a people who had permitted a great wrong, slavery, to go unpunished. Like the Egyptians in the Old Testament, whites had not listened to the voice of God and "in their hardness of heart refuse to let the oppressed go free." Had even the war, however, allowed blacks to make any gains? Ruby answered, "In *no wise*." Instead of being called on "as equals" to organize regiments to aid in the suppression of rebellion, blacks were "*more* denounced, *more* contemned" than they ever were before. Ruby pointed to mob assaults on blacks in cities, days of attacks on blacks in Toledo and Cincinnati, Ohio, New Albany, Indiana, and Chicago, to prove his point. He also condemned President Abraham Lincoln's meeting with black leaders where the president suggested that free blacks should leave the country to "oblige the whites, as they [blacks] are the cause of this civil discord," a loose interpretation of the president's suggestion that without the presence of blacks in the United States no war would have occurred, made at the White House on August 14, 1862, during a discussion about settling freed slaves in the Isthmus of Panama."[28]

Ruby recognized that most blacks considered the United States their home, but he counseled them to declare that the future of the race was not to be "eternally the *pariah* race." He pointed to the Puritans as a people who had left their homes to avoid persecution and contended that blacks had even more reason for emigration. They should not, he declared, "pursue the stay-here-and-fight-it-out policy" if it was to the lasting detriment of their race. Instead he urged them to join with an "independent people." The Haitian people had "thrown wide their arms of brotherly love" to the free blacks of the United States. Together, he believed, they would be able to build "a nationality which shall stand through all time a monument of African independence and glory!" Ruby, at the age of twenty-four, and as a result of his time in Haiti, had become a strident black nationalist.[29]

Unfortunately for Ruby, when it came time to return to his Haitian home, there was nowhere to go. The entire Haitian project collapsed while he was in the United States. Redpath resigned his post as director of the Haitian Emigration Bureau and moved in new directions that included book publishing and editing, working as a war correspondent, and ultimately serving as the first superintendent of the freedmen's schools in Charleston, South Carolina, following the war. With Redpath's departure the publication of the *Pine and Palm* ceased. Ruby's articles appeared in the September 4 edition, which turned out to be the last edition of the journal. While possibly somewhere between five hundred and two thousand free blacks may have taken advantage of the program since its inception prior to 1862, few remained in Haiti after Redpath left. With Redpath gone, Ruby must have seen no future there.[30]

Ruby found himself without a cause. Unhappy with the situation in the United States, as indicated in his last letter to the *Pine and Palm*, he could hardly be happy back in Portland. There he went back to work as a baker with his brother William. The United States government finally agreed to the use of black troops and began allowing free blacks and escaped slaves into the army in the spring of 1863, but they were placed under white officers and paid less than the whites who served. Ruby and his brother William registered for conscription in Portland in July 1863, but neither rushed to volunteer for service. At the time he registered, Ruby listed his job as "porter," a disappointing station for a young man who had believed himself to be a part of a social revolution. One can imagine the questions in the mind of the man who had been struck by the possibilities for his race that he had seen over the town gate at Mirogoâne. God had given the black race, along with all men, the chance to rise above the level of the brute, to remake themselves in his image. How, in the America to which he had returned, would it be possible to rectify the damage slavery had done, to bring the "broad light of civilization and religion" needed to rise above the degradation and ignorance created by slavery? What could his role be in this mission of redemption for his race? In 1863 he did not see it as joining the army. Instead, Ruby turned his face to the South, where as an educator he hoped to do what he could to bring the light of civilization and religion to the people degraded by slavery.[31]

CHAPTER III

LOUISIANA

I pen you these few lines, trusting they may prove of especial benefit to those who say that the black man, when freed, cannot take care of themselves.—
George Ruby in the Liberator, *February 26, 1864*

In late December 1863 George Ruby left Portland and sailed to New Orleans. He never explained what prompted this move, but given his commitment to the creation of a society that would allow blacks to achieve their fullest potential, he possibly believed that work among the freedmen in Louisiana offered him an opportunity to continue his efforts. Louisiana certainly offered him the opportunity to show that progress could be made even among the men and women only recently freed from slavery. The city of New Orleans had surrendered to Union forces only eight months before Ruby sailed. Many of the surrounding parishes came under Union control in the months following the arrival of federal troops. When that happened, hundreds of slaves left their masters and fled to the city. The black population of the city swelled with these refugees, forcing a response by the Union Army. One of the measures implemented by General Nathaniel Banks to assist the freedmen in their move from slavery to freedom was a school system. The schools needed teachers, and Ruby was qualified to teach. He could help the former slaves take the first step towards improving their lives. After accepting a place as a teacher, Ruby dedicated the next two and a half years to educating the former slaves. In that work he showed himself to be a good teacher, a capable administrator, and an even more outspoken advocate for his race.

In addition to these goals, Ruby may have wished to join his two brothers in Louisiana. His brother William had accompanied Brig. Gen. George Foster Shepley to Louisiana as a mess cook when that Maine attorney had been sent there as military governor in May 1862. His brother Horatio also was in the South and involved in numerous engagements with the Union Army along the Mississippi River, although his role is unclear. George also wanted to enter the army on his return from Haiti and accepted a position as a servant with an officer in the Army of the Potomac, but then he cancelled his plans when he remained in Portland to fill his father's position as porter in the Custom House after his father became ill. When his father returned to the job, George left for New Orleans, a local paper ascribing his motives to a call that was "suiting his aspirations."[1]

Ruby arrived in New Orleans in early January 1864. He initially did much the same thing that he had done in Haiti, demonstrating a self-confidence and set of social skills that allowed him to easily mix with all classes of society. He introduced himself to leaders of the black community and public officials. He soaked up the unique character of New Orleans with its upper echelon of blacks, many of whom had been free before the war. Despite pressure on them to leave the state in the decade leading up to the Civil War, the city still had over ten thousand of this class present. They possessed wealth, education, and culture beyond that of the newly freed who had come to the city after the Union occupation, and Ruby, perhaps because of his experiences in Haiti, moved easily among them. In his roughly three years in Louisiana, he established comfortable relationships with men who would become political leaders later, and he maintained those connections through the rest of his life.[2]

As in Haiti, Ruby was an acute observer of conditions in New Orleans and an inveterate letter writer. The letters that he sent to northern newspapers contained his perceptive observations on conditions among the freedmen and also showed his optimistic view of the possibilities the war had presented for his race. On February 4, 1864, he sent his first letter to William Lloyd Garrison's *Liberator*. The purpose of the letter, he wrote, was to elaborate on the condition of the freedmen in New Orleans. He did so in the hopes that it would convince Northerners of the capabilities of his race. He trusted that his letters might prove "of especial benefit to those who say that the black man, when freed, cannot take care of [himself]." He found that the addition of the freedmen and women to the population of New Orleans had swelled the total black population, including those who had been free before the war, to at least 35,000 blacks, a sizeable increase over the 26,000 who had lived there in 1860. Even though many of these men and women had just escaped from slavery and had suffered all of the oppression of the institution, they impressed him. He observed, "[T]heir intelligence and character, I have simply to say, that no people in like circumstances show a brighter record than they." They had, he believed, made immense economic and moral progress and he detailed their wealth, their religious activity, and the progress of the schools. Considering that many black residents had been free for only two years, he saw "[m]arvelous progress."[3]

The men of the Louisiana Native Guard regiments, many of whom had been free before the war, particularly impressed Ruby. He found the men especially noteworthy because they had performed gallantly and had "withstood the repeated and long continued assaults of prejudice." He cited Captain James H. Ingraham, a veteran of the Battle of Port Hudson who had assumed command of E Company of the Guards following the death in that battle of Captain André Cailloux, as the basis for his impression. Ingraham told Ruby that since the national forces had arrived in Louisiana, he had "harder work in fighting *Northern* prejudice, than he ever had in fighting the rebels." Ingraham welcomed Ruby to his home, a fact indicative of Ruby's easy rapport with the local Creole elite, and showed him the battle flag of his regiment. Ruby found the flag to be stained with blood. Ingraham told him that it was the blood of Anaelma Placianio, the color-sergeant of the regiment who had been shot through the head in a charge against the

Confederate lines at Port Hudson. The banner and the story awed Ruby, and he wrote of it, "Precious memento of [N]egro intrepidity!"[4]

Ruby's letter also recognized the political currents and the factions that existed among the city's white Unionists, especially concerning their views of the place blacks should hold in a reconstructed state. Reporting that an election to establish a civil government in the state would be held on February 22, Ruby wrote that at a convention to nominate candidates, white Union delegates had split on the nominees. The rift had occurred between what he described as "conservative Union men (or Copperheads)" and what he described as more radical men. Blacks in New Orleans opposed the conservatives because they believed that, if empowered, the conservatives would create a government that "will give them [Negroes] no more rights than in the palmy days of slavery." Blacks preferred a candidate to have been strongly antislavery, believing that if that sort of delegate was elected blacks would have "their right, as citizens acknowledged." Ruby found that blacks in New Orleans were not satisfied just to be free. They wanted the right of suffrage as well. Ruby sympathized with the blacks in their desire for the vote.[5]

Ruby found the schools that had been created in New Orleans after the Union occupation particularly impressive. He visited some of the schools where he found the children were doing well. He believed that educational efforts among the freedmen "promise grand results for the originators." Ruby detailed how General Nathaniel Banks had created the schools the previous fall in the belief that education would be a major factor in facilitating the transition of slaves from enslavement to freedom. He believed that the men appointed to run the schools were well-chosen for the work. He praised the men of the Commission of Enrollment that Banks appointed to organize these schools and the naming of Lieutenant William Stickney, an officer of the Eighth Vermont Infantry, an abolitionist, and what the New England Freedman's Aid Society described as a practical teacher, to administer schools for freedmen in New Orleans. Ruby applauded Stickney's creation of a system based on the New England educational system—graded schools with common textbooks and education in morals and character as well as in the traditional curriculum. When Ruby arrived, Stickney had opened seven schools, four in churches and the rest in private homes, staffed by sixteen teachers. With his usual eye for detail, Ruby noted that the system paid teachers salaries of between fifty and eighty dollars per month.[6]

Ruby took note of one of the schools that would have immediate importance to him. That school was located in the Coliseum Baptist Church on New Orleans's Coliseum Square. Jonathan W. Horton, a native of Massachusetts who had been a minister in Milford, New Hampshire, when the war broke out, pastored the church. Horton had gone to St. Helena Island off the coast of South Carolina after the capture of Port Royal to work among the freedmen and became "deeply interested in the spiritual welfare of the freed colored men." In 1863 Horton decided to go to New Orleans, where the military commander allowed him to take over the Coliseum Baptist Church. He formed a school at the church and also introduced the Young Men's Christian Association. Contemporaries considered Horton to be devoted to the rights of blacks and observed that he vigorously supported them in their efforts to secure those rights. Ruby took a position at Horton's school and probably began teaching only a short time after he arrived in New Orleans. He initially headed a class of adult freedmen in the night school. This opportunity must only have confirmed Ruby's own views, for Horton's position on the rights of the freedmen coincided closely with his own. The commitment of the forty-year-old Baptist minister must have assured the idealistic twenty-six-year-old of the rightness of his decision to come to Louisiana.[7]

Ruby's teaching career changed when General Banks ordered changes in the school system on March 22, 1864. He realized the need to expand the system into the rural parishes, and he created a Board of Education charged with developing schools outside of New Orleans. His General Orders No. 38 empowered the board to acquire lands and pay for the construction of schools. The board also had the authorization to employ teachers, purchase educational materials, and establish the curriculum for the schools. Critically, the general authorized the board to levy a tax on real and personal property to support the schools, thus providing a solid financial foundation for the system. Ruby resigned from Horton's school and went to work as a teacher in the new system on June 21, 1864. While working for the new schools he met two men who would play important roles in his later life. Lieutenant Edwin M. Wheelock, a Unitarian minister from New York, abolitionist, and officer of the Seventy-Sixth United States Colored Infantry, served as a school supervisor in the system. Benjamin Rush Plumly, a recruiter of black soldiers and an abolitionist from Philadelphia, headed the board.[8]

The new system first appointed Ruby as head teacher in Reggio, Saint Bernard Parish. He remained there until October 1865. The town, or what little actually existed, was the center of a sugar-growing region located some twenty miles to the east of New Orleans. In addition to a large black population, the area contained many families who had emigrated there from the Canary Islands at the end of the eighteenth century. Little is known about the conditions that he faced in this rural school because no school examiners visited while he taught there, although the school probably appeared and operated much like the other schools outside of New Orleans described in the Board of Education's report at the end of 1864. That report described the rural schools as still in a primitive stage, with the classes held in sheds or buildings seized by the federal authorities. Often such facilities were barely usable. One teacher reported that his school had no floor or windows, and frequent rains required him to move his students into a corner to keep them from drowning. The government often failed to pay the teachers, and locals refused to sell them anything on credit. Food was hard to find, with "strong pork and sour bread" standard fare. Teachers faced hostility from local whites who, according to the report, hated the schools with "all the virulence of ignorance and complexional caste." Ruby's persistence in such conditions showed once again his dedication to the cause of black improvement.[9]

Ruby's classes and his students were probably also similar to the other schools described in the board's first report. Most of the students were ill prepared for classroom work, but on the whole, according to reports from the country parishes, they were eager for an education. Ruby must have adhered to the standard curriculum. Given his religious background, he likely provided the moral and character instruction typical of the New England system as well. Whatever his approach to education, Ruby produced what administrators considered good results in his tenure at Reggio. In their evaluation of Ruby, school supervisors gave him high marks as a teacher and considered him to be a skilled administrator. When a school inspector finally visited the Reggio school after Ruby left in 1865, the inspector reported that under Ruby's leadership the school "had flourished." The high estimation of Ruby held by his superiors in the school system marked him as a teacher who had even greater potential and paved the way for advancement in the system.[10]

Ruby's new opportunities arose as the school system changed. In June 1865 the system came under the control of the Bureau of Refugees, Freedmen, and Abandoned Lands. This government agency had been created the previous March by Congress specifically to deal with the issues connected to the items in its title, although freedmen's affairs came to dominate its efforts. Unfortunately, when Congress created the bureau it failed to provide the resources needed to support its operations. Initially in Louisiana this failure did not present a problem for the schools because General Banks's taxes continued to pay for them. As a result, the bureau's schools initially continued to operate much as they had under the army. The one exception was that the assistant commissioner of the Freedmen's Bureau, who took charge of affairs in Louisiana, abolished Banks's board of education and replaced it with a Superintendent of Education responsible to the bureau. This meant that Rush Plumly lost his job and eventually moved to Texas, where Ruby encountered him later. Wheelock also lost his job but in mid-July received an appointment as secretary of a newly created board of education.[11]

Ruby remained at Reggio during the first months after the Freedmen's Bureau took control of the school system, but in October he moved back to New Orleans, where he assumed the position of first assistant teacher in the Frederick Douglass School. At some point that same month, he assumed the job of temporary principal, then resigned his position as teacher to accept the principal position permanently on November 1, 1865. Ruby's new school had 435 students and ten teachers. A visitor to the Frederick Douglass School shortly after Ruby's tenure there described it in a letter to the *National Era*, a black newspaper in Washington, DC. The age differential in the classes struck the writer in particular, and he noted that he saw at one end of a class "little urchins" and at another a fifty-year-old man. The latter had given up earning more money in the job he had previously held in order to learn to read and write. There was also a night school for adults who paid a dollar a month for tuition. Some of the night students, the correspondent wrote, were "gray headed, and wore spectacles." The greatest irony for the author was the fact that the school met in an old slave market. Over the door a sign read "*Virginia negroes for sale by I. Bruin*," still legible "beneath the black paint (*black*, figuratively as well as literally) which the hand of Freedom has drawn over the words."[12]

The school apparently had been poorly run prior to Ruby's arrival. Past examiners had graded it as unsuccessful and attributed problems to the previous principal. That principal had failed, according to the examiner, because of his "want of attention & thoroughness." In the first report made after Ruby took charge, the examiner indicated that he expected Ruby to make improvements, although little had been done since he had just taken over the job. Ruby must have already made a name for himself within the system since the examiner predicted that his appointment would "no doubt tend to improve the general order of the school." That much was to be done was evident. The examiner recognized that success would be difficult, for while he gave Ruby's teachers high marks, he found that most of the students were indifferent to an education and had been making little progress.[13]

One month later the examiner returned to the Frederick Douglass School. This time he found it "under better discipline and order" and praised the change in principal as having worked. Ruby improved the school not only as its principal but also as a teacher. He taught the A level of the Intermediate Department, focusing on reading, spelling, and definitions.

Ruby also required the students to synopsize their lessons. The examiner found that Ruby had greatly improved student performance in that department and described students' work for Ruby as "very good." After the very negative report given to the school under its previous head, the examiner also praised the improvement that Ruby had achieved in the work of his teachers, whom he now found to be working well. The report attributed to Ruby the phenomenal change that had taken place in the school's performance in only a month. It concluded that what had taken place reflected well on the new principal's character.[14]

The first two reports on Ruby written by bureau examiners expressed admiration for his administrative skills and for his abilities as a teacher. A third, made in January 1866, heaped even more praise on him, stating that the management of the school was "bettered in almost every particular." The examiner offered particular commendation for Ruby's directing all of the teachers in the school to work with their students on using proper English. In an observation that spoke to the goals of middle-class white educators and perhaps those of Ruby as well, the report described the students in the school as "a mixture of creoles, French, plantation negroes, and wild men." As a result, on the ground the examiner found the students unsatisfactorily talked in a "gumbo" language that the examiner thought "abominable." Ruby had paid particular attention to changing those students who always were "talking French or gumbo." As a result, in a comment that said much about how the examiner saw the freedmen, the report indicated that Ruby was "fast getting them civilized" and their behavior had become "less like cannibals." Educational progress, the report concluded, had been as great as any other in the system.[15]

Even as Ruby settled down to his new job at the Douglass School, his future became uncertain when the Freedmen's Bureau's school system began to encounter financial problems. In November 1865, Brigadier General Joseph S. Fullerton, an Ohio Civil War veteran with little sympathy for the freedmen who acted as assistant commissioner of the bureau in Louisiana, suspended the taxes that General Banks had imposed to support the schools. This action cut off the major stream of revenue for the schools. In addition, President Andrew Johnson's pardoning of many former Confederates allowed them to reclaim the property that had been seized during the war. Some of this property had been used as sites for schools or to produce additional revenue, and with its surrender the system lost buildings and money. As a result of Fullerton's orders and the reclaiming by former rebels of their property, the Freedmen's Bureau found itself without funds to pay for its teachers, and in December 1865 the assistant superintendent of the Freedmen's Bureau for Louisiana reported that teachers' salaries were three months in arrears. By January the school system owed the teachers and other creditors over $80,000. As a result the superintendent began closing schools, although he promised to restore them if a new system of funding could be devised. In March 1866 the Freedmen's Bureau devised a new system to support rural schools with a tax of 5 percent on the wages of rural laborers. In towns and cities students would pay tuition of a dollar or a dollar and a half to attend school for a year. Neither plan promised much money, so the bureau schools cut all teacher salaries from an average of sixty-five dollars to thirty-one dollars per month. The new system disheartened the teachers and supervisors. In his semiannual report, the national superintendent of the bureau concluded that the new system was only partially successful, and that the Louisiana schools had entered a "chaotic period from which it will take time to recover." He remained hopeful that support for the schools might come from the various benevolent associations in the North, but the system had clearly collapsed. The number of students had dropped precipitously from 19,000 to 2,239. Only fifteen schools remained out of the seventy-three that existed at the system's height. The number of teachers had fallen from 265 to 150. The superintendent confessed that the figures might even be worse.[16]

Ruby, like most of the other teachers in the freedmen's schools, probably lost his job in January, but he became an important part of the effort at reorganizing the schools that began in March 1866. The bureau's assistant superintendent appointed him as a traveling agent to go to the parishes outside of New Orleans and assess whether or not schools could be created and maintained in the countryside. In the months after his appointment he went to parishes across central, eastern, and southern Louisiana. His observations showed him to be an astute analyst of local conditions, and his willingness, as a black man, to go into some of these parishes revealed him to be fearless in carrying out his duties. On his first trip he traveled north of New Orleans to Port Hudson, where he examined plantations in that vicinity, then rode overland to Clinton and Jackson in East Feliciana Parish. The latter communities were in the middle of rich cotton growing country, and East Feliciana Parish had produced 23,332 bales of cotton in 1860. At that time the black population outnumbered the white by 10,593 persons to 4,681, and he believed it a likely area for schools. Ruby returned to Port Hudson and then made his way downriver through the large sugar plantation parishes with their heavily black majority populations along both sides of the Mississippi.[17]

The trip disappointed Ruby for the most part. Everywhere he went he found that the collapse of the first Freedmen's Bureau schools had brought an end to educational efforts, and that little local effort had been made to create new schools. In the midst of a dismal picture overall, he did find some reasons for optimism. At Port Hudson he found a freedman who had begun building a schoolhouse that could accommodate a hundred students on land rented by another freedman near the Union garrison there. Ruby held a meeting with the freedmen, and they assured him that they desired a school and promised to finish erecting the building. Ruby believed that as many as fifty students would come to the school, even if that meant that they had to pay the dollar-a-school-year tuition since most of the parents were not working on contracts that could be taxed to support a school. Ruby also believed that a "lady teacher" could find room and board with a "well to do freedman" who would willingly offer his home to a teacher. He found circumstances equally favorable at Bayou Sarah and St. Francisville, towns he visited along the river to the north of Port Hudson. While blacks wanted schools and in some cases could support them, Ruby warned that their success would depend on their protection by the United States Army. At Port Hudson, the most likely place to establish a school, he found the post command supported the schools. Ruby believed, however, that without the officer's backing, the school could not succeed because of white hostility to the education of blacks and the "spirit displayed by some 'reconstructed' rebels in the vicinity."[18]

Ruby found the potential for schools to be limited along the Mississippi River, but when he moved away from the river he found conditions even less favorable. When he reached Clinton and Jackson he learned that the freedmen in both towns were interested in having a school. At a meeting Ruby held in Clinton the freedmen even formed a committee of "their most influential men" to look into finding a place where they could build a school. The freedmen in Clinton particularly impressed Ruby, who always looked for proof of black accomplishments. He observed that many of them were "good mechanics and farmers" and lived well. On the other hand, they understood that whites did not want black schools, and they warned Ruby that his mission was a dangerous one. The whites in Jackson were particularly threatening, and Ruby reported that they were rebels in sentiment and that they "hate a 'Yankee,' the Freedmen's Bureau and do not wish a colored school." While the local mayor appeared to have "tolerably right feelings" on the school, even he believed it best for the freedmen to have a southern teacher. After his visit, Ruby concluded that while schools might be located in Clinton or Jackson, it would be neither "safe nor desirable" to try to open one in the countryside.[19]

Ruby rode from Jackson to East Baton Rouge and then on to Baton Rouge, where he found the freedmen equally anxious to have schools established. At a meeting in the latter community the officers of the Sixty-Fifth United States Colored Troops donated one hundred dollars to purchase tuition tickets for those children who were too poor to pay for their schooling. Moving south from Baton Rouge, Ruby found some of the schools created previously by the bureau were still in operation, and he thought teachers could be paid under the proposed tuition system. In most places, however, the teachers had left when they were unable to meet their expenses with the money raised through tuition. Of the schools still in operation, Ruby found most to be run by good teachers, although given his own sense of morality he did not hesitate to condemn one male teacher who he learned was "guilty of conduct lascivious and degrading in its character." He hardly represented the sort of individual who could responsibly develop the morals and character of his charges. Ruby sought his replacement. He ended this first tour through parishes between New Orleans and Port Hudson at Elmwood Plantation, near Camp Parapet in Jefferson County. Ruby made his first report to the superintendent of education on April 12, 1866. He indicated that a little over a thousand prospective students lived in these parishes and desperately needed schools. He noted, however, that given the hostility of whites to black schools almost everywhere he went, the best chance for the creation of schools would be where either the United States Army or the Freedmen's Bureau were strongest and could offer protection.[20]

After his return from the Port Hudson area, Ruby set out almost immediately for a visit to parishes to the east of Lake Pontchartrain and along the state's border with Mississippi. This journey challenged not only his commitment to his task but also his basic courage. He intended visiting St. Tammany, Livingston, and Washington parishes but determined after arriving and consulting with the local bureau agents, planters, and freedman that so few freedmen lived in the Livingston and Washington parishes it would be impossible to sustain schools there. He did believe that enough freedmen lived in the vicinity of Madisonville in St. Tammany Parish that a school could be sustained there. The land in these parishes differed considerably from the rich agricultural lands he had visited near Port Hudson. Not only was the black population smaller, but he thought the countryside was poorer as well. He believed it was not possible to sustain profitable agriculture, and that even if they wanted schools, the freedmen would be incapable of paying tuition. There were some plantations around Madisonville, but elsewhere piney woods covered the land, and raising cattle was the primary occupation. One planter, a lawyer who had owned one of the largest plantations before the war, told Ruby that the plantation had never been profitable and that he had relied on his professional income to support himself. When the slaves were freed, the man simply let them go to "shift for themselves."[21]

Ruby went on to Amite in St. Helena Parish, where he immediately discovered that the black population was too poor to support schools. He described the entire population around Amite as impoverished. Many of the freedmen worked in local sawmills, and employers did not pay them until they sold their lumber and had the cash to pay out. The freedmen who worked on farms generally worked on shares and thus were as cash-poor as the sawmill workers. Even though the situation was inauspicious for creating a school, Ruby still met with the freedmen to discuss the matter on the evening of April 26. Ruby had received word earlier that many whites were hostile to his work and to the idea of educating the freedmen, but that evening he came face-to-face with the terror that many freedmen in the countryside experienced every day. As the meeting began, he informed bureau headquarters that he had the "honor to have two dozen of these poor 'chivalry' enter the building enmasse [sic] with cudgels in their hands." These "poor whites," he observed, were "intensely rebel in sentiment, hating all Yankees most heartily, disliking the trouble of education for themselves and children, resent the idea of schools for freedmen and do all they dare to intimidate and frighten the blacks about the matter." The mob of whites frightened the freedmen, who showed reluctance to enter the meeting rooms. Ruby, however, calmed them down and informed them that if they created a school, "<u>no</u> person could molest them." The whites muttered at times, but Ruby believed that when they saw he was not easily frightened, they "slunk gradually away leaving the meeting to the freedmen." The confrontation in Amite may have been the first time that Ruby faced danger from a white mob, but it would not be the last. After the affair in Amite, Ruby went on to examine conditions in Greensburg, then returned to New Orleans.[22]

Ruby continued his examination of existing schools and the prospects of schools that May in an extended trip of inspection in the parishes to the southwest of New Orleans. On this journey he first went to Terrebonne

Parish, another of the state's major sugar-producing parishes, visiting plantations in the vicinity of the town of Houma. Writing in the same descriptive style he had used in his letters from Haiti, Ruby's account showed how the environment could impress him. Terrebonne Parish had, he wrote, "the richest soil and a larger number of cultivated plantations than any parish I have yet visited." He found, as he had in the Port Hudson area, that many of the freedmen wanted schools, but problems existed. The chief one, as he had found elsewhere, was financial. Here he discovered that many freedmen rented their land and consequently "work for themselves." As a result, they would have no cash until they sold their crops at the end of the year. Schools could not be sustained unless the bureau could find teachers willing to wait until the end of the year to be paid. And, of course, local whites evinced the usual hostility to any sort of black education. Still, at least one school existed.[23]

In his report from Houma, Ruby blamed the local Freedmen's Bureau agent, not the racism of local whites, for the failure of an educational program to develop. Ruby did not believe the agent to be a morally upright man. When Ruby visited the local schools one of the teachers told him that the agent had declared that he cared "nothing for the darkies and is heartily tired of them." "I cannot refrain from writing," he informed headquarters, "that if Bureau Agents in their parishes are seen the major portion of the day loitering in the 'Coffee Houses' and 'Billiard Saloons' of the town they inhabit, it cannot be considered strange if planters and others, the solid men of the community and parish, should be prejudiced towards the Bureau." Ultimately, Ruby believed that if the agents of the bureau were firm and essentially upheld the laws they were committed to enforce, more peaceful relations could be created. His views reflected his continuing optimism that if circumstances changed and the government actually supported the improvement of the freedmen through education, peace would be achieved along with the betterment of race relations.[24]

Ruby went on from Houma to Thibodaux in Lafourche Parish, about twenty miles away. There he found several schools in existence, but there was as much white hostility there as had existed at Houma. The freedmen wanted schools, but many could not afford the new tuition system. Once again, he found the local bureau agent to be inadequate and of little help in furthering the cause of education among the freedmen. In this case the freedmen complained "quite bitterly" that the man catered and deferred to the prejudice of the planters, and asserted that the agent actually assisted the planters in oppressing the freedmen. Ruby believed that some truth lay behind their complaints, and he proposed his own solution. Opposition to the education of the freedmen had to be "overcome," and he believed this could be done only by "firm and judicious measures" carried out by the bureau agents. Again, he counseled the necessity that the bureau put men in place who would carry out the law, further advancing his optimistic view that good laws, if enforced, could solve racial problems.[25]

After Ruby's extensive travel reporting on the possibilities for creating schools, the bureau sent him back to East Feliciana Parish, the parish where he had found so much open hostility to their creation, to open schools. He found a teacher for a school in Clinton, then went on to Jackson to arrange a school there. He discovered that while he had been welcomed as a school agent investigating the possibilities for a school, the local whites would not stand for him actually creating a school. He attempted to rent one of the many vacant buildings in the town, but no one would rent to him. He soon began to receive threats and heard from black residents that whites had said that he "could not keep a negro school there." He immediately enlisted the help of the local Freedmen's Bureau agent and went to the town mayor, informing him that he was an agent of the government and that if he was molested, the perpetrators would be punished. On July 2, 1866, he opened a small school in the home of the freedmen with whom he boarded.[26]

Ruby's efforts provoked a violent response from local whites almost immediately. Late that night a party of fifty men with blackened faces surrounded the house. Ruby, finding himself and the other inhabitants of the house threatened with revolvers, gave himself into the hands of the mob. They carried him about a mile and a half out of Jackson to Thompson's

Creek. They beat him until he could not walk and told him that they "did not want to have any damned nigger school in that town, and they were not going to have it." Ruby escaped the mob by throwing himself into the creek and swimming across the stream. Somehow he got to a federal soldier who helped him bind his wounds and escape to New Orleans.[27]

Ruby reported the matter to authorities in New Orleans and pushed for the mob's arrest under the Civil Rights Act of 1866. That law, passed on April 9, had created a national citizenship and guaranteed, relevant to this situation, the same security of person and property enjoyed by white citizens. The law further prescribed any person convicted of depriving another of these rights to be guilty of a misdemeanor and fined a thousand dollars or committed to imprisonment for up to a year. The law gave the federal courts exclusive authority in such cases and gave various federal agencies the power to institute proceedings; the agencies included district attorneys, marshals, deputy marshals, and commissioners appointed by the various federal courts. Ruby probably was not the first but certainly was among the first to take advantage of the new statute in an effort to secure redress under the its provisions.[28]

Several days after the assault, Lieutenant James DeGray, the bureau agent at Clinton, accompanied a party of federal soldiers to Jackson to arrest the men who had murderously assaulted Ruby. They arrested nine of the party and took them to New Orleans for trial. On July 18, 1866, a hearing was held before a US Commissioner's Court, and Ruby appeared at the hearing to testify against the nine. The commissioner ordered the men tried the following November. He offered them bail at $20,000 each, and when they could not make that amount, he sent them to jail. Their lawyer appealed the decision to the commissioner, asking for a writ of habeas corpus. The commissioner, however, declared that notwithstanding the president's proclamation, he did not believe peace had been established. Indeed, he believed that the men had, in their actions against Ruby, intended to resist the United States government and, thereby, committed an act of treason. An officer of the Freedmen's Bureau attended the hearing and indicated the bureau's intention of holding the prisoners in custody until they could be tried, no matter what the decision on bail.[29]

Violence provided a framework for Ruby's last days in Louisiana when a riot, better called a massacre, broke out in the city on July 30. In New Orleans, Unionists had expressed growing concern over the development of the political scene under the Reconstruction policies of President Andrew Johnson. His lenient policies allowed ex-Confederates to gain control of the Louisiana legislature that assembled in November 1865. That legislature then enacted Black Codes restricting the rights of the freedmen, laws that provided relief to Confederate debtors, and grants to corporations dominated by former Confederates. It also authorized an election for local officials in New Orleans the following March that allowed ex-Confederates to regain control of the city's government. In response, Governor J. Madison Welles, who had been elected in part with the support of these men, abandoned them and determined to fight their return to power by reconvening the state constitutional convention of 1864. A critical component to undermining their power was to change the state constitution to allow black suffrage. Welles's convention was scheduled to meet at the Mechanics' Institute in New Orleans on July 30, twelve days after Ruby's appearance in court to testify concerning the violence carried out against him.[30]

In the days leading up to the convention, tension grew between the supporters of the state legislature and city government and the supporters of the convention. The latter held a mass meeting on July 27 at which speakers supported the call for black suffrage but also warned of potential violence, pointing to the massacre of blacks by whites in Memphis that had occurred the previous May. At least one of the speakers that evening warned the audience that they should be prepared to respond if attacked. On the morning of July 30 several hundred blacks gathered outside the Mechanics' Institute to show their support for the convention, and a party of some two hundred black Union Army veterans marched to the hall through the streets of New Orleans to demonstrate their support for the convention and to join those at the institute. The marchers were met by mob of white men who began throwing bricks. When the marchers threw the bricks back, the confrontation broke out into a widespread melee that moved towards the convention hall. The city police, rather than protecting the blacks, turned on them, joining the mob. As a result the men who had gathered outside the convention hall in support of the meeting were assaulted and many of them shot down or beaten to death. The mob ultimately broke into the hall itself, shooting and beating to death many of the men present, including delegates. General Philip Sheridan, commander of the Fifth Military District, later described the riot as nothing more than a "massacre by the police."[31]

Ruby was in New Orleans at the time and, given his own determination to secure equal rights for blacks, he may have been at least an onlooker if not among the demonstrators on the day of the riot. He certainly was friends with prominent supporters of the drive for black suffrage such as Dr. Louis Charles Roudanez of the *New Orleans Tribune*. White Unionists whom Ruby knew were also present, including Ruby's former employer B. Rush Plumly. Plumly was not in the convention but looked on with a reporter for the *New York Times* and later testified before the military commission created to investigate the riot. Whether Ruby was present or not, the events must have had an impact on him as they did on every other individual who had been working towards full freedom for the former slaves. If for no other reason, he must have been affected by the fate of Rev. Horton, the man who had hired him when he came to New Orleans in 1864. Horton, who had delivered the prayer at the beginning of the convention's session, was still in the hall at the time the riot broke out. As the violence mounted, Horton carried a white flag of surrender to the door of the convention hall. When he attempted to wave the flag through the door the crowd outside shot into the door, wounding him in the arm and hands. When the crowd broke into the hall, someone beat the wounded preacher with a club, fracturing his skull. When rescuers arrived they carried Horton to the United States Marine Hospital on Tchoupitoulas Street where he lived several days longer, dying on August 5. The New Orleans riot signaled the extent of the hostility that men like Ruby who supported Reconstruction and the

Murder of Rev. Jonathan W. Horton, head of Ruby's first school in New Orleans, in Massacre of July 30, 1866 (*Harper's Weekly*, Aug. 25, 1866).

expansion of black rights faced. At the same time, the riot helped bring about a reversal of national policy towards the former Confederate states and opened up new hope for change in the South. Horton became a martyr in the fight for black civil rights. When he was taken back to Boston for burial, the city held Horton's funeral service at the city's Tremont Temple, where large crowds attended and prominent Bostonians, including the governor of Massachusetts, spoke.[32]

The "Great Riot" had another impact, as far as Ruby was concerned. The national superintendent of education for the Freedmen's Bureau noted in one of his reports on the freedmen's schools that the affair had "disastrous results" on school efforts in Louisiana, "blasting . . . the hopes of both the freedmen and their friends." Subsequent political excitement, he believed, had been adverse to the interests of education in the state. Whether the total blame can be placed on the "Great Riot" is unclear, but certainly the freedmen's school system was on the verge of collapse by the fall of 1867. Efforts to continue the schools through a tuition system were fruitless, since paying tuition was beyond the means of the vast number of freedmen who found themselves slowly relegated to a new poverty as tenant farmers. Without tuition, the funding was never enough to meet the massive needs for education among the freedmen. The failure of the schools forced Ruby to turn elsewhere both for work and to continue his efforts in support of his race. In Louisiana he had shown bravery and commitment to that effort. He remained convinced of the importance of education in allowing his race to move forward. His Louisiana experience may also have convinced him that he must look to politics to effect his goals.[33]

CHAPTER IV

THE MOVE TO TEXAS: TEACHER, BUREAU AGENT, AND FLEDGLING POLITICIAN

Mr. Ruby is a very intelligent mulatto. . . . He is an energetic man and has great influence among his people.—General Charles C. Griffin to General Oliver Otis Howard, May 24, 1867

Ruby had no job and no real future in Louisiana after the failure of the Freedmen's Bureau's school system. New opportunities for Ruby and other teachers among the freedmen in Louisiana appeared, however, when the bureau initiated a school system in Texas. In the fall of 1865, General Edgar M. Gregory, assistant commissioner of the bureau for Texas, brought Ruby's acquaintance Edwin M. Wheelock to the state from Louisiana to organize these schools and serve as superintendent. Wheelock encountered problems initially because, as in Louisiana, the bureau had no way of providing financial support. The lack of funds forced Wheelock to create a tuition-based system similar to the one that failed in Louisiana. Still, by the end of 1865, he had created twenty-six schools with 1,691 students. By the end of April 1866, Wheelock had expanded his system to include nearly ninety schools and 4,710 students. Opportunities for school work increased when General Joseph B. Kiddoo replaced General Gregory as assistant commissioner in April 1866 and began funding the schools with fees attached to labor contracts, making possible a further expansion of the system. At the beginning Wheelock had trouble finding teachers willing to work with the freedmen, but the failure of the Louisiana schools gave him the opportunity to hire the necessary staff. By April he had forty-five men and women teaching in Texas, and he reported that he had succeeded in part by bringing in "trained instructors" from the "wreck of the Louisiana school system." Indeed, in his May report Wheelock explained that the teachers had "mostly been drawn" from Louisiana and that he had been able to take advantage of the failure of the Louisiana schools to bring in "trained & competent teachers" who were "accustomed to the negro" and used to the southern climate. George Ruby, who had known Wheelock in Louisiana, followed the Louisiana teachers into Texas. He arrived in Galveston in September 1866.[1]

Ruby would have found Galveston in some ways similar to New Orleans although, with only a little over seven thousand inhabitants, a much smaller place. Like New Orleans, it was the major commercial city of the state. Prior to the Civil War and still afterwards, the city dominated the state's export market. Regular shipping routes connected it directly to New Orleans, the east coast of the United States, and Europe and made it the avenue through which much of the trade of the state passed. In 1860 two-thirds of Texas's cotton crop passed through the port of Galveston on its way to manufacturers. The completion of the Galveston, Houston, and Henderson Railroad's bridge into the city in 1860, just before the war's outbreak, gave the city even greater access to the cotton producers in the state's interior and promised even more trade. As the center of this lucrative commerce, Galveston was also the location of much of the state's financial and provisioning business. With two daily newspapers, it was also the center of communication for the state.

The city had suffered during the war. Trade had been cut off by the Union blockade, and for a time it had even been occupied by Union troops. By 1866, however, the city's merchants were quickly rebuilding their businesses. The establishment of the United States Army's headquarters in the city and that of the Freedmen's Bureau added to its initial postwar prosperity. In addition to its roles in economics and communication, and in part because of them, the heart of political power in Texas also lay in Galveston. The city ultimately offered Ruby more opportunities than teaching school.[2]

Galveston, however, had little in the way of the elite black society that Ruby had found in New Orleans. While New Orleans had a relatively wealthy and culturally sophisticated free black community prior to the war, Galveston had virtually none. The census of 1860 showed only two free blacks in the whole of Galveston County. While blacks constituted a majority of the population in New Orleans and the surrounding parishes, they represented a minority both in the city of Galveston and Galveston County. Before the war there had been 1,520 in the city, a number equal to only a little more than twenty percent of the total population. The number of blacks had increased during the immediate postwar years and by 1870 numbered 3,236, but most of the newcomers were men, women, and children who had left plantations seeking their freedom in the city. While Ruby did not have the social and cultural opportunities offered in New Orleans, the absence of that black social and economic elite presented new opportunities for him. While there must have been black leaders among the slaves in the city prior to the war, none appeared to have emerged in the postwar community. If Ruby, different from the former slaves in his education, his background as a free man, and in many cases even in his light color, could link himself to the freedmen, a greater possibility existed that he could play a significant role in the city. Ruby identified with the former slaves racially. The question that Ruby faced was whether or not the former slaves could identify with him.[3]

On October 15, 1866, Ruby began teaching at School No. 2, located in the Colored Methodist Church at Twentieth Street and Broadway. In his October report to the state's superintendent of education, he indicated that he had just arrived and taken over his school and that he did not yet have a large attendance. He taught at a school that offered both day and night classes. The day school had ten boys and twenty-one girls enrolled. The night school was even smaller, enrolling two men and three women. He operated the schools in conformity with the regulations that Wheelock had issued, with day school lasting from 9:00 a.m. to 2:30 p.m. each day from Monday through Friday. The night school sessions were held each weekday evening from 7:00 to 9:30 p.m. Wheelock made it clear in his regulations that he believed that reading, writing, and arithmetic were the subjects of primary importance for the freedmen and admonished his teachers to make these studies prominent. Through his career as a teacher Ruby showed himself to be skilled at instilling this material and probably did as good a job in Galveston as he had done in Reggio and New Orleans. The downside of his new job was that during his first month at the school he brought in $37.44 from his students' tuition. This was considerably less than he had been making when the Louisiana schools had been fully funded. Still, it was employment and kept Ruby engaged in his efforts in behalf of his race. Noting that he had been on the job only half a month and that few students had yet enrolled, the ever-hopeful Ruby assured his supervisor that he believed the prospects were good for both his day and night school.[4]

Increasing the number of students in the school proved to be a slow process. At the end of October, Ruby had only added two boys and four girls to his day school, increasing the total to thirty-nine. The night school, however, had grown from the original five students to thirty-three. This increase in enrollment boosted his income to sixty-six dollars. In his report for October, Ruby informed bureau headquarters that nothing of special importance had occurred during the month, but he believed that the students in both of the schools were "doing well." In December the number of students continued to increase in the day school, reaching forty-one, although the night school remained at thirty-three. His students continued to perform well and earned praise from the bureau commander. On Christmas Eve, General Kiddoo attended a school exercise. The children presented a program to the general that included declamations and singing. The teachers, Ruby and an assistant, distributed awards for meritorious conduct. At the end of the evening Kiddoo spoke to the children and the audience. Exactly what he said to them is unknown, but the reporter who attended from a local newspaper indicated that he gave them all "wholesome advice."[5]

Ruby was teaching, but, as in New Orleans, he was aware of the political situation developing around him. In December 1866, he wrote a letter to the editor of the *New Orleans Tribune* that discussed affairs in Texas.

The previous summer a state civil government had been created in the Texas under the Reconstruction plan of President Andrew Johnson. The new government had done much to limit the freedom of the newly freed slaves. The state legislature had passed so-called Black Codes that denied blacks the right to vote, hold office, serve on juries, or even testify in court cases that did not involve other blacks. These laws excluded blacks from the public school fund and even required racial segregation of public transportation such as boats and railroads. Additionally, the new governor, James W. Throckmorton, did little to protect the freedmen from the personal violence that had exploded in the postwar years. Ruby did not elaborate on all of the causes of their condition, but he described the situation for blacks in Texas as bleak. He noted that recent reports from General Philip Sheridan about Texas affairs were accurate. On October 20, 1866, Sheridan had informed General Grant that he had "little security from professions of Texas loyalty" and judged the moral standards of the state's white citizens by the fact that "nothing is said or done over the murder of very many negroes in the settled portions of the State." Ruby agreed and stated his belief that "Positively, Unionism, black or white, is not safe anywhere here beyond the military limit."[6]

At this point Ruby knew that Congress was already considering intervening in the Reconstruction process and reversing the relatively mild policy implemented by President Johnson. He voiced his support for an idea advanced in 1864 by Congressman Thaddeus Stevens of Pennsylvania that the former Confederate states should be treated as conquered provinces and thus treated as other territories that were under the control of Congress. In such cases, territorial governors were appointed and the territories admitted as states (in this case readmitted) only on their acceptance by Congress. Stevens's theory had never been crafted into law, but Ruby thought there was no alternative to such a measure, given the South's refusal to accept the legitimate results of the war. Ruby informed the editor of the *Tribune* that he thought the only course, given the circumstances, was for the national government to create provisional governments for the "conquered territories" and then root out the rebels "who assume in the face of four years of carnage and sacrifice of treasure, to rule with the venom of slavery." He hoped that Congress would have the "backbone" to provide justice for the Unionists of "this foully ruled State."[7]

Congress finally acted that spring, although not in the way that Ruby had envisioned. On March 2, 1867, in the midst of growing conflict between President Johnson and Congress, Congress passed the First Reconstruction Act over the president's veto. The act divided the South into military districts under commanders who were to supervise a new program of Reconstruction, and the governments that had taken power under the Reconstruction plans of President Johnson were declared provisional. In Texas, this meant that Governor Throckmorton, the state legislature, and judges, all elected in 1866, now served only so long as the local military commander believed they were working to implement the congressional plan. The congressional program required the former Confederate states to hold new constitutional conventions and write new constitutions that met the approval of Congress. When the people of the states ratified these constitutions and also approved the proposed Fourteenth Amendment to the US Constitution, they would be restored to their normal relations within the Union. The important part of the act for Ruby was the requirement that in the election of delegates to the required constitutional convention, blacks would be allowed to vote. This opened the way to the participation in politics that Ruby's father had fought for in New York and Maine and that Ruby's friends had wanted in New Orleans. The legislation inevitably brought Ruby into politics.[8]

Even though Ruby remained focused on his job as a teacher, he immediately connected himself to the Texas Republican Party, initially organized by white Unionists in the spring of 1867, and the Loyal League, a patriotic organization created in the North during the war and introduced into the South to help the new Republican parties mobilize and organize black voters. The teaching job, however, may have come to look less promising as a vehicle to change race relations. Through that spring his school's student numbers fluctuated greatly and never reached any size. This fact may have undermined any hopes that he could achieve a livelihood as a teacher and led to his greater investment in politics. In the report he filed for January 1867, Ruby indicated that attendance in his school bounced back from the low evidenced in December, with fifty-four boys and sixty-two girls in his day school and thirty men and sixteen women in the night school. Ruby even believed that the enrollments that month amounted to a breakthrough for the survival of his school. With his students paying a total of $55.00 in tuition, he reported that for the "first time since my labors here as a teacher I hope to pay my expenses from money received for my duties as such." The next month, however, even though the number of students increased, some failed to pay their tuition, and Ruby's income was only $40.00. Still, he remained optimistic, reporting that the school was in a "very fair condition as to discipline, etc." He felt it had made a "commendable degree of progress." The problems mounted in March as the number of day students in his classes actually increased, but the night school dropped to only three students. Still, the freedmen paid $62.50 in tuition, even better than in January. At this point Ruby remained hopeful, commending especially the "eagerness displayed by the adults in learning." In April, the number of students in his day school remained roughly the same, but, because the building being used for the night school was being used for other purposes, he was able to meet only two nights a week, and student numbers dropped further. The tuition he received for the month reflected the change, dropping to only $31.25. Ruby once more was in the red financially. Despite the financial problems that he faced, Ruby had established a good reputation as a teacher in Galveston. One of the local Galveston newspapers, though owned by a prominent white Unionist, had shown little sympathy for the work of the Freedmen's Bureau; nonetheless it complimented Ruby's efforts, describing him as "a colored teacher of education, character and ability, and as we believe, an honest man."[9]

Ruby continued to teach through the spring of 1867, but at the same time he became deeply involved in politics. He was in some ways on new ground as he entered Texas politics. His father had sought to create organizations that blacks controlled, and George had hoped for a black nation run by blacks in Haiti. Now, in a state where whites comprised the majority, he became a part of a biracial coalition in order to secure the goals of equality for his race. At the beginning this meant that he often had to take roles subordinate to leadership positions, although even this was a breakthrough since a black man had never played any role at all in state politics prior to this time.

Ruby began by joining the Loyal League. A letter written on April 10, 1867, and sent to General Charles Griffin, then head of the Military District of Texas, created under the authority of the congressional act, indicated that he had not only become an officer of a state league organization but had also become active as a league organizer outside of Galveston. Ruby signed himself as a member of "Texas State Council, U.L.A." Formally known as the Union League of America but usually referred to as the Loyal League in Texas, the league had been created during the Civil War to provide support for the Republican Party and for the war. It was a secret organization with rituals that demanded the loyalty of its members and support of league goals. National leaders of the league introduced it into the South following the intervention of Congress in the Reconstruction process. It was to be used to organize the freedmen in support of the Republican Party. White Unionists, subsequently, brought it to Texas, and a league council meeting probably first took place in Austin in mid-April 1867. Councils in other towns organized shortly thereafter. The secret character of the league made it possible for freedmen and white Unionists to participate in Republican politics without fear of the violent retribution levelled at men openly Republican in the South. Through its rituals, which involved oaths to protect the national government and patriotic songs, the league provided the means to educate the freedmen on their new responsibilities as voters and promoted their loyalty to the party as loyalty to the nation. As with the league in the North, in Texas the organization mobilized voters to support the

Republican Party, and throughout its history in Texas it successfully accomplished this goal.[10]

Ruby's first role in the league was as an organizer, selecting men to create league councils in the surrounding counties. He quickly became aware of the complexities involved in such work among the former slaves. His April 10 letter to General Griffin indicated that efforts to organize a council in nearby Brazoria County had not been successful. Ruby informed the general that he had sent Rev. Houston Reedy, who was also black and an organizer for the African Methodist Episcopal Church, to Columbia as an agent of the league to organize the freedmen and prepare them to register to vote. When Reedy got there, however, he encountered the Rev. Joseph Welch, a white missionary among the freedmen for the Methodist Episcopal Church involved in attempting to bring the freedmen of Brazoria into the ME Church. Welch told the freedmen that Reedy, whom Welch considered a competitor for the souls of blacks in Brazoria, was an "emissary of the rebels." As a result, blacks in Brazoria threatened Reedy's life and only the intervention of the local sub-assistant commissioner of the bureau convinced the freedmen that Reedy had only good intentions. Ruby complained that Welch's motives in "traducing Mr. R. were churchly ones," but that as a result Reedy had been unable to create a local council. Ruby did not ask the general to intervene in the situation but did inform him that the problem's effect had been to "materially retard the growth of so important a movement for our people as the Union League Organization."[11]

The conflict in Brazoria County would not be the last problem Ruby faced. At some point the Galveston council elected him president, and his problems increased. The two daily papers in Galveston, the *Galveston News*, operated primarily as a Democratic newspaper, and *Flake's Bulletin*, edited by a conservative Unionist Ferdinand Flake, both opposed the league, so they readily reported on the troubles Ruby encountered as head of the organization. That tendency exposed internal tensions within the league without providing much information on how the council actually worked.

Several months after the Brazoria County problem, Ruby had to address an internal fight between two important white members over which of the two should be backed by the league for a potential appointment to the mayor's office. The two parties were B. Rush Plumly, whom Ruby had known in Louisiana and who now headed a street car company that he had built in Galveston, and Jesse Stancel, an attorney and a former officer in the Second Texas Cavalry, US. At the time the military possessed the power to remove the sitting mayor, and both Plumly and Stancel wanted the job. Ruby decided to get the local council to throw its support for Plumly. Ruby now faced brutal criticism from the press. In fact, the basis for Ruby's decision in this matter is not known, but his critics now attacked him as nothing more than the creature of his white political friends in the Freedmen's Bureau. *Flake's Bulletin* called him a "tool" of Plumly and of Dr. Robert K. Smith, another northerner associated with the Freedmen's Bureau, the health officer for the Port of Galveston, and the United States Direct Tax Commissioner—all outsiders who came to the city after the war. Prior to this time newspapers had referred to Ruby as an honorable man; now *Flake's* described him as a "selfish and scornful negro" who thought Plumly and other men involved with the bureau to be "his God." These whites were nothing more than "negro pickpockets, and Ruby their tool." For the first time *Flake's* attempted to undermine Ruby's connection with the black voters of the city, suggesting not only that he simply represented the interest of white outsiders but also suggesting he was not fully black. *Flake's* published an anonymous letter supposedly written by a freedman but more probably penned by a supporter of Stancel that called Ruby a "yellow negro." It would not be the last time that his opponents attempted to suggest that as a mulatto, Ruby hardly represented his black supporters.[12]

Ruby unquestionably was connected with a large number of northern whites who were in Texas at the time and had become involved in politics, men called carpetbaggers by their opponents. No evidence, however, supported *Flake's* assertion that they controlled him. Ruby had many political connections by the spring of 1867, and the breadth of these associations was made clear in the men who took leadership roles at a Republican rally on May 15, 1867, the first Republican gathering where Ruby made a public appearance and played a role. Both Dr. Robert Smith and Rush Plumly were present. Other white northerners attending included Edwin M. Wheelock, superintendent of the bureau schools, and George W. Honey, a Methodist minister who had moved to Texas from Wisconsin as a special agent of the American Missionary Association. While involved with these so-called carpetbaggers, Ruby also found himself associated with several Galvestonians who had lived in the city prior to the war. These included Major Oscar F. Hunsacker, the legal counselor to General Griffin; Wilson H. Nichols, a general broker in the city; and Judge Daniel J. Baldwin, United States District Judge for the Eastern District of Texas. In addition to Ruby, several other black men played important roles in the meeting, including John DeBruhl and Stephen Paschal, both former slaves.[13]

The meeting had been called to provide public support for the congressional plan of Reconstruction. When electing officers, the delegates showed their recognition of Ruby's role as a leader in the new party by electing him one of the secretaries, along with Wheelock. He also made one of his first known speeches to the gathering that evening. The delegates approved resolutions that conformed with many of the goals that had been central to Ruby's family for decades, resolutions that provided some indication of his own views of what constituted equality at this time. They declared their belief in the right of all men to equal protection from the government—the right to vote, the right to sit on juries, the right to hold office, the right to equal education in the common schools, and an equal and undisputed share in the benefit of the Homestead laws and all other laws passed by the government. The meeting also provided Ruby with the opportunity to demonstrate his courage during the speech of Stephen Paschal. A melee broke out when an unidentified man in the audience called Paschal a "damned liar" when he asserted that given opportunities equal to those possessed by whites, he could outdistance them. Someone fired shots, the largely black audience of five hundred panicked, but Ruby, rather than running, helped settle the gathering down by having the band play.[14]

Ruby, now finding himself involved in Reconstruction politics, decided to leave the schools to devote more of his time to league organization and preparing for the upcoming election. In May he submitted his last report as a teacher for his Galveston school. In it he indicated that because the school building was being used for other purposes in the evening, he now had to discontinue the night school. He believed, however, that under his supervision the "progress of the school . . . have been . . . commendable and highly creditable to the pupils." By the time he left, the number of students in his day school had increased to 129 boys and girls. The night school, however, already in trouble because of the loss of the use of the building, came to a virtual close. The amount of tuition that was paid amounted to only twenty-five dollars. Teaching school in Texas was not a lucrative affair; indeed it brought in hardly enough to live on. Ruby's experience paralleled that of the teachers in other schools in the state system. Despite the positive reports of the new superintendent, Lieutenant Joel T. Kirkman, the schools had actually made little progress. As in Louisiana, the fee-based system hardly met the needs for education among the freedmen. At the end of June 1867, Kirkman could report only forty-four day schools and eleven night schools in the entire state. Fifty-three teachers worked in the schools instructing 2,975 students, both school-age and adult pupils. The exact number of school-age children in the state at the time is unknown, but the 1870 census found 88,638 black children between the age of five and eighteen in the state. The schools had received little support from the bureau and almost no financial assistance from charitable groups that were working in other Southern states, and as a result had provided an education for probably less than 3 percent of those who needed schooling. Given the bleak outlook for his school and his increasing political activity, Ruby resigned.[15]

After his resignation, Ruby found a new job that allowed him to become more involved in politics, to gain a broader grasp of the problems faced by blacks throughout the state, and to make himself known outside of Galveston. The new job fell under the auspices of both the Freedmen's Bureau and the Military District of Texas. General Charles Griffin, military commander of the District of Texas and assistant commissioner of the Freedmen's Bureau in Texas, named Ruby an inspector. His job would be to visit areas outside Galveston and report on bureau activities. The real purpose of the appointment, however, was to encourage the registration of blacks to vote. Griffin's immediate problem in the spring and summer of 1867 was preparing the state for an election of delegates to the constitutional convention required by Congress. That required the registration of voters, and Griffin was particularly intent on ensuring that all potential black voters be registered. He wanted men in the field to expedite that process. Ruby's appearance at the Galveston meeting in May, his role in the Galveston Loyal League, his association with prominent white supporters of Congressional Reconstruction, and his race gave him obvious advantages in securing appointment as one of Griffin's agents. On May 24, General Griffin asked General Oliver Otis Howard for permission to appoint Ruby. He described Ruby as an "intelligent mulatto" who had been engaged in the education of the freedmen in Louisiana and Texas since January 1864. He praised Ruby as being energetic and demonstrating "great influence" among the freedmen. Griffin planned to place Ruby in the field to observe bureau activity but also to encourage the organization of the freedmen. Griffin believed that using Ruby would allow the bureau to better reach out to the freedmen and that "much good [could be] accomplished which cannot be by others."[16]

Howard granted permission to hire Ruby, and on June 1, after receiving word that he would be hired, Ruby resigned his teaching position to take on his new job. On June 7 General Griffin officially named him as an inspector and awarded him a salary of one hundred dollars per month, a sizeable increase over what he had been making as a teacher. Ruby went on his only inspection tour shortly after the July Republican convention adjourned. His reports indicated the extent of his assignment from Griffin. Griffin had given him "private instruction" and ordered him to report on "how matters exist," essentially to provide information on the state of affairs politically. Ruby also operated under the bureau's Special Orders No. 77 to report on the organization of schools and to encourage the development of temperance societies. His reports were as detailed as those he had written in Louisiana and showed Ruby to be an acute observer of local conditions, a capable arbiter of problems that interfered with the success of the bureau, and an active organizer of the freedmen.[17]

Ruby's tour of inspection covered nine counties and lasted for over a month. The trip would have been arduous and exhausting, even though the railroads had changed the speed with which contemporary travelers could move through the state and made possible the extensive character of his journey. Ruby probably took the Galveston, Houston, and Henderson's 8:00 a.m. train to Houston where he would have arrived at 11:45. From there he would have taken the Houston and Texas Central's 2:15 p.m. train to Millican, arriving there at 6:30 if the train was on time. In only a day it was possible for him to get deep into the state's interior, covering some 132 miles. After this initial rush into the state, however, his journey reverted to pre-railroad travel, having to take one of the Sawyers stagecoaches for the rest of the trip northward, along the east bank of the Brazos River to Sterling in Robertson County, Marlin in Falls County, Waco in McLennan County, Hill County, and his farthest point north in Ellis County. From there he moved east into Navarro County, then back to Waco and southward to Austin through Bell and Williamson counties. He returned to Galveston from Austin, and he wrote his report to the superintendent of education in mid-August. The exact number of miles that Ruby covered in this tour cannot be known, but he probably traveled over seven hundred miles on train, stage, and horseback in the five to six weeks that he was on the road.[18]

Ruby submitted two reports to the bureau, each sent to Lieutenant Joel T. Kirkman, who served as the assistant adjutant general, as General Griffin's assistant, and also as superintendent of education for the bureau. Several general themes ran through his reports as he described the various places he visited. First, he found whites in most of these places to be "unreconstructed" and hostile to the freedmen and white Unionists. They generally manifested their hostility with opposition to black schools. They also readily used violence against the freedmen in any conflict. Ruby showed a certain optimism in all of this, believing that in many cases the racial tension that existed resulted from the failure of local bureau officials, for a variety of reasons, to protect the freedmen and hold whites responsible for their actions against them. If only the bureau's representatives acted, he believed that peace could be restored. In his letter to Kirkman in the latter's capacity as assistant adjutant general, Ruby advised that the white "people need a little rough handling" to create more favorable relations. If the bureau could simply put "energetic faithful" officers in place, Reconstruction could be successfully concluded. As for blacks, he reported them generally fearful of their relationship with whites, but anxious for schools and ready to be active politically.[19]

At Millican in Brazos County, Ruby found that the freedmen and Union men believed the area to be in a state of upheaval with murder rampant. He believed that much of the problem in the county was due to the illness of the sub-assistant commissioner, whom he found unable to do his duties. The freedmen, on the other hand, believed that he was not sick but afraid to confront the widespread violence directed by whites against them. Despite the violence, Ruby found that the freedmen in Millican wanted to create schools and to organize politically. Ruby gave at least one talk to a large number of freedmen, urging them to form their school and also speaking on the importance of temperance. He reported "a great deal of success" in the latter matter, writing that he had obtained over two hundred signatures of men and women taking a temperance pledge. The positive response he received within the black community may have been due to two prominent local leaders. He found the two voting registrars there, a Mr. Kelsey, probably Erastus Kelley who had moved to the county from New York, and George T. Brooks, a black Methodist minister, had emerged as community leaders among the local freedmen. The freedmen had asked Kelsey to become the teacher in the proposed school and Brooks to be his assistant.

Ruby reported the two men willing to teach the freedmen and also ready to help organize the freedmen politically. Ruby informed headquarters, "I organized here . . . ," the blank indicating that he had created a league council. Kelsey headed the organization chartered by Ruby, while Brooks acted as his assistant. Brooks remained an active participant in league activities until his murder by whites the following year.[20]

Ruby moved on to Sterling in Robertson County, where he met the sub-assistant commissioner assigned to that area. He described Sterling as a small town that consisted of "several general stores, three saloons, a blacksmith shop, two livery stables, a post office, two churches, and Masonic lodge," in the midst of a county that had been one of the state's richer plantation areas. The war had profoundly changed the county, with thousands of slaves being brought from Arkansas and Louisiana to keep them from being emancipated by Union forces. Equal numbers of white settlers also had arrived through the 1860s. Such upheaval may account for Ruby's summary of conditions there as being "a terrible state of affairs." Former rebels had openly vowed to kill the bureau agent and did not fear any punishment, for they thought soldiers located in a nearby post would not do anything about it. As for the freedmen, Ruby reported that the local whites "murder and outrage the freed people with the same indifference as displayed in the killing of snakes or other venomous reptiles." Ruby found no outright Unionist other than the bookkeeper on the Ranger Plantation. The owner of that plantation wanted to create a school on his land that fall, but Ruby did not believe any black schools could be created, given white hostility. He was able to secure fifty signees on a temperance pledge at the Ranger Plantation, but he could organize no league council. Again, Ruby believed that the local bureau agent contributed to the problems. He found the agent determined to do his duty and to be popular among the freedmen, but he had been sick and unable to effectively carry out his job. The situation in the county was difficult enough that Ruby expressed relief when he left it. "I did not deem it wise or expedient to stay too long in Robertson County," he informed headquarters.[21]

Ruby left Sterling after completing his duties there and moved on to Marlin in Falls County, some thirty miles away. Falls County had experienced disruptive growth similar to that in Robertson County, but when he visited a point above the falls on the Brazos River, he found conditions "quiet and orderly," a situation he attributed to the fact that the economy there relied less on plantation agriculture. He also believed that the local bureau agent played a role in this relative peace, insisting once again that good agents made possible good relations between whites and the freedmen. He characterized the sub-assistant commissioner, Colonel F. B. Sturgis, as a "judicious, firm officer who endeavors to do his duty." Sturgis impressed Ruby particularly with his commitment to working out peacefully the differences between freedmen and planters. Following his initial report, however, Ruby tempered his praise of Sturgis, relating that he had found that many of the freedmen thought that Sturgis did not represent them fairly in their dealings with local planters. He also heard from white Union men who backed up the freedmen's criticisms and contended that the agent refused to listen to the complaints freedmen made about their employers. They contended that local planters abused their workers as a result of Sturgis's indifference. In a subsequent letter to headquarters Ruby reported the freedmen's concerns, writing that he had counseled them to work out their complaints with the agent. He suggested that the men go to Sturgis and explain their concerns. He also visited with the colonel and told him how the freedmen felt about him and found the agent willing to address the issue. Even in the face of the concerns of the freedmen and white Unionists in the neighborhood, he defended the agent, suggesting that he might only have "unwittingly" frightened the freedmen. In the end, he believed that he had reduced the friction that had existed on his arrival.[22]

Ruby's praise of Sturgis in the face of his apparent failure to fairly represent the freedmen in their labor contracts may have been based on the agent's willingness to be politically active. Ruby's report indicated that he thought that organizing the freedmen in Falls County would be difficult. He found that once the actual registration of blacks as voters had begun, tension between blacks and whites had increased. He remained optimistic about the effort, however, because he found Sturgis supportive of the registration effort and the Republican Party. He believed Sturgis ready to support the party's recruitment of black voters. In a second letter written from Marlin, Ruby observed that Colonel Sturgis had shown his willingness to "act in harmony with the party."[23]

As to the rest of his report on Falls County, Ruby proved as diligent as ever in his efforts. He visited three plantations, the Stallworth, Falls, and Roberson operations, and found the planters more favorably disposed towards black education than in Robertson or Brazos counties. In addition, he found the freedmen already supporting Sunday schools and ready for regular schools to be created. On the three plantations, he apparently did little towards political organization, but he did address a "large number" of freedmen on their new rights when he visited the Stallworth Plantation. In his talk to the gathering he mainly pushed the same message that he had delivered elsewhere, telling his audience of the great importance of education and temperance. He believed that his listeners, both freedmen and planters, had listened with a "great deal of attention," and that he had convinced many of them to take the temperance pledge. Some had even expressed their determination to hang their temperance pledge "as pictures" on the walls of their houses and cabins.[24]

Ruby continued up the Brazos River from Marlin, next stopping in Waco in McLennan County and then moving on to Hill and Ellis counties. The further up the Brazos he travelled, the fewer freedmen he encountered. A sizeable black population lived in McLennan County, a legacy of the plantations that existed in the Brazos bottoms. The white population, the majority working on small farms or ranches away from the river, nearly doubled that of the black. He did not seem to see the area as one where political organization was viable. Instead he spent much more time talking with the freedmen about their need for education and temperance to improve their lot, pushing the self-help and uplift philosophy that had long informed his own ideas concerning the improvement of the race and race relations. He attracted a large crowd in Waco, where he delivered a speech on the need for education and temperance. The fact that three hundred freedmen signed a temperance pledge after his talk pleased him. Further up the Brazos in Hill County he found even fewer freedmen than in Waco, although some did live along the Brazos River bottoms and in the town of Hillsboro. In Hillsboro, a town he called "a squalid affair of a few tumble down houses," he found two Union men who would contribute "moral support" but little else for black schools. Whites in general, however, offered no support for black schools. In Ellis County he found even fewer freedmen, but "evil doing" between the races existed. Little could be done, however, because the local bureau agent at Milford had too small a force to suppress criminal activity. Ruby saw no possibility that a school could be maintained given the circumstances.[25]

After Ellis County, Ruby began his return trip. From Milford he began a part of his trip that challenged not only his physical endurance but his commitment to his job and his courage. He initially intended to investigate conditions in Bosque County, to the west of Ellis County, but decided he should not go. He received reports that dangerous and unstable conditions existed there and that he might be murdered if he appeared. Instead he went east from Milford, probably riding horseback or in a buggy, to the town of Dresden in the western part of Navarro County. He found a large number of freedmen there but doubted that a school could be created because of white hostility. In the countryside outside of the town, "rebel" inhabitants terrorized the freedmen with "brutal and murderous acts." Near Spring Hill, "a miserable rebel hole," he did find one planter willing to let his freedmen have ground for a school and a church and a white Unionist willing to teach it. He believed that the willingness of the prospective teacher, Captain Charles Winn, to teach a black school in a "community of unreconstructed rebels" showed the importance Unionists placed on black education. Ruby never reached the eastern part of the county and ultimately abandoned plans to go into Leon and Freestone counties along the Trinity River. White Unionists and freedmen informed him of the pervasiveness of violence in those counties. He reported that having received word of the "difficulty of travelling and the danger incurred" he decided to turn back.[26]

Dissuaded from an expedition into the plantation regions along the Trinity River, Ruby headed back to Galveston through Austin. Along the way he visited Belton in Bell County, where he found a school of approximately sixty children with a freedman as a teacher in a "poor struggling village rough and uncouth in looks as are its inhabitants." Moving further south he found Salado to be more to his liking, although few freedmen lived in the vicinity. Salado, however, was "an extremely moral one for this county and Texas, no whisky I learned being sold and but one freedman taken out and hung within a year." In a stop at Georgetown in Williamson County, he found whites generally "unreconstructed" but fairly friendly towards the proposed freedmen's schools. A school there was already in preparation, with the freedmen having purchased a house and lot for their schools. Ruby proposed that the bureau aid them in their efforts at paying for repairs to the house, which he estimated would cost two hundred and fifty dollars. At this point in his trip Ruby's reports indicated that he was hastening home, heading for Austin and then back to Galveston.[27]

Ruby returned home even more convinced that successful Reconstruction required the bureau or the government to support education. He thought schools necessary not only for the advancement of the freedmen but also to give support to the white Unionists he encountered on his trip. He found the Unionists treated with incredible hostility by their former enemies. He wrote, "They are socially ostracized and debarred even from school privileges by their rebel neighbors." Ruby seldom spoke or wrote in any detail about what he meant when he advocated civil and social equality, but in this case he urged that if the government created schools for the freedmen, the children of white Unionists should also be allowed to attend. Ruby always denied he had any intention of imposing himself on the society of contemporary whites, but his recommendation for the schools provided one of the first instances where he clearly indicated that he believed in equal access to public institutions regardless of race.[28]

The possibility that Ruby might be able to actually effect change in Texas improved while he was on his journey. The government of Governor Throckmorton offered little help in enforcing the labor contracts of the freedmen or suppressing violence against them, but that impediment was removed at the very time Ruby headed home for Galveston. General Griffin had urged General Philip Sheridan, commander of the Fifth Military District, to remove Governor Throckmorton and other officials put in office in the 1866 election almost as soon as Griffin arrived in Texas, contending that the governor impeded the general's efforts to reconstruct the state. Sheridan had not believed he had the authority to remove the governor, but Congress passed the Third Reconstruction Act on July 19, 1867, and opened the way for Sheridan to act. On July 30 the general removed the governor as an "impediment to the reconstruction of that [Texas] state" and in the next weeks began to remove other officials from the state to local level. In Throckmorton's place, Sheridan appointed former governor and wartime Unionist Elisha M. Pease. The general's action opened the way for Ruby and other supporters of Congressional Reconstruction to play an even greater role in reconstructing the state.[29]

On August 16, Ruby wrote a letter to Governor Pease soliciting a political appointment, noting that they had recently met, probably when Ruby passed through Austin on his return from his inspection tour. General Griffin endorsed Ruby's request, praising Ruby's skills at political organization and noting that since Pease knew Ruby, the general need not add more information. Ruby's associates in the Galveston league, Oscar Hunsacker and Rush Plumly, also added their endorsements. On August 22, Pease removed one of the men holding the position of notary public in Galveston and replaced him with Ruby. The position was not necessarily an important one among the appointments at the governor's disposal, but it did represent a major step for Ruby. It meant that Ruby, who had already established himself as an important leader in Galveston, was known among bureau officials, and had begun to develop connections with blacks beyond Galveston, now had become noticed by the white Republican politicians in Austin. The appointment did not bring a salary with it, but it allowed Ruby to charge fees for any documents he notarized. More critically for any political aspirations he might have had, the appointment marked Ruby as a politician with connections not only in Galveston but with prominent politicians holding state office.[30]

Accepting this position, even though it was not considered a salaried civil job, disqualified Ruby for service in the Freedman's Bureau. Ruby resigned. In the communication accompanying his departure from the agency, Ruby demonstrated a character trait that manifested itself more frequently through his career. Aware of what he contributed to the bureau's work and possessing considerable self-confidence, he refused to accept behavior directed toward him that he considered condescending. On October 1, bureau headquarters in Galveston had requested that the headquarters in Washington revoke Ruby's appointment as an agent since he had taken an appointment as an officer in the civil government. When he received the order revoking his appointment, the paperwork inexplicably listed him as a clerk. Ruby quickly replied to the assistant adjutant general in Galveston that the revocation was inaccurate since he actually had worked as an agent. Ruby did not take kindly to the slight and insisted that his rank in the bureau be recognized. This slightly unhappy episode brought an end to his career with the Freedmen's Bureau. In his time with the bureau he once again demonstrated himself as a hardworking individual, both persistent and courageous in his pursuit of the bureau's and his own goals. Out of the bureau, he now continued to devote himself to creating a more equitable society in the political arena opened up to him by Congressional Reconstruction and where he already had shown considerable skill.[31]

CHAPTER V

EMERGENCE OF A POLITICAL LEADER

Ruby said that by his color, he would represent the black man, by his brains, talents, and culture, he was fit to represent the white man of this or any other State.—Statement attributed to George Ruby, Flake's Bulletin, *December 8, 1867*

A major aspect of George Ruby's character was ambition. He had displayed it when he showed white Portland that a black youth could graduate from the city's high school. His Haitian adventure and the letters that he wrote home revealed that he believed himself capable of assisting in the improvement of the conditions of his race. The same belief in himself was evident in his teaching career in Louisiana and Texas. He had proven himself skilled at political organization and leadership as well. Having left the Freedmen's Bureau, Ruby's ambition turned now to a desire to hold political office, to secure a position where he would be able to help craft laws that provided the framework for society and shape them in such a way as to secure equal treatment for his race. Congressional Reconstruction created the first opportunity for him to obtain such a position when it provided for a new state constitutional convention with delegates elected by an expanded voter base that included blacks. Ruby eventually aimed at attaining the seat for the district that included Galveston. Following his resignation from the bureau, he proceeded to develop support among black voters in that district. He also had to attend to white Republicans. He needed support from at least some of them. He also needed to deal with those who, while willing for blacks to have a vote, did not believe they should aspire to office. Through the summer and fall of 1867, Ruby successfully built the support he needed for success in the convention election, showing again his skills at gaining voter support.

Ruby's activity as president of the Galveston league council and in the city's Republican Association allowed him to play a significant role in Houston on July 4, 1867, when the state Republican Party held its first convention. Ruby was a notable participant even though white politicians, particularly the state's antebellum Unionists, dominated the proceedings. Former governor Elisha M. Pease served as chairman, and Judge James H. Bell, who had introduced the league to the state that spring, also played a prominent role in the proceedings. Many of the whites Ruby had joined to create the Republican Party in Galveston attended, including Wheelock and Honey. Ruby was, nonetheless, an active delegate. On the first day the chairman of the convention named him to the committee on credentials. Delegates elected him one of the meeting's vice presidents, an action that showed that even at this early stage, the men involved in the creation of the state's Republican Party recognized his importance. White hostility towards the convention, which the Democratic *Galveston News* called the "Radical Negro Convention," created a situation alarmingly like that in New Orleans the previous year. The same paper reported that at one point "a riot was imminent and was only prevented by the stoical determination on the part of this people [local whites] to pocket grave insults." Such stories in the opposition press presented Ruby and the other delegates with the reality that for most white Texans, the new party had embarked on a revolutionary journey that could, and often in the future would, meet violent white opposition.[1]

The convention adopted resolutions similar to those embraced in Galveston, committing the new party to many of the goals that the Rubys, father and son, had sought previously. George Ruby had found a political home. The delegates began with declarations of their support for the National Republican Party and for the Reconstruction measures that had been passed by Congress. The resolutions called for the removal of all civil officers in the state who had participated in the rebellion and who were hostile to the Reconstruction acts. Several specific resolutions appealed directly to Ruby, including one that supported the establishment of a free public school system for the benefit of all children of school age "without distinction of race or color." Another resolution advocated the enactment of laws allowing all citizens "without distinction of race or color" to secure homesteads out of the public lands. Contending that the lives and property of loyal citizens were not yet protected in the state, the delegates also passed a resolution asking the military commander to ensure these basic rights. Overall, the new party committed itself at least ideologically to a government offering all Texans opportunities to improve themselves through education and homesteading but also to the larger task of guaranteeing the equal rights of all the state's citizens. Ruby had a platform that, if carried out, tied him to this biracial coalition seeking to control the upcoming state convention and the subsequent government.[2]

Unfortunately, the personal interactions that helped Ruby build support among voters and especially black voters are difficult to discover. The lack of letters, diaries, or even newspapers that spoke for his potential constituents make it impossible to know what attracted them to him. Perhaps Ruby had a head start in developing his voting base as a result of his work as a teacher. All contemporary sources indicate that the black communities throughout Texas wanted schools, and the men and women most vocal in stating this desire were probably leaders in their communities. Ruby's job put him into contact with such individuals. Possibly they saw him as a man of their own race who could help them get schools. He also had an additional advantage. He was a Congregationalist committed to temperance and moral reform. As a religious person he would have found support among black ministers. His religion may also have worked to his advantage at a time when Baptists and Methodists vied, as they had in Brazoria County, for church members. Congregationalists were not involved in the competition, so Ruby may have been seen as unbiased and not favoring one group over the other. In addition, he may also have been seen as a man who could get things done because of his connections with the white officers of the

Freedmen's Bureau, the military, and even Governor Pease and the state government.

While discovering the personal connection between Ruby and his constituents is impossible, Ruby's words and actions do show what he thought his constituents wanted and probably what he believed they needed to hear. In his speeches he emphasized the connection between himself and the black population among potential voters, never suggesting that he was anything but black, despite his light skin color. He desired, like them, a government that would provide education, opportunities for economic advancement, and protection. He also let them know that he might actually be able to secure such goals by demonstrating his ability to work alongside and even influence the white men who held power in the state. Having secured his appointment from Governor Pease, Ruby worked to influence the governor's removal and appointment policies, an effort that not only might produce desired appointments but also would show that he could work with white politicians. In one instance, in October he sent a request from himself, several other Republicans, and league members in Galveston asking Pease to recommend to General Joseph Reynolds that Reynolds name E. M. Wheelock superintendent of the bureau's freedmen's schools. The letter revealed that Ruby understood the complexities of appointments at the time, as he informed Pease that he and his cowriters believed that the governor's personal support of Wheelock would be more favorably received than support coming from Wheelock's friends. They feared that their own recommendation would be seen as "savoring too much of party pressure" and that a "suggestion coming from you would be all powerful and produce the desired effect." Pease apparently acceded to their request and recommended Wheelock, and Reynolds appointed him. On October 12 Ruby wrote the governor and thanked him for his "kindness and consideration." At the same time, he informed the governor that he would make more requests in the future for the governor's help in the appointment of loyal men to government positions and particularly for help in matters addressing "our present evils." While Ruby did not specify these evils, the development of a conflict between Galveston's Republican organizations and the city's chief of police was the evil referenced. This letter indicated Ruby's growing role in local Republican organizations, for he informed Pease that future correspondence would not be of a personal nature but would be from him as a representative of the Loyal League or of the Galveston Republican Association, the non-secret public Republican organization just created in the city.[3]

Registration of black voters and the educational efforts of the Republican Association and the Loyal League in Galveston brought increasing newspaper coverage. That attention provided further insights into Ruby's role in the two organizations and how the two actually carried out their mission. In Galveston, the Loyal League consisted of the most dedicated Republicans and included both blacks and whites. The league council usually considered important issues such as policy, recommendations for appointments in government positions, or who to nominate for offices. Ruby, as president, was able to play a major role in developing the local Republican Party's basic program. After having made its decision, the league passed its proposals on to the Republican Association for consideration in its public meetings. The association invariably ratified the action of the league. A meeting of the Republican Association on October 8, 1867, provided more detailed information on how the machinery of local Republican politics worked and Ruby's role in it.[4]

Ruby chaired the October 8 meeting, where members discussed who should be able to vote on the party's candidate for the city's delegate to the upcoming constitutional convention. While not apparent at the time, the result of the meeting had significant implications for Ruby's future. Rush Plumly, reputedly wanting the nomination, introduced a resolution to exclude all persons disfranchised under the provisions laid out by Congress from voting membership in the association. The resolution effectively would have kept out of the organization any Galvestonian who had voluntarily supported the Confederacy. It would have left control of nominations in the hands of the newly enfranchised blacks, a few white Unionists, and the Northerners who had come to the city after the war. The resolution provoked an immediate and hostile response from Jesse Stancel, also a potential candidate for the delegate position. Stancel, a resident of Texas before the war, clearly would have benefited from a voting base that included other prewar residents. Stancel got backing from several prominent members of the league council and the association, including William E. Parker, a South Carolina Unionist who had come to Texas after the war and been named one of the voting registrars by General Reynolds; George W. Honey from the American Missionary Association; George P. Douglass, an agent with the United States Treasury Department; and Vergie Lemmon, a black man who was one of the vice presidents of the league and probably a drayman.[5]

In the subsequent debates the opponents of Plumly's resolution claimed that they only wished to bring into the association white men who had accepted the results of the war, although to do so would have unquestionably altered the voting base in the organization by bringing in more whites. Plumly offered a compromise that would have excluded only those who had voluntarily joined the rebel army or who were not disfranchised by act of Congress. His opponents refused the compromise. Ruby left the chair to make his position on the matter clear. He agreed with Plumly and argued that former rebels should be kept out of the association. Whether or not Ruby had decided to run for the convention is not known, but his position had significant implications for his chances of receiving the nomination. A larger white presence in the association would not have helped his chances. Ruby's support of Plumly, if Ruby already had decided to run, made good political sense. When the members of the association voted, George Douglass, acting as secretary of the meeting, recorded the resolution as having failed. The debate was not over, though.[6]

At the association's next meeting, Ruby chaired the session once again and moved immediately to correct the earlier minutes to show that Plumly's resolution to exclude former rebels from full membership had passed. Ruby stated that the vote for the resolution had been overwhelming, with 106 votes supporting Plumly and only 47 votes cast in opposition. George Douglass, who was responsible for the previous minutes, defended himself, saying that Ruby had declared the motion lost and that was the reason he had recorded the resolution as having been defeated. Ruby replied that it was Douglass who declared the resolution lost and that the meeting had adjourned before the minutes could be corrected. Ruby pushed forward despite Douglass's opposition and moved the correction to a vote. Ruby's supporters were a decisive majority in the meeting and immediately voted to correct the minutes. Ruby's control of the chair during the discussion of the minutes and subsequent debates allowed him to successfully block efforts by the opposition to open up the membership of the association. The result was to Ruby's future benefit. The maneuvering also showed that by this time he controlled the majority of voting members of the association.[7]

Shortly after the conflict over its membership the Republican Association became involved in another dispute that allowed Ruby to show his mastery of the association and the Loyal League. This incident involved the Galveston police chief, Major Robert H. Perry, a former officer of the Union Army who had been appointed to the position by General Reynolds in mid-August. Galveston's Republicans initially welcomed Perry's appointment and praised his efforts to establish a professional force. Within a week after he took up his duties, however, complaints began to develop among blacks as to his treatment of prisoners. He put both men and women prisoners, mainly blacks, to work cleaning the streets, wearing red flannel badges on their arms. Blacks considered the practice to be demeaning. Criticism intensified when he fired several black police officers and even jailed one. The situation reached a critical point when Perry assaulted one of the city commissioners in a dispute over the use of city carts. Then, in an incident that cost him the support of Rush Plumly, the chief broke Plumly's son's jaw while the youth was under arrest. As a result the city council suspended Perry, although it was not certain that the removal was legal since Perry's was a military appointment. Facing pressure from Plumly and the black community as well, the Galveston City Council removed Perry.[8]

The Republican Association met on October 21, and Rush Plumly introduced three resolutions concerning the Perry situation. The first approved the action of the city council in removing Major Perry for his "grave violations of law, and for gross misuse of his authority, in the brutal and inhuman treatment of peaceable citizens in the street, and of persons in custody in his office." The second asked General Reynolds to ratify the suspension. A final resolution called for the appointment of a committee of five members to present the facts of the case supporting immediate dismissal to General Reynolds. Various members of the association spoke in favor of the resolutions, charging that Perry not only demeaned his prisoners but went out of his way to arrest blacks to clean up the city. Ruby also spoke, indicating that the league had concluded Perry must go. Ruby said that even if an official were his friend or his brother and had struck a prisoner he would vote for removal, and he called Perry a "disgrace to the country." Ruby admitted that Perry was efficient but believed the chief guilty of outrages, particularly in his attack on young Plumly, a "defenseless prisoner." In a broader sense, Ruby wanted Perry gone because the chief was "not a friend of the colored people." As a representative of his race, he stood with them. The meeting subsequently chose Ruby to be one of the men to visit General Reynolds, along with voting registrar William E. Parker and three other white members of the association. With Ruby speaking for black voters and with even white members of the association demanding Perry's removal, Reynolds agreed to the association's demands. In the public mind, Ruby had demonstrated not only that he would work for his black constituents but that he could actually achieve results. The Perry incident further strengthened his position as a representative of Galveston's black community and especially its black policemen.[9]

At the end of the Perry affair, Ruby displayed another characteristic that may have solidified his support among black voters. He showed a willingness to stand up to his white critics. On October 25 he responded to an article that had appeared in *Flake's Bulletin* that complained that the Loyal League had been involved in the business of removing the chief. Ruby's role in removing Perry certainly indicated league involvement, but Ruby insisted that the move against Perry had not originated in any secret meeting. The opposition to Perry had been widespread and openly discussed in the association. He went beyond defending the decision-making process concerning Perry to make a broader attack on the editorial policies of the *Bulletin*, as well as the rest of the white press, and on the character of local publishers. Ruby stated that he had come to view the staff of the *Bulletin* as political enemies and noted that everyone agreed that it was "customary with some journalists to leave a wide margin of truth especially where the acts of their political opponents are concerned." His usual position on getting involved with newspaper controversies, especially where "the advantages of reply are all on one side," was to avoid them. In this case, however, he had concluded that when a Union organization was "persistently abused by a vituperative writer, on account of the individual acts of some of its members, justice demands a fair statement of facts."[10] Whether or not Ruby intended to run for a seat in the constitutional convention was not apparent through October and November, but his role in the discussion of membership in the Republican Association, his action in the Perry controversy, and his public run-in with the Galveston newspapers unquestionably set him up as a possible candidate. By early December, however, his opponents within the league and among the Conservative Republicans like Ferdinand Flake were convinced that he would seek the nomination. On December 8 the *Bulletin*'s "Smooth Epithet," the pseudonym of its local reporter, claimed that Ruby had announced to some individuals that he intended to go to the convention as the delegate from Galveston. Supposedly, he had said that would happen "notwithstanding" any opposition. He reputedly declared that he would go as a representative of his race. The reporter wrote that Ruby said he had control of the league and that its members would support him in preference to anyone else. "They alone," he cited Ruby as saying, "can and will elect" him. At least in the reporter's opinion, Ruby believed that he did not need any white support to be nominated and elected to the convention. Whether or not Ruby had spoken to anyone about his intentions at this point or really believed he needed no white support is unclear. Given his various white associates, the latter is unlikely.

The reporter may simply have been spreading rumors to undermine a possible Ruby candidacy. The piece unquestionably played on racial tensions in Galveston when it suggested a black man did not need white support to hold political office. Ruby never responded to the article. No matter what strategy Ruby might have intended, two weeks after the publication of the *Bulletin* article he did declare himself to be a candidate.[11]

The *Bulletin* reported on December 19, 1867, that the league's Galveston council intended to meet on the twenty-first to nominate Republican candidates for the convention election. The article hinted that Ruby was a candidate and suggested that the idea that he would run had created tension in the council. The item suggested that some of the white men in the league wanted white men as delegates and that this conflicted with the desires of "a colored man who wants to go himself." The "colored man" obviously was Ruby, and the *Bulletin*'s account brought up its earlier charge that he intended to represent Galveston County. This time they put words into his mouth, writing that he had said that "by his color, he would represent the black man, by his brains, talents, and culture, he was fit to represent the white man of this or any other State." With considerable irony, the reporter wrote that it "would be a pity that one so highly qualified should not be chosen." Again, the reporter played up the idea of racial tension existing within the league and playing a part in the nominating process. The same report indicated that the league also intended to nominate Dr. Robert Smith for the Galveston-Harris County floater position. The writer of the piece predicted that the contest in the league was "fair to be bitter."[12]

Race undoubtedly did play a role in the league's and Republican Association's decision-making, and it did show up, as suggested by the *Bulletin*, in the determination of some white members to keep a black man from receiving the nomination. Some opponents to Ruby were men who had their own ambitions regarding the convention, but Ruby's race was perhaps even more important to others. Once the nominating process began, however, Ruby demonstrated that he had control of the two Republican organizations and that his opponents had little chance of stopping him. On the evening of the league council's meeting, the *Bulletin*'s reporter slipped into the hall. He stated that as he approached the council's meeting rooms he encountered a half dozen freedmen guarding the entrance to the hall with drawn swords and that sentries were in place two blocks away to prevent the uninitiated from attending. Ruby was in the chair, and after some procedural issues, he moved that the body take up the question of nominations. His opponents at this time tried to block him, contending that the meeting had not been called to make nominations. Ironically, some of his long-time allies, including Rush Plumly and E. M. Wheelock, supported the move, possibly because of their own desire to go to the convention and their realization that Ruby had the votes for the nomination. Vergie Lemmon, the league vice president who had voted to open up the association earlier, also protested. Lemmon denounced the right of the league to dictate nominees to the Republican Party at secret meetings held at three o'clock in the morning. The majority in the council overrode the opposition, however, and went ahead with the nominations. In their vote they selected Ruby for the seat from Galveston and Dr. Robert K. Smith as the floater from Galveston and Harris counties. Little opposition developed in the vote, with the majority of council members present being black and supporters of Ruby. Ruby's opponents either withdrew from the meeting or remained quiet when the members moved to approve the nominations by acclamation. In his acceptance speech Ruby told his audience that he had always worked for his race and that he would continue to "stand by them always." He already recognized, however, that in a white majority county he ultimately would have to attract white votes and stated that he believed he was capable of representing the white race as well as the black.[13]

On December 24 the Galveston Republican Association met to consider the league's action. When opponents to endorsing the nominees contended that the original agenda did not include such business, the majority of members present voted to alter the order of business to take up the nominations. That vote indicated clearly that Ruby's supporters were in the majority and that his opponents could not block his nomination. With no further discussion, an unnamed member introduced a resolution endorsing the nominations of George Ruby as the Republican Association's delegate from Galveston and Dr. Robert K. Smith as the floater delegate for Galveston and Harris Counties. The members of the association moved immediately to make the vote unanimous. Ruby then addressed the association, probably in the same vein as he had addressed the league council. The newspapers did not publish his exact remarks, but reports indicated that he thanked the members of the association for giving him the opportunity to run and that the rest of his speech had been "pertinent." After taking his seat he had been "highly applauded." The group went on to pass additional resolutions pledging the members of the association to support the nominees.[14]

Ruby had effectively used the league and the Republican Association to assure his nomination. Those who opposed him in each organization, however, were not content to allow his actions to go unprotested. The day after the association meeting, a letter published in the *Bulletin* by George W. Honey and others contended that the December 24 meeting had not been authorized by the association's executive committee and that its actions were not only invalid but not binding on members of the city's Republican Party. The men who signed the protest promised that another meeting would be held to select the legitimate candidates for the election. At least one of the men listed as signing Honey's letter denied later that he had given permission for his name to be used and contended that Honey represented nothing more than a "handful of disappointed aspirants." The dissidents did meet on the evening of December 31 to consider whether or not to nominate their own candidate but failed to agree on what they should do. They ultimately encouraged James A. McKee, a Galveston businessman, to run against Ruby, and William H. Goddard, a local attorney and partner of a former Galveston resident and abolitionist, Lorenzo Sherwood, to run against Smith. Other candidates also lined up to contest Ruby and Smith, including Jesse Stancel, who had by now been in repeated conflict with the leadership of both the league and association.[15]

The white Republican opponents of Ruby had readily supported black suffrage but failed to see that blacks not only might run for office but also had a legitimate right to do so. On the evening of January 31, 1868, former governor Andrew J. Hamilton attended a meeting of the Galveston council of the Loyal League and addressed the issue of black office-seeking, articulating basic reasons for opposing this. Hamilton had been the provisional governor appointed by President Johnson in 1865 to direct the reconstruction of the state. Hamilton had delayed the process, not trusting the former Confederates, and felt justified in his beliefs by the results of the state election in 1866. He had gone to Washington where he had been a major advocate of black suffrage. Ruby's nomination had been one of the logical consequences of that action. In his speech Hamilton recognized that fact and congratulated his hearers on nominating a "negro candidate" who he had heard was a "person of intelligence." He nonetheless addressed the problem black candidates presented for many whites, and he urged the members of the league "not to attempt to have many." He believed that doing so would be "more than the party could carry" and that many white voters would not vote for blacks. In the upcoming election Ruby did not need those white voters, but his ultimate test as a politician in the long run would be whether or not he could secure their support and hold on to his black constituency.[16]

Given the registration figures, Ruby's chances of winning the election were good. He had successfully established himself as the leading black politician in Galveston. His career as a teacher, bureau agent, and then emerging politician had unquestionably established his credentials among the black community. That was the community that could determine the election. When registration closed, blacks represented the majority of eligible voters. Figures published by the army indicated that 953 blacks had registered while only 801 whites had signed up. Conservatives complained that the full white vote had not registered and may have been prohibited from registration, even though the number actually exceeded the number of whites who had voted in the 1866 election. That the registration board actually turned down very few potential white voters suggests that rather than being prevented from registering, many whites simply decided not to do so.

As a result Ruby had an advantage, but he still had to assure a full turnout of black voters, and they had to be unified in their support of him. Prior to the opening of the polls, the city's Conservative newspapers still believed that Ruby's election was uncertain. Ferdinand Flake of the *Bulletin* predicted that there would be a "substantial" contest.[17]

Voting began on Monday, February 10, 1868, and continued through the following Friday. During the five days of voting, Conservatives who had come to support McKee and Goddard remained hopeful that they could defeat Ruby and Smith. They believed that a full white turnout and a lackluster one among blacks would produce victory. Rumors that black voters would not vote as expected for the Radical candidates but would cast their votes for McKee and Goddard also fed their optimism. On the evening of the second day of voting, the Conservative candidate for the floater's position worked to rally support, appearing with his rivals at a public meeting in Galveston. He chastised those who had not already gone to the polls, admonishing those who had registered to do their duty and vote. The editor of the *News* still believed, even after the polls had opened, that Conservatives might pull out a victory if only they would vote, so he urged them to act. Their voting, he wrote, was "the only means left us for our protection" and indicated that the crowds of blacks who had been around the polls on the first days were no longer there "to annoy white voters." A piece in the *Bulletin* concluded that Ruby could be defeated but observed that some Conservatives had said they would vote for Ruby as a criticism of the proposed convention. The writer warned them against such a course. He cautioned that in other former Confederate states, Conservatives had done the same thing, only to get both an undesirable constitutional convention and black delegates. This approach, he believed, was "like playing with edged tools—rather dangerous." If they elected Ruby to the convention, he believed that they would "howl about negro officers, ignoring the fact that they have helped make him so."[18]

Ruby dashed Conservative hopes. Those hopes proved to be little more than daydreams from the opening of the polls. On the first day of the election, observers from the *News* indicated that 480 votes had been cast and that all of them except for about a dozen went to Ruby and Smith. The report also observed that nearly all of the men who cast their votes were "of the recently liberated and enfranchised race." It also noted as something of significance that there had been no disorder or fighting, and the policemen on duty to protect the polls had nothing to do. The *Bulletin* also reported that turnout was large, with lines backing up from the ballot boxes for a hundred or more feet. Like the reports in the *News*, those in the *Bulletin* indicated that few whites had voted. The continued attendance of black voters at the polls and the size of their turnout even led to a shortage of workers in Galveston, since many had left their jobs to cast their ballots, determined to exercise the franchise for the first time. Through all five days of the election observers found that the peaceful conditions continued. Whites voted fast and left the polling areas. Blacks still flocked to the polls. On the final day of voting, a report in the *News* indicated that only a hundred ballots had been cast and that, as on previous days, most of the voters were black. While votes had not been counted, the *News* reporter believed that Ruby was "far ahead of his competitor" in an election that had seen a large turnout.[19]

The official returns verified Ruby's success in consolidating black voters in his support. The results made the basis for his victory clear. First of all, blacks had turned out in large numbers. Almost 92 percent of the men who had registered—879 voters—went to the polls. Only 319 whites voted, about 39 percent of the total white registration. All of the blacks had supported the league's position favoring a constitutional convention, a result indicated by the army's official tabulation. Ruby received nine hundred votes, a result that suggested that almost all if not all the blacks who went to the polls voted for him. If that was true, the results assured him of office in the immediate future but posed problems for his future political ambition, since he received only twenty-one white votes. If more whites registered, maintaining his power ultimately required that he find a way to bring them to his support. That remained in the future. For the moment, Ruby had crushed his opponent, James McKee, who received only 245 votes.[20]

The Loyal League gathered on the evening of February 15 to celebrate

Ruby's victory. The members, gathered on the street, fired a "feu de joie" with thirty to forty pistols. The members also appeared determined to punish those men who had refused to support their candidates. That evening they singled out George Honey for his opposition to the council's ticket. He had already been criticized prior to the election for openly talking against the league's candidates. On the night of the fifteenth, the league expelled Honey from the council. Governor Pease had recently appointed Honey to the position of clerk of the state's supreme court, and the league also resolved to work toward having him removed from that position. Honey contended that he had already resigned from the league. The *Bulletin* printed a letter written by him to Ruby on February 13, in which Honey observed that he believed the league had been organized to "protect loyal men from injustice." Instead, he wrote, "designing demagogues have wholly perverted the same." As a result Honey believed he could no longer lend his influence to its councils. Honey was simply one deserter, but his actions made it all the more critical for Ruby to find some way of maintaining the support of the men he had associated with in the Freedmen's Bureau and to broaden his base among whites.[21]

In the wake of the election, both the *Bulletin* and the *News* speculated as to what the results signified for electoral politics in this new era of black suffrage, and also what could be expected from their black delegate. Much of their allegations and speculation were attempts to undermine the legitimacy of the election, suggesting that the election did not reflect a true democratic process. The newspapers did this by suggesting first of all that black voters had not been open to rational appeals by other candidates but rather had voted machine-like under the influence of the Loyal League. They drew their conclusions in part from the fact that Ruby and Smith had received virtually the same number of votes, a fact that suggested, to them, that black voters had not seriously considered the character of the candidates but had simply voted the way the league's leadership had told them to vote. The votes suggested, to these editors, the "completeness [sic] of the machinery with which the League is armed." Newspaper coverage also insisted that the successful candidates had depended completely on black votes and that black voters had not listened to white leaders but rather to men of their own race. They suggested that this was irrational, or certainly unexpected. One of *Flake's* editorials observed that it was clear that the black voter was going for political counsel to "the man of his own color—that he has more confidence in his own color than he has in the white man. This was not calculated upon at the beginning." *Flake's* concluded that Ruby was the real force in the election and that Smith owed his election to Ruby. In the end, the conclusion was that the men elected did not represent the whites of Galveston.[22]

The editor of the *Bulletin*, who, though a Republican, had never supported black suffrage, also had difficulty understanding what appeared to be the almost unanimous support of Ruby by black voters. He refused to see it as the rational choice of a man who represented the interest of the black race but suggested that the vote might have been accomplished by the use of intimidation at the polls by members of the Loyal League. He reported that unnamed parties had expressed their unhappiness with the results of the election and alleged that on the final day of the voting a committee of the league had been present at the polling place. The members of this committee reputedly examined the ballots of prospective black voters and took away the ballots that were not those for the league's nominees. The writer for the *Bulletin* did not know whether the allegations were true or not and did not wish to unsettle the election, but he did see the election as indicative of how fully organized the league's machinery had been in ensuring support for its candidates. In another article on the vote the same editor attributed the results to the "clannishness with which the negroes voted their own ticket straight." He concluded that this could only mean that blacks were not voting their individual interest but rather were simply voting "as they were told by their leaders." This failure to accept the possibility that blacks possessed legitimate political interests, and that they voted for Ruby because they thought he would meet those interests, was a view of black voting behavior used by men like the editor of the *Bulletin* and then those who failed to receive the black vote for much of the rest of the nineteenth century.[23]

Another question white newspapermen in Galveston raised following Ruby's successful campaign was whether or not he would have any sway in the convention and if his victory meant that Galvestonians were now under "negro domination," a condition where Ruby would carry out some sort of black agenda to the detriment of whites. At the time, the editor believed that Ruby would have little influence in the convention. "Like the stone in the soup," he wrote, "they [the black delegates] will add neither strength nor flavor." He believed that they would talk and make speeches, but "precious little will be their influence." Such speculation, clearly resting on the racist views of the editor and his belief that whites across the state accepted those views as well, would be tested when the convention finally met.[24]

Conservatives perceived the election of Ruby and other black delegates as a political disaster. They immediately began a campaign to discredit Ruby in white eyes, charging that he had ambitions beyond holding office and that he might desire social equality. Such ambitions, in their view, were beyond those appropriate for his race. Robert Josselyn, the former Confederate and rabidly racist editor of the Conservative Party's *State Gazette* in Austin, speculated on whether or not black delegates would be invited to the parties and receptions given by the governor. Were they to mingle with the "wives and daughters of our best citizens to partake of our best society"? If in the future a man like George Ruby, "said to be 'an excellent and educated man,'" was to be elected comptroller and fifteen blacks elected to the legislature, would the governor invite them to social affairs and would they attend? Could they be excluded? The editor believed they would have to be allowed to attend, but then where was the "stopping place"? In an apocalyptic vision of white racism, he asked if there would be rounds of dancing and "a feast of reason and a flow of soul? A rushing and a gushing and a blushing? A gingling [sic] and a mingling and a tingling?" Ruby and the other black delegates had raised questions in white minds that challenged the very soul of their racial views, threatened their world. Given such views, the opposition that blacks faced in achieving success as politicians would be hardly surprising.[25]

In another item in the anti-black *State Gazette*, Josselyn facetiously proposed Ruby for the presidency of the state convention. In so doing, that editor raised the specter of social equality that would result from Ruby's rise to political power. In this case, the *Gazette*'s editor asked where Ruby would board and who would be honored by having their meals with him. He also asked who would furnish the "fine linen sheets, between which the great Ruby shall repose and dream of future honors?" He did not doubt that Ruby already was considering a position in Washington, perhaps the United States Senate, perhaps even the "Presidency of the model Republic." The editor of the *Bulletin* responded that since the *Gazette* had proposed Ruby as their candidate, they would provide the lodgings.[26]

In the end, the editor of the *State Gazette* concluded Ruby could best serve in the office of the comptroller. Others speculated as to how far this revolution would go. In April the *Bulletin* published rumors that Dr. Smith had gone to Washington where he was working to secure the Galveston postmastership for Ruby. Such reports had been in circulation for over a week. While the writer was unsure as to whether or not the rumors were valid, the newspaper did not hesitate to publish them. Later in May, as President Johnson's impeachment trial proceeded in the Senate, other rumors spread that the Loyal League was in the process of putting together a slate of candidates for federal offices in Galveston to be proposed to Congress or the president's successor in the event that Johnson was actually convicted. This time Ruby was reputed to have been their candidate for special agent of the Treasury Department. In every case his attackers appealed to the racist sentiments of their readers and suggested that Ruby represented a threat to racial norms in aspiring to take jobs and power traditionally exercised by whites alone.[27]

Conservatives disparaged Ruby after the election, but he had established himself as a successful politician. Recognizing that fact, the Texas

Republican Executive Committee that had been created following its July 4, 1867, convention named him delegate to the Republican Party's national convention in Chicago on May 20. In preparing to go, Ruby was forced to take steps that raised questions about his financial situation at the time. His fees as a notary had not provided him enough to pay for a trip to Chicago, and he reportedly called on the members of the league for help in raising the funds. The editor of the *Bulletin* advised the city's blacks not to support a trip for a delegate not elected by all Republicans in a traditional way and to "keep your money, it will do more good in time of sickness than he can accomplish for you at Chicago or anywhere else." Ruby by this time had clearly established himself within Galveston's black community, and he successfully raised enough money to attend the convention.[28]

On the way to the convention Ruby became involved in an incident that gained him national attention. As in Louisiana in 1866, what happened gave Ruby another chance to demonstrate his intention of ensuring that black people were protected under the Civil Rights Act. The incident occurred on his voyage from Galveston to Brashear City, Louisiana. On April 14, 1867, he left Galveston for New Orleans on the steamship *Morgan* with two other delegates: R. K. Smith (Doctor Robert K. Smith), who had also been elected to the constitutional convention, and William E. Horne, the recently elected delegate to that convention from Fort Bend County. The ship had already gone to sea when Ruby tended the twenty dollars towards the eighteen-dollar fare necessary for a first-class passage. The purser refused, stating that he would "not take the onus for the precedent." Ruby then talked with Captain J. N. Lewis of the *Morgan* and told him that he did not desire to "obtrude himself on any one, but he wished decent accommodations." The captain informed Ruby that it was the owner's instructions that he followed and that the ship's rules allowed black people into the passenger cabin only to permit them to occupy mattresses on the floor at night, "coupling his refusal (after Mr. Ruby had indignantly left him) with grossness of language and deportment to Mr. R's friends, unbecoming a gentleman." Smith and Horne both offered to let Ruby share their rooms, but Lewis replied that he would only allow Ruby a deck passage. Ruby, consequently, spent the twenty-six hours of a "tempestuous and rough Gulf passage" on the open deck. After arriving in New Orleans, he immediately filed a complaint against the Morgan Steamship Company and demanded $5,000 in damages.[29]

Conservative newspapers in Galveston immediately interpreted Ruby's action as an effort to gain what they defined as social equality, seeing the event as confirming their charge that Ruby was a social radical. An editorial in the *Bulletin* responded to Ruby's complaint by suggesting that he might have the moral right to have a room or even a first class dinner but that "a majority of the travelling public have a prejudice against persons of Mr. Ruby's race sitting at the table." Consequently, Ruby had no right to demand a "violation of the usual custom." The editor believed that he had no legal action possible under the Civil Rights Act. Ruby's friends responded to charges that he had intended to break social barriers by insisting that he had not asked to sit at the table with white passengers but had only wanted a stateroom and that his meals could be served there or elsewhere. Oscar Hunsacker informed the editor of the *Bulletin* that Ruby had no intention to "obtrude himself on anyone, to violate any social or other custom of the travelling public." He obviously did want to have equal access to the facilities of a public means of transportation.[30]

The Morgan case showed Ruby's basic view of what he meant by social equality. In this case he wanted to be treated equally in a public conveyance. Past actions also indicated that in addition to basic civil rights, the vote, and equal protection under the law, Ruby defined social equality as equal access to public institutions like schools that opened up new opportunities for blacks and even entry into private businesses that served the public. For Ruby, social equality simply meant being treated equally in the public sphere. For conservative newspapers, however, such goals marked Ruby as a real revolutionary. At this time they saw equal access to public places like restaurants and governmental institutions such as schools as the first step towards an amalgamation of the races. One correspondent of the *Galveston*

News called the acceptance of Ruby's ideas of social equality "sentimental treason." In another letter to the *News*, "An Old Texan" called social equality the "open door to universal depravity, a mongrelization [sic] of colors of civilization, and of progressive depravity." Ruby and those who opposed him had radically different views of what social equality meant.[31]

Ruby's case did not come up before the United States Commissioner in New Orleans until April 29, 1868. Dr. Smith appeared for Ruby, since Ruby may not have been in the city, testifying on what he had seen take place on the *Morgan*. In his testimony Smith emphasized the unwillingness of the captain to allow Ruby to room with him and the refusal of the purser to accept the twenty dollars offered for the room. He also testified that at no other point in their trip together had there been such discrimination. They had ridden the train from Brashear City to New Orleans together. They had shared a room in the Orleans Hotel. Ruby had sat at the table with the other boarders with no complaints. He stated his belief that Ruby was a very intelligent and highly educated young man. The captain and the purser testified for the steamship company, offering only that it was the policy of the company not to "admit colored persons into the cabin." In addition, they suggested Ruby had not suffered any real harm from his deck passage since the sea may have been rough but the ship never was in danger. The commissioner ruled in favor of Ruby, although he was awarded only $250 in damages rather than the $5,000 he had demanded. After the decision, Ruby and Smith went on to Chicago.[32]

Ruby found his first Republican National Convention uneventful, at least in terms of playing an active role. It is hard to imagine, however, the excitement that he must have felt to have become part of the process of choosing a candidate for president of the United States when only two years before he could not have voted. The Texas delegation represented a state that had not yet been returned to the Union, and its status initially was in question. The regular delegates voted on the first day, however, to allow the Texans to be active participants in the convention. While white Texans took places on all of the convention committees, Ruby was left out. He was overshadowed by the presence of the white delegates. Men like Robert K. Smith, Alfred Longley, and A. J. Bennett had all served in the army during the war and had made themselves known at the Sailors and Soldiers Union meeting held before the party convention. Jack Hamilton, who headed the delegation, was a well-known character in the North for his role in supporting the overturning of Presidential Reconstruction and received the only personal attention from the Northern press. The only mention of Ruby appeared in an item in the *Chicago Republican* that indicated that his appearance had produced considerable conjecture because of his "peculiar physique." It went on to note that he was a man of "fine personal appearance, denoting extreme vitality and mental vigor." As a result of his light color, however, "bystanders" wondered if he was a Mexican, a Creole, or a Negro.[33]

On May 29 Ruby returned to Galveston on the steamer *Josephine* in the company of Smith, former Governor Hamilton, and other convention delegates, this time experiencing no problems with his accommodations. He appeared at a mass meeting to endorse the Chicago convention's nominees for president and vice president at the AME Church on the evening of June 2. Ruby addressed the crowd and used his speech as an opportunity to show himself as a man who understood larger economic and social issues and who would represent both blacks and whites in the upcoming convention. His speech focused on what he had seen on his journey to and from Chicago, a trip that had taken him to Louisiana and then by rail through Mississippi, western Tennessee, and Illinois. What he saw convinced him that the nation was on the verge of a better future. In the Southern states he traveled through he discovered that laborers had settled down and worked cheerfully. The political situation, under the protection of the military authorities, appeared to be steadily improving. In addition, he found the economy to be modernizing with the introduction of labor-saving machinery. On the whole, he believed the situation hopeful for the freedmen. A stable economy also boded well for the merchants whose livelihoods depended on the revival of the South's agricultural economy. The optimistic picture that he drew showed Ruby was willing to see infinite possibilities even in the

Reconstruction South. Matching as it did his view of conditions in Haiti in 1862, his characterization of conditions at this time suggests that Ruby still had a very positive outlook on life.[34]

Ruby may have accomplished little in Chicago, but by the time he returned to Galveston he had established himself as a representative of his race, at least among the freedmen of that city. An event that occurred shortly after his return provides possible insight into how blacks in Galveston had come to see him, although the report came from the *Bulletin*, whose staff often misrepresented all news surrounding Ruby. On his return to Texas, Ruby had gone to Austin to participate in the constitutional convention, and rumor spread in Galveston's black community that he had been assassinated. A reporter wrote that the rumor had spread quickly and that he had been told by a black man that "President Ruby is killed, shot at Austin." The reporter had responded by asking the man what organization Ruby was president of. The man responded that he was "President of Galveston." Another black joined in, contending that he actually was "President of all Texas." While any article on Ruby that appeared in the *Bulletin* must be viewed carefully, the story suggested that Ruby's constituents in Galveston had come to see him not only as a representative of their interests but as a significant player politically.[35]

On June 15 an event took place in Austin that showed that the view of blacks in Galveston had a great deal of validity. On that date the state Loyal League organization held elections to choose officers for the upcoming year. Judge James H. Bell, a close associate of Governor Pease, had introduced the league into the state in 1867 and probably still headed the organization at this time. Newspaper coverage of the league meeting portrayed him as the front-running candidate and likely to be reelected. Despite this foregone conclusion by the press, Ruby challenged Bell for the office. When the vote was counted Ruby won, defeating Judge Bell by one vote. With that vote Ruby emerged as a state figure in the Republican Party, not simply a local leader. His victory provided an additional indication that blacks and black leaders in particular refused to remain simply in a supporting role. Ruby and others wanted actual power as well.[36]

The response of white-owned newspapers indicated the earthshaking character of Ruby's election. In Galveston, the *Bulletin*'s editor contended that Ruby's victory had occurred only because Judge Bell had not made it known at the commencement of the meeting that he was interested in the presidency. When Ruby won the presidency, a correspondent for the *Bulletin* wrote that the council's proceedings "do not give eminent satisfaction." White men would now have to deal with a black man who controlled the organization. The *News* in Galveston also recognized the revolutionary character of what had taken place, concluding that the Republicans had "caught in the negro a real Tartar." No one would have imagined that a virtually unknown black man would defeat Bell, "at one time Associate Justice of the Supreme Court" for any position, much less that of the "Grand Mogul of said saintly combinations." The Democratic *Houston Telegraph* also jumped on the discomfort that Ruby's election created among many white Republicans. In an editorial paralleling that of the *News*, the editor of the *Telegraph* noted that Bell had run for the supreme court in the Confederate state government and been defeated, had failed again in 1866 in an effort to get on the court, and now had lost a race "with a carpet bag negro for the Presidency of a secret political society, and the negro from Philadelphia has beaten the learned and distinguished 'native of Texas.'"[37]

Ruby's career between August 1867 and his arrival in Austin for the constitutional convention in June 1868 represented a rapid rise to political power. He successfully gained control of the two Republican organizations in Galveston necessary to that rise to power. He overcame opposition to his course from within his own party. As his ambitions became better known, he also began to face attacks that focused on his race, characterizing him as a man with ambitions beyond his ability who also disrespected whites. Despite all of this he managed a successful election campaign. In the upcoming convention he would have to prove that he could effectively act in the interests of his constituents, that the attacks upon him were spurious and did not represent his real character. He would need to determine a way not only to represent the black constituency responsible for his gaining office but also to prove to white Galvestonians that he could look after their interests as well. Winning whites to his support represented a formidable task given how his opponents portrayed his basic hopes for a more equitable society. The constitutional convention provided a difficult test of his abilities as a politician.

CHAPTER VI

CONVENTION DELEGATE AND RADICAL REPUBLICAN

He is an educated man and has a very neat and genteel appearance, seem[s] to be quite a ready debater, and evidently 'feels his oats' in the position he occupies.—Characterization of George Ruby in Dallas Weekly Herald, *June 20, 1868*

George Ruby arrived in Austin for the constitutional convention on June 1, 1868, one of ten blacks among the ninety men elected to the convention. His campaign had indicated that he hoped to represent the interests of his black constituency, in particular, in the convention. Without question he hoped to help draft a document that provided for racial equality before the law. Precisely what these provisions might be was not clear when he arrived. As a Republican leader he backed the party's platform and its support of the Fourteenth Amendment with its guarantee of citizenship and equal rights to the freedmen. A similar guarantee in the state constitution would certainly be something he might want to incorporate. Texas Republicans had committed themselves to the creation of a public school system in their 1867 convention. From his experiences as a teacher he would have wanted to insure that system included black students. Although he did not push the idea in 1868, he might even have envisioned a system of integrated schools such as had existed in Louisiana.

The state party had endorsed a constitutional provision for a homestead law. For the thousands of freedmen left at the end of the war with no access to land, equality before the law demanded that they have access to the state's lands. To advance such an agenda, Ruby had to face a different political environment from what he faced in Galveston. In Galveston he had a black voting majority to work with. In the convention he was part of a small black minority. Even if all the black delegates voted together, which they would not, advancing an agenda required that he work with white delegates, most of whom were Unionists but few of whom were of the same character as the men he had worked with in Galveston. For the most part, it was unclear how far Southerners would go to work with a black man. Ruby used the convention to build alliances with whites to secure a constitution that would guarantee equality, at least for all of the state's male citizens.

Creating alliances with white Republicans was not easy. As indicated, most of Ruby's white political associates did not fully share his vision of a racially equitable society. The fact that white Republicans quickly broke into factions only tangential to the concerns of Ruby and the other black delegates made creating these alliances even more problematic. The most troublesome of the splits among white Republicans that Ruby had to negotiate centered on what contemporaries called the *ab initio* issue. At the time Texans formed the Republican Party in 1867, most of the party's leaders favored declaring all of the state laws passed, and state, county, and even city government actions taken since secession, to be null and void from the beginning, or ab initio. This included the acts of the Eleventh Legislature in 1866. Implementation of ab initio would have nullified the seizure of Unionist property during the war, the criminal prosecution of Unionists, the legislature's allowing the state's railroads to repay their debts to the state in Confederate money rather than gold as originally required, and many other such measures that Unionists and then Republicans considered supportive of the Confederacy and ultimately hostile to their own interests. The unity among the white Republicans, however, had not lasted. Governor Pease and former governor Jack Hamilton, elected to represent Travis County in the convention, came to oppose a general nullification, possibly because of the damaging impact it would have had on the state's railroads if they were forced to repay in gold the monies to the school fund they had paid in Confederate paper during the war. Jack Hamilton's brother, Morgan, representing Bastrop County in the convention, and Bexar County's James P. Newcomb both supported ab initio. The two sides refused to compromise. Ruby had not taken a public stance on the issue when the convention assembled. Unless the two sides reached an agreement, Ruby would have no choice but to ally himself with one of the groups to gain support for his own agenda at the convention.[1]

Initially Ruby tried to stay clear of such factional disputes among the white delegates. He demonstrated this reluctance when he attended a public meeting in Austin held by the local council of the Loyal League on June 13. The original purpose of the meeting is unknown, but the meeting took a pronounced ab initio turn when Morgan Hamilton, possibly the strongest advocate of ab initio within the party, took the stage to speak. George W. Whitmore, the delegate from Smith County and another ardent advocate of the issue, joined him. Both men spoke in favor of making ab initio a major goal of the convention. Whitmore reputedly said that any man who did not support the idea should be considered a "rebel." As the newly elected president of the state Loyal League, Ruby would have been expected to attend the meeting, but his presence did not necessarily indicate his own support of ab initio. In fact, when Ruby was asked to speak, he told the audience that he believed party unity was more important than supporting any particular ideology. The reporter for the *Austin Republican,* the newspaper spokesman for Governor Pease, congratulated Ruby for counseling harmony. The reporter praised Ruby, who, joined by Charles W. Bryant, the black delegate from Houston, spoke of the importance of the party maintaining unity to create a "*Free* Constitution, placing White and Black upon a perfect equality before the law" rather than going "wild about *ab initio.*"[2]

Ruby's future course on policy might have been unclear, but from the beginning, he actively participated in the body's proceedings, and he earned the reputation of being a delegate who understood the ins and outs of a convention and who looked out for the people who supported him. Ruby's earliest effort in the convention aimed at obtaining a place on the convention staff for one of his Galveston supporters. His work to this end showed his ability to negotiate the complexities of the elective process. Max Mobius was a former white Union soldier who had worked as a clerk in the army's Bureau of Civil Affairs in Galveston. He became a member of the league in Galveston and was one of Ruby's allies. On June 2, Ruby nominated Mobius as a candidate for the position of Enrolling Clerk, a position that involved preparing official copies of the actions of the convention. Mobius faced three opponents in the race for the position, but Ruby actively campaigned for his candidate. On the first ballot Mobius received forty-five votes against a combined thirty-four votes for the other three candidates. This victory showed that Ruby already possessed considerable influence in the convention, but he showed further skills and attracted more attention when he helped the Republican leadership ensure control of the convention by supporting a resolution that demanded each member of the convention swear an oath that he would support, protect, and defend the Constitution and laws of the United States. The vote on this measure, opposed by the Democrats on the floor, passed with sixty-four delegates voting for it and twenty-two against. That vote was the clearest early indicator of the strength of the Republican Party in the convention. By the third day, Ruby had emerged as one of the floor leaders of his party, introducing party-sponsored resolutions to appoint delegates to the various committees assigned to drafting the new constitution. That Ruby would play an important role in the process was made apparent when the president of the convention, Edmund J. Davis, named Ruby to the important Committee on Political and Legislative matters, a committee assigned to examine the political condition of the state and the state's position relative to the national government. Ruby subsequently served on other significant committees, including the Education Committee, the group tasked with developing provisions for a school system, and the Division Committee, the one assigned the controversial task of considering whether or how to divide the state into new states. The Division Committee proved particularly important as the convention progressed because white Republicans would divide over it along the same lines as they had on ab initio.[3]

In the early days of the convention, Ruby's actions attracted considerable attention from newspaper reporters who were present. They appeared particularly interested in observing how a black man would perform in a political body like a constitutional convention. Their initial expectation was that, as a black man, Ruby would be subservient to the whites. Ruby failed to meet these expectations, exhibiting behavior that often led these white reporters to describe him as acting inappropriately for a man of his race. One of the first portraits of Ruby at work came from the correspondent for John W. Swindell's *Dallas Herald*. On the first day of the convention, Ruby went to the front of the hall to pick up a list of officers, and he stopped to talk with the reporter. Ruby asked him what newspaper he worked for. When the reporter told him his paper was the *Herald*, Ruby replied that it was a "fine paper, though strongly opposition." The reporter answered that it was published by a good man. Ruby, in turn, said that he must be since he "evinced brains more than many did in a better cause." The reporter was not impressed by Ruby's ability to engage a white man in what might be considered a socially skillful manner but instead saw the encounter as reflecting a certain abrasiveness on Ruby's part and a readiness to be overly familiar with a white man. That correspondent held much the same sort of view of all the black delegates, whom he found to be "very forward and . . . not at all backwards, not even modest." Ruby seemed particularly aggressive and made himself, in the words of the reporter, "quite conspicuous," a judgment not intended to be favorable. In a second article on Ruby, the reporter for the *Herald* further elaborated on his view of Ruby, describing him as "an educated man" who had a "very neat and genteel appearance." He also found him to be "quite a ready debater." Again, rather than seeing these as positive attributes, he found Ruby's possession of traits as off-putting. He concluded that Ruby "feels his oats" and aspired to be a party leader, ambitions that the reporter believed made Ruby unpopular with many of the white Republican delegates and actually produced jealousy among them.[4]

The reporter for the *Galveston News*, the state's principal paper associated with the Conservative party, wrote much in the same vein, recognizing Ruby's skills but refusing to recognize any of the characteristics usually associated with a good leader—self-confident, diligent, hardworking, knowledgeable, and intelligent—as something desirable in a black man. Ruby impressed the reporter for the *News* with his performance in a debate over how much money delegates should receive each day for their service. Some of the white delegates had proposed the convention pay the delegates eight or fifteen dollars per day. Stephen Curtis, one of the black delegates, said that he did not need to be paid for his loyalty and thought five dollars per day would be appropriate. Ruby agreed with Curtis and indicated that five dollars would satisfy him as well. The reporter thought that Ruby had done well in the discussion. "Ruby is bright," he wrote, "his language good." Like the reporter for the *Herald*, however, he found Ruby's persona to be annoying and too forward, even impertinent. He concluded, "[I]f he would get over his pertness [he] would do very well." Within two weeks the same correspondent became more critical of Ruby, contending that he was "losing ground." The reporter wrote that he had come to realize that Ruby was "not the smartest man in the Convention." He pointed to Ruby's resolution asking that members be provided with maps of the state, hardly an unreasonable request, as evidence of his "impracticable" and "foolish" actions. The characterization of Ruby by the reporters for the *Herald* and the *News* made clear from the start that a black politician in Texas would face criticism and hostility, no matter how skilled he might be.[5]

Ruby had insisted that Republicans in the convention should avoid fighting over ideological issues and focus on the basic tasks of completing a constitution that met the requirements of Congress, but he quickly found that the issues that divided white Republicans refused to be suppressed or compromised. When they began to appear for consideration on the convention floor, Ruby had little choice but to take sides. On June 5, Andrew J. Evans from Waco, a prominent Republican lawyer and jurist, introduced a resolution declaring that the convention would not recognize as valid any legislative action by the state government after secession that was not sanctioned by Congress, the first effort at getting ab initio recognized. This resolution went to committee and then came back to the floor on June 16, opening the way for an extended debate. Evans subsequently became the primary spokesman on the floor for the ab initio idea, although he found strong allies in Morgan Hamilton, James P. Newcomb, and Edmund J. Davis, president of the convention. Former Governor A. J. Hamilton, Morgan Hamilton's brother, led the opposition on the floor. Debate on the issue continued almost daily, with the convention sitting as the Committee of the Whole, all the members discussing the issue in a secret session. Ruby, after having avoided aligning with either side up to this time, spoke on the issue on June 25.[6]

The June 25 speech marked Ruby's move into the ab initio camp. Ruby never explained what convinced him to favor ab initio. Not all of the black delegates supported it, so Ruby's decision was not inevitable. Still, black Texans plainly had an interest in the issue. No clearer statement of that interest had been made than that of Attorney General William Alexander when he resigned following Governor Pease's proclamation on October 25, 1868, that ruled against ab initio and contended that the laws in question must be considered "rules of government." That proclamation had been intended to put the question of the legality of government actions from secession up to that time to rest, but it only provoked Alexander, who had already issued an opinion that these acts were illegal, to resign. He published his letter of resignation and in it provided a lengthy explanation of his reasons. Alexander pointed out that at least eighty-three laws passed by the Constitutional Convention of 1866 and the Eleventh Legislature were hostile to the United States government and loyal citizens. Another two hundred laws rewarded former rebels in one way or another. Alexander also contended that some twenty-four of these laws discriminated particularly against the freedmen and needed to be annulled. Alexander did not list all of the laws he questioned, but they certainly would have included such legislation as the provisions of the Constitution of 1866 that denied blacks and their descendants the rights of citizenship and dedicated the state's school fund to whites alone. The Eleventh Legislature also had been particularly aggressive in its efforts to limit the freedom of blacks with apprentice, contract, and vagrancy laws. Access to justice was limited by denying blacks the right to serve on juries or to testify in court against whites. Laws even required the railroads to provide separate accommodations for blacks. These measures certainly were of interest to Ruby and to the majority of his race. As long as Republicans were unified, they might be addressed internally, but with the party splintered, Ruby had little choice but to unite with the ab initioists.[7]

Ruby's service on the convention's education committee may also have influenced his course on ab initio. That committee did not issue its report until July 23, but its members early understood that if laws passed by the state government during the war remained in force, the state's school fund would be bankrupt. The railroads built in the state prior to the Civil War had borrowed millions of dollars from the school fund prior to the war. In 1864 the legislature had allowed these railroads to substitute the payments on their loans in state warrants, paper money issued by the state government, rather than in gold, as had been required by the legislation originally loaning the money to the railroads. The companies had unloaded their worthless state money on the fund. If the law authorizing the substitution of state warrants for specie was invalid, the railroads would owe the school fund some three hundred thousand dollars to replace the worthless state warrants. In addition, the railroad companies owed the state overall some $2.5 million for the money they had borrowed. Ruby's education committee recommended the companies and their equipment be sold to fund the creation of a public school system. If invalidating the provisions of the Constitution of 1866 and the laws of the Eleventh Legislature that denied full freedom to the freedmen was not reason enough to support ab initio, Ruby's interest in securing a free education for the children of his race was another reason for his alliance with white ab initioists.[8]

The exact content of Ruby's July 25 speech is not known because debates were held in the convention meeting as the Committee of the Whole and were not officially recorded. Remarkably, the official party newspaper, the *Austin Republican*, never even mentioned the session. Democratic newspapers in Galveston, however, did note it, and in their comments provided the substance of Ruby's remarks. The speech was given as a reply to a lengthy attack against the ab initio doctrine made by Jack Hamilton. Ruby charged that Hamilton failed to understand the need for the doctrine and that Hamilton's mind was "trammeled by the ideas of slave times." He should, according to Ruby, consider the needs of "Young America," possibly referring to the newly enfranchised African American voters. He went on to lecture Hamilton on the need to maintain harmony in the Republican Party and suggested that the former governor's position was taken simply because he had not been consulted on the matter. The correspondent of the *Galveston News* suggested that Hamilton had closed Ruby's mouth with "a few courteous words," although it is hard to imagine Ruby being intimidated by the former governor. The *News*'s man went on to condemn the Galveston delegate for a speech that he considered "pert, a quality very pretty in a little girl, but not at all suitable to a legislative body." Ruby's maiden speech obviously shocked white observers and marked a significant moment in his efforts to connect himself to enough delegates to advance his own agenda. He had taken a clear position on this troublesome issue and had begun to establish himself as an ally of the white advocates of ab initio in the convention, men like E. J. Davis, James P. Newcomb, and Morgan Hamilton.[9]

Three days later, an exchange between Ruby and Henry C. Pedigo, a white delegate from eastern Texas and a supporter of Jack Hamilton, showed that Ruby's break with Hamilton had become personal as well as ideological. Pedigo lectured Ruby and the other black delegates on their obligation to Hamilton, who was "responsible for negro suffrage in the Southern States." He reminded them that Hamilton was worthy of their confidence, and they did themselves an injustice when they opposed him. Pedigo's comments implied that blacks had no real interest in the issue. Ruby rose in reply, unable to let the charge go unanswered. Ruby called Pedigo's assertion that blacks should have confidence in Hamilton a slander against black people. He went further to charge that Pedigo's remarks were "personally odious to him and that he did not wish such remarks to be made again." The exchange showed an increasingly self-confident Ruby in debate and a willingness to go against some of the state's best-known politicians to resist their efforts to pursue policies detrimental to the interests of his constituents. As in the exchange with Hamilton, however, the hostile newspapers in Galveston saw his encounter with Pedigo as further evidence that Ruby was assuming a role inappropriate to his race. The correspondent of the *Galveston News* who described Ruby's remarks concluded that they gave further evidence of the "haughtiness with which the colored delegates are bearing themselves," and predicted that many white Republicans would soon realign with the Conservatives.[10]

Efforts to include provisions in the new constitution that would have nullified the acts of the state government after 1861 came to nothing. Following days of debates, Jack Hamilton introduced a substitute for the original ab initio resolution. Hamilton's resolution declared only the Ordinance of Secession, laws contrary to the Constitution of the United States and national acts, laws in aid of the Confederacy, and laws aiding disloyal men at the expense of the loyal to be null and void. It recognized the principle of ab initio but provided considerable latitude in interpreting what laws aided the Confederacy or led to results at the expense of loyal citizens. This included enough latitude to allow the railroads to claim their debts had been faithfully paid. This was unacceptable to ab initio supporters, but on June 29, the delegates sitting as Committee of the Whole passed Hamilton's resolution. The vote was not part of the convention record, but the correspondent of *Flake's Bulletin* believed that the substitute received a favorable vote, forty-two to thirty-seven. The supporters of ab initio then moved to table the substitute, effectively ending further discussion. Ruby cast his vote with the ab initioists along with all but one of the other black delegates. Ruby's role in bringing together the majority of black delegates behind ab initio is not known, but the vote showed that a bloc of the black delegates now existed. Not only Ruby but most of the other black delegates also had seen the relevance of ab initio to their future. For Ruby, the fight over ab initio began an alliance with the white men who supported the measure that remained through the rest of the convention and much of the rest of Reconstruction.[11]

Ruby's association with the supporters of ab initio may have influenced the direction he took on a second issue that split the Republicans and one that his committee assignment on the Division Committee made important for him personally, the possibility of dividing the state. Interest in a division of the state had its roots in prewar white politics. Pressure came particularly at the time from people in the eastern and western sections of the state and reflected their belief that the politicians and business interests of Galveston, Houston, and Austin dominated state government and state funding, all to their detriment. After the war, the supporters of division publicly argued that splitting the state into two or more parts would produce havens for wartime Unionists and create a state truly loyal to the national government. In 1866, for example, convention president E. J. Davis had urged Elisha Pease to support dividing the state along the Brazos River, a move that would have divorced San Antonio and other southern communities from a state controlled by Galveston and Houston, creating what Davis believed would be a loyal state in the west. The question was of little consequence to Ruby's black constituents, but many of the white delegates who supported ab initio supported division. This was particularly true of delegates from the southern and western parts of the state, a group that included Davis, Newcomb, and Morgan Hamilton. As he allied with them on ab initio, Ruby also tied himself to these men on the question of division.[12]

Ruby became involved in the debate over division on June 8 when the Committee on the Division of the State first took up the issue. Given Ruby's electoral base in Galveston, his work on this committee required considerable diplomacy since Galveston's white businessmen were not interested in dividing the state and depriving themselves of the interior markets to the east and south. The editor of *Flake's Bulletin* had made it clear that Ruby should look to the city's interest and urged its readers to contact the delegate to make their wishes known. If Ruby intended at any point in the future to expand his base of support to include the white businessmen of Galveston, there was no question that he needed to heed that advice. Ruby may have ultimately assumed that his best course in the convention was to maintain his alliance with the ab initio men who supported division to get the sort of constitution he wanted. At the same time, while he aligned himself with the divisionists, he attempted to bring about a division that best protected Galveston's business interests. On June 24, the majority of the committee reported a proposed ordinance on division that supported a bill in Congress sponsored by Fernando C. Beaman of Michigan that would have divided the state but recommended that the boundaries proposed by Beaman be changed. The suggested change would have moved Dallas, Collin, and Grayson Counties and the city of Dallas into a new state formed by eastern Texas. The change would have removed what was becoming one of the richest agricultural regions in the state from the Galveston and Houston market and shifted its trade eastward to the Sabine River. Ruby, along with Erwin Wilson of Brazoria County, the two representatives of central Texas on the committee, issued a minority report proposing that the original boundaries of the Beaman Plan be maintained, keeping these three counties and Dallas in a central Texas. Ruby's move was a calculated one and necessary politically. He had to maintain support in the convention, but he also had somehow to attract white support at home.[13]

In the instance of division, the movement stalled in the convention when its proponents divided among themselves on boundaries for proposed states and how best to proceed. After several weeks of debate and increasing disagreements among divisionists, on July 14 James W. Thomas of Collin and Denton Counties introduced a resolution that would put an end to all discussion of division until Congress authorized action on the question. The most fervid divisionists opposed the measure, but in a vote on July 16 a majority voted against a move to table the Thomas resolution. When taken up again, a subsequent vote approved the resolution and effectively ended debate on the question for the rest of the convention. The majority of black delegates voted in favor of Thomas's resolution. Ruby, however, showed that he had linked himself more strongly with what now appeared to be an ab initio-division faction of the Republican Party. He was among the thirty-seven men who voted against Thomas's measures and attempted to continue debate.[14]

Ruby's masterful stance on ab initio and division linked him to allies he deemed essential to gaining support on matters of greater import to him as a black man. Of these, none was possibly more important than his desire for the convention to take measures to suppress the violence, usually directed at blacks and white Unionists, that had increased following the advent of Congressional Reconstruction and the extension of voting rights to blacks. In the spring of 1868, the state witnessed the introduction of the Ku Klux Klan, an organization promoted by both the state and the national Democratic parties with the specific goal of driving black and white Republicans from power. The Klan's appearance had taken place contemporaneously with conservative belief that Texas might be back in the Union by the end of that summer and that voters would be able to participate in the upcoming presidential election. During the first session the convention's Committee on Lawlessness and Violence reported that 428 freedmen and 470 whites had been murdered in the state since the war's end. Noting that most of the freedmen had been killed by whites, the committee concluded that a war of races was taking place and that the war was "all on the part of the whites against the blacks." With political violence on the increase, Governor Pease recommended in his address to the convention that the new constitution disfranchise enough former rebels to ensure political power would remain in the hands of the loyal citizens of the state for the foreseeable future, but the delegates looked to other means to suppress the violence as well.[15]

Among the measures that Republicans considered were raising a loyal militia and creating a police force of detectives to suppress the rampant violence. On July 6, Ruby became involved in a bitter debate that took place over a resolution introduced by E. J. Davis to authorize him to ask Congress for permission to organize a militia. Two white conservative delegates, Lemuel D. Evans, a conservative Unionist and ally of Jack Hamilton from Titus County, and William H. Mullins, a former Democrat and conservative politician from Cherokee County, objected to the measure, charging Davis with attempting to impose an "unmitigated and cruel despotism" on the people of Texas. Evans denied the validity of the report on violence and contended that its authors simply wanted a pretext for creating a police force and militia to suppress their political opponents. He went further, using words that actually undermined his contention, when he suggested that for peace to be restored blacks had to accept their minority status and that it was in their interests to accept that "the political forms should rest and remain, with the more numerous race." Mullins joined Evans in opposition, speaking in even more antagonistic terms about the Republican Party's desire to create an army of "forty thousand black men, just released from the manacles of slavery and not yet emerged from the long night of ignorance and superstition in which their souls have been enveloped for centuries . . . to patrol the premises of their former masters." He believed such measures were unjustified by the report on violence and would only open old wounds, and predicted that they would lead to violence, saying "midnight will again be made hideously luminous with the glare of the incendiary's brand and torch, consternation and death will stalk broadcast throughout the land; the earth will again be drenched in blood, and wail of despair and grief that will go up from this devoted country will be sufficient to appal [sic] the ear of Heaven!"[16]

Ruby offered a forceful reply to the two speakers. He charged them with using words that would excite their supporters to "deeds of violence and bloodshed on Union men and Republicans." Should that happen, they would be as responsible as the men who actually committed the violence. The guilt would be on their heads. He went on to challenge their view of blacks. They appeared fearful of "negro equality, afraid of a race who have been oppressed and downtrodden for two hundred and fifty years." They represented blacks as being belligerent to whites and asserted that they even brought murder and outrages on themselves by their insolence and lawless conduct, in a sense blaming the victims for the crimes against them. This was vilification, Ruby insisted, and failed to perceive the reality of his race. He declared that blacks were God-fearing and possessed more than any other Christian characteristic the willingness to turn the other cheek to their persecutors. If any of Evans's and Mullins's fear of blacks was justified, Ruby suggested, it was that the freedmen would outrun them in the race for improvement, progress, and honor. In what must have been a particularly infuriating point to Conservatives, Ruby countered their suggestion that in relationships between whites and blacks, one or the other had to go down by saying that this "axiom has been ocularly [sic] demonstrated to us time and again by the gentleman and his friends in the licentiousness so common hitherto, and the fruits thereof daily manifest in the faces of their descendants," a clear accusation of white sexual impropriety. "The black race will be annihilated' [they said]. Judging from their works in the past we may prognosticate for the future, should they and theirs have the dominion, that the 'unfortunate blacks' will be bleached out by their policy."[17]

The violence that concerned Ruby intensified while the constitutional convention was in session. Only a short time after Ruby's response to Evans and Mullins, a riot took place in the town of Millican in Brazos County on July 15 and 16. Referred to by whites as a riot, it might more accurately be described as a massacre. In a confrontation between local whites and blacks an unknown number of blacks were killed, including the local black preacher and voting registrar who headed the Loyal League in the county. Local whites contended the entire affair was caused by blacks, although all of the casualties were blacks. Ruby was certain that the affair was political and that whites had initiated the confrontation intending to crush the Loyal League in Brazos County. On July 21 he introduced a resolution into the convention calling for the appointment of a special committee to investigate the murders and, concerned for the safety of the committee, that the military send an escort to accompany it. In the end the committee never went to Millican. A change in military command in Texas caused the committee to back off. On July 28 General Joseph J. Reynolds assumed command of the Fifth Military District, now with Texas separate from Louisiana, and the convention asked Reynolds to investigate the Millican affair rather than send its own men. The violence in Millican underlined the necessity of including safeguards for the rights of the freedmen in the new constitution, especially when Reynolds did nothing about the murders.[18]

Ruby's increasingly public role in the convention and his alliance with the ab initio-divisionist faction of the Republican Party brought more intense criticism of him from the Conservative and old Democratic newspapers of the state. They turned him into an example of the black man who would not be satisfied simply with equality before the law but who wanted social equality as well, a characterization intended not just to defame Ruby but to suggest that the entire Republican Reconstruction plan aimed at a social revolution. The newspapers clearly intended their attacks on Ruby to have this broader purpose, and at times they even sank to publishing fallacious reports that intimated Ruby's radical ambitions. The Democratic paper in Austin, the *State Gazette*, was the worst offender in these appeals to the racial fears of its white readers. When the ladies of the Austin Presbyterian Church gave a supper as a fundraiser for their church, an article in the *State Gazette* contended that Ruby had asked to attend. Desiring to go to a supper given by white women was proof, according to the article, of Ruby's desire for "negro equality" and represented behavior totally inappropriate for a black man. In fact, Ruby never asked to attend the supper, and the newspaper actually published a retraction, burying it in a small item. Once published, however, the rumor helped fix Ruby's reputation as wanting to break down racial barriers. It also ruined the women's fundraising event since, at least according to the *Gazette,* many people did not attend because they expected Ruby to be there.[19]

In another such story, the *State Gazette* published a claim that Ruby had sought a ticket to attend a musical performance given by a German theatrical company at Buaas Hall. The venue was a saloon, beer garden, and hall on Austin's Pecan Street, licensed by the state government and theoretically open to all. The *Gazette* reported that the men who put on the event denied Ruby admission. The head of the column with the account read, "Negro equality repudiated by our German citizens." As in the case of the Presbyterian supper, the *Gazette*'s story had no factual basis. Ruby had asked Julius Schuetze, a German delegate to the convention from Bastrop County, if the group would mind if he attended. Schuetze then asked the president of the association if there would be any objection to Ruby's presence, indicating that he had seen blacks attending other theatrical productions and concerts where admission was paid for. The president of the association responded that he had no objection to Ruby's attendance, and Schuetze bought a ticket. Ruby was unable to attend, however, because he had another engagement. The story that Ruby had been denied entry to the performance, Schuetze said, was "basely fabricated."[20]

Ruby triggered even further hostility when he stood up for himself against insults and insinuations from his opponents. Following a debate on the convention floor in which former governor Hamilton once again contemptuously dismissed what Ruby was saying, an action referred to in an article in *Flake's Bulletin* as a snub, Ruby complained to the reporter who had filed the article, contending that he had attacked his manhood. The reporter replied by asking Ruby whether or not Hamilton had snubbed him. Ruby said that even if it were so, the paper should not have mentioned it. At this point Ruby also said that if the reporter did anything like this again there would be a fight. As usual in a fight with a newspaper, the newspaper man had the last word. In the correspondent's response to Ruby, he alleged that the delegate had complained twice before to him about the accounts he had sent to the *Bulletin* but that he did not intend to engage Ruby further. The reporter suggested that Ruby was too easily offended and that his testiness was a matter of common talk among other delegates, who were mortified at his "assumption." Ruby should be more deferential, he insisted. Had not Ruby's rights and privileges been given him as a free-will offering, he asked, rights that white men had struggled to give him? Where had Ruby been in the past war? Where were his brave deeds then? Such deeds, he asserted, were out of place in the present. In his view, Ruby's "unseemly assumptions" created a "stumbling block and a hindrance to the men of his race." He should acknowledge his debt to the men who had fought on the battlefield for the privileges he enjoyed. Ruby, he concluded, overrated his natural abilities and his acquired attainments at least 50 percent. Ruby, of course, had no platform he could use to counter such attacks, and they continued, as hostility towards Ruby increased even as he strengthened his own position in the convention and within the party.[21]

In August, as the constitutional convention moved into its third month, the state Republican Party held its second convention in Austin. The convention quickly broke down as the ab initio-division split with their opponents over the direction that the Republican Party should take. The breakup would have enormous consequences for Ruby's political future. Delegates to the convention gathered in the hall of the House of Representatives in the state capitol on Wednesday, August 12, while the constitutional convention went into a temporary recess. The party's gathering proved contentious as many of the issues that had divided the party in the constitutional convention spilled over into proceedings. Ruby's role in the party's internal fights was a critical one, and in the convention Ruby played a major role in determining the future course of the party. By this point the division among the white Republicans had reached the stage where there appeared to be little chance of reconciliation. The friction caused by the fights over ab initio and division was made worse by the fact that the chairman of the state executive committee, John L. Haynes, had packed the convention with anti-ab initio and anti-division delegates, many of them representing and voting for counties that did not send actual representatives. On the second day of the convention, this fixed majority voted not to include an ab initio plank in their platform. As a result a number of the delegates, led by E. J. Davis and James P. Newcomb, walked out of the convention, then reassembled that evening to discuss what course of action to take. Ruby attended the meeting of the bolters that evening to see what would happen, although he reportedly had not agreed at that time to go with them. A reporter for the *Austin Republican* also attended the meeting and found the hall of the House of Representatives to be filled. Angry speeches asserted that the Conservative Republicans had refused to harmonize and that the bolters must move to a formal organization. They formed a committee on address and another to prepare an acceptable platform, steps that ruptured the Republican Party. Ruby had at this point aligned himself with whites who supported ab initio, division, and a desire to suppress violence, but he was initially uncertain what position to take regarding the creation of a new party. He had always counseled harmony. Although he spoke at the meeting, he did not immediately endorse its action and stated that he wanted to see what platform they drafted before acting. According to the reporter for the *Austin Republican*, he made it known that if it was not more radical than the one being considered in the regular convention, he would not support it. Exactly what he considered to be more radical was unclear, though, and the meeting adjourned to reconvene the next day without Ruby endorsing its actions.[22]

On the evening of August 14 the bolters met again. This time they introduced a platform clearly aimed at appealing to Ruby and black voters in general. It offered a much more radical agenda on racial issues than anything considered by the regular convention. The platform contained some planks that would have been expected of the bolting white delegates: support for ab initio and division. It also included a plank that proposed state encouragement of manufacturers and railroads. In addition, however, the platform called for no proscriptive measures to be placed on the qualifications for holding political office in the new constitution, a goal particularly desired by blacks who would have been kept from holding office if the constitution imposed lengthy residency or property-owning requirements. It also endorsed the creation of a public school system without regard to race. Without specifically outlining the various implications of ab initio, it came down strongly for that measure with all of its potential, including the possibility that former slave owners might have to pay wages to their former slaves from the date of the Emancipation Proclamation, and the possibility of securing a restoration of the school fund if the railroads had to repay the debts they had paid in Confederate currency and bonds. The platform met Ruby's demands, and he endorsed the course of the convention and its platform. When the bolters moved to create a new party, Ruby joined and was named a member of the new organization's executive committee. The split now saw two Republican parties in the state. This faction usually was referred to as the Radical Republican Party after the August breakup. The Jack Hamilton–E. M. Pease faction came to be known as the Conservative Republicans. Ruby's decision was a significant one. As head of the Loyal League, Ruby had the potential of determining which of the two factions survived by bringing the support of black voters to it.[23]

The constitutional convention reconvened after the Republican convention adjourned. Committees began making reports, but both Radical and Conservative Republicans showed no interest in rushing to a conclusion and considered adjourning the convention until a later date. In part this was purposeful, to ensure that Texas would not participate in the upcoming presidential election. An article in the *Austin Republican* congratulated the delegates on the decision, observing that if the convention had completed its work and ordered an election before the November election, the state would have seen "civil conflict." Indeed, the editorialist had recommended such a delay six weeks earlier. He pointed out that one of the Conservative members of the convention, the term usually applied to the former Democrats in that body, had "boasted that he and his friends intended to march on the polls and vote, without regard to the disfranchising clause in the Reconstruction Laws, if they had to do so with shot-guns and six-shooters in their hands." Using the excuse that the convention had run out of funds necessary to operate, Republicans, united at least for the moment and with Ruby supporting the move, voted to adjourn on August 31 with plans to reassemble on Monday, December 7.[24]

Ruby returned to Galveston after the convention adjourned. His formal linkage with the Radical Republicans promised to bring the league's support to that faction. At the same time, his actions in the convention prompted an aggressive effort by Conservative Republicans in the city to undermine his role in the league. The *Bulletin*, now largely behind the Conservative Republican faction, questioned whether or not Ruby could be supplanted. The paper's editor recognized that a good deal of opposition to Ruby's leadership had emerged and that this opposition hoped to replace him. He wrote that "influential members" of the Republican Party believed that they could "throw Ruby off and burst up the organization, the power of which is greater than they control." The editor was not sure, however, that displacing Ruby was possible. His opponents could withdraw from the league, but the editor doubted that a rival political organization could be created among the blacks. Another item several days later went into greater detail about the problem with Ruby and the league. This article suggested that some of the "best white men" did not like Ruby and apparently believed he had political aspirations that they needed to stifle. The *Bulletin* warned again that it could not be done. The blacks were in the majority for the moment. The article indicated that Ruby's opponents believed that he now aspired to be the lieutenant governor, but the writer expressed surprise that with his hold on black voters Ruby did not aspire to something even higher. That hold was so strong that the author believed any effort at removing Ruby would simply "enthrone him in the hearts of his race, and possibly in the gubernatorial chair."[25]

The warning in the *Bulletin* did not prevent Ruby's opponents from acting. On his return to Galveston he faced an immediate attack on his leadership in the local council. On September 4, the *Galveston News* reported that a meeting of the Galveston league council had been held and that an effort had been made to remove Ruby as president. Colonel Jesse

Stancel, who had been at odds with Ruby in the past and now held the post of federal Register in Bankruptcy at the recommendation of Governor Pease, initiated the effort. As an associate of the governor and now a Conservative Republican, Stancel probably acted not just on his own initiative but may rather have responded to suggestions from the state leadership of his Republican faction. Stancel ran into opposition, however, from Rush Plumly, who by this time had reestablished himself as an ally of Ruby. The report indicated that the ab initio question had been discussed, although its relevance to the council's leadership was not mentioned, and then the meeting turned to removing Ruby. Plumly thwarted Stancel's efforts. Plumly's success, however, did not end continuing efforts by the Conservative Republican to pry control of the league from Ruby's hands.[26]

An even more vigorous attack on Ruby's control of the league surprisingly came not from Conservative Republicans but from Dr. Robert K. Smith, the other delegate to the convention from the Galveston area and a man who had long been one of Ruby's white friends in the league. The hostility between the two appeared to have emerged out of an altercation that took place in Austin on August 2. A visitor to the capital city from Galveston apparently told Ruby that Smith had written a letter to someone in Galveston impugning Ruby's character. The content of the reputed message is not known, but given subsequent events, Smith may have charged that Ruby had failed to look after the interests of his black constituents and had not worked for them in matters concerning ab initio and the school system. Smith possibly also suggested that Ruby was bribed to back away from his support for these measures. Smith's accusations were clearly false. His motivations were not clear, but he may have been trying to ingratiate himself with the Conservative faction. That possibility receives some support from Smith's plans to accompany Jack Hamilton to Washington that fall to meet with members of the Grant administration. Whatever the reason for Smith's charges, Ruby encountered Smith on the convention floor. The two exchanged harsh words and Ruby called Smith a "damned lair." Smith in turn grabbed Ruby by the throat. The sergeant-at-arms separated the two and prevented anything more serious, but the hard feelings remained. Back in Galveston, Smith moved to further undermine Ruby.[27]

Smith renewed his attack on Ruby at a meeting of the local league council on Friday evening, September 4. The officers of the league had asked Smith and Ruby to attend the meeting and explain their actions at the convention. The editor of *Flake's Bulletin* wrote that the particular reason for that meeting was concern among the members about the failure of ab initio and the end to their hopes that (1) they might be allowed to recover the wages from their former masters from the date President Lincoln announced his emancipation proclamation, and (2) that the school fund would be restored to permit the creation of a free public school system. Ruby did not attend, but Smith was present, and he immediately went after Ruby, charging that he had betrayed his black constituents. He had not stood up for their concerns. Instead he had linked himself to white Republicans whom Smith denounced as opposing the interests of blacks, calling them scoundrels and thieves. The meeting came to an end when Rush Plumly, at this time president of the city's Republican Association, walked into the meeting and Smith assailed him as well, calling him "hard names." Smith even drew his revolver on Plumly, but Plumly refused to be goaded and retorted that Smith was drunk and he would not quarrel with a drunken man. The confrontation brought an end to the meeting.[28]

Ruby responded almost immediately to Smith's criticism. On the evening of September 5, the day after the row between Smith and Plumly, Ruby appeared along with E. J. Davis, president of the convention, at the African Methodist Church, where he had been invited to talk about events at the convention. Ruby defended himself, arguing that much of what he attempted to do in the convention was thwarted by members of his own party. He maintained that there actually was little difference between many of the Republicans and the rebels. Conservative Republicans, whom he linked with Smith, had even attempted to include a clause requiring extended citizenship before holding office to keep freedmen from office, but that had been defeated. He also talked about the school system, saying that he knew blacks did not as a general rule want their children to go to school with whites, but he objected to having their segregation written into the constitution. Any assertion that he had not done all he could to work for the interests of his race, he insisted, was a lie.[29]

The following Monday, September 7, Ruby appeared before another gathering of the freedmen in the African Methodist Church and once again addressed their questions about the convention. As on the previous occasion, he defended his actions in a way that the reporter for the *Bulletin* described as being "with more deliberation than he was accustomed to speak," and also that his defense was "creditable." Smith was present and asked to speak. It appeared on the previous evening that the two had reconciled themselves, but Smith went on the attack once again. Smith said that he had listened to Ruby and wanted to expose him. Smith charged that Ruby had been bribed by Plumly and a lobbyist named Sloanaker for $600. That showed, Smith claimed, that a "Maine free negro" was worth less than a slave before the war, when male slaves often sold for $1,000. Ruby believed he "owned the colored people," Smith claimed, but that was a mistake. Ruby did not. When Smith left the building Ruby spoke and defended himself, saying that as a gentleman he should not note what a drunk had said, but that Smith had lied. He was not for sale. When asked further questions, he told the questioners to refer to General Davis and Mr. Newcomb for his record in the convention. The reporter for the *Bulletin* in his account of events that evening probably accurately portrayed what Smith was trying to do when he speculated that Smith was trying to gain the confidence of black voters and turn them against Ruby.[30]

The dispute between Smith and Ruby worsened on the evening of September 9 at a meeting of the Galveston Republican Association. Rush Pumly was in the chair that evening, and Ruby asked permission to make a personal statement. Given permission, Ruby said that he had been "maligned and defamed" by Dr. Smith. He continued, saying that Smith was drunk when he made the charges that Ruby had sold himself, but since some believed him, he felt the need to defend himself further. The one mistake he had made, he said, was to have been responsible for the election of Smith. He called on Capt. Bennett, secretary of the convention, to state his votes on ab initio and other propositions. Bennett responded and indicated that Ruby had cast the right votes on all such matters. Following Ruby's talk, Plumly took the floor and said that the charge that he had given Ruby $600 was a lie and that Smith knew it. He also accused Smith of saying that Ruby had been bribed because Smith himself had been bribed. Ruby interjected, yes, with railroad money, a charge that was possibly true because of Smith's votes in favor of railroads. Subsequent speakers urged party harmony, but the conflict that evening was not played out.[31]

When the meeting adjourned Ruby walked down the aisle to exit, but as he moved through the crowd Smith and one of his associates, a Dr. S. M. Haslea, followed him. Exactly what happened at this point is unclear. One account said that Ruby pushed Haslea aside and hit Smith hard enough to knock him back into Plumly. Smith then pulled out his pistol and tried to cock it when the chief of police intervened. Ruby was quickly surrounded by his defenders. Later, Ruby denied having struck Smith, and the reporter for the *Bulletin* could not tell who hit whom. Others said that Smith struck Ruby, and at the same time Haslea cut at Ruby with a Bowie knife. All three men were arrested and charged to appear the next morning before the city's Recorder Court. Ruby was charged with assault, Smith for carrying and drawing a concealed weapon, and Haslea for cutting with a Bowie knife. The reporter gave a clear indication of the sympathies of the crowd in favor of Ruby when he noted that had the chief of police not been present, the crowd was so incensed they would have killed both Smith and Haslea.[32]

The subsequent trial turned into a circus, with large numbers of freedmen packing the courtroom. All of the major participants appeared to testify. Each gave testimony defending their own actions the previous evening. With so much contradictory testimony, the chief of police's account ultimately must have been given the greatest credence by the City Recorder, for the court's decision reflected the facts as he gave them. Ruby was fined twenty dollars for hitting Smith. Smith, strangely given the character of his crime, was fined twenty dollars for pulling his gun and attempting to shoot Ruby. The recorder fined Haslea fifteen dollars for his attack with the Bowie knife. The affair provided another opportunity for the opposition press to attack Ruby and also the very character of Reconstruction. The *Dallas Herald* provided an account of the fight between the two delegates taken from the *Bulletin*, then went on to condemn them both. They had shamed the citizens of Galveston, who had to bear being misrepresented by a "pair of beautiful birds, who could not get a respectable vote of respectable people for the meanest office men are ever elected to." These two men, the article went on, "are to make a constitution for white men and decent negroes [sic] to live under." The affair represented a "burlesque upon so-called republicanism."[33]

The editor of the *Bulletin* believed that in the end, the result of the fight between Ruby and Smith had not worked to Smith's advantage. Instead, it had only strengthened Ruby. The editor recognized that many freedmen legitimately wanted to know whether or not their representatives had worked in their interest while in Austin. They were especially concerned with Ruby's stand on ab initio, education, and other such matters. The editor maintained that they should realize that Ruby had "stood by his race and color in all that the most radical of them demanded." As far as he understood, Ruby had even gone the "whole hog" on a resolution put forward by Newcomb that would have legitimized children born out of wedlock, a measure that Newcomb intended as a means to legitimize the children of slave women and their white masters. The editor remarked that he did not agree with Ruby on most of these measures and thought he had done wrong to support them. He censured Ruby and stated his belief that he should never have been sent to Austin. The editor, however, recognized that Ruby had "stuck close to the notions of those who sent him."[34]

The appearance in court ended the open confrontation between the two men. The future careers of the two showed that Smith had failed to undercut Ruby's hold on either the Galveston council of the league or the state league. Smith went to the North to campaign for Grant. Ruby's activity during the rest of the recess is unknown, although he continued to be an outspoken advocate of stronger measures by the federal government to suppress the violence rampant in the state. In early November he held a council meeting in Galveston that passed resolutions insisting that outside the towns of Texas a state of war existed. The resolutions pointed particularly to the assassination in Jefferson, Texas, of Ruby's colleague from the convention, George W. Smith, as proof of the character of the violence. Smith, the delegate from Marion County and prominent leader of the league in the town of Jefferson, had been murdered by a white mob calling themselves members of the Knights of the Rising Sun in Jefferson that October. Ruby's supporters proposed a solution, urging military authorities to arrest everyone near the scene and to hold them hostage until the community surrender the murderers. Reflecting an already changing attitude among Conservative Republicans about their Democratic opponents and the desire for some sort of coalition against their Radical opponents, the Conservative's *Austin Republican* refused to print the resolutions. The *Republican*'s editor even denied that the conditions described by Ruby existed in Texas and contended that Ruby actually intended his resolutions to censure the administration of the District of Texas by General Joseph Reynolds. If the military pursued such an "atrocious" policy, he claimed, it would lead to a state of war. For Ruby and his black constituents, however, the situation already amounted to a state of war. Ruby's attention to such matters and his presence at the November meeting was proof, however, that Ruby had won against Smith. Ruby still controlled the league.[35]

Ruby returned to Austin when the convention reassembled on December 7. That body continued to meet for nearly two months. In that time Ruby kept a lower profile than in the first session. Attracting little attention in the press and making few open statements in the convention itself, his voting record showed that by this time he had forged a permanent alliance within the Radical Republican movement. On measure after measure, despite the fact that other black delegates often strayed from the Radical position, Ruby remained true to it. When the question of division reemerged,

Ruby supported the Radical party's successful passage of a resolution that sent six commissioners to Washington to argue for congressional action in dividing the state after the Radicals had failed to secure that goal in the convention itself. He also stood with the Radicals in their efforts to include voting restrictions on former Confederates in the new constitution. On January 29 the committee delivered a proposed article that would have required a number of individuals to swear that they had not supported secession before they could register to vote. Most of those excluded were men already excluded under the Reconstruction acts or the proposed constitutional amendments, but the January 29 proposal also intended to punish the men who viciously attacked Republicans. The list included members of secret orders (such as the Ku Klux Klan, who had appeared in Millican, and the Knights of the Rising Sun, who had murdered George Smith), ministers who encouraged violence from their pulpits, and newspaper editors to be sanctioned. Ruby had a clear interest in this measure, but Jack Hamilton, now leading a combination of Conservative Republicans and Democrats, managed to introduce a substitute that excluded only those named by congressional acts. They subsequently managed to order a July election to be held on the proposed constitution. Ruby and the Radicals failed to defeat Hamilton's substitute, and the subsequent decision to hold an election represented a major blow to Radical efforts to exclude former secessionists from the political process and assure the control of the government by loyalists. These failures also ultimately had a direct effect on Ruby's political career. On this issue, after the passage of Hamilton's substitute, Ruby made one of his few efforts to add an item to the constitution when he proposed a declaration addressing the efforts of Conservatives and Democrats to reduce the black vote when they gained power. Ruby's declaration stipulated that the use of violence or threats of violence, bribery, or labor contracts as means of manipulating black voters would be crimes. Linking voting to hiring workers was defined by Ruby as bribery. Given the direction the convention had moved by this time, the declaration failed, with only eighteen delegates offering support.[36]

The Radicals did not want to see the constitution go to a public vote and began pressing for adjournment once the convention had decided to send a delegation to Congress to push for division. A combination of Conservative Republicans and Democrats, however, managed to stop that from happening in the weeks that followed, but after the passage of the suffrage and election provisions, the Radicals made even more earnest work of their efforts at breaking up the convention. One historian described the atmosphere in the hall as "seething with excitement" as the convention approached its end and the two factions maneuvered to secure their goals. Part of the excitement centered on Ruby when one of the assistant doorkeepers of the convention and a supporter of Jack Hamilton, Scipio McKee, a black league member from Galveston, physically attacked Ruby on the streets on February 1. The attack supposedly came because Ruby had criticized McKee for his failure to perform his duties and for his hostility towards another black member of the convention. No damage was done to Ruby, but he attempted to have McKee removed from his post for the attack. In a show of partisanship, the Hamilton faction blocked the effort. The convention had devolved into physical confrontations such as this when the Radicals decided to bring the convention to an end not by adjournment but simply by breaking the quorum. On the morning of February 4, Ruby joined other Radicals in support of a resolution expressing their disapproval of the proposed constitution, particularly because of its suffrage provisions. A day later Ruby, along with James P. Newcomb and Benjamin F. Williams, resigned as delegates. Their resignations actually dropped the number of members attending below 50 percent and at least theoretically meant that the convention no longer had enough members to do business. Ruby tendered his resignation, claiming that the convention had lost "through many of its members, all regard for dignity and honor" and that a continuation of the session would end only "in disgrace to the entire country." In the midst of volatile parliamentary maneuvering, E. J. Davis attempted to adjourn the convention, only to have the Conservative Republican and Democratic delegates, who refused to leave the hall, attempt to elect a new president.

On the morning of February 6 this group met but were advised to disperse. That afternoon Davis declared the convention adjourned. The following day the Conservative Republican-Democratic group did as well. General E. R. S. Canby, then commanding the military district, acted to gather up the papers of the convention and publish them.[37]

In the end, after five months in Austin during the two sessions of the convention, Ruby did not sign the proposed constitution. In this he aligned with the other Radical members of the convention. Only forty-five delegates signed the constitution, less than half the number of delegates who had been elected. Almost all of the major Radical delegates left Austin without signing, although at least five black delegates did sign. It is possible, however, that the latter had their names signed to the document by the victorious Conservatives. Ruby, having finished with the convention, turned to other matters, including a trip to the North with the committee sent there by the convention. He also pondered his next step in his efforts to influence the course of Reconstruction in his newly adopted state.[38]

CHAPTER VII

THE ELECTION OF 1869

Ruby has more influence with the negroes than any other man in Texas.—
Weekly Houston Telegraph, *Sept. 2, 1869*

In February 1869, Ruby joined Morgan Hamilton, E. J. Davis, James R. Burnett, James W. Flanagan, William M. Varnell, Edward Degener, James P. Newcomb, and George W. Whitmore, all whites who were part of the Radical faction in the constitutional convention, on a trip to Washington to meet with members of the Grant administration and Republicans in Congress to argue for a division of the state and a delay of any election. Ruby visited the offices of the *New Orleans Republican* on his way and discussed the situation in Texas. According to the editor, Ruby said that the Radicals would oppose the adoption of the new constitution and that Ruby was particularly critical of the document's suffrage clause. His objection was that it allowed too many rebels who remained disloyal to vote and that it would assure the rapid return of former rebels to power. Ruby admitted, however, that all Republicans had not yet agreed on what should be done regarding the proposed constitution and that a majority coalition on these issues had not yet come together. Ruby went on from New Orleans to Washington, arriving there in early March. His efforts in Washington, the subsequent state election, and the campaign of 1869 saw Ruby expand his connections nationally, further develop his power base at home, and play an even larger role in the course of Reconstruction in Texas.[1]

When Ruby arrived in Washington he found a subtle change in conditions for his race. On this trip he was able to stay with his white colleagues in the same boarding house at 389 Third Street. From these headquarters, Ruby and the other delegates worked to gain the backing of national Republican leaders and the new Grant administration for their cause. Ruby played an important role in this effort. He initially met with former general Nathaniel P. Banks, now a member of Congress from Massachusetts. Ruby carried with him a letter of introduction from Rush Plumly. The letter informed Banks that Ruby would be able to inform Banks "correctly of our state of affairs." According to Plumly, as head of the Loyal League, Ruby possessed "more influence that is effective than any of the many among us, an influence which he uses wisely." What happened in that meeting is unknown, although Banks subsequently became a supporter of the claims of the Texas Radicals. On March 7, Ruby accompanied the committee on a visit with Senator Benjamin Wade of Ohio, one of the more radical Republicans in the United States Senate, an outspoken critic of President Johnson's reconstruction program, and a man who from the beginning looked more favorably on their claims for national Republican support than on the claims of Jack Hamilton. Later Ruby and the other Radicals met with Ohio Congressman Robert C. Schenck, a member of the House Select Committee on Reconstruction, the body that would make recommendations concerning the Texas election. After this meeting the committee claimed that their ideas received a favorable response. In the midst of this round of lobbying visits, the Texans also met Senator Charles Sumner of Massachusetts. Sumner appeared to accept their claims that they were the true representatives of Republicanism in Texas. In the meeting Sumner welcomed Ruby in particular and told the group that he hoped that he would see black men like Ruby sent to Congress from Texas in the future.[2]

The decision as to whether or not to hold a convention ultimately rested with Congress and the Congressional Reconstruction Committee. The convention's Radical delegation and Jack Hamilton, representing the interests of the Conservative Republicans, testified before that committee on March 30 and April 1 and 3. E. J. Davis spoke for the Radicals and argued in favor of a delay in the election and a division of the state, although he admitted that action was unlikely in the sitting Congress. He argued that the election should be delayed in part because the constitution as written was objectionable, pointing to the suffrage clause in particular. He also maintained that an early election even as late as July would see lawlessness and crime work to prevent a fair vote. Jack Hamilton attended the committee hearings on the day that Davis testified and disrupted the meeting with asides and questions directed at Davis. Despite Hamilton's efforts at countering Davis's arguments, by the end of the testimony important congressmen, and especially Benjamin Butler, chairman of the committee, had concluded that the Radicals rather than Hamilton represented the true Republican interest in Texas. Butler recommended that the Texas election be postponed until the claims of the Radicals could be considered further. Responding to Butler's proposal, Congress passed a bill overriding the state convention's election mandate but turned the question of when to hold an election over to President Grant. Jack Hamilton's supporters believed that the president would go ahead with the July election, but Grant's position on the question was uncertain at the time.[3]

On April 1, Ruby accompanied committee members led by Morgan Hamilton for a meeting with the president at the White House to determine his views and whether or not he agreed with Morgan's brother Jack that the election should proceed. The meeting lasted three-fourths of an hour, and Washington newspapers reported that the president gave little indication of what he would do. That was good news, especially after the Conservatives had concluded that the president favored them. When Ruby returned to Galveston he told a Republican meeting that the president actually had been more positive about the claims of the Radical delegation than suggested in the newspaper reports. Ruby thought that he accepted the Radical delegation's characterization of conditions in Texas as being bad enough to warrant a delay in the election. According to Ruby, the president told him that he would deal with the violence in Texas and that "wrongs and outrages in Texas should cease, even if he had to garrison the whole State."[4]

In addition to his efforts to influence northern political leaders, Ruby used his trip to try to influence northern popular opinion and convince the public that conditions in Texas were bad. To accomplish this end he published a widely circulated article entitled "Condition of Texas—The Freedmen and what they are doing" in the *New York Evening Post.* The article subsequently appeared in other Northern newspapers, including the *National Anti-Slavery Standard*, a black journal published in New York. Ruby devoted much of the article to why the Radicals objected to the proposed constitution, making many of the same points that he had made in his interview with Congressman Banks. He considered allowing unreconstructed rebels to have suffrage again to be one of the major problems. The suffrage provisions in the constitution would, he said, allow "every unrepentant, violent and murderous rebel ruffian in the state" to vote without any guarantee of their loyalty. Further, the new constitution included no safeguards to protect voter registration or the polls. While the convention had considered the organization of a militia to maintain peace and security, the Conservatives made no provisions for one. Ruby did not doubt that in such circumstances these former rebels would vote to put themselves back in power and that they would then reverse the course of Reconstruction. The immediate result would be legislation that would prevent blacks from holding office and then possibly even an attack on black voting. He attributed such a flawed document to Democrats and Conservative Republicans who came from the large slaveholding class that had controlled Texas before the war and resisted giving up their power. He singled out Jack Hamilton in particular for producing such an objectionable document.[5]

Ruby's letter also described the condition of the freedmen in Texas, providing a much more favorable report than he did on the political situation. The black people of Texas seemed to justify his belief that, once freed, they would rapidly show the capacity of their race to improve, and what he saw happening among blacks differed considerably from that seen by whites. The freedmen in western Texas particularly impressed him, and he saw their progress as a justification for the state's division. A state of western Texas would allow that progress to continue, providing opportunities that did not exist in the older plantation areas of the state. He reported that about three-eighths of the black population lived in western Texas, an area he described as west of the Colorado River. Although he found them measurably poorer than blacks to the east of the river, he found them to have made more progress than blacks elsewhere in the state. They had achieved greater success in getting an education and securing a livelihood. After only four years of freedom a third of them owned property. They had created churches and schools in most cases without assistance from the people of the North. They had shown themselves to be "thrifty." They appreciated, Ruby thought, a truism once stated by the abolitionist Wendell Phillips, "The negro knows what land means, with him Liberty is seldom seen save on the pedestal of an acre." In addition, Ruby found that the blacks in western Texas experienced fewer of the outrages that took place elsewhere in the state. Ruby's letter to the *Evening Post* provided his most extensive view on how he had come to support division in the constitutional convention.[6]

Ruby did not discount progress made among the freedmen elsewhere in the state, but he saw most of that taking place in the towns and cities. There blacks worked many of the trades, as mechanics, blacksmiths, painters, and tinners. These craftsmen, "industrious and frugal," made good wages and amassed wealth. Individual freedmen had made enormous progress also in gaining an education. He pointed in particular to Stephen Curtis of Brazos County, one of his fellow delegates to the convention, as representative of the achievements of former slaves. The oldest man in the convention at sixty-two years of age, Curtis learned to read after Congress had extended the vote to blacks. Acquiring the right to vote incited his desire to acquire that skill. Now he not only read but also wrote a small and legible hand and was "a wonder to his friends." All was not good, however, and he recognized that on the plantations and farms east of the Colorado River blacks usually worked on white-owned land on shares. Even with hard work, however, they could keep little that they made, being "generally robbed or murdered." Despite such problems, he remained optimistic and reported that "the colored people of Texas 'are rising.'"[7]

Ruby also used his position as president of the Loyal League to gather support for the Radicals. Ruby attended at least at one Loyal League meeting in Washington, where he spoke about what he considered to be the real conditions in Texas to counter the efforts of the Conservatives to convince northern politicians that Texas was at relative peace and that there should be no problem in readmitting the state to the Union. Ruby used a copy of *Flake's Bulletin*, a Conservative newspaper, to list the crimes against blacks, to counter the Conservative's story, and to contradict Jack Hamilton. After having read stories of six murders, he asked his audience whether or not Hamilton had become the Andy Johnson of Texas, a man who, like the president, had abandoned the Republican Party. Ruby gave his own answer, telling the audience that Hamilton could "be anything he wanted to be." In New York City Ruby also spoke to the Loyal League club there after the club had welcomed him and given him free access to its rooms.[8]

In addition to lobbying for northern support for the Radical cause in Texas, he also spent this time in the North attempting to raise money for a Radical newspaper in Galveston. This was the first time that Ruby attempted to get into the newspaper business but not the last. In this effort Ruby carried with him the endorsement of E. J. Davis, Morgan Hamilton, and James W. Flanagan, among the commissioners from the convention. Their letter provided insight into his white colleagues' perception of him at this time, describing him as well qualified to undertake the publication of a newspaper and loyal to the Republican cause. His course in the convention, they wrote, had been "firm and consistent" and he had gained a reputation second to none in the convention for his "ability and unswerving fidelity to the cause of the nation and the people he represented."[9]

Ruby remained in the North for a time after his efforts in Washington and New York and paid a short visit to his family in Maine. He found himself to be something of a hero when he arrived. Locals saw him as a son of

Portland who had made a name for himself. His supporters in the Portland community gave a banquet in his honor where Ruby gave a speech on what he encountered in Texas. Probably the speech included many of the points that he had made in his letter to the *New York Evening Post*, which revealed his concern over whether or not Texas could have a truly free election and praised African Americans there in moving forward from their days as slaves. Certainly he aimed at having Maine's citizens put pressure on their congressmen to support the aims of the Radical Republicans.[10]

Ruby returned to Galveston from his trip to the north in early May only to find that despite what had appeared to be successful testimony before Congress, gaining the support of prominent Republican Congressional leaders, and a good meeting with the president, the Radicals had not succeeded in getting the Grant administration to recognize them as the legitimate representatives of the Republican Party. They had asked the president and the various cabinet officers to place their men in the various patronage positions in Texas, but instead the government's appointments seemed to favor the Jack Hamilton faction. The Radicals had proposed Nathan Patten, a manufacturer who had previously lived in Waco, for the collector's position, and Ruby for the post office, appointments that would put two of the most lucrative positions in the state in Radical hands. The Conservatives had recommended John L. Haynes for the Galveston customhouse and James A. McKee for the city's post office. Grant named Haynes and McKee. That decision produced considerable optimism among the Hamilton supporters, who also believed that they would still get their July election. The Radicals remained hopeful, however, and pressed for a change in Washington's policy.[11]

If the president did order an early election, the Radicals still had the opportunity to take control of the state government at the polls. Ruby, immediately on his return to Galveston, made it clear that he intended to run for office, although what office was not immediately clear. To secure that office he turned to organizing the local league council. On the evening of May 3 he addressed a large crowd at the Colored Methodist Church in Galveston.

George W. Honey, the former Freedmen's Bureau official who now was a minister in the city and had reestablished his alliance with Ruby, introduced him, calling Ruby an "old, steady and tried friend." Ruby reported on the trip to Washington in a speech that lasted almost two hours. He described at length his view of what had occurred in the capital city. When the delegation arrived in the North they found that many there did not understand that all Union men were not Republicans. They had to make that clear and also to convince northerners that Jack Hamilton and his supporters were not Republicans either. Hamilton, Ruby said, actually had gone over to the rebels. It was equally important for his audience, described by the newspaper reporters present as largely black, to know that was true. Hamilton had gone north and tried to convince federal officials that the "men who were hanging and killing colored men were ready to become good Republicans." Hamilton even maintained that no black men were being hurt or injured. Ruby had made it clear that such claims were lies. In the end, Ruby's address not only told his audience what he had been up to, it also made it clear to his black listeners in Galveston that they could not count on Jack Hamilton to protect them. It was a first step in lining up black voters for himself and the Radical party.[12]

In his ambition for office Ruby received some encouragement from the developing Radical press. The editor of a new Radical newspaper in Houston started by James G. Tracy, the *Union*, recognized Ruby as "probably the representative colored man of this State." As such, the editor believed, Ruby controlled a significant source of voting strength, "a formidable political element," and he believed their "rights will not be ignored." To lead them in their efforts to assure their rights, the editor hoped that Ruby's friends would "bring him prominently before the public on the republican ticket." The very suggestion of Ruby running for state office produced an intense and hostile reaction in the Conservative press. The *Houston Telegraph* took the lead with an editorial that urged Republicans to see the error of their ways and hoped that each man who "loves his race and his country, [would be found] standing shoulder to shoulder to save it from the most dire calamities," meaning the election of Ruby. The *Telegraph*'s editorial saw the possible election of Ruby as bringing about the "absolute ruin and degradation" of the state.[13]

The splintering of the Republican Party complicated Ruby's political plans in the late spring and early summer of 1868. Ruby had aligned himself with the Radicals, but he had always believed that Republicans must remain together in order to gain office. That the two sides could be reconciled became less likely when Jack Hamilton nominated himself to run for governor while he was still in Washington. Worse, Hamilton said that he would not run as a party candidate because he hoped that he could gain the support of those Democrats willing to accept the results of Reconstruction. He further argued that if the Republican Party actually ran a candidate, the Democrats would respond by organizing as well, and he did not believe men who supported Reconstruction could win an election in such circumstances. Radical Republicans disagreed, contending that they must remain aligned with the national party and be uncompromising in their support of Congress and its policies. As a result, on March 29 Morgan Hamilton, acting as chairman of the Radical Republican Executive Committee created the previous August, published a call for a Republican convention to meet on May 10 in Galveston to "consult measures for the good of the loyal people." Ruby backed Hamilton's decision to hold the convention. Ruby wrote to his fellow Radical James P. Newcomb that he believed the Morgan Hamilton convention definitely should be held. He believed that many Conservative Republicans had been demoralized by Jack Hamilton's abandonment of the Republican Party. The Radicals, as a result, should move promptly, vigorously, and wisely to achieve success. In Galveston he began organizing the league to elect desirable delegates to the May 10 convention.[14]

Ruby's course in this interparty conflict because more complicated, however, when Republican newspaperman James Tracy began a new movement to reconcile the Republican factions. Tracy, a thirty-nine-year-old Illinois native, although a prewar resident of Texas, had founded the *Houston Union* that spring. He published Morgan Hamilton's appeal for a convention but indicated that he was not yet ready to support either wing of the party. He thought that victory could be achieved only by "wiping out all past differences and uniting our forces upon a liberal, but strongly Republican platform." Tracy wanted John L. Haynes, head of the Republican executive committee named at the 1868 convention, to call for a convention to meet at the same time as the Morgan Hamilton convention so that some sort of reconciliation could take place. Tracy found an ally in Edwin M. Wheelock, now editor of the *San Antonio Express*, who agreed that Republican success could not be achieved with Jack Hamilton running on his own. At a meeting of the Conservative Republican faction's executive committee, under the control of Jack Hamilton's most ardent supporters, Wheelock unsuccessfully urged that Hamilton go into a party convention. When Haynes's executive committee refused to agree to a party nominee, Tracy wrote of Jack Hamilton and his supporters, "They have declared themselves in favor of themselves" and not for the interests of the state's Republicans. Tracy called for Republicans to "rouse themselves, and shake off the politicians that have been riding them so long." A convention, he believed, would lead to harmony. Opposition could only be for one of two reasons—they were afraid to submit their claims to the people, or they were unwilling to see loyal reconstruction. Tracy then joined with Wheelock in calling for their own Republican convention to be held in Houston on Thursday, May 27, and urged Morgan Hamilton to postpone his own convention and join the May 27 meeting.[15]

Ruby remained committed to Morgan Hamilton's May 10 convention. E. J. Davis also believed that meeting should be held, and he urged Tracy and his supporters to attend the May 10 meeting. Davis thought that if nothing else the two parties could establish the basis for some sort of reconciliation and then hold an actual nominating convention in July. Ruby, however, was ready to make nominations in the Morgan Hamilton meeting. Ruby brought the Galveston league in line behind it, and he then maneuvered in the subsequent open meeting of the Republican Association to be named one of the delegates. On May 8 the association gathered at Galveston's Varieties Theatre, where Rush Plumly presided and George W. Honey served as secretary. Ruby maintained a low profile initially, but he clearly had control of the delegates. When the body turned to the election of delegates it chose Ruby and Plumly. In addition, the meeting named thirteen alternates, a list of the prominent white and black Radicals in Galveston and league members that included Honey and newly emerging black leaders such as John DeBruhl, Johnson Reed, Stephen Paschal, and Richard Nelson. All of these men continued to play a role in Ruby's subsequent political career.[16]

On May 10, delegates from twenty counties appeared at Morgan Hamilton's convention. Most of the delegates, including alternates, came from Galveston and Harris Counties and consequently constituted only a small representation of the state's Republicans. Tracy was among the delegates from Houston, and he came intent on healing the rift between the two factions. Ruby early on emerged as the principal representative in the convention for Morgan Hamilton, who remained in Washington at this time. Early in the meeting he introduced a resolution that he had received from Hamilton that voiced approval of the proposed Fifteenth Amendment to the United States Constitution, an amendment that promised to protect black voting rights. The resolution also supported the postponement of the election until the "terror should cease." Because of the widespread lawlessness, it insisted a free ballot could not be made in most of the state. In addition it recommended that the suffrage clause of the proposed constitution, the clause that had opened up the suffrage to many former rebels, be submitted separately from the rest of the constitution. This would have made it possible to adopt the constitution, return to the Union, yet still keep many former Confederates from voting. Hamilton's resolutions also included a part that condemned the legislation that had been passed by the constitutional convention. Ruby, however, could not keep the convention focused on the resolutions and the course Morgan Hamilton had laid out. Tracy urged reconciliation, and many of the delegates appeared hopeful that something could be done. Following the floor maneuvering, W. H. Mann of Galveston offered a resolution to adjourn and meet again in Houston on the fourth

Monday in May in conjunction with the convention called by Tracy. Ruby opposed the move, but the majority, although passing Hamilton's resolutions, voted to adjourn and meet again with the proposed Tracy convention. Tracy, in turn, rescheduled his meeting for June 7.[17]

Ruby had opposed the adjournment and the new convention, but he moved ahead once the decision had been made and began efforts to ensure that the Radicals had some control over the Houston meeting. Ruby began appearing at Republican rallies. His efforts focused particularly on securing delegates to the Houston convention who would support E. J. Davis, who was backed by Morgan Hamilton and was the man most people considered to be the favored Radical candidate for governor. In mid-May, Ruby wrote to James P. Newcomb, his fellow Radical from the constitutional convention, and indicated that he did not intend to argue politically with the men who had proposed the Houston convention. He said that he was willing to appear at Republican meetings even if they were sponsored by men he considered not to be wholeheartedly Republican, one of the few statements he ever made about the character of James Tracy. On such occasions, however, he said that he would do what he could to ensure that the Radicals would have a majority. He urged Newcomb to send "proper men" from San Antonio, contending that if "[p]roperly managed, we are sure of victory for Gen. Davis" and the Radical agenda.[18]

Ruby's early campaigning took him into the plantation country along the Brazos River. His first campaign event outside of Galveston may have been one he attended in Navasota, in Grimes County, on May 22. At this mass meeting, a crowd of some four to five hundred people was present. The correspondent reporting the event indicated that blacks comprised the majority of those in attendance. Ruby and others spoke, urging the election of Radical delegates to go to Houston, and the meeting apparently did so. Two days later, Ruby attended another mass meeting at Huntsville in Walker County. The meeting there proceeded in much the same way as in Navasota. Ruby's speech explained the principles of the Republican Party and elaborated on the character of the divisions among Republicans and how they had developed. He worked particularly hard to convince the audience that Jack Hamilton had abandoned Republicanism and that only the Radicals represented the truc party. Edward H. Quick, the *Houston Union*'s reporter and Republican operative traveling with Ruby, did not detail the content of the talk, but he described Ruby's speech in Huntsville as falling "like a clap of thunder upon the ears of his race." He believed that the speech had made a "lasting impression on the colored people present" and concluded that mobilizing black voters behind the Radical party required Ruby's presence. Quick believed that black voters could be brought to support the Radicals and could determine the election's results if Ruby "could continue on the stump during the present campaign."[19]

Ruby, in addition to making campaign appearances, also took the first steps towards getting the Loyal League in order prior to an election. At the beginning of May he issued a circular, sent to the local councils, advising them to get ready for an election. "Never before in our political history," Ruby wrote, "has there been such need of prompt, vigorous, and united action by our order." He maintained that the issues loyal men faced were a matter of "life or death." He warned that the enemy, "the rebels and their sympathizers," meaning Jack Hamilton among the latter, would do anything to keep blacks from doing their duty. As a result, he urged prompt reorganization of every council that had regular meetings in order to prepare for an active campaign. Members of the league owed it to themselves to be true to "ourselves, our country, and our people." When he appeared at Republican rallies in Navasota and Huntsville, he likely also made efforts to establish league councils in those places.[20]

Ruby's efforts encountered considerable opposition from whites and particularly white planters as he stumped the plantation counties, an antagonism that suggested they saw him as a potentially influential spokesman for the Radicals and, therefore, dangerous. In Walker County, landowners attempted to keep their workers from attending Ruby's speech by using a variety of techniques that included intimidation and threats. In some cases landowners actually drove men who attended the meeting off their farms.

Other landowners charged their workers $2.50 a day for being away from their work, an enormous fine. An observer noted that this ploy had actually backfired when A. J. Hamilton appeared later and the planters encouraged their hands to attend his speech rather than trying to dissuade them. According to "Scallawag," a correspondent from the county, the freedmen were told, "Don't you want to go and hear the speech to-day, going to have a fine time, you had better a' go. I won't charge you nothing for this day, just take and hitch up my mules in the wagon and all go in." Such behavior resulted in the opening of the eyes of black workers to the differences between Ruby's party and that of A. J. Hamilton. They saw that Ruby represented those hoping to assure their freedom while Hamilton was in league with the landowners and their old masters.[21]

That Ruby was effective or at least perceived as effective by the opposition also was evidenced when A. J. Hamilton singled out Ruby for special attention in his campaign speeches. Hamilton appeared in Houston on May 26 to speak in favor of his own candidacy and to explain his support of renewed suffrage for former rebels in particular. Hamilton insisted that he had been the man who had first advocated the right of blacks to vote. He similarly believed that all whites must vote as well. His speech then attacked those who advocated blacks standing together as a bloc in the upcoming election. Men who advocated this behavior desired a black man's party and needed to be watched. He pointed in particular to Ruby and then tried to distance him from local blacks, intimating that as a free black before emancipation and possibly even because of his color he could not identify with them. The proposed constitution, he insisted, was as good as blacks would get. "Ruby, with his curly hair, dainty hands, and kid gloves, might tell you differently," he warned, "but he would not tell you the truth if he could." Who was Ruby? he asked. Had he been heard of during the war? Did he ever roll a bale of cotton? Did he ever do anything honest or useful? "He only wants office," Hamilton insisted. He urged blacks to defer to whites, to work to change their own behaviors and improve their conduct in order to correct public opinion that discriminated against them, and not seek office and privileges beyond their moral qualifications. In a speech at Gonzales he essentially called out Ruby, stating that he could "beat any of the bob-tailed ponies they can put upon the track. I want to meet the odoriferous Ruby—fifteen minutes will do." That he was forced to focus on Ruby indicated how dangerous he and his campaign managers thought the Galvestonian was to Hamilton's own political aspirations.[22]

The meeting arranged by Tracy at Houston convened on June 7 and proclaimed itself the Republican State Convention. A committee on permanent organization recommended Tracy as president of the meeting, and the delegates elected him. Ruby attended as a delegate from Galveston, along with United States Marshal William E. Parker and Spenser Hardwell, a black minister and political activist who would be assassinated in his pulpit later in the campaign. While Ruby was not named a convention officer, the actions of the convention indicated that he had accomplished much of what he intended in ensuring that a majority of the delegates supported Radical candidates, even if they did not always support the Radical agenda established in 1868. The correspondent for the *San Antonio Express* believed that Ruby, Nathan Patten, and J. P. Butler were the "leading spirits" in the convention. Tracy recognized Ruby's influence in the convention's actions when the chair appointed him to be a member of the important platform committee. In that committee Ruby attempted to ensure that the convention opposed the proposed constitution and fought a proposed plank that accepted the document. In the end the committee recommended acceptance of the constitution, although Ruby may have been responsible for including a phrase that characterized the document as "imperfect and objectionable." Ruby was more successful in managing the nomination of E. J. Davis. Tracy had looked for a compromise candidate, but Ruby moved for a suspension of the rules to unanimously elect E. J. Davis as the party's candidate for governor. The delegates overwhelmingly adopted the motion. Ruby also nominated his associate from Galveston, George W. Honey, for the office of state treasurer, but Honey declined the nomination. Tracy recognized Ruby's importance to the new party and the upcoming campaign when the chairman named Ruby to the party to notify Davis of his nomination and accompany the candidate to the speaker's platform for his acceptance speech.[23]

On the last day of the convention Tracy gave Ruby an additional role in the upcoming campaign when he named him to a committee on address, which would prepare a formal statement for publication to explain the Radicals' assessment of the political condition of the state. The committee issued their report on June 11. Ruby's endorsement of the report indicated that he finally had accepted the work of the convention and the address's basic conclusions concerning the political situation in the state. Its opening observed that "Texas to-day is no nearer reconstruction than at the close of the war." Most former secessionists were still "bitterly hostile" to the government, congressional policy, and the principles of the Republican Party. It went on to assert that the security of life and property was uncertain, justice often not given, and "party hate penetrates the social circle, and lawlessness and crime yet prevails." The address blamed Jack Hamilton for many of the failures of Reconstruction, calling him a man who had been trusted but then deserted his party. He had made himself the candidate of the Democratic Party for governor and declared that he would not accept the nomination of a Republican convention. If elected along with a Democratic legislature, loyal men would see none of the constitutional provisions guaranteeing their rights carried out. Blacks would see measures imposing property and intelligence qualifications on them before they could vote. Loyal men faced a clear choice. On the one side were the Radical Republicans, united by "eternal principles of truth" and sustaining the policies of Congress. On the other side was a mass of whites made up of Democrats, secessionists, Knights of the White Camellia, the Ku Klux Klan, and renegade Republicans. The address pleaded for men "by all you hold dear, by the love you bear your wives and children, and by your patriotism and love of country" not to be deceived by Hamilton and instead organize, even in the face of threats and intimidation, to stand firm behind the Republican Party.[24]

In the days after the convention, Ruby now set about stumping in support of the Radical candidates and the constitution. On the evening after the convention, adjourned Republican leaders in Houston asked Ruby to appear on the platform at a rally for E. J. Davis and the other candidates sponsored by the Republican Association of Harris County. The members of the association and many of the delegates from the state party convention formed on the town's Fannin Street and marched to the home of James Tracy, where the featured speakers addressed the crowd. Davis was the featured speaker, but Ruby was the principal black speaker addressing the crowd that evening. While in Houston, Ruby also met with other delegates to the convention who came from the Third Congressional District, the district that included Galveston County and much of central Texas. To prepare for the upcoming campaign the group created a congressional executive committee and named Ruby to head it. The job of the committee was to prepare for a district convention to nominate a candidate for Congress, a convention the committee decided to hold in Bryan on August 3, the first Tuesday of the month. The chairmanship of the committee also meant that Ruby would have to work to assure that the convention chose a Radical candidate. All of this assumed, however, that the president did not order an early election.[25]

Ruby returned from Houston to Galveston and continued campaigning in preparation for an election. On June 16 he appeared at a meeting to ratify the nominations and the platform of the Houston convention. The hostile reporter of the *Galveston News* related that the crowd in front of the county courthouse numbered only several hundred, including women and children. He described Ruby's speech on this occasion as being particularly vitriolic, although its content did not appear to veer in any way from the view of the political scene published by the Houston convention. Ruby reportedly attacked the opposition as not only political opponents but, in the end, as disloyal as well. Ruby denounced President Andrew Johnson and A. J. Hamilton for their failure to uphold the loyal people of the state. In the end he appealed to his listeners and particularly the blacks in the audience to "stand by their rights and Gen. Davis." Ruby then introduced a resolution that endorsed the nomination of General Davis and the other nominations of the convention and pledged the delegates to support the nominees. The crowd sounded their unanimous approval of the resolution. A correspondent for Tracy's *Houston Union* provided an alternative view of the gathering to that given by the *News*, describing it as the most enthusiastic meeting ever held in the county.[26]

Ruby also went back into the field, carrying his campaigning outside of Galveston. Having accepted the results of the Houston convention, he now promoted General Davis as the Radical candidate for governor and advised his listeners to vote for the new constitution. On June 19 he appeared in the morning at the "Emancipation Day" celebration held in Bryan. A local observer believed that almost six thousand people attended the celebration, a celebration, in the words of one of the speakers, of the "anniversary of their liberation." Ruby appeared first on the platform. A correspondent of the *Union* described his address as "very courteous," although it seemed to be very similar to the one condemned by the reporter for the *News* that Ruby had given three days earlier. According to the man for the *Union,* Ruby's remarks made a "marked impression" on the crowd. On the same day after the celebration he went to Navasota, about thirty miles south of Bryan and reachable in several hours on the Houston and Texas Central Railway's line, where he spoke again. Once more he attacked Hamilton's loyalty. E. H. Quick, traveling with Ruby as a party operative and as representative for the *Union*, believed that Hamilton had been "laid in the shade." Quick estimated that the crowd that heard Ruby speak in Navasota may have numbered in the thousands.[27]

Ruby travelled less after the Emancipation Day appearances in Bryan and Navasota, as it was clear by the middle of June that President Grant did not intend to order an early election. Even though not on the road, Ruby continued his efforts at mobilizing the league. On July 1 he issued another circular to the subordinate councils. This circular indicated that by this time a major problem facing the Radicals was a lack of money to fund speakers and publications. When he had returned from his earlier trip to Grimes and Walker Counties he had informed Newcomb that he found no parties in those communities with enough money to support a party newspaper.

Now he urged local councils to organize and to help raise the needed funds. He advised the councils to tax each member twenty-five cents to be sent to the State Grand Council for a fund to be used to support the campaign. He believed this was essential since he thought that Jack Hamilton's supporters had money and were willing to use it. By mid-July he was pleading with E. J. Davis for money and complaining that he did not have adequate resources. Davis realized how important Ruby was to the campaign and attempted to raise funds so that he could electioneer, particularly in the counties between Austin and San Antonio. It is not clear, however, that much support ever came.[28]

Ruby also worked to obtain support for the campaign from the league's national organization. On July 15 he wrote to Thomas G. Baker, national grand secretary, asking for whatever help the organization could provide. "As our very existence is involved in the political contest now pending," he wrote, "may we not hope for speedy and effectual aid for the maintenance of Free Speech, Free Press and an unswerving fidelity to the Union?" Baker forwarded Ruby's appeal to Republican operative William E. Chandler, a newspaper editor from New Hampshire and manager of Grant's campaign in 1868, for consideration, begging him to carefully consider Ruby's claims. Ruby had been optimistic that the National Grand Council would send money, but the money never came. Instead, Governor John W. Geary of Pennsylvania, then president of the National Grand Council, promised to send campaign materials and several speakers to campaign in the interest of Davis. Like the hoped-for money, the speakers never appeared, a failure that suggested diminishing support by northern Republicans for the idea that they could create effective Republican parties in the South.[29]

Ruby went back on the road, despite inadequate funds, to campaign for Davis in late July. On July 24 he talked in Brazoria County, once again assuring his black listeners that they owed their support to Davis and working to convince them of Hamilton's political treason. Hamilton, he argued, had defected from the principles of the party. A local correspondent for the *Houston Union* said that Ruby charged Hamilton with "chicanery and duplicity." The writer believed that Ruby had frustrated the efforts of Hamilton and his friends to "hoodwink the Republicans of Brazoria." Ruby also paid attention to other "self-nominated" men who were running for office alongside Hamilton, especially Andrew P. McCormick, a lawyer, planter, and supporter of Jack Hamilton who had determined to run for the state senate from the district that included Brazoria, Matagorda, and Galveston Counties. McCormick, reportedly, "winced and withered" under Ruby's attacks. For the first time following the mass meeting at Brazoria, Ruby's name began to be considered as a possible candidate for the legislature in the upcoming campaign. The article suggested that "[o]ur people" had begun to insist that Ruby run for the state senate from their district, the very one that McCormick had announced for. The correspondent believed that the people of the district, where two of the counties had black majorities, would support his election with a large turnout.[30]

In the midst of his campaigning Ruby found that he was not yet free of Dr. Robert K. Smith's efforts at undermining him. On the evening of July 28, shortly after his return from Brazoria County, Ruby attended a meeting of the Republican Association in Galveston. Smith was also there, and when the doctor spoke he brought up his previous charge that Ruby had betrayed his constituents. This time he claimed that Ruby had sold his vote in the constitutional convention on an emigration scheme for $400. When the meeting adjourned the two men clashed as they left the building. Smith claimed that Ruby refused to let him leave the building and then, "with force of arms," violently assaulted him, pushing him into his seat, and demanding satisfaction. The next day Smith charged Ruby with assault. Smith's action forced Ruby to appear in the city's Recorder Court, where the judge dismissed the case and charged the costs to Smith. Democratic newspaper correspondents concluded that Smith probably had provoked the incident to delay Ruby from getting to Bryan prior to the upcoming convention for the local senate district. The editor of the *Galveston News* wrote that Smith thought he might keep Ruby from arriving early so that the doctor could control the convention. A correspondent for the *Houston Telegraph* agreed, believing that the entire affair had been a "preliminary exercise" to their encounter in the convention. The latter believed, however, that Ruby had the "inside track" in controlling the convention.[31]

Smith's ploy, if designed to weaken Ruby's power in the convention, failed to prevent Ruby from reaching Bryan in time for its opening on August 2. As temporary chairman of the meeting he carefully orchestrated its proceedings. The convention subsequently named Nathan Patten, a Radical and friend of Ruby's from the constitutional convention, as permanent president. James Tracy also played a major role in the convention and, with Ruby's apparent support, secured the Republican nomination of William T. Clark, a former brigade commander in the Union's Army of Tennessee, Medal of Honor recipient, and founder of Galveston's First National Bank, for Congress. Clark's choice reflected Tracy's efforts at attracting white businessmen who might agree with the national Republican Party's economic policies to link themselves with the Texas Republican Party. Tracy believed that Clark was acceptable to the Galveston business community and would attract support from businessmen who seldom took part in elections. Tracy later extoled Clark as a man committed to encouraging immigration and liberal subsidies to railroads and promoting a free and comprehensive system of public schools. Tracy put Clark's name before the convention, and Ruby, possibly agreeing with Tracy's strategy, moved that Clark be elected unanimously. Tracy named the executive committee for the congressional district, appointing Ruby to serve as the committeeman for the Twelfth Senate District. By the time of the congressional district convention Ruby and Tracy had reached a political understanding and were working together despite their earlier differences.[32]

Ruby returned to Galveston to attend a meeting at the African Methodist Episcopal Church on August 7. The purpose of the meeting was to ratify Clark's nomination. Ruby appeared on the stage with Clark, further establishing his connection with Tracy's effort at creating some sort of systematic party organization and trying to broaden Republican support. The congressional nominating convention and the Galveston ratification meeting marked a major shift in political alliances for Ruby. He had been closely connected with Morgan Hamilton in the spring, and as late as the June 7 state convention he remained opposed to the proposed constitution. He had participated in that convention, however, and emerged from it as a member of the state executive committee. His role in assuring the nomination of General Clark linked Ruby more closely with Tracy but also indicated he may have realized that while his power base remained the black population of Galveston, his political future depended to some degree on support from whites. Support of Clark provided that possible linkage, indicating that at least economically, Ruby would continue to work to support the business interests of his adopted city as well as the concerns of his black supporters. The move evidenced a political awareness of his unique circumstances. He had not abandoned the more radical positions taken during his earlier years, but he now faced the need to build a constituency broader than his black base.[33]

The Galveston Association's meeting to endorse the Clark candidacy was also the beginning of Ruby's efforts to be nominated for election to the seat from the Twelfth Senate District, the district encompassing Galveston, Brazoria, and Matagorda Counties. Prior to the Bryan convention a mass meeting of Republicans in Brazoria, representing party members in Brazoria and Matagorda Counties, instructed the delegates sent to Bryan to also attend any convention to select candidates for the state legislature and to cast their votes for Ruby for the state senate. No convention was held, but at the August 7 ratification meeting in Galveston those in attendance also endorsed Ruby for the senate. The final resolution passed at the meeting stated that Ruby was their first choice for the senate and applauded the resolutions passed earlier in Brazoria. The Galvestonians pledged their cooperation with the people of the other counties in the district to assure Ruby's election. They assured their "brothers" that they believed Ruby was "able to meet the emergency, and competent to battle for and maintain the true principles of Republicanism . . . against the enemies of our cause." A correspondent for the *Houston Union* said that the nomination was unanimous, that the "voice of the people was distinctly given, and the continuous applause was deafening."

Ruby took the endorsement of the two meetings as an official nomination. As he campaigned for the state ticket, he now began to canvass for his own election. The correspondent for the *Union* announced that Ruby had "entered the ring against the Hamilton mule, who is bound to be distanced in the race."[34]

Ruby's official selection as the party's nominee took place on August 25 at a meeting of the Republican Association in Galveston. No formal convention was held, but the purpose of this meeting was to confirm his nomination. That meeting revealed strains within the Republican Party that continued to exist through the rest of Reconstruction and ultimately limited its effectiveness. The only reports of this meeting came from the staff of the *Galveston News*, and by this time its editorial policy was totally hostile to Ruby and tended to portray him in racist terms intended to undermine any possibility of securing white support. The paper's reporter characterized disagreements within the party organization over the nomination as being a division on the issue of race. At this meeting, at least according to the correspondent for the *News*, objections were raised against Ruby's candidacy from what the correspondent called the "decent portion of the party." This group apparently believed that a white man should represent Galveston and was willing to "dispense with the services of the individual who 'claims to be a negro.'" This charge, that Ruby was not really black, was intended to destroy his credibility among black voters. George P. Douglass, deputy United States marshal, put Ruby's name in nomination and several members rose to object, urging a delay in making nominations. Rush Plumly, Ruby's former associate and friend, appeared to be the head of this opposition, possibly motivated by his desire to have the senate nomination for himself. What the correspondent for the *News* called the "negro supremacy" group in the party had insisted on ratifying Ruby's nomination, however, and pushed aside the objections. If the account of the meeting is correct, Plumly and the other men the reporter called the "respectable portion of the party" left and indicated that they might not support the party's nominee. He wrote that they declared that they would not "gratuitously outrage the community in which they reside" by nominating a black man.[35]

In a story written by the editor of the opposition *Galveston News* and couched in a way to suggest black racism on the part of Ruby, Ruby responded to Plumly with a speech that the editor called "a most violent and intemperate harangue." Ruby went after Plumly in particular, then declared that the platform of the party rested entirely on the question of color. Ruby stated that he was a colored man and that as a colored man he had been nominated and as a colored man he would run the race. Plumly replied that he was a true friend of blacks and that he had worked to do away with the question of color and did not wish to see it laid as the basis of principles for government of the Republican Party. Ruby, he said, was playing the demagogue. If Ruby proceeded along these lines, Plumly said that he would not support him. Plumly allegedly warned that if the issue of color was raised, four million blacks were not destined to rule thirty million whites and that if they so acted, blacks would be inviting their own political destruction. Plumly apparently went on to call Ruby arrogant. The reporter for the *News* turned the exchange into a claim by Ruby that he had the right to the nomination because of his race, but a subsequent card published in *Flake's Bulletin* by the officers of the Republican Association denied that was his intention or what he had said.[36]

A subsequent meeting of the Loyal League, on Friday, September 3, attempted to heal the breach. Again, the only report of the meeting came from the staff of the hostile *Galveston News*. *Flake's Bulletin*, equally hostile to Ruby, did not bother to report the meeting. The article in the *News* maintained that the council had considered what to do about Plumly's reputed defection and whether or not the "irrepressible Ruby" needed to have his "dimensions" curtailed. The item contended that the members of the council had become concerned as to whether or not the Republican Party could achieve its goals without Plumly, whom the *News* considered the brains of the organization. In an openly racist attack on Ruby, the piece concluded that the greatest admirers of the "saffron-faced Senator that is to be have suddenly discovered that like a certain other ape often spoken of the higher he climbs the more necessity he has for a long tailed coat." Whether or not any resolution took place at this meeting was unclear.[37]

Ultimately Ruby carried the day against Plumly. In a letter to Newcomb after these meetings, Ruby explained that Plumly had been encouraged by "the rebels" to consider running for the senate after initially deciding to run for the house. To accomplish this he had to push Ruby aside and to do so he managed the nomination of John DeBruhl, another black man, for the house during a meeting of the Galveston council of the Loyal League. Ruby argued against this, insisting that the nomination of two black men would threaten "credence to the story the enemy assiduously circulates of a 'Black man's party.'" When Plumly continued to push, Ruby threatened to withdraw from the race. Ruby believed that Plumly actually hoped this would happen, but when Ruby's friends advised him to remain in the race he decided to do so. In the end, Plumly, rather than DeBruhl, ran for the house seat from Galveston.[38]

At the same time that Ruby maneuvered to become the Republican candidate for the Twelfth District, he also remained active in efforts to undermine support for Jack Hamilton and his party in Washington. At this point most federal appointments in Texas remained in the hands of supporters of Hamilton. These positions provided the appointees with the money needed to sustain the Hamilton candidacy, and gave Hamilton the appearance of having the backing of national Republicans as well. As president of the Loyal League, Ruby had attempted to influence men in the north to oppose the constitution the previous spring. Throughout the summer, representatives of the Davis party had been in Washington working to undercut faith in Jack Hamilton, and by August they appeared to be making headway. As a result, the Radicals renewed their attacks on Hamilton. Ruby joined in and, uniting with other members from the Bryan convention, sent a letter to Secretary of the Treasury George Boutwell to denounce Hamilton as heading a party that included the Ku Klux Klan. The immediate purpose of this letter was to get Boutwell to replace John L. Haynes as collector of customs at Galveston, and the writers pointed to Haynes as a prime mover in the Hamilton movement and a man who, as head of the old Republican executive committee, had stood in the way of the achievement of unity and harmony among Republicans. At this point Boutwell and other members of the cabinet swung to Davis and began removing Hamilton supporters from federal positions. In the process, Ruby received an appointment as deputy collector of customs for the Port of Galveston. With the position he gained a salary of two thousand dollars per year plus a portion of the revenue collected in the port, an amount that allowed him to carry out an active campaign for the senate seat. The Democratic *Galveston News* reported that "loyalty had at last been rewarded, merit appreciated, and color indicated, by the appointment of that delectable biped, the Ruby, to the post."[39]

While Ruby had worked to gain support for his senate campaign and had made earlier appearances for the party, his first public campaign appearance took place on October 19. On that date he spoke in Galveston, accompanied on the stage by former Confederate General William H. Parsons. Parsons, who had commanded a brigade in the Confederate army during the war, was the Republican nominee for the senate seat from Houston. Parsons was the first speaker and spent most of his effort attacking the Republican credentials of Jack Hamilton and explaining why he supported General Davis for governor. Robert Smith, Ruby's nemesis at this time, managed to gain the stage, where he once again denounced Ruby. Ruby followed Smith, and when he rose to speak someone in the audience cried out that Ruby, compared to Smith, was "the best *nigger of the two*." Ruby responded by thanking the person who had made the remark for his kindness in defining his nationality, pointing out that some people in the press were inclined to dispute the fact that he was black. Ruby then turned to more substantive matters. He spoke on the prejudice of color and the need to move away from it. He pointed out that claims by Hamilton's supporters that the Radicals wanted to start a war of races was absurd. He alluded briefly to the attack by Smith but refused to reply in kind, indicating that he would not deal in personalities. Ruby's address, according to the reporter for the *News*, was "decidedly the most sensible, moderate speech of the night."[40]

Ruby also campaigned in Matagorda and Brazoria Counties, the other parts of his district. The exact dates of his appearances in those communities is unclear, but a correspondent for the *Houston Union*, probably E. H. Quick again, reported that when Ruby appeared in the town of Matagorda the people there were "enthusiastic over his arrival." Quick believed that even "old hack conservatives unwillingly concede his election over all others." A different correspondent for the *Union* wrote that when Ruby appeared, officials had lighted the courthouse so that he could speak and that a large number of people assembled to hear him. This correspondent reported that the audience listened with attention and that Ruby's speaking delighted all present. Rather than hearing a radical speech, however, Ruby spoke in a conciliatory tone, leading even some of the bitterest Democrats who attended to praise it and acknowledge Ruby to be a "kindhearted and reasonable man, and one of fine attainments." The correspondent believed Ruby's election was a fixed fact. Ruby secured the support of the white county judge in the county on this trip, a fact that assured he would get a good turnout in his favor. Ruby also appeared in the town of Brazoria where his speech reportedly had a similar effect.[41]

Back in Galveston, Ruby attended another meeting of the Republican Association on November 19, this one held at the black Baptist church, to endorse the complete slate of candidates that the party had put forward in Galveston. This gathering indicated that the differences within the party finally had been settled. Ruby remained at the head of the local ticket as the candidate for the state senate. George Douglass, in addition to his new position in the custom house where he was a colleague of Ruby, became the party's candidate for county sheriff. Rush Plumly settled for being the candidate for the state house of representatives. In addition, John DeBruhl, whom Plumly had attempted to use against Ruby the previous August, was on the ticket as the candidate for Justice of the Peace in the city's Fourth Ward, Second Precinct. The men attending the rally voted unanimously in their endorsement of the candidates. Galveston Republicans appeared to be internally at peace going into the election.[42]

Through the months leading up to the election Ruby had emerged as a prominent figure within the Republican Party. He was, perhaps, even better known by this time than he had been during his time in the constitutional convention. The price of his growing reputation and political power was a steadily increasing attack on his character and his race by his opponents. By the time of the election they had made every effort to ensure that white voters would not support him. *Flake's Bulletin*, a supporter of his opponent A. P. McCormick and firmly in the Jack Hamilton camp, attacked him repeatedly following his announcement for the senate. The editor assailed him in an August article, criticizing him for having attempted to influence the national administration against Hamilton. In an attack typical of the assaults whites levelled at blacks across the South, the *Bulletin*'s editor belittled his subject, contending that he simply was not qualified to represent Galveston. Ruby was, according to the editor, "a colored man, with that sort of sharpness and shrewdness that a gentleman's body servant is apt to pick up. . . . [W]e recognize in him simply a conceited, puffed up man, inferior in intellect and original talent to many of his race, whose ambition would never lead them to imagine themselves great men." A later editorial insisted that they did not oppose him because he was black but because he wanted an office which "he is incapable to exercise the function of." Objections raised later were based on his advocacy of a proscriptive voting policy and ultimately because he was head of the Loyal League, "a mischievous and pernicious secret political organization."[43]

The Democratic press joined in, not hesitating, as had *Flake's*, to emphasize the issue of race. The *Galveston News* went so far as endorse McCormick, even though he was a professed Republican, because he thought it critical to prevent the "disgrace" brought on Galveston by Ruby's election. The principal Democratic newspaper of the state, the *Texas State Gazette*, echoed the sentiment of the *News*. Its editor wrote, "It would be a great misfortune and disgrace to the State for this man to be elected." He went on to argue, "We cannot and should not elect G. T. Ruby, *even if it defeated reconstruction.*" The election of a black Republican to represent an important city was seen as irresponsible. The *Houston Telegraph* added to the opposition, insisting that Democrats should come to the support of a single candidate to defeat Ruby, contending that "every patriot in Texas is interested in his defeat, and the people of the 12th District should see to it that he shall not be elected."[44]

As the election approached, however, observers concluded that Ruby's election probably was inevitable. The editor of the radical Republican *San Antonio Express*, clearly biased in favor of Ruby, believed that the candidate would run away from McCormick and welcomed the possibility. He believed that Ruby had no superior in "the refinement of his tastes and manners" and that Ruby ranked "well as a man of fine intellect and excellent attainments." The editor of the *Houston Telegraph*, a Democratic journal, was not ready for Ruby's election, but he understood the demographics of Ruby's district. He pointed out that at the last registration the Twelfth District consisted of 2,679 black and 1,121 white voters. This made his election almost certain. There was no doubt, he wrote, that "Ruby has more influence with the negroes than any other man in Texas." They looked upon him as the "'grand president' of their race, and his election will be hailed by Radical negroes all over the State as a *triumph of color.*" They would vote for him and he would win unless the opposition made sure that he faced only one opponent and if whites turned out to register en masse during the next registration. He believed that would assure Ruby's defeat. The view was the most optimistic one for the men opposing Ruby.[45]

The election began on November 30 and proceeded for four days. While potential violence disrupted polling in some parts of the state, the election proceeded quietly in Ruby's district. From the beginning Ruby appeared personally assured of his election. On December 5, the day after the polls closed, he was in Houston with E. J. Davis and the Radical nominee for Congress, William T. Clark. The reporter for the *Houston Union* encountered him and found him optimistic and "in the finest spirits." As the returns came in, his optimism proved justified. In Brazoria County the total vote on Tuesday and Wednesday, the first two days of the election, was 856 votes. Of this number, "Beholder," a local correspondent, believed that Davis and Ruby had each received over 600 votes and that the Republican majority in that county would be fully one thousand votes. "Beholder" reported that the "desperado element" in the county had threatened violence against the leading black citizens because of their role in the election and would deliver as soon as federal troops were removed, but that their threats had not diminished the turnout. An unofficial report that ultimately proved to be accurate from Brazoria on December 5 gave the full vote in that county as only 1,036, not the large turnout predicted, but that the Republican ticket had won. Davis bested Jack Hamilton by a vote of 601 to 435. Ruby's vote was not as dominating as anticipated, but he still beat McCormick by 599 votes to 427. Galveston also was relatively close, but Ruby received 1,170 votes to McCormick's 955. In Matagorda County, however, Ruby crushed McCormick with a vote of 398 to 30. Overall, Ruby defeated McCormick by a vote of 2,167 to 1,421, a 746 vote majority. The returns suggested that Ruby had not made inroads among white voters, however, as Plumly, running for the house and seen by Jack Hamilton Republicans as an acceptable candidate, actually received more votes than Ruby in all three of the counties. His 739 votes in Brazoria, 1,492 in Galveston, and 421 in Matagorda represented 484 Republican voters who supported this white candidate for the house as opposed to the black candidate for the senate.[46]

The Radical victory in Galveston owed much to Ruby, his associates, and black voters. A correspondent for the *New Era* in Washington, DC, recognized Ruby's importance, informing that journal that the Radical victory in the district "in a great measure was brought about by the vigorous and efficient efforts of Hon. G. T. Ruby of Galveston county, Rev. Johnson Reed, and the Hon. Richard Nelson." Reed and Nelson, both associates of Ruby in the league and the Republican Association, would continue to be part of the party apparatus that he created. All of them, the correspondent wrote, had worked "zealously and ably in the interest of the party in this

District." Ruby's future, however, depended on more than simply mobilizing his black base of power. The vote clearly indicated that in the long term, maintaining power in Galveston required him to bring white voters to his support. Whether or not he could do that depended at least in part on how well he managed as senator to fulfill the interests of Galveston's businessmen. Even more critically, his ability to attract white votes hinged on whether or not he could overcome the racism of many of his district's white voters and the willingness of his opponents to use his race as a weapon against him.[47]

CHAPTER VIII

TEXAS STATE SENATOR

Mr. Ruby is an honor to the people and his State.—Houston Union, *September 24, 1870*

George Ruby's victory in the 1869 election made him one of two African Americans elected to the state senate. He served there with Matthew Gaines of Washington County, the other black senator. As a senator Ruby faced two major challenges. In the constitutional convention Ruby proved skillful in the maneuvering necessary for success in any legislative body, even though he failed to secure goals he considered essential to the protection and advancement of his race. A reluctance by white delegates to fully accept black aspirations for equality before the law and protection from the violence that pervaded the state helped account for that failure. Even white delegates from his own party undermined his efforts. Unable to effect a program strongly committed to the protection of equal rights in a body dominated by Republicans, Ruby faced an even worse situation in the Twelfth Legislature, where Republicans outnumbered Democrats by only four votes, seventeen to thirteen. On race issues, all of the seventeen Republicans could not be counted on, and Ruby had to find some way of advancing the interests of his black constituents despite this lack of support.

In addition to finding allies in the senate, Ruby had to find some way of developing support from among whites in his district. Population figures for his district were not known at the beginning of his time in the senate, but observers generally agreed the district had a white majority and that

Ruby could not survive on a black vote alone. The 1870 census confirmed this estimate. Brazoria and Matagorda Counties had large black majority populations, with blacks outnumbering whites in Brazoria by 5,786 to 1,791 and in Matagorda by 2,120 to 1,254. In Galveston, however, whites outnumbered blacks by 12,053 to 3,236. When combined, whites constituted roughly 58 percent of the total population in his district. In 1869 the failure of many whites to register allowed Ruby to gain office primarily with the support of black voters. Now, success in the senate and as a politician in the long term demanded that he find some way to overcome the reluctance of whites in his home district to work with him. The first two sessions of the Twelfth Legislature tested Ruby's ability to find votes in the senate and at home.

Ruby attended the first session or the Provisional Session of the Twelfth Legislature when it met in Austin on February 8, 1870. He appeared on the senate floor that day, took the oath of office, and was seated. The body did not get down to real business until February 11, when it informed General Reynolds and Governor-elect Davis that it had completed its organization. The president of the senate included Ruby in the committee sent to notify Davis that the senate had organized and to request him to transmit any messages he wished to send. Davis determined that since Texas remained outside the Union he was only the provisional appointee of the military commander and could not send a formal message. He, however, did send lawmakers a copy of the proposed Fifteenth Amendment to the Constitution of the United States. That amendment demanded that the rights of citizens to vote should not be denied or abridged on account of "race, color, or previous condition of servitude." In December of 1869, Congress had made ratification of the amendment a condition of Texas's readmission to the Union.[1]

On Monday, February 14, the senate began to deal with the proposed amendment when it considered resolutions ratifying it. Senators quickly approved the amendment by a vote of twenty-three to four, with four men absent. Ruby, obviously, voted yes. Senators subsequently ratified the Thirteenth and Fourteenth Amendments, although each of these already had become part of the national constitution. On the constitutional amendments, Ruby had the honor of bringing them to a final vote on February 18 when he moved for a suspension of rules so that the Thirteenth Amendment might be read the second and final time as required under the senate's rules. Subsequently the Fourteenth and Fifteenth Amendments also passed for the final time. Ruby's first significant role in the session as a representative of the Radical party took place three days prior to the final vote on the amendments when the senate considered the appointment of a public printer. Ruby nominated the publishing firm of Tracy & Siemering, a new partnership of the editors of the *Houston Union* and the *San Antonio Express*, which intended printing an official newspaper of the state and the Republican Party in Austin, the *State Journal*. In offering this resolution, Ruby acted for Governor Davis and indicated his close connection with the men in the executive branch. In the end, the printing went to Tracy after Siemering withdrew from the proposed partnership, but the administration and the Radicals had a newspaper in Austin.[2]

After the adoption of the amendments, the senate turned to other business. The votes in the election of United States senators and a resolution to remove the disabilities of former Confederates still prevented from voting showed the close division within the Senate between Republicans and the Democrats. In the election of United States senators, two positions had to be filled. Since both senators could not hold a six-year term, senators considered candidates for staggered terms, the first with a term ending in 1875 and the other ending in 1877. In the election for the seat for the long term, Morgan Hamilton ran against Horace Broughton, the candidate backed by Jack Hamilton's supporters. While the Senate did not hold a roll call vote, Ruby obviously favored Morgan Hamilton, with whom he had been politically connected since the spring of 1868. Hamilton defeated Broughton by a vote of seventeen to eleven, a tally that showed the small size of the Republican majority. Roughly the same margin held with the election of Lieutenant Governor James W. Flanagan to the short term by a vote of eighteen to ten. A vote that more clearly showed the problem Radical Republicans would have in advancing a progressive agenda, however, took place when the senate considered a resolution that asked the Congress to remove the political disabilities of all citizens of the state. Republicans tabled this resolution by a vote of fifteen to thirteen. Ruby and the other Radicals voted with the majority, but some Republicans associated with the Jack Hamilton faction joined with Democrats in the minority. This vote showed that the Davis administration, when it officially took office after the readmission of Texas to the Union, could not always count on men of its own party on some measures. That vote promised trouble for the sorts of laws Ruby envisioned as critical to securing a better place for blacks in Texas. On February 24 the senate adjourned, having completed the work necessary to secure the state's readmission to the Union.[3]

Shortly after the senate adjourned Ruby left Texas once again for a visit to his family in Maine, although he also had political reasons for the journey. The first part of his trip took him to Portland. George's father, Reuben, had been in Washington, DC, for a time during the war but had moved back to Portland, where he worked as a janitor in the Portland Custom House. While his position appeared to be relatively insignificant, in fact political parties in power usually filled government offices with their political allies. Prestige came with any salaried government job and reflected a favored status within a political party. Reuben's post in the Custom House indicated that he had been rewarded either for his own political activity or that of his son. The younger Ruby did not spend much time in Portland. After only several days he headed for Washington, DC.[4]

In Washington, Ruby renewed efforts at making connections with Republican leaders at the national level. His goals were to influence their view on conditions in the South and probably to pressure for delay in removing all controls over the former Confederate states. On March 29, he attended a meeting in Washington "for the benefit of the Georgia negro legislators, Bullock, *et id genus omne* [and everything of that sort]." In September 1868, the Georgia legislature, controlled by white Democrats, had expelled its black members, contending that the recently adopted constitution did not confer office-holding rights on them. In response to the legislature's action Republican Governor Rufus Bullock persuaded Congress to restore federal military rule. The actions of the legislature suggested that Democrats could not be counted on to uphold the results of the Civil War or Reconstruction, and Ruby spoke at the meeting to protest what had happened in Georgia and warn congressmen that the same could happen elsewhere in the South. Pointing to Texas, Ruby spoke of the "trials of the loyal men" and the "summary manner" in which they had been disposed of by the Ku Klux Klan. He contended that in the entire South most whites considered being a Confederate soldier more glorious than being a federal soldier. Congress, he argued, must be done with their "*nonsense and legal cobwebs*—to brush them away, and do justice to the loyal men of the land."[5]

Ruby also took the opportunity presented by his trip to mix with the black elite in Washington and New York City. By this time, that group readily accepted him into their circle, evidenced by his receipt of an invitation to the wedding of two black socialites in New York City. The wedding involved Cordelia Downing, daughter of a well-known New York caterer, and Mark R. DeMortie, a commission merchant in Richmond, Virginia, and also a partner in a Chicago real estate brokerage. Others on the guest list indicated the prominence of the couple and their families. Ruby was included along with United States Senators John S. Harris of Louisiana and Hiram Revels of Mississippi, and Frederick Douglass. Ruby could not make the wedding, but he did send the young couple a "pair of very heavy silver napkin rings."[6]

His election victory, his early activity in the senate, and the circles he moved within in the North indicated not only Ruby's success as a politician but also suggested that he had even greater ambitions. The speech he gave in Washington particularly suggested that he had aspirations to have influence for his race and the white Republicans of the South not only at the local level but also at the national level. In the Washington speech, for the first time on a national stage, he made clear his hope that a community could be created where political freedom and opportunity for all of its members regardless of race would exist.

Ruby's chance to advance his goal of an equitable society, at least as a legislator in Texas, came with the restoration of the state to the Union and the restoration of civil authority. Ruby was still in the nation's capital when President Grant signed the bill readmitting Texas to the Union on March 30, 1870. On April 16, General Reynolds completed the reestablishment of civil government in the state when he issued a proclamation turning over authority to the officials elected by the people. Ruby had returned to Texas by the time of General Reynolds's proclamation and was in Galveston when the city's citizens celebrated the state's restoration to the Union on April 18. Richard Nelson, an associate of Ruby in the league council, wrote to Fredrick Douglass's *New Era* in Washington describing the occasion. The local Republican Association prepared for the event at a meeting on April 10. The men named to put together the celebration included another of Ruby's protégés, young Norris Wright Cuney. Cuney, the son of a white planter and a slave mother, had been sent to the North for an education before the war and returned to Texas sometime after the war, settling in Galveston. Cuney, of all Ruby's associates, would have the most prominent career as a politician and as a leader of the state Republican Party in subsequent years. The organizers of the meeting intended to include non-Republicans on the committee, but they excluded them when several of these men objected to including a celebration of the ratification of the Fifteenth Amendment at the event as well as readmission. Opposition to black voting certainly had not died among many white Galvestonians. At ten o'clock in the morning on Saturday the 18th, a crowd assembled at the AME Church, and headed by a "splendid colored band" marched to the western suburbs of Galveston, where a celebratory picnic was held. That afternoon the speechmaking began, and at 6:00 p.m. the Revenue Cutter *Delaware* fired a twenty-one-gun salute in honor of the occasion. A crowd reckoned at three thousand in number marched from the picnic grounds to the courthouse by torchlight for speeches. The featured speakers that evening included Ruby, the only black man on the speaker's platform. Nelson wrote that the celebration ended when Nathan Patten, collector of the port, proposed three cheers for the admission of Texas, a proposal responded to with "immense enthusiasm by the vast throng."[7]

Prior to the reassembling of the Twelfth Legislature, some observers, including Conservative Republicans, expected Ruby to be a leader in the legislature in advancing the Davis government's legislative agenda. Their expectations proved true. In the weeks leading up to the opening of the Called Session of the legislature, the special session called for by Governor Davis at the end of the Provisional Session, even Jack Hamilton's *Austin Republican* mentioned Ruby as a likely candidate to be elected president pro tem of the senate to fill the place of James Flanagan, who had been elected to the United States Senate in the Provisional Session. Alfred H. Longley, editor at the time, saw Ruby as an example of a black man who had achieved a level of culture and who would serve as a model for others of his race. Of course Longley may simply have been playing once again on racial tensions within the Radical Party, but the editor of the *Houston Union*, a Radical journal, believed Ruby had an important role to play. After visiting with Ruby on his return from the North, the then editor of that newspaper wrote that Ruby could be instrumental in "doing away with the bitter prejudices against them [black people] on account of their political enfranchisement." His sociability allowed him to be at home among people of both races and a variety of backgrounds. The editor believed on the eve of the convening of the Twelfth Legislature that racial prejudice hopefully might be put aside. Certainly that was essential for Ruby's success as a legislator.[8]

The regular session opened on April 26, 1870, and Ruby initially really did appear slated to be elected presiding officer of the senate. The correspondent for the *Galveston News* described Ruby as the "most formidable opponent" among the men who ran for the position. He even believed Ruby to be superior to others in his knowledge of parliamentary law. Ruby's fate, however, hinged on the struggles among the various regional factions within the Radical party for recognition. Ruby had the advantage of coming from the Third Congressional District, the district that had essentially put the Radical Republicans into all of the state offices. The fact that at least two other men from the same district wanted the position worked to Ruby's disadvantage. When these two withdrew, Ruby remained a viable candidate. His friends pointed out that no other black man held a state office and that his race should be recognized by electing him to this important position. Senators from eastern Texas, however, insisted that their section should have the prize and, in the end, Webster Flanagan, son of the newly elected United States Senator James W. Flanagan, managed the election of Donald Campbell, another man from eastern Texas. In a close election, Campbell beat Ruby, reportedly by a single vote. Ruby's opponents welcomed his defeat and saw it as a possible check on Ruby's ambitions. The possibility that Ruby might be chosen as the senate's presiding officer proved overly optimistic.[9]

When the senate organized, the members drew lots to determine the length of their terms. Ruby drew a six-year term, assuring that he would hold his seat at least until 1874. On the same day he also received his committee assignments. He had a place on the Committee on Contingent Expenses, a relatively unimportant committee. Significantly, however, Don Campbell, as president of the senate, named him to two of the more important committees of the senate—the Committee on the Militia and the Committee on Public Lands. He subsequently received a place on the important Judiciary Committee as well. Through the term, in addition to his service on these and other special committees, much of what Ruby worked on involved the commonplace business of any legislator, introducing bills of interest to his constituents, or attending to the resolutions and petitions that they sent to him. In the course of the session he put ten resolutions before the senate, introduced twenty-one bills, and offered amendments to three bills being considered. Eight of the bills that he introduced dealt with either the incorporation of railroads or the modifications of their charters. Three bills incorporated financial institutions in Galveston. In addition, he introduced legislation to create a Geological and Agricultural Survey and a Horticultural Society. Such efforts, in behalf of corporations controlled by white Galvestonians, were essential if he was to gain any support from them.[10]

Ruby's efforts on behalf of Galveston business interests supported the activities of some of the city's most prominent men, men he desperately needed to support him if he were to have a political future in Galveston. T. H. McMahan, one of Galveston's prominent merchant bankers and a co-owner of McMahan Banking, headed the Texas Mutual Life Insurance Corporation, one of the businesses Ruby worked to incorporate. Ruby's support of Texas Mutual potentially associated him with other men listed as board members of the new corporation, including Allen Lewis and Jesse Batts, two other of Galveston's leading businessmen, and A. J. Ward of the firm of Ward, Dewey & Company. Ward and his company had other Republican connections as Ward later acquired the lease of the state prison system. Relatively unknown black men, however, sought Ruby's help to incorporate the Beneficial Society of Galveston. The men associated with this burial society included William A. Clark, a boatman who worked in the Customs House, Charles Redmond, a laborer, and Ruby's political associate, Richard Nelson. The Savings & Trust Company of Texas, another company backed by Ruby, included among its incorporators a socially diverse group that ranged from Congressman William T. Clark and Joseph B. Simpson, a lawyer, to Republican activists like Samuel A. Dodge and at least one black man, Johnson Reed.[11]

The men Ruby attempted to ally with were known in the financial and benevolent institutions that he supported. His connections are not as clear in most of the railroad corporations that he supported, since none of these companies ever received a charter. The route of these proposed railroads, however, indicated that most of them had the backing of Galveston businessmen. All of the lines he backed, except for the Austin & Pacific, directly served the business interests of Galveston, whose merchants worked to control trade into the interior of the state. The Houston & Henderson Railroad, for example, would have replaced the previously chartered Galveston, Houston & Henderson. This railroad's backers hoped to make it a part of the Galveston & St. Louis Railroad, a line intended to tie Galveston to the markets in St. Louis by way of the farming lands in eastern Texas. The Galveston & El Paso Railroad also represented the ambitions of Galveston businessmen to tap into the commerce of western Texas and ultimately the Pacific coast. Because Galveston newspapers actively supported the Galveston & El Paso and published information on it, that railroad is the one where the backers are known. In this case Ruby once again supported an effort by T. H. McMahan, the Galveston banker who was part of the newly incorporated Mutual Life Insurance Corporation. As the senator from Galveston, Ruby was the natural sponsor of such legislation, but his actions in favor of local business interests offered at least the potential of securing for him their political support.[12]

Ruby's most important work relative to private legislation, in the long term, was his support of the Houston Ship Channel, an internal improvement project that at the time appeared to benefit both Houston and Galveston in their efforts to establish themselves as the center of trade for all of Texas. The men responsible for the corporation, styled the Buffalo Bayou Ship Channel Company, included some of the most prominent men in the Galveston and Houston banking and business communities. The incorporators included Alfred S. Richardson, an officer of the Houston and Texas Central Railway; John Shearne, director of the navigation company and merchant in Houston; Thomas W. House, a wholesale merchant in Houston; Robert O. Love, editor of the *Houston Mercury*, a business newspaper; Abram Groesbeck, a director of the Houston and Texas Central; Joseph R. Morris, mayor of Houston; and Henry R. Allen, a merchant associated with the firm of McIlhenny, Willis and Company. The bill sponsored by Ruby authorized the company to construct and maintain a ship channel from within the city of Houston along Buffalo Bayou and into the Gulf of Mexico at Bolivar Channel. The company could charge vessels to use this channel, making it a potentially lucrative enterprise. Such a channel actually threatened Galveston's role as the chief port of the state, but at the time Galvestonians believed that it would work to their benefit as well. Explaining Ruby's stand on the ship channel, the correspondent for the *Houston Union* reported in mid-July that as people had come to understand the purpose of the ship channel it had come to be seen as a work that would benefit the entire state. "I may mention," he wrote, "the fact that Senator Ruby and the rest of the Galveston delegation all support it."[13]

Ruby's sponsorship of legislation beneficial to the business community of Galveston and introduction of measures for the incorporation of a horticultural society and a state geological and agricultural survey earned him initial praise from men who had not supported him in the election. The correspondent for *Flake's Bulletin* offered a positive portrait of Ruby to that newspaper's readers in mid-May. He described the senator from Galveston as being a recognizable individual, "with a nose like a hawk and an aggressive countenance he looks the man that will be active, up and doing." He also found Ruby to be a man of culture and possessing considerable shrewdness. *Flake's* correspondent had been critical of Ruby in the constitutional convention, but now he found that he had "improved very much during the last year." He noted in particular that he had "abated, or else conceals the egotism that made him offensive in the constitutional convention," although he found that he still "loves the melody of his own voice." Overall, he reported, "truth compels me to say that he is one of the most gentlemanly Senators on the floor." He only feared that Ruby had a relatively low idea of political morality, in short suggesting once again that he was open to bribery, although he believed in this willingness to accept favors in return for his support he measured up to most of the other men on the senate floor. A subsequent item published by *Flake*'s observed that all of the black legislators acted in the legislature with more decorum than some of their white colleagues. The author once again praised Ruby, who he thought had "conducted himself admirably."[14]

Ruby's support of the legislative program advanced by Governor Edmund J. Davis, critical to Ruby's hopes for the safety and progress of his own people, however, produced less favorable assessments by *Flake's* and the *Galveston News* as the session went on. The governor set his legislative agenda in his address to the legislature on April 29. Davis touched on a wide variety of issues, but three subjects were of particular importance to Ruby. These had been matters that had attracted Ruby to the Radicals in August 1868, and then to the Davis faction during the 1869 elections. The first, considered by Governor Davis of primary importance to all of the people of the state, was the passage of laws to suppress crime and violence and restore law and order throughout the state. To accomplish this end, the governor recommended several measures. The first was the passage of a law creating an efficient and well-organized militia. As part of a militia bill he recommended the creation of a national guard, an active militia, to be paid for by a tax on those individuals wanting to avoid militia duty. The national guard would be a smaller force of volunteers who would be more disciplined than the regular militia and would be better armed and equipped and could be called quickly into service when needed. Davis pointed to other states that had adopted such a measure and believed that they found the smaller force more easily handled and more effective. He looked to the militia as a means of sustaining the laws in extreme emergencies. Ruby and other black voters desperately needed such a force to avoid the widespread race-related election violence that had occurred in 1868 and 1869.[15]

Ruby's belief that measures had to be enacted that would suppress violence received additional recognition with the governor's request that the legislature create a state police force, a state-wide law enforcement agency that served as a prototype for the later Texas Rangers, which emerged after the end of Reconstruction. Davis pointed to cases where county officials were too weak to enforce the law or were indisposed to do so. Many criminals moved across the state, jumping from jurisdiction to jurisdiction, thus thwarting their pursuit by local officials and escaping capture. A state police that could move across county boundaries, he believed, would allow the pursuit of such men and help to suppress the crime he found rampant in the state. Davis further recommended that city police, county sheriffs and their deputies and constables be made a part of a general police force and subject to the orders of the chief of the state police. The governor believed that the system could be created without great expense and would be efficient in "pursuing and bringing to justice offenders," and, pointing to the presence of Ku Klux Klan-like bands, "in destroying lawless organizations." Additionally, he encouraged the legislature to provide funds to help the counties build secure jails.[16]

The governor also backed another measure that coincided with Ruby's belief that the government must suppress violence, a modification of the state's criminal code. Davis wanted laws that provided particularly severe punishment on "mobs of lawless men assembling and operating in disguise, for the carrying out of some unlawful purpose." These men, again involved in organizations similar to the Ku Klux Klan, had directed their violence particularly against black voters. In case after case no one had been punished for such activity. Indeed, Davis believed that in some locations such action was "protected and encouraged by the majority of the people." Such activity, he insisted, was the most dangerous to public security. The fact that in some cases local authorities refused to act made it necessary, the governor believed, to give the governor the authority to act in such cases. Davis recommended that he be given the power to temporarily establish martial law in such cases. He believed that intervention would seldom be required because the very existence of such a power would probably produce an end to such violence. In another proposed change in the criminal code, Davis suggested that the legislature enact restrictions on the carrying of arms. Section Thirteen of the newly adopted Constitution's Bill of Rights specifically addressed the issue and gave the legislature control over the bearing of arms not present in the earlier constitution, reflecting the belief by the governor and others that limiting the number of firearms in circulation would reduce crime.[17]

After proposing solutions to the problem of violence, the governor turned to fulfilling the constitutional mandate for the creation of a public school system. Davis believed this was critical, thinking that a liberal system of education exercised a civilizing influence and that the success of Republican institutions and universal suffrage depended on universal education, a view similar to that held by Ruby. To fund the schools, in addition to the various funds provided for by the constitution, Davis proposed collecting the amount owed the school by the state's railroads and paid back to the school fund in Confederate paper money. In particular he proposed selling those railroads in default on their payments to the school fund, although he believed the situation warranted the sale of all the railroads that had borrowed money from the fund. He noted that some had suggested that the railroads that paid the interest then due and made regular payments thereafter should be relieved from forfeiture. That required special legislation, he said, and contended that if such legislation was not passed, he would sell the railroads to recoup the funds owed the schools.[18]

The final issue of particular importance to Senator Ruby in Davis's message was the governor's recommendation on whether or not the state should fund new railroad enterprises. Davis recognized that the public wanted the development of some sort of railroad system, built with state support, but he urged caution. It was not apparent to the governor that any honest and feasible internal improvement enterprise, including railroad companies in particular, required anything from the state beyond a liberal charter and right of way. The state's dealings with "the vast number of schemes of the sort that have never progressed further than to encumber our statute books, and obstruct the ground to other more responsible companies," was evidence of the problems with state support. Davis pointed out that despite the state giving away vast amounts of land, the railroad companies actually had built few miles before the war. If the legislature concluded that aid was necessary, however, he recommended that it be limited to a railroad crossing the state from Red River to the Rio Grande and linking Texas to the railroad systems to the north and east. That was all, he believed, state finances could bear. Ruby, by contrast, represented a district where business interests were entangled in numerous railroad enterprises and wanted state support to further those companies. Railroad legislation in the Twelfth Legislature presented Ruby with his most difficult decisions as a senator when forced to decide whether or not he should stand with the governor or go with the men he ultimately needed to remain in power.[19]

Ruby's support for much of Governor Davis's program meant that the early positive assessments of his actions in the legislature lasted barely into the third week of the session. His positions, especially those that tended to address the concerns of black voters, usually aroused white opposition. The issue that raised early concerns with Ruby in the Conservative and Democratic press was his support of Joseph W. Talbot for the position of state superintendent of schools. Talbot had been important as an advocate of the schools in the constitutional convention and was a likely candidate for the job. His appointment turned into a fight in the senate, however, when he faced opposition because he would not take a firm stand against the possibility of creating integrated schools. The constitution did not require integrated schools, and Talbot had no interest in creating them. He realized, however, that segregated schools would be financially impracticable in some communities and that public schools would succeed only if integrated. The balance of power in the senate between Radicals and their opponents was close, and four Radicals refused to support Talbot, making it impossible to secure the senate's consent. Ruby had never been an advocate of integrated schools, but like Talbot he understood the potential financial implications of segregated schools and could see that in a segregated system his race would be discriminated against. When the governor refused to withdraw Talbot's name, a contest developed in which Ruby came to Talbot's support. In the end, however, the senate refused to consent to Talbot's appointment. The fight over Talbot showed how, on issues regarding race and particularly on assuring blacks of their rights, the Radical party in the legislature was not united.[20]

Surprisingly, the governor's Frontier Protection Bill, generally supported by all Republicans and even some Democrats, had detractors. The bill authorized the creation of ranger companies, similar to the antebellum rangers, consisting of local citizens in frontier counties who would meet Native American tribes who raided in them, providing members of the company with weapons and pay. The opposition focused primarily on the potential cost. The correspondent for *Flake's Bulletin* criticized the bill as being "very expensive," pointing particularly to the pay for the men who would serve. He indicated that a moderate estimate of the cost to the state would be $1.5 million per annum. One of the major opponents to the bill was United States Senator Morgan Hamilton. Hamilton based his opposition in part on the cost of the measure, but he also believed that the federal government should provide such protection along the frontier.[21]

Despite the opposition, few in the senate proved willing to vote against it, and Ruby gave what may have been his maiden speech on the senate floor on June 7 in support of the measure. Ruby recognized that opposition to the bill existed, accepting that some Texans opposed it because they objected to the way it dealt with Indians. Others opposed it because of the cost to the state. Still others were against it because they did not believe that the use of the military would produce the desired results. Ruby said that, to his thinking, none of these were adequate reasons to oppose the bill. In an argument similar to the ones he used to favor his own long-sought goal of action to protect the freedmen, Ruby contended that the "utter and absolute regard that we should entertain for human life" demanded the measure. He went on to deprecate the fact that the Indians had to be dealt with by military means, but he also decried the existing policy of the national government that attempted to move the Indians onto reservations where they would be fed and clothed. He had earlier agreed with Senator Albert J. Fountain from El Paso, who had complained that the government fed and clothed the Indians so they could raid the frontier. That policy had been wrong from the beginning, and it had helped produce the reasons that had "forced upon us to-day the protection of our frontier by such a bill as is before us." At some point after Ruby's speech, the senate voted on the bill and passed it by a vote of twenty-four to three.[22]

The various police measures that Governor Davis requested also ran into serious opposition in the senate, and Ruby's support for them outraged many of his opponents back in Galveston. When the senate took up the governor's militia and state police bills, the Jack Hamilton Republicans and Democrats met them with determined opposition. As the bills moved through the senate and Ruby actively supported them, he came under increasing criticism in Galveston. Conservative Republicans publicly objected to the cost of such measures. Democrats more commonly condemned them as unconstitutional, contending that they created a standing army and gave the governor almost dictatorial power. The house passed the Militia Bill on May 21 and followed with the State Police Bill on June 6. As early as May 12, however, two Radicals in the senate indicated that they would not support either of the proposed bills and the Radical majority in that body was too small to suppress Democratic delaying tactics without the vote of these two men. Initially the opposition attempted to block consideration of both measures by breaking the quorum, a parliamentary tactic that had been used effectively by Jack Hamilton in the constitutional convention. Both bills languished as the administration looked for ways to get the bills on to the senate floor. Through consideration of these measures, Ruby actively supported them. A letter Thomas J. Powell, the assistant sergeant-at-arms in the senate and another ally of Ruby, wrote to the Loyal League in Galveston on June 9 pointed to the Galveston senator as working hard at this time for the Militia Bill. Five Radicals, he wrote, stood in the way of the passage of the Militia Bill, the "great panacea for all the ills that now beset our (loyal) people." Ruby, Powell assured his readers, stood behind the Militia Bill "like the everlasting hills, true to his Country, his God, and the people." Everything that he had done was for their benefit and prosperity. The writer noted that Ruby was always at work and ready to carry out his duty.[23]

The desertion of the five Republicans made passage of the bill impossible, but the administration worked behind the scenes to secure the needed votes. The measure finally came to the floor for debate on June 16. The next day, June 17, Ruby spoke in favor of the Militia Bill. The correspondent for *Flake's Bulletin*, strongly hostile to the bill, agreed with its opponents that it violated "no less than twenty-three sections of the Constitution." He believed these violations were plain for anyone to see, and they included an imposition of military authority over civil authority. Ruby argued against such a conclusion and contended that the bill made the militia subordinate to the governor and asked, was not the governor, by the constitution, the head of the civil government as its executive? If so, then civil government remained in force. Although the correspondent disagreed with Senator Ruby's conclusions in the latter's defense of the bill, he did believe that Ruby was the only Radical to actually argue that it was constitutional. The correspondent asserted, in the usual condescending way, that this was a fallacy of argument "worthy only of a school boy of ten years old." Nonetheless, he assured his readers that Ruby's words were "nearer an argument in the bill's favor on constitutional grounds than anything which fell from the lips of any Senator on the floor."[24]

The actual text of his speech suggests, however, that Ruby was not as concerned with the constitutional character of the bill as the *Bulletin*'s correspondent implied, and that Ruby saw Reconstruction as a revolution. In the speech noted at the beginning of this book, Ruby insisted that the changes brought about by Reconstruction had changed the very character of government, and that change was still in progress. The arguments concerning constitutional limits on actions made no sense when the very character of constitutions was changing. It was then that he showed an erudition that must have startled many on the senate floor, referring to John Maynard, and Thomas Babington Macauley, and England's Glorious Revolution. Like Maynard, Ruby agreed that the nation and Texans were "out of the beaten path," and that this required extraordinary actions. Violence had to be suppressed and by whatever means possible.[25]

The Militia Bill finally passed amid "great excitement at the capitol," in the words of the correspondent for *Flake's Bulletin*. When the vote to pass the bill in its final form came up on June 21, at least two of the Radicals who had previously opposed it now said that they would vote in favor of it. Thirteen members of the opposition, however, left the floor and broke the quorum needed for the senate to proceed. The thirteen later denied their intention had been to break the quorum, although their action effectively did so and delayed action. When they returned to the floor, the president of the senate ordered them to be placed under arrest so that they could not leave the floor again and block consideration of the bill. When the vote came, the president released four of the members to reconstitute the quorum and to vote. The bill then passed by a vote of fifteen to five. Only a failure to secure a fourth-fifths vote prevented the bill's final passage. The next day, the bill went forward for final passage, again by a vote of fifteen to five. The eight senators arrested the previous day remained under arrest, thus preventing the use of any parliamentary maneuvering to block the vote. Throughout the controversy over the bill, Ruby stood with the administration. Indeed, at least one Democratic newspaper blamed him for the entire business. Explaining the arrest of the senators, the editor of the *Dallas Herald* opined that the arrests probably were done "through the influence of the immortal nigger carpetbagger, Ruby."[26]

When the senate took up the Police Bill, the Radical leadership in the senate managed to keep the bolting senators under arrest to avoid the same sort of parliamentary maneuvering that the opposition had used attempting to block the Militia Bill. This time debate on the bill was limited. The president of the senate allowed enough senators who were under arrest and who would help constitute a quorum to take their seats. On June 28, the bill passed readily with roughly the same vote as had the Militia Bill, fifteen to six. Ruby made no remarks while the senate considered the bill, but in the vote he stood with the administration and the majority in securing its passage.[27]

Contemporary newspapers paid particular attention to the rulings that allowed the senate to proceed with several of its members under arrest, but they also puzzled over the fact that several of the Radical senators who had said they would not vote for the bill decided to support it. They speculated that the governor had managed to pressure the railroads to influence those senators by threatening to veto all railroad legislation until the Militia and Police bills passed. This put on hold two major pieces of legislation critical to two of the biggest railroad companies in the state. The Southern Pacific Railroad had a proposed incorporation bill that guaranteed that the company would receive state land for each mile of track built. The bill circumvented the constitutional prohibition on grants of land to railroads incorporated into the 1869 constitution by contending that the new charter was a continuation of the charter of the Memphis, El Paso, and Pacific Railroad, an antebellum railroad that had received a grant of land. The Southern Pacific had the support of powerful Republicans, like Senator James W. Flanagan and his son Webster, and Democrats, including former governor James W. Throckmorton. The Houston and Texas Central Railway had a relief bill in committee that its backers considered critical to its future operations. The bill provided relief for its indebtedness to the state caused by its nonpayment of interests on state bonds during the war by allowing the road to exchange its existing bonds for new ones. The measure also allowed the school fund to be invested in Central's new bonds. Among supporters of the Central's relief bill was Representative James G. Tracy, at this point not only in the legislature but still the chairman of the Republican State Executive Committee. To get action on the railroads, the railroad lobbyists supposedly, at least according to newspaper accounts, threw their support to the governor's Militia and Police bills. One report, never proven, alleged that $55,000 in railroad stock had been given to one group of senators to secure the Militia Bill's passage.[28]

Whether or not Governor Davis supported some sort of compromise is unknown. When the bills came up in the senate, however, some of Davis's strongest supporters, including Ruby, voted in favor of their passage. When the senate considered the Southern Pacific Bill on June 13, Ruby and most

Republicans voted to support it, and in an unusual alliance of Radicals and Democrats the measure carried with a vote of twenty to six. The six who opposed the bill were men from the interior of the state who were anti-railroad throughout the session. This voting bloc consisted of S. W. Ford from McLennan County, Phidello W. Hall from Robertson County, Theo Hertzberg from Menard County, Mijamin Priest from Cherokee County, William A. Saylor from Brazos County, and Matthew Gaines from Washington County, the other black senator. The Texas Central legislation passed the senate on July 27, with Ruby once again voting with the majority. This time the vote carried twenty-one to six, with the opponents who had voted against the Southern Pacific legislation remaining together.[29]

Surprisingly, if a deal had been made, Governor Davis vetoed both of these bills. Possibly, again if some sort of bargain had been made, the vetoes were simply to signal the governor's opposition to any extravagance in supporting the railroads, since he knew that the legislation's supporters had enough votes to pass the bills over his veto. Ruby, however, now shifted his position. When the senate looked to override the governor's veto of the Southern Pacific bill, Ruby and others who had supported it initially voted to sustain the governor, thus defeating the bill. The Texas Central bill was another matter, given Ruby's efforts to build some sort of support among Galveston businessmen. That railroad promised to route even more business from the state's interior to Galveston. When the senate took up the Texas Central veto, Ruby voted to override it, joining a majority of senators to give relief to that company. Unfortunately, Ruby never said anything about his decision-making in this case, although his votes undoubtedly served the interests of his district.[30]

A vote that caused Ruby much trouble in the future came when the senate took up the incorporation of another railroad, the International. The projected line had the backing of a prominent northern railroad promoter, John S. Barnes, and, locally, Houston businessman Thomas W. House. The company intended building a line from northeast Texas and the south bank of the Red River to Laredo. Ultimately, it would have tied Texas by rail to northeastern markets through St. Louis. The bill incorporating the railroad proposed generous state support, offering the company state bonds of $10,000 per mile. Unlike the Southern Pacific, the International had prominent backers within the administration. It also represented the type of railroad that Governor Davis had envisioned. When it came to a final vote, Ruby, unquestionably backing a measure favored by Davis, voted along with most of the Republicans and Democrats in the senate in favor of incorporating the line. Unfortunately, from when the senate first took up the International bill, rumors spread that its financial backers were spreading money among legislators in order to get the bill passed. The source of the rumors is unclear. With Davis's backing the railroad did not need to bribe anyone. Nonetheless, Ruby's opponents took up these rumors and suggested that he had been bribed. Their charges plagued him for some time afterward.[31]

Ruby may have supported the interests of the Galveston businessmen when he voted for the railroads, but his efforts produced no discernible results. They needed him and used him, but they refused to openly support him. Race certainly played a role in this refusal, for Ruby also introduced bills that reflected his desire to protect the rights of his race. That put him at odds with the very businessmen he needed to sustain his political career. His sponsorship of a new city charter for the city of Galveston was such an instance. In late June, Ruby introduced the bill. The editor of the *News* contended that the bill originated in the Loyal League's local council, and Ruby openly claimed responsibility for it. Three of the bill's features were clearly a product of Ruby's concerns. First, the bill removed property qualifications for office holding, a measure that would have allowed poor blacks to hold office. Second, the bill would have allowed men without property to vote in municipal elections. Third, the proposed charter required officeholders only to be citizens of the state and did not impose local residency requirements, opening the way for blacks who moved to Galveston from the countryside to hold office. The bill would have made city government in Galveston more democratic, opening it up to the hundreds of freedmen who had come to the city since the war. The bill immediately provoked opposition from the city's businessmen and from the two principal newspapers, the *News* and *Flake's*. The editor of the *News* summed up the outrage of property interests in the city when he wrote that "with no property of their own, it is deemed but right they [property less residents] should have the right of taxing those who have property." The charge of its opponents that the bill represented the interests of Ruby and his associates appeared to be confirmed on July 8 when a mass meeting of men at Freedmen's Hall endorsed the "Ruby charter" and selected names to be recommended to the governor to fill the various offices until the next election.[32]

In their public statements on Ruby's bill, the opposition ultimately emphasized a proposal in the charter that would have allowed city authorities to authorize public improvements without the consent of the taxpayers as the reason for their opposition rather than emphasizing the voting rights issue. They thus masked their opposition to more democratic government with the assertion that they opposed the potential for corruption. Hostile newspaper editors contended that the entire charter was nothing more than a conspiracy to allow Tom Ochiltree to put down Nicholson pavement in the city without any restrictions on how much Ochiltree charged the city. At the time Ochiltree represented the American Nicholson Pavement Company, a northern company that specialized in using wood blocks to pave streets. Ochiltree had concluded, according to Willard Richardson, editor of the *News*, that the best way to get the contract was to "harmonize with our Radical friends." Richardson called what was taking place the greatest "crisis in the history of Galveston." Flake, referring to the measure as the Ruby-Patten-Ochiltree bill, contended that what he called "the conspirators" sought to confiscate the property of the city's businessmen for their own use. It would inevitably lead, he believed, to a heavy increase in taxes to put in a pavement that would be installed by Northerners. In the same article Flake unleashed a barrage of criticism against Ruby, who, he contended, failed to represent the interests of Galvestonians, meaning as always propertied white Galvestonians. He concluded that Ruby might next have a project to do with the Galveston Fertilizing Company, "a project doubtless in which he is well qualified to take part."[33]

Despite the turmoil created by Ruby's support of measures unpopular with many whites in his district, his loyalty to the administration earned him consideration from the Davis government as the session progressed. In July, Davis reappointed Ruby a notary public for Galveston. The position provided no salary but it gave a certain amount of prestige, kept Ruby in contact with his constituents, and did produce some income in the fees that he could charge for notarizing documents. The governor also considered appointing Ruby to the Galveston City Council after he removed three of its members. That would have been a better job, since the office had a salary. Ruby, however, refused the appointment and, in his stead, Davis appointed one of Ruby's associates, Johnson Reed. The correspondent who had covered the session for *Flake's Bulletin* wrote on August 17 that Ruby's decision not to take the position had led him to conclude that "Ruby is shrewder than we supposed." Ruby had managed to acquire several other good offices that gave him the resources needed to be an effective politician, including his legislative office, and he did not really need the salary. Ruby's refusal to take the position appeared, as a result, particularly astute. It gave the job to a man who, the reporter believed, was a rival for Ruby's leadership position in Galveston. He thought Ruby understood there would be no glory in being on the council and it might, in fact, lead to a "might deal of opprobrium." Giving the job to Reed would ruin Reed, who, the correspondent assumed, would wake up one morning to find that he had made nine enemies. The correspondent found Ruby's maneuver to be a "sharp trick." In the end, he concluded that "[f]or the leadership of the colored men he [Ruby] has but few rivals."[34]

Ruby's support of the administration also put him in the position to influence other political matters and particularly political appointments.

Galveston newspapermen believed, with reason, that Ruby held veto power over the appointment of the local district judge. *Flake's Bulletin* complained following the session that no one had yet been appointed judge in Galveston. During the session Governor Davis had been ready to appoint someone. In the end, however, the editor wrote that Davis "would send none in for this district because Mr. Ruby was hard to please." When Ruby left the state for several months at the end of the session, a judge still had not been appointed. The editor believed that because of Ruby's control over the appointment, naming someone to the position would have to wait until the senator's return. That Ruby may actually have had the power to determine who held the position received some validation when, after Ruby returned, Governor Davis did finally appoint a new judge.[35]

Throughout the legislative session Ruby not only dealt with his work as a state senator but also retained considerable influence in the local council of the Loyal League, even though he had surrendered the presidency of the Texas State Council. The latter body held its annual meeting in Austin in May, and delegates voted James Newcomb to be the new president after Ruby declined to run. The shift made sense. Newcomb had access to clerks and to funds for printing. This access allowed him to develop the organization more fully. Ruby remained involved in the state leadership, however, and still received letters from around the state asking for his opinion on a variety of issues. In early June, for example, he received a letter from Sabine Pass informing him of the existence of a "secret organization of Rebels" that met in Beaumont. The informant told Ruby that this group planned to prevent any person belonging to the Republican Party from settling in their community. Further, they planned to oppose the education of all blacks, "except so far as they see proper to enlighten them." The purpose of the letter was to keep Ruby informed of developments at the local level and to request his assistance in responding to such threats. Ruby thus remained aware of local conditions among blacks.[36]

Local councils also turned to him for political advice. On July 30 several "black citizens" of Henderson asked his opinion on the political situation, writing to Ruby because "in casting about no fitter person than yourself, being one of our race, is presented, to whom we may appeal for advice." They questioned the loyalty to the Republican Party of state senator Web Flanagan, who had been one of the movers of the ill-fated Southern Pacific Railroad bill in the state legislature. The blacks told Ruby that white friends, probably in the league, had told them that Flanagan had deserted the party and its principles. They, however, were slow to believe so because they had "as a race, turned out from field and plough, from axe and hoe at the last election" to support him. They wanted Ruby to advise them. Ruby replied on August 8, indicating that differences of opinion had arisen among Republicans on the Militia and Police bills and that Senator Flanagan differed as to the remedy. This was, Ruby believed, an honest expression of opinion. Difference also had occurred on questions of internal improvements, the governor having views directly opposite to those of Flanagan and other members of the legislature. Unwise acts had been committed, although Ruby did not point to anyone in particular. Ruby concluded by advising the citizens of Henderson that "all of us are liable to err." Apologizing for not being able to come personally to visit them, he urged them to move forward in organizing their county.[37]

Ruby challenged the stereotypes of blacks held by many whites, although the opposition repeatedly used stereotypes to attack him. Still, his activity in the senate forced even some of his enemies to reassess Ruby. The Austin reporter for the *Galveston News*, never one to appreciate Ruby, believed that during the session Ruby had proven himself to be a tactician "of more than ordinary ability." In addition, the *News*'s man thought him to be the "ablest man in the Senate on the Radical side of the House," even better than Senator Parsons from Houston. Of course such praise also tended to pit Ruby against white leaders such as Parsons and was only a small part of the generally negative press given to Ruby by the *News*.[38]

Seldom examined by later historians, the pages of the Radical press offered more fulsome praise of the senator from Galveston. A reporter for the *State Journal*, the administration's newspaper, offered one of the most graphic portraits of Ruby printed during the session. That article described Ruby physically as of medium size, "slight but compactly built." His complexion was considered "light olive." He had what the author considered "fine phrenological development." The author considered his mind to be "well cultivated." In his private life he was portrayed as industrious and his habits irreproachable. In the senate he was a deliberate speaker, "his words are well chosen, and his periods nicely turned." The author found that when Ruby spoke the entire house listened "with deference." He considered him to be a "fair and gentlemanly debater." In addition, he was "well posted in parliamentary usage." Recognition of his abilities had led to the president of the senate to frequently call him to the chair where he had shown considerable "executive ability." The author predicted that if Ruby's life was spared, there would be a "brilliant future" for a man still only twenty-nine years old.[39]

After the session adjourned Ruby received even more lavish praise from the Republican press. The reporter for the *State Journal* acclaimed Ruby as being "assiduous in the discharge of his official duties, and faithful to the trusts committed to his charge." The reporter was particularly impressed with the logic of his speeches and the fact that he did not occupy the floor when he had nothing to say, which differed considerably from what the reporter for *Flake's Bulletin* had indicated in the past. For the *Journal*'s correspondent, Ruby's speaking style was "marked by force and precision of logical utterance." The reporter again noted his skill as a parliamentarian and his frequent call to preside over the body. The correspondent of the *Houston Union* summed up Ruby's performance in the legislature as one in which he won the respect and esteem of his fellow senators, regardless of party. Ruby had shown himself to be a man of "courteous bearing, of refined and affable manners, of dignified deportment, and excellent temper." The *Union*'s correspondent believed that unquestionably there was no more perfect gentleman in the senate. The fact that Ruby always "counselled forbearance and moderation whenever the vexed and often bitter question of the two races was brought up" particularly impressed the man from the *Union*. This reporter summed up the general impression many had of Ruby when he wrote, "Mr. Ruby is an honor to the people and his State." Even a writer for the *New Orleans Republican*, a newspaper with which Ruby had connections, mentioned Ruby. He described him as "one of the ablest and most intelligent members of the Legislature of our sister State." He was clearly recognized as an accomplished individual, although he was still considered an outsider by the white businessmen he represented in Galveston.[40]

Ruby returned to Galveston following the adjournment of the second session of the legislature and quickly went to work strengthening his political base and perhaps reaching out beyond it. He was in the city by August 21, busily at work maintaining his connections with the state's party leaders. Showing himself to be a party loyalist, Ruby wrote to Edward H. Quick, who was then editing James Tracy's *Houston Union*, and sent him a check for one hundred dollars. He asked Quick to credit it to his account for an indefinite subscription to the *Union*. Ruby stated that he did so to show that he appreciated Quick's "services to the party and your friends," appreciation shown in a tangible way with a monetary subscription. Quick replied and expressed his thanks for the recognition of his efforts to sustain the Davis administration given by such a prominent Republican. Ruby, in making public his subscription, provided a model for others in the party to support their local Republican newspapers, as well as endearing himself to Quick.[41]

Ruby also attended meetings in Galveston to explain his actions in the legislature. On the evening of August 26, he attended a gathering sponsored by the Loyal League. The meeting was a prelude to problems he would encounter in the future, for in it he met Louis W. Stevenson, a man who would replace Robert K. Smith as Ruby's local nemesis. Stevenson, at the time, worked as a representative for the Grand Council of the state's Loyal League under Newcomb's direction. Newcomb had sent him to Galveston to organize new league councils in the Galveston area. Stevenson, in addition, was ambitious for political office. In his politics he was uncompromisingly Radical, and he clearly believed that the Republicans in the legislature had sold their votes to the railroad interests and given away the school fund. Now he took advantage of Ruby's voting on railroad matters to criticize him. In a letter to Newcomb, Stevenson described Ruby's speech as a "lame affair" in which he dealt in generalities and, except for his account of the passage of the Militia Bill, never told his listeners how he had voted. In fact, Ruby had little to hide concerning his votes. The meeting, despite Stevenson's account, was uneventful with no one criticizing Ruby, and it closed after passing resolutions that endorsed the governor's vetoes of the railroad bills.[42]

After the August 26 meeting, in a letter to Newcomb, Stevenson made accusations concerning Ruby's honesty that mirrored the claims made in the conservative Republican and Democratic papers. Stevenson believed that Ruby had been bribed to support the International Railroad. His only evidence was that on Ruby's return from Austin, the senator had announced that he wanted to purchase real estate. He then bought a house and two lots on Mechanic Street in the residential section on Galveston's east side, paying $3,000 down and promising to pay the remaining $2,000 of the purchase in the future. That Stevenson was maneuvering for position himself and trying to undercut Ruby was clear when he informed Newcomb that he believed that the Republican Party in Galveston could never be developed until the administration saw that only "respectable men are appointed to office," an unabashed suggestion that he and not Ruby was just such a man.[43]

Stevenson did not keep his criticism of Ruby to himself. The editor of *Flake's Bulletin* picked up his accusations and used them to attack the senator. Like Stevenson, he charged that men had been bribed to pass the International bill and that Ruby had been one of the men bribed. There was no proof of this, but, like Stevenson, *Flake's* based the charges on the fact that Ruby had returned from Austin and bought a residence on Broadway. The cost of the dwelling had been, according to the editorial, $5,000. The editor could not understand how on a legislator's pay and mileage he could have saved enough money to make the purchase. "As a place to make poor men rich," he concluded, "Austin beats the world."[44]

In the end, no one ever produced any proof that Ruby took money from the railroads. Ruby denied the charges, and nothing suggested that he had become wealthy from railroad bribes. In fact, Ruby's various positions probably made him quite comfortable financially and easily capable of the purchase of his new home. Ruby made roughly $1,000 as a state senator, plus additional reimbursements for travel. In addition, he still drew $2,000 a year while acting as the special deputy collector of the Port of Galveston. That salary was only his base, however, since under the moiety system in place in the Custom Service, Ruby also drew a share of both the revenue collected and any fines and penalties imposed by the collector on shippers. With the collector in Galveston bringing in nearly $300,000 in revenue in 1870, Ruby may easily have doubled his base salary or made even more. Additionally, he had any fees that he made as a justice of the peace and a notary. His family may even have helped, although it is unknown whether or not they still had any of the money his father made during the California gold rush. If Ruby made $5,000 annually, the down payment on his home hardly seems noteworthy. The 2019 value of that amount can be variously computed, but it potentially ranged from $96,900 to $153,000 per year. Unproven charges provided Ruby's opponents with a good way of undermining his position as a leader but did not necessarily reflect the reality of Ruby's financial condition.[45]

Despite the accusations, the charges appeared to have little impact on Ruby's relationship with his constituents. He moved on. He had completed a successful stint in the first legislature following the readmission of the state to the Union. He had seen the implementation of Republican promises through the work of the legislature. He had accomplished much good for his white constituents through his support of corporate charters and for his black voters with his backing of the administration's efforts to bring about law and order and create public schools. Much remained to be done, however, for the school law proved ineffectual, and even the police and militia laws required modification. Whether or not any of this produced any support for Ruby from whites remained to be seen. He would return to the legislature in its regular session to continue his efforts, but before he did he journeyed to Washington to take care of official business and also to attend to a personal matter.

CHAPTER IX

PATRONAGE POLITICS, MARRIAGE, ARGUING AGAINST RACISM, AND THE REGULAR SESSION OF THE STATE LEGISLATURE, 1870–1871

Mr. Ruby, with his ardent love of republicanism, since the suppression of the Rebellion has been a leading spirit in the councils of the 'Lone Star' State, and stands conspicuous among the rising men of the New South for his loyalty and just perceptions of the true policy of our Republican government.

—New National Era, *October 6, 1870*

When the called session adjourned, Ruby had several months free before he had to return to Austin for the beginning of the regular session. These months were eventful ones. He initially travelled to the North with fellow Texas Republicans to lobby for the removal of several federal officials who the Davis administration believed had done little to further the party's legislative agenda. He also further established himself as a spokesman for blacks in the South with appearances at several important events where he associated and established contact with prominent black social and political leaders. In addition to participating in political efforts, Ruby got married. When he returned to Austin in January 1871, he faced many of the same challenges that he encountered in 1870. The question remained unanswered as to whether or not he could build biracial support for himself. It remained uncertain whether or not he could fulfill the promise and expectations that many of his political colleagues had for him, expectations that required a coalition to be built.

Ruby had been forced on his return from Austin to defend his votes on railroad legislation to his supporters in the league and Republican Association, but after several public meetings he left Galveston, departing for Washington on the steamer *Josephine* on August 29. The immediate purpose of the trip was political. When he arrived in Washington he met with other Texans on the same mission. These men included Congressman Clark; Collector Patten; Senator William A. Saylor, the representative from Brazos County and the special mail agent for Texas; and Representative James P. Butler from Grimes County. Also present was Tom Ochiltree. Ochiltree, the former secessionist and Confederate officer who had become a Republican and supported Grant in 1868, had by this time come to be seen as someone with influence in the Grant administration. Texas newspapers reported that the group intended to lobby for the removal of federal office holders in Texas who party officials believed had done little to support the party or the Davis government. A correspondent in Washington reported to the *Galveston News* that they wanted "more *active* Republicans" put in place. By active they meant men willing to contribute some of their government salaries to the party and certainly to support the party's basic agenda. The men they singled out all drew good government salaries and were only lukewarm in their support of the Davis administration. James A. McKee, the postmaster at Galveston, may have been on the top of the list of the appointees they wanted removed. McKee had been a former supporter of Jack Hamilton and never moved fully into the Davis wing of the party. They also sought the removal of Angier M. Hobbs, who held the job of assessor of internal revenue in the First District of Texas, the district that included Galveston and Houston. John N. Camp, the assistant assessor of internal revenue, also was on their list. Hobbs and Camp both owed no loyalty to the Texas Republican Party and held their appointments through the patronage of northern politicians. Hobbs, a forty-eight-year-old native of Virginia, arrived in Texas after the 1868 election with no family and a residence in Galveston's Exchange Hotel. Camp had held numerous appointments earlier, including serving as counsel in Jamaica during the Lincoln administration. The three men together drew salaries that equaled nine thousand dollars, a significant sum. Davis's supporters believed that well-paid government officials should use at least some of that money to help party activity. Hobbs and Camp had neither made contributions nor offered vocal support. McKee actually worked against the administration. The lobbying effort by Ruby and his associates did not produce immediate results, however, and the struggle over these lucrative and important patronage positions created internal problems throughout the Reconstruction era, with officials in Washington seldom concerned with the plight of Texas Republicans.[1]

Ruby's trip may have been for political reasons but it also had a personal aspect, ending in an event that provides one of the few insights into his personal life. While in Washington he married Lucy V. Nalle on September 19. The marriage came about as the result of either a whirlwind courtship or a meeting of the couple on one of Ruby's previous visits to Washington. The latter is possible, since Lucy Nalle came from a well-known Washington family, and George had visited among the black elites when he had been in Washington earlier. Lucy's parents were Charles and Catherine Nalle. Charles had been a slave in Virginia, and at some point he and his family had escaped and moved to Troy, New York. In Troy he had gone to work for the mayor as a coachman and had lived there quietly until his former owner tracked him down. In 1860, slave catchers captured him when he returned from work and took him before the United States commissioner to be returned to his old master under the Fugitive Slave Law. A large crowd of free blacks helped him to escape the officials, and then took him, according to different accounts, either into the countryside or into Canada. In 1870 Nalle and his family lived in the District of Columbia, where he had worked variously as a coachman and as a messenger in the Post Office Department, a patronage job that guaranteed his family a good living. Catherine, his wife, worked as a dressmaker.[2]

Lucy, Ruby's new bride, was eighteen years old at the time of their marriage. She, like Ruby, was of mixed race. The 1870 census listed both of her parents as mulattoes, and an item in the *Boston Post* described her as being a quadroon, although that term may have been used only to explain the lightness of her skin rather than any exact lineage. Other newspapers described Lucy as being a "white blonde," nearly white with freckles. An item in the *Troy Whig*, reprinted in the *New Orleans Republican*, provided a slightly different description, saying that her hair was straight and tinged with red. When Ruby met her she was working, like her mother, as a dressmaker. The reporter for the *Whig* noted that Lucy "was always distinguished as a young lady of considerable accomplishments." Senator Ruby, he noted, should congratulate himself on the fact that he had done "well in his choice of a help-meet."[3]

The new couple left Washington for Portland to meet Ruby's family, but they stopped on their way in New York City, where Ruby had been invited to attend a reception for Ebenezer D. Bassett, the United States minister to Haiti. Ruby, who never hesitated to introduce himself to prominent individuals wherever he moved, probably knew Bassett from the time that he spent in that country. The visit to New York began with an embarrassing slight that demonstrated that racial prejudice did not exist just in the South at that time. Ruby inquired of ten of the city's best hotels whether or not they would "admit a colored gentleman and lady as guests." Every one of them refused to accept the couple. This insult received attention throughout the national African American and the Southern press. The New York Hotel, where former Confederate president Jefferson Davis stayed when he was in the city, informed Ruby that the hotel was already booked. Most of the hotel owners' replies had been polite, but the proprietor of the Astor House replied to Ruby that the Astor House was unwilling to take on people of color because if they let "colored people" into the parlors and dining room it would "raise the devil with the other guests." As a result, George and Lucy were forced to rely on friends to put them up in the city.[4]

On September 22, George and Lucy attended the reception for Bassett at the Cooper Institute. An item in the *New York World* described the young couple, and its portrayal gives some insight into their financial circumstances at the time. They appeared to be comfortable financially. The *World*'s reporter devoted considerable attention to Mrs. Ruby's appearance and dress. It was the *World*'s reporter who had described Mrs. Ruby as a "white blonde." As to her dress, the reporter wrote that Lucy wore a dress "in green silk, with an opera cloak thrown over her shoulders. She held a fan of white down, with an ivory handle, and wore green kids, white necklace, pearl ear rings, gold locket and bracelets, a seal ring, a diamond ring, and a white bonnet trimmed with green satin." George had on "full evening dress and wore diamond studs." Whatever the Rubys' actual assets may have been, and they probably were considerable, the *World* pictured a well-off couple, certainly a successful one.[5]

Men and women of considerable prominence coming from a wide variety of professional and political backgrounds attended the reception. Ruby's presence at the affair showed the degree to which he had been accepted among the black elite in the city. Particularly important guests included Edward J. Royce, president of the Republic of Liberia, and James M. Priest, the ex-vice president. Rev. Henry Highland Garnett, former abolitionist and pastor at the First Colored Presbyterian Church in New York City, and James J. Spelman, a member of the Mississippi House of Representatives, were also present. That such people considered Ruby to be a significant public figure became obvious in the course of the gathering. Following introductions of the honored guests, the hosts of the reception decided that speeches should be given. Ruby had not expected to give a speech. He was, after all, on his bridal tour. The crowd, however, called on him to make an address and he gave a well-received impromptu speech. The reporter for the *New National Era*, an African American newspaper published by Frederick Douglass in Washington, DC, described Ruby as being not only a man of good upbringing and education but also "gifted with more than ordinary talents and powers of oratory." The same article pronounced Ruby as being "among the rising men of the New South for his loyalty and just perceptions of the true policy of our Republican government." Well received, Ruby's presence and his future history showed him using such opportunities to build networks of personal and political connections that extended beyond Texas.[6]

Ruby's speech that evening emphasized the "baleful influence" of what he called the caste spirit in the United States, a term used by many of his contemporaries to describe white racism. Described as a man with the "advantages of travel and a wide range of society," he used his experiences to contrast the discrimination that he had encountered in the United States with the "wider spirit of toleration and charity" of other nationalities with whom he had been acquainted in his travels. He spoke of experiences in his own life that had made him aware of such differences. Following Ruby's speech Aaron M. Powell, the white editor of the *National Standard*, addressed the crowd and pointed out the reality of Ruby's observation, pointing to the problems that he and his wife had finding a hotel. Powell decried what he called the "still prevailing notions of caste" alive in the nation. The reporter for the *New York World*, who told of Powell's comments, suggested that Powell had put the one damper on the whole affair.[7]

Ruby's connection with Ebenezer Bassett, the minister to Haiti, also became apparent in the social gathering that followed the formal remarks by the minister and others. Following the speechmaking, the crowd at the reception moved from the Cooper Institute to the Powel Hotel for a dance and late supper. The orchestra, performing numerous "popular airs" for the dignitaries, included a rendition of "Come Where My Love Lies Dreaming," a Stephen Foster song about two lovers, in honor of the senator and his wife. The dancing began with a grand march where Lucy Ruby, "Mrs. Senator Ruby," entered on the arm of Minister Bassett. Ruby followed in the company of Mrs. Bassett. The reporter for the *World* reported that after the formality of the proceedings at the institute, the young people enjoyed the "mirth and gayety of the ball," followed by a supper at 12:30, and more dancing that followed. The Rubys had played a central role in an occasion called by the reporter of the *World* a gathering of the "combined wealth, intelligence, and refinement of colored New York."[8]

After the events in New York, the Rubys travelled to Portland for a reception and so that Lucy could meet George's family. On October 7 the mayor of Portland held a reception for the young couple in the town's city hall. A social gathering was held in the mayor's office before the formal reception, with local black dignitaries attending, including Elbridge P. Talbot, black politician and employee of the post office, and George's father and stepmother. The party entered the reception room together where they met the public. Lucy wore her bridal gown, and its description further showed the considerable financial resources of the new family. Her dress had on it what the *Portland Press* described as "a plentiful supply of diamonds and pearls." Ruby, on the other hand, was dressed in a plain suit of black. Following addresses by Talbot and then Rev. Shailer, the white Congregational minister, who remarked on Ruby's times at Portland High School, George gave a short response that focused on his experiences in Texas, probably remarks similar to those he had given in New York. The *Press*'s reporter described his talk as being given in a "fluent and graceful manner." The following day the couple left Portland to "visit friends and make a tour of the country."[9]

The tour of the country did not last long, for on October 10 Ruby returned to New York City to attend a conference at the Cooper Institute sponsored by the Reform League of New York that considered the "Social Status of the Colored Race." He had been asked to appear by A. M. Powell, whom Ruby had met at the reception for Minister Bassett. Powell advertised Ruby as "a well-known and influential Senator, representing the Galveston District," and "a sterling man, an eloquent speaker." Once again, Ruby associated with some of most prominent African American leaders of the time. In addition to Powell, Senator James J. Spelman from Mississippi, who had also been at the reception for the United States minister to Haiti, was one of the speakers. Also appearing at the conference was Rev. William F. Butler, African American pastor of the important Zion Methodist Episcopal Church in New York City, an organizer for that denomination, longtime advocate of political equality, and a founder of the Negro Republican Party. Doctor E. Darwin Hudson of New York City, a specialist in surgery and artificial limbs who had been a member of the American Anti-Slavery Society, was one of the other speakers. The audience included Ebenezer Bassett, the Haitian minister, and Henry Highland Garnett, prominent African American supporter of immigration and former abolitionist.[10]

Powell presided over the meeting and began reading letters of support from prominent black activists like Frederick Douglass and former abolitionists such as Wendell Phillips. Ruby spoke first. He began by apologizing for his poor delivery, telling the audience that he had a "severe indisposition occasioned by the sudden changes in temperature of your Northern climes." He turned to the substantive part of his address when he said that he was present not because of any personal interest as a member of the "caste" towards which discrimination was exercised, but rather because of his broader belief in the "genius and spirit of our government, the absolute equality of all men before the law, and appreciating heartily the important interests at stake, —dear to us as a people and a nation." As to the American system of caste, he thought it based on "the flimsiest and most whimsical of all pretexts." It should be, in his opinion, "sneered at and ridiculed" except for the fact that so many American citizens suffered from its existence. While the pretexts upon which white prejudice existed might be baseless, such feelings nonetheless produced "the most bitter and vindictive feelings." The discrimination that resulted from those feelings had to be addressed. Some whites, he said, believed that a bill introduced by Mr. Sumner, a bill that demanded equal access of blacks to most public facilities, pampered blacks now that their political rights had been declared. The Constitution now declared the equality of the races, but he noted, "declaration is not security." In the end, he believed that the last remnant of slavery had to be abolished by destroying prejudice against color by government actions such as proposed by Sumner, laws that punished those who discriminated. He suggested that every member of the Reform League should bring public pressure to abolish caste "effectually and completely." In the end, he was optimistic and believed that schools, an informed press, and the dissemination of knowledge would bring an end to a system that was a "hideous relic of barbarism." He urged the members to "persevere in the work until the common brotherhood of humanity, stripped of all the accidents of color, nationality, or condition of life, be everywhere recognized."[11]

The meeting subsequently passed resolutions much in tune with what Ruby had long advocated and very similar to the legislation introduced by Senator Sumner into Congress. The resolutions deplored the fact that despite the guarantees of the Fifteenth Amendment, a "spirit of caste" existed that excluded blacks from hotels, saloons, staterooms of steam boats, sleeping cars on the railroads, workshops, places of amusement, equal educational opportunities, and social recognition. As a result, they asked the Republican Party, the party that had done so much to end political proscription based on color, to move forward with additional legislation to protect blacks from the injustice they suffered at the hands of licensed hotel proprietors and chartered corporations. The people attending the meeting supported in particular a proposal by Senator Charles Sumner supplementary to the civil rights bill. They further observed that the Democratic Party, with its persecution and intimidation of black voters and with its habitual maligning and caricaturing of black people in the North, preserved a "wicked consistency with its former championship of slavery," and, as a result, the Democratic Party proved that it did not deserve black support, a fact realized all too well by George Ruby. Not only politicians but also Christians were abjured to educate people as to the common brotherhood of mankind, where there would be no "invidious distinctions on account of either race, sex, or nationality."[12]

George and Lucy returned to Galveston in mid-November, along with either Alice or Agnes Nalle, one of George's sisters-in-law. The *Houston Union* thought it noteworthy to mention that the couple occupied a stateroom on their trip on the steamer *Josephine*, and that they had received a reception that was much different from what Ruby had been given in 1869. The party did have their meals served in their cabin rather than with the white passengers, but they had a first-class cabin. Ruby, according to the article, was seen "ashore with great politeness by Captain Ichabod." They arrived on November 15 and settled down in Ruby's home at 563 East Mechanic Street, an integrated neighborhood of residences and a few shops in the eastern part of the city, about fourteen blocks from his office in the custom house. The couple's nearest neighbors consisted largely of office workers, clerks, and bookkeepers. On a moonlit evening shortly after his return, the Galveston Cadet Band came to their home and provided a "moonlight serenade."[13]

Rather than congratulating him, Ruby's enemies used his marriage and particularly his choice of brides as another opportunity to attack him. The fact that he married a woman who appeared white allowed the editor of *Flake's Bulletin* to recycle an older charge that Ruby actually was not black. "It is well known that Mr. Ruby is not a negro [sic]," the editor wrote in an article on the marriage. Even blacks disowned him socially, the editor contended. The editor of the *Galveston News* attacked him for not marrying a Texas woman. "Among all the daughters of Ham residing on Galveston Island, was there no beauty fair enough to be the wife of the Hon. State Senator?" the editor asked. Attacking his political leadership role, the editor went further, "How will he account to his brethren of the Loyal League for passing their sisters in contempt and selecting for his wife and the partner of his Senatorial bosom the daughter of white folks? And as if to intensify his insult and aggravate his affront he chooses a fair blond—a beautiful blonde—perhaps, for all that we in our ignorance know, one of those fair creatures who accompany the ineffable Lydia in her travels." Pointing to the fact that his bride was dressed in green, the editor contended that it might mean Ruby would "go back on the whole race and swear himself an Irishman." In the end he contended that Ruby was ashamed of his race, a man who denied his color.[14]

Ruby had little time to enjoy his new marital status on his return to Galveston, as he returned quickly to political work. On November 17 he attended a gathering of Republicans in Galveston's Morian Hall. He apparently still felt compelled to defend his work in the legislative session the previous summer, for he talked about the general and special laws that had been passed. A reporter for the *News* indicated that he once again defended himself against accusations that he had been bought by the railroads, contending that he had "devoted himself to the interest of his constituents without any regard to persons or politics." He denied that he had been involved in any acts of corruption and pointed to what was known of his character and particularly to his refusal to go to Austin's saloons and "similar places of congregation" as a defense against the contentions of those who charged him with corruption. The reporter for the *News*, never one to praise Ruby, agreed that he was right so far as he went, leaving an insinuation that he still might have done something shady. On the other hand, he agreed that Ruby "pressed the bills of political and personal opponents as vigorously as those presented by his friends."[15]

The Morian Hall meeting may have been the first step towards what a correspondent from Galveston for the *Houston Union* suggested was Ruby's effort to "reorganize and establish on its old footing the Republican Party in this district." That goal included keeping peace among the fractious elements of the Galveston party in particular. Ruby, the correspondent wrote, "sees the importance of preserving harmony and unity in the party." He was untiring in his efforts to produce that end. The goal was to prepare the party for the campaigns that would take place in 1871, the year of the first general election since 1869. Perhaps he already knew at this time that there would be trouble. Nonetheless, he hoped to "oblige the Democratic party to suffer the odium of another inglorious defeat." Following a November 30 meeting of Galveston Republicans to consider whether or not they should hold a convention to nominate candidates for justice of the peace, probably the same correspondent for the *Houston Union* related that the party, "after a period of suspended animation, have at length given a sign of returning life and vigor." Ruby was present at the meeting and the gathering nominated Richard Nelson, another one of Ruby's protégés from the Loyal League, for the justice position in the city's First Precinct.[16]

Ruby returned to Austin in early January 1871 for the Regular Session of the Twelfth Legislature. From the beginning the opposition press, once again, paid considerable attention to Ruby's performance. In this session his opponents became even more critical, seeing less that they liked in his performance as a senator. His more strident advocacy of Governor Davis's agenda and his own advocacy of measures to secure equal rights for blacks may account for this growing hostility. His opponents usually attacked him indirectly and did not draw attention to his support of Davis or equal rights. Instead they portrayed him as a black man aspiring to a status beyond the reach of his race. They accused him of seeking social equality, not equal rights. He had barely arrived in the capital city when the Democratic Party's state newspaper, the *Austin Statesman*, celebrated what had been an embarrassing encounter for Ruby. In the first week of the session Ruby and Don Campbell, president of the senate, went to the Avenue Hotel to visit General George P. Buell, a friend of the Davis administration but also the prospective engineer of the Trans-Continental Railroad that was backed by former Governor James W. Throckmorton, his associate Benjamin Epperson, and also former governor Andrew J. Hamilton. At the time Republicans in the legislature were considering Buell as a prospective candidate for the United States Senate to replace Morgan Hamilton. The landlady at the hotel stopped Ruby at the front door and informed him that "colored men" were not admitted as guests to her hotel and asked him to leave. Ruby apparently did so without comment and made no trouble. The reporter for the *Galveston News* complained that Ruby considered himself a martyr as a result and contended that the landlady had every right to exclude anyone she wished from her hotel. Publishing the story, however, once again made it clear that Ruby's opponents considered him a threat to the racial status quo. Other Democratic newspapers picked up the story and broadcast it throughout the state.[17]

Ruby took such hostility in stride. In the five months after the session began on January 10, he played an increasingly important role in support of the administration even as he continued to work for the particular economic interests of his district. He received even more important committee assignments in this session than he had in the called session. In the course

Interior of Texas Senate Chamber at time of Ruby's tenure (*Frank Leslie's Illustrated Newspaper*, May 22, 1880).

of the session he served on the standing committees on Federal Relations, the Militia, Education, the Judiciary, Private Land Claims, Committee on Election and Privileges, and Engrossed Bills. He chaired the committees on Private Land Claims and Engrossed Bills and may also have been chair of the Committee on Election and Privileges at some point. He served on numerous important select committees as well, including one to make recommendations regarding Governor Davis's veto of the previous appropriations bill, another to develop amendments to a law passed in the previous session providing pensions to veterans of the Texas War of Independence, and still another to develop acts necessary to put into effect the provisions of the new constitution regarding taxes. He also continued to demonstrate his role as a parliamentarian, again taking the chair on several significant occasions.[18]

As in the previous session, he introduced and supported special legislation that created institutions of importance for his district and his constituents. For the most part he succeeded in getting resolutions on the books and bills passed. He secured passage of a bill creating the Galveston Seaman's Home and also the Galveston Agricultural, Horticultural, and Industrial

Association. The latter was an organization created to promote and encourage the development of agriculture and floriculture in Texas. In addition, unique to Texas at this time, the association required its members to "discourage cruel treatment of every kind to domestic and other animals, to prevent the same in every instance possible." This admonition included reporting offenders to local police agencies. For Galveston's Magnolia Grove Cemetery Association, he managed to get a bill passed preventing the sale of intoxicating liquors or the establishment of saloons, gambling houses, or houses of ill-fame within a half mile of its boundaries. He also introduced successful bills confirming previously unconfirmed land grants or bounty warrants from the Texas Revolution for numerous Galvestonians and their heirs.[19]

He continued his work for Galveston's business interests, work essential for a state senator, still trying to gain political backing for himself from the white business community. In the course of the session he introduced bills incorporating enterprises such as the Galveston and Brazos Navigation Company, the Grand Trunk Railroad Company, the Island City Gas Company, the Port of Galveston Wharf Company, the Texas Cotton Spinning and Manufacturing Company, and the Texas Dry Dock Company. Not all of these received their charters, but two particularly important companies did. These showed Ruby's continued willingness to represent some of Galveston's most important businessmen, including some of his bitterest political opponents. The Texas Dry Dock Company, created to assume the charter of a previous dry dock company, included backers such as George Sealy, cashier for Ball, Hutchings and Company, one of the city's most important commission and banking firms, and Charles Fowler, a prominent ship captain and sponsor of projects improving Galveston Harbor. The Texas Cotton Spinning and Manufacturing Company's backers included James A. McKee, the city's mayor and postmaster whom Ruby had attempted to have removed the previous autumn; John Sealy, brother of George Sealy; Abraham P. Lufkin, a prominent cotton merchant; and Francis R. Lubbock, the former Confederate governor. He also introduced a bill to incorporate the Galveston Trunk Railroad. In this case in particular he acted in the interests of men who openly opposed him politically. The principal supporter of the proposed company was John S. Thrasher, businessman, local politician, and Democrat. The Galveston Trunk Railroad represented an effort by Galveston business interests to ensure they had a direct connection with the mainland by building a double track line from Galveston to Houston or anywhere else where the city could connect to the state's other railroad systems. Thrasher and his backers had already looked into encouraging other lines to build their own roads into Galveston, and they intended the Grand Trunk as a fallback if none of those roads decided to build into the city. Ultimately, concerns that the proposed company might be controlled by Houston railroad interests and would be a stranglehold on Galveston led the city's commercial interests to oppose the bill. Ruby, at that point, backed away from it and the bill wound up buried in committee.[20]

Even more than in the previous session, Ruby became a leader on the floor in advancing the legislation introduced by Governor Davis. On January 18, Ruby moved that the senate receive the message usually sent by the governor at the beginning of each session outlining possible concerns and needed legislation. Davis devoted much of his message to financial issues, encouraging the legislature to implement tax programs that were fair and yet raised the money necessary to fund the operations of expanded government programs, including the state's asylums and penitentiary. He also asked for the legislature to pass a bill that organized the school system demanded by the constitution and initiated in the previous session. He requested legislation to fund and arm the state militia and state guard authorized in the previous session. As for railroads, the governor remained adamant that the legislature should provide no further support to these companies. Against his advice and overriding his veto, the legislature had provided bonds to fund the International Railroad in the previous session. Davis believed that the legislature's action had committed the state to enough debt and to do more would be irresponsible. In the course of the session, Ruby would stand by the governor on most of his program, working on the floor to assure passage of its components. Once again, however, he would break with the governor's recommendations on railroads, voting in the last week of the session to support another major railroad company opposed by the governor.[21]

Implementing Governor Davis's legislative agenda proved difficult, when, almost from the beginning, in the senate Republicans were divided. The divisions that emerged over railroad policy in the previous session persisted, with Republicans who had been advocates of railroad legislation voting together with Democrats to organize the senate and place their own men in the various offices rather than Davis's allies. In the struggle Ruby worked to keep Davis's supporters in control. Webster Flanagan, son of United States Senator James W. Flanagan and an ardent supporter of railroads in the Called Session, led the breakaway coalition. That the administration might not have control of the senate looked probable in the selection of the body's nonlegislative officers. The first test came when the senators considered the choice of the assistant sergeant-at-arms. Ruby, acting for the governor, nominated Thomas Powell to oppose a man supported by Flanagan. Flanagan's candidate won by a vote of sixteen to twelve. Other contests went the same way. Flanagan's control, however, hinged on the outcome of a contested seat, that of Senator Edward L. Alford, a Democrat from Fayette County. Alford had been removed from the senate in the previous session and a special election had been held to replace him. A Republican, Richard Hildebrand, won that election. Alford, however, remained on the rolls and claimed that he still held the seat at the beginning of the session, contending that he never vacated it. Following the selection of the senate's officers, the first business of the session, the senate took up the question of Alford. Ruby immediately moved to seat Hildebrand and have Alford removed from the rolls. The president of the senate rejected Ruby's motion after the senate tied, fourteen to fourteen, on the resolution. The vote indicated that the administration still did not have firm control of the senate and that the accomplishments of the previous session—the schools, militia, and state police—might be reversed. Faced with this threat, Ruby joined with other supporters of the governor to lobby Republicans who appeared to have abandoned Davis to come back to his support. Their efforts finally convinced or manipulated enough wavering Republicans to reverse course that on January 17 they believed they had enough votes to remove. They quickly voted to remove Alford and seat Hildebrand. The administration now had a majority, although a narrow one, and on January 18 they discharged all of the previously elected officers of the senate. Ruby nominated Charles M. Campbell for secretary of the senate and the senate elected him by a vote of twenty to five, with many of Flanagan's supporters realizing that with the Davis party in control there was no point in resisting the governor's will. Ruby renominated Powell for assistant sergeant-at-arms. This time Powell won by a vote of seventeen to one, with all Republicans now back together and the Democrats refusing to vote. Ruby and other administration backers had not only regained control of the senate, they had also broken up the Flanagan-Democratic coalition.[22]

Ruby and the Republican majority then attempted to remove Morgan Hamilton from the United States Senate. Hamilton had been a thorn in the side of Governor Davis from the moment he arrived in Washington, working to prevent the sale of the bonds appropriated by the previous legislature to fund the frontier protection forces. Republicans in the legislature, backed by Davis, contended that Hamilton had been elected prior to the state's readmission to the Union and that another election was necessary. On January 21, Ruby, again representing the administration's interests, introduced a motion on the senate floor to consider a house resolution providing for the election of a United States senator. The measure passed through its three readings on the floor, and, on January 24, a majority in the senate voted in favor of naming General Joseph Reynolds to a six-year term beginning on March 4, 1871. The following day in a joint session the legislature voted for Reynolds, with only Democrats voting against him. In this case the Davis administration failed to secure its ultimate goal. In March, the United States Senate refused to seat Reynolds. The majority in that body held that Hamilton had been legally elected and recognized him as the state's senator, thus thwarting the governor's and legislature's efforts to get rid of him.[23]

Ruby's support of the governor led in most occasions, however, to favorable results. In February the Militia Committee received Governor Davis's report on his declarations of martial law in Hill and Walker Counties, and that report went to a special committee that included Ruby. Hill County had been a center of violence throughout Reconstruction. In 1869 the election judges had left the county to count the ballots, fearing for their lives. In addition to political violence, gangs of outlaws operated in the county committing numerous outrages, attacking black farmers, taking away their guns, and in some cases murdering them. As a result of the problems, Governor Davis had threatened to declare martial law as early as October 1870. When state police arrested the son of a prominent resident of the county, James J. Gathings, for the murder of a black couple that December, local whites responded by arresting the members of the state police for an illegal search of the Gathingses' house. Fearing for their lives, the state policemen escaped. In January 1871, Adjutant General James Davidson led a contingent of police back into the county. Determining that civil authorities could not maintain law and order, Davidson issued the governor's declaration of martial law, arrested Gathings and his associates, and fined them the cost of the intervention. After two days Davidson lifted martial law. In Walker County, a shooting fray in a district courtroom, the freeing of men arrested for the murder of a black man, and the refusal of local citizens to assist in the pursuit of the men responsible led to a martial law declaration in that county in February.[24]

The governor's actions in both cases produced condemnation by senate Democrats. Ruby became the chief defender of the governor's and Adjutant General Davidson's actions. The main issue involved how Adjutant General Davidson dealt with collecting the fines usually levied in such cases, allowing the men he arrested in Hill County to pay the charges rather than levying a tax on the entire community. Further, contemporary Democratic newspapers charged that the declarations of martial law were an abuse of power and a violation of the rights of the people in situations where local authorities remained capable of defending the law. Suggesting similarities to events that precipitated the American Revolution, the *Waco Examiner* intimated that Davidson had threatened to quarter his troops among the people, refused the men arrested the right to consult with lawyers, and informed these men that they would be tried by a military commission and sent to the penitentiary before any appeal could be made to a civil tribunal. In the case of Walker County, local citizens protested that civil authorities could have dealt with the outbreak of lawlessness there and no need for martial law existed. Such charges led to the senate's consideration of the legality and character of the governor's action. Ruby's Militia Committee considered the case and heard complaints and received the governor's account of the incidents. On February 18 Ruby and two other members of the committee submitted their report. In it they concluded that conditions in the counties justified the governor's actions, that he had acted legally, and that "no excess has been committed." Even though one of the committee members submitted a minority report that criticized Davidson's fining of the Gathings party, the senate voted to accept Ruby's report. Ruby and his fellow committee members ensured that the legislature took no action against the governor.[25]

As a legislative leader for the Davis administration, Ruby also played a major role in the expulsion of James E. Dillard, the senator from the Third District, Cherokee and Houston Counties. Early in the session a resolution was introduced on the floor of the senate that recommended an investigation into whether or not Dillard had the right to hold his seat. He unquestionably had received the majority of votes in the election, but the secretary of state had received numerous complaints that Dillard's supporters in Cherokee County had threatened and intimidated Republican voters, thus making the results null. Dillard's opponent, George W. Lane, had carried Houston County, but he had been badly beaten in Cherokee County by a vote of 889 to 384. If the senate threw out the Cherokee vote, Lane, a Republican, would be seated, giving the Davis administration a greater majority. Proving that intimidation took place and changed the character of the vote would be difficult, however, for the numbers polled in the special election in the Third District paralleled closely the racial composition of the county, where whites outnumbered blacks by two to one, and the 1869 registration had shown roughly the same proportion. On January 27, Ruby introduced a resolution that the case be considered by the Committee on Election and Privileges, a committee where Ruby sat. Ruby faced some opposition to this move within his own party, but he successfully brought together enough Republican senators to send the request to the committee and begin an investigation of the election.[26]

Ruby officiated as the presiding officer in the hearings on Dillard's seat, and after the committee had finished with testimony, he crafted the majority report. The committee issued the report on March 30, 1871, and concluded that the testimony collected in the county provided specific and convincing evidence that black voters had been kept from voting. Incidents of intimidation included a confrontation at the polls between whites and a group of blacks, probably members of a local Loyal League council, who had marched to the polls behind a national flag and with a drum beating. The whites had moved to seize the flag and the drum and after a short confrontation the blacks retreated. The report determined that only the refusal of the blacks to resist kept the encounter from turning violent. The blacks, however, left without voting. A minority report contended that because the voter turnout paralleled that in 1869, no intimidation had taken place. The senate delayed action on the report, however, when the printed testimony turned out not to include affidavits secured by Dillard in support of his case, and the committee had to carry out an investigation into where the documents had gone. The disappearance of the documents led Dillard's supporters to argue that the senator should have the opportunity to secure new affidavits, thus effectively delaying any decision until after the session would conclude. Ruby, however, would not be thwarted in his efforts to remove Dillard.[27]

The disappearance of the affidavits threw the investigation back into the committee, where Ruby helped carry out an investigation of their disappearance. The problem of the affidavits effectively delayed consideration of the committee's reports for over a week. The newly created *State Gazette*, the publication of the state's Democratic Party, charged that Ruby sat as the presiding officer of the committee specifically with the intention of embarrassing Dillard. Not only, they asserted, did the Republicans intend to rob Dillard of his seat, but the Republican caucus meant to make his removal "as humiliating as possible," by calling "a negro Senator" to officiate. The Republican Party's newspaper, the *State Journal*, replied that Dillard could hardly have been humiliated since Ruby was "superior to Dillard in personal appearance, intellect and manners." Dillard, in the view of that paper, was not Ruby's equal.[28]

On April 10 Ruby presented the majority report from the committee, recommending the senate proceed with the vote on the original recommendation to expel Dillard. Ruby noted that the missing testimony was from the same men and of the same character as that provided in a similar case involving the representatives elected from Cherokee County in the house of representatives. The senate voted to accept the report, with even the Flanagan Republicans siding with the majority. On the next day the senate voted on the question of expelling Dillard, and again the Republican majority held together to vote in favor of removing him. The concluding vote produced a bitter confrontation between Dillard and the two black members of the senate. Edward H. Quick, a reporter for the *Houston Union* who was in Austin covering the legislature, reported Dillard was "wild with excitement" and called Ruby a "carpet-bag Jew" and Senator Matt Gaines a "flat-footed nigger," threatening to break his cane on the head of the latter. Gaines had replied that the time had passed for "colored men getting their heads broke by Democratic desperadoes." Ruby responded with what the correspondent of the *Houston Union* called a "withering and dignified rebuke." Unfortunately no record of his remarks remains.[29]

Ruby's support of administration wishes on an immigration bill also reflected his continuing connection with the governor. It may also have been a part of his efforts at broadening his constituency, although it led temporarily to a break with Senator Gaines. William H. Parsons of Montgomery County, head of the Republican legislative caucus and a man close to the governor, introduced the bill which created a Bureau of Immigration. The specific provision of the draft bill that caused a problem was that it empowered the superintendent of the bureau to appoint agents to encourage immigration from the northern and southern states, Great Britain, and the countries of the European continent. The bill ran into trouble when Matt Gaines introduced an amendment to send an agent to Africa to encourage immigration from there as well as Europe. The amendment produced considerable argument. Parsons opposed it. Ruby also spoke against it.[30]

Ruby felt that he needed to explain his opposition, particularly after the debates on the Gaines amendment where white Democrats declared that they wanted no more blacks brought into the states and attacked the black race as inferior to the white. One senator, Ebenezer L. Dohoney from Lamar County, spoke in opposition of ever sending an agent to Africa, explaining that he believed such an immigration would bring men into Texas whom he considered a lower type of man. On April 14 Ruby took the floor in the senate to reply to such statements and particularly to respond to any characterization of Africans as "degraded or unfortunate." Ruby said that he objected to the amendment, but he opposed the project because it would be expensive and had no provisions for defraying the expenses of immigration. Few in Africa would be able to come to Texas on their own. Africa, however, needed no apologies from him. "Egypt and Arabia," he said, "peopled by some of the races of Africa had given birth to the sciences and arts of civilization." The English had recognized the contributions of Africa when they had received the Queen of Madagascar, "the question of color not being raised." Senator Dohoney had suggested that the African was inferior to the white man. Senator Ruby asked Dohoney to tell him the color of Adam. Dohoney admitted that he could not.[31]

After rancorous debate, on April 18 the senate voted down the Gaines amendment, and Parsons's original bill went on to passage two days later. It did not, however, bring an end to the dispute nor the bad feelings that had developed between Gaines and Ruby. Ruby's stand against Gaines on the immigration bill turned Gaines, at least temporarily, into a political enemy.

On April 20 Gaines published in the *Galveston Republican* a letter that attacked Ruby and Parsons for their opposition to his amendment. Gaines contended that the same privilege should be extended to Africans to settle in Texas as was given inhabitants of Germany, France, and Great Britain. Gaines complained that white legislators were willing to take the money that came from the hard labor of blacks to attract white immigrants but refused to look out for blacks. This, he contended, would fill the country with white labor and result in poor black people losing their jobs. "Senators in the Senate . . . said that the amendment was for buncomb [sic]," he wrote. "I deny the charge made on me," he continued, "and hurl the same back in the teeth of Senator G. T. Ruby and W. H. Parsons and all others that have said this of me. Buncomb [sic] is not any man, if Parsons and Ruby and all others are legislating for buncomb [sic], I am not. I am seeking the right of all the poor colored people of this State." He went on to charge that Ruby and the other Republicans who opposed his amendment had their hands in the pockets of "hard-laboring classes of the poor whites and blacks."[32]

In an ironic twist, given the fight over African immigration, Ruby joined with Gaines on the day after the passage of the immigration bill to support a resolution urging the annexation of Santo Domingo. Both Ruby and Gaines served on the select committee to consider the resolution introduced by Elisha Petit, one of the senate's more radical Republican members. The Santo Domingo issue had come up in large part because the United States had sent commissioners to Santo Domingo the previous February to negotiate annexation. The committee introduced a report that provided strong support for Petit's resolution. The committee's report saw annexation as an opportunity for the United States to extend its territorial reach into the tropics and to expand its institutions southward. They saw Santo Domingo's acquisition as the first step toward turning the Gulf of Mexico into a great inland sea belonging to the United States. Ruby joined with Gaines and other Republicans to move the resolution on to passage. The primary source of opposition came from white Democrats.[33]

In addition to his support of the various measures put forward by the Davis administration or connected to Republican interests, Ruby also worked to advance measures he personally desired. In particular he wanted the passage of laws that ensured that blacks would receive equal treatment in public spaces. His experiences in New York and his later problems in Austin's Avenue Hotel had shown him the baleful influence of racial prejudice across the nation and how it served as a barrier to full freedom for his race. His introduction of Senate Bill No. 221, "An Act to Enforce Compliance by Public Carriers with the Provisions of Section Twenty-one, Article One, of the Constitution," represented a positive effort to bring an end to the sort of discrimination he had confronted. Section 21, part of the Constitution's Bill of Rights, provided that no citizen should be deprived of any "right, privilege, or immunity" on account of race, color or previous condition. Equal access to public facilities had been central to Ruby's activity up to this time, and his bill would have put teeth in the Constitution's guarantee of equal rights by punishing those who failed to live up to the provision. He presented the bill on the floor on March 7. In pushing the bill forward, however, he faced strong opposition from the Democrats in the senate and lukewarm support from some white Republicans.[34]

On April 24 the senate took up Ruby's bill. Democrats immediately attempted to send it back to committee. Ruby spoke against recommitting the bill, stating that he wanted to "settle the fate of the bill, on the grounds of justice." Failing to send the bill back to committee, the Democrats then began to add pointless amendments. Ruby accepted one amendment that allowed conductors and ship captains to set aside separate accommodations for women and persons accompanying them. After the addition of the amendment, the Republicans in the senate pushed the bill through on a party line vote. Democrats unanimously voted against it, using the occasion to insist that Ruby really intended the bill to break down social barriers between whites and blacks. The reporter for the Democratic *State Gazette* characterized the bill as just another effort by Ruby and his white associates to bring about "negro equality." After the senate's approval, however, for unknown reasons, the bill failed to become law. On April 26 the senate sent the bill to the House of Representatives, only to have it sent back to the senate for reconsideration. On May 8 the senate considered the bill again and once more passed it on a party-line vote. Sent back to the house on May 9, the house failed to act on it before the session ended and the bill died. Ruby failed to secure a measure that was of the utmost significance for him, facing once again the racism not only of his openly hostile Democratic opponents but the lukewarm support for black equality that existed even among his white Republican colleagues.[35]

In addition to Ruby's advocacy of a state civil rights act, he also supported two measures that originated in the house that sought to remove the limitations white society had attempted to put on the freedom of their former slaves immediately after the war. These bills repealed two of the more onerous of the bills that had been passed by the Eleventh Legislature and that had been intended to restrict the freedom of the newly emancipated blacks. The apprenticeship law had created the possibility that young blacks could still be held in some sort of bondage until they reached the age of twenty-one. The labor law of the Eleventh Legislature had essentially forced blacks back to work on the farms and plantations where they had been prior to emancipation. The two laws had been part of the reason Republicans had embraced the idea that all laws passed since 1861 had been nullified from the beginning, or ab initio, hoping to eliminate such controls. Although these laws had not been enforced as a result of decisions of the military in 1867, the laws remained on the books in 1871. On May 5 the senate took up House Bills 299 and 300, the proposed legislation that repealed the apprenticeship and labor laws. Ruby supported repeal and voted for it when the two bills came up for a vote. Although he had not originated them, their passage represented another major step towards the true freedom for his race that Ruby had long fought for.[36]

As in the previous session, Ruby was a faithful supporter of Governor Davis's program but once again broke away on a railroad bill. This time the issue was a bill to provide state support to the Southern Pacific and the Southern Transcontinental railroad companies. These two companies proposed to build parallel rail lines from the eastern border of Texas to the western, with the intention of coming together somewhere in Shackleford County. The men who proposed this bill hoped that both of these lines ultimately would be taken over by the Texas Pacific line that had been chartered by Congress, and that the Texas Pacific would push the line on to the Pacific Ocean. The reasons for his support are unclear, since except for the International charter he had opposed new railroad charters and helped maintain the governor's vetoes of those that had gotten through the legislature. The fact that Webster Flanagan, who had not been a strong supporter of other bills of interest to Ruby, sponsored the legislation added to the uncertainty about Ruby's reasoning. What made this bill unique was a section that allowed the state to call in the three million dollars in bonds offered to each of the roads in the previous session and exchange them for land grants if the constitutional restriction on granting lands to corporations could be effected, thus potentially avoiding the bonded indebtedness of the state. Perhaps like other Republicans, Ruby came to see the construction of the lines as not only necessary but inevitable. He may also simply have submitted to the wishes of the businessmen of Galveston.[37]

The bill, entitled "An act to encourage the speedy construction of a railway through the State of Texas to the Pacific Ocean," came on to the floor of the senate on April 24 and received extensive discussion. Much of that debate focused on the proposed route, with legislators intent on ensuring that the line went through their local communities. The bill received strong support from both Democrats and Republicans, including the two black senators, Ruby and Gaines. It went on to the governor to be signed on May 18. On May 24 it came back with the governor's veto. As with Davis's veto of the International Railroad in the previous session, the governor pointed to what he considered to be the uncertainty that the men involved ever would actually build the railroad and expressed particular concern over the debt that the railroad created. The six million dollars, he pointed out, ultimately dwarfed the budget of the entire state government, including the newly implemented school system. When the senate received the veto, however, it moved quickly to override it, passing it over the veto on the same day it was received. Ruby never explained why he had abandoned Davis on the measure.[38]

Despite his action on the Southern Transcontinental legislation, Ruby was perhaps the governor's most loyal supporter in the session. He also played an increasingly active role as a party leader in the senate, helping to guide some of the party's most important legislation into law. He had been with the governor in the creation of a public school system and securing its funding. He had continued to back Davis's efforts at establishing law and order through the use of the police and the militia. He supported the governor's efforts to pacify the frontier. He had played a major role in finally accomplishing most of the goals his party had pursued since its creation. His opponents frequently disparaged him, and his very success provoked increasingly hostile attacks, attacks that usually appealed to the racism of whites. The *Houston Times*, at the end of the session, suggested that Ruby, along with Congressman William T. Clark, might better be employed as "barbers and dining-room servants." Republicans, however, believed that he had shown himself to be a superb leader of their party. The editor of the Republican *Houston Union* summed up what he believed many of the men with whom Ruby worked thought of the senator from Galveston. "[T]here is not even a Democratic State Senator," he wrote, "who does not recognize in Senator Ruby a gentleman of unexceptional courtesy and dignity." The attacks on him, he believed, showed how little devotion to the nation and its government existed among the state's Democrats. Calling the Democratic Party a "sham Democracy," he insisted that their disparagement of Ruby showed that the party possessed "not the least infusion of the old high-bred gentility and courtesy of the South." Indeed, the party of the men who attacked Ruby was "bogus in its coin, cockle and tares in its wheat, shoddy in its material, and apostacy [sic] and hypocrisy in its faith." Ruby was the political gentleman. The legislative session, however, showed that even a gentleman would have to fight against opponents, and that such men existed not only in the opposition party but within his own party. An upcoming congressional election in 1871 challenged Ruby's ability to hold his party together in the face of increasing internal factionalism.[39]

CHAPTER X

THE CONGRESSIONAL ELECTION OF 1871

Though by all odds the best of all candidates or aspirants in this district, Clark is certainly a poor politician.—George Ruby to James Newcomb, June 29, 1871

Ruby and the Texas Republican Party faced a critical test in 1871. Texas would hold its first congressional election since 1869 in the autumn of that year. This time, it faced a serious challenge from a reorganized Democratic Party. Ruby chaired the executive committee for the Third Congressional District with the responsibility of organizing the district convention and ensuring that a viable candidate received the party's nomination. The role was of particular importance because the Third was the most likely of the four Texas districts that the party could retain. It ran roughly from the Gulf Coast towards the northwest between the Colorado and San Jacinto Rivers until it reached Bosque, Hill, and Navarro Counties and embraced not only black majority counties but many almost totally white ones. If mobilized, however, black Republicans still should be able to keep the district Republican if enough whites could be added to their vote. The 1871 election would test whether or not Republicans had managed to attract any white votes, a step critical to future success, but from the beginning Republicans became involved in a bitter internal struggle that tested Ruby's ability to control his own party rather than allowing him to work at expanding the party's base.

Ruby was in Austin attending the legislature when the state party organization announced its plans for the upcoming election. James Tracy, the chairman of the state Republican Party, took the first step in planning for the election when in early March 1871, he called on Republicans to prepare for the contest. Tracy, as chairman, hoped to create a more formal process of choosing candidates, and as a result he created a more systematic procedure for doing so. He advised that local Republicans first create party committees at the county level, then committees in each state senate district. The county committee would then call a convention, set up by the senate district committee in its district, to elect delegates. The senate district convention would then choose delegates to the congressional district convention. This process reflected Tracy's desire to make the nominating process more transparent. It also represented Tracy's intention of reducing the power of the Loyal League in the nominating process, ending the League's ability to select candidates in secret. According to Tracy, following the process would resolve internal differences in a regular manner and in a way that "no conflict of authority can arise." The conventions, he concluded, would be "fair for all concerned" and would not be as liable to be "used in the interest of individuals or cliques." Ruby responded to Tracy's call later in March by announcing that the party would hold a congressional district convention in Houston on June 8 to nominate the Republican congressional candidate. Ruby's announcement set the number of delegates to be elected from each of the senate districts and recommended that Republicans immediately create party organizations in each of the counties. Ruby, however, did not specify that they be organized under Tracy's plan, even though he probably intended that the local organizations adopt the process outlined by the state committee. This oversight proved disastrous in terms of party unity.[1]

Ruby ordinarily should have had little trouble in preparing his district for the upcoming election. The party actually held the seat from the district; the incumbent, William T. Clark, wanted to run again, and he should have been able to promise enough patronage to ensure his nomination. Some members of the party, however, did not like Clark. He had been the nominee in 1869, with Republicans thinking that his background might help build that coalition of blacks and business interests that Ruby also worked toward. A native of Connecticut, Clark had practiced law in Iowa prior to the Civil War. Joining the Union army as a lieutenant in an Iowa infantry regiment, he had risen to the rank of brigadier general by the war's end. He was sent to Texas at the war's end with the army, but following his discharge he remained in Galveston where he founded the First National Bank and served as its first cashier. He had the background and connections that could potentially attract white businessmen in Galveston seeking the support of the federal government for everything from the improvement of Galveston Harbor to the construction of railroads from the city to the hinterlands. His work had not gained much support for the party though, and many Republicans believed he had forgotten about them altogether. James Tracy and Secretary Newcomb, however, believed Clark should go back to Congress. Ruby had the very difficult job of carrying out the wishes of these party leaders in the face of a groundswell of opposition in the district.[2]

Clark, in addition, was not a very good politician. While he worked for white business interests, with uncertain gains politically, he failed particularly to take care of his existing political base among black voters and court favor with key black leaders. Even Ruby felt snubbed by the congressman. The resistance to Clark's nomination from blacks emerged shortly after Ruby announced the convention. Particularly troubling was the opposition of Senator Matt Gaines. In a letter sent on March 30 to Republicans belonging to the Loyal League and published in the *Brenham Inquirer*, Gaines wrote that Republicans in the district had "done enough for William T. Clark," implying that Clark, in turn, had not done enough for the people of his district. Gaines went on to say that "we have good men at home who know better what we need in Texas." Gaines may even have thought that he was among the "good men at home" who should be considered, although he did not make his own ambitions clear. Gaines's letter indicated dissatisfaction not only with Clark but with the leadership of his party, including party chairman James Tracy, who he believed intended using Ruby's convention to get Clark renominated. Gaines urged Republicans to defeat the "Tracy movement" and charged that Tracy thought he could run the Republican Party by himself. Gaines said that he refused to submit to Tracy's manipulations. In the same letter he also indicated he would oppose the renomination of Charles Stockbridge, one of the representatives from Washington County, who he believed was like Tracy in believing that he could run the party without the support of others. Gaines's desertion of Clark was potentially catastrophic for the party and also to Ruby's control of black voters in the district. Gaines, along with Ruby, was one of the black leaders who had the most influence within the black community. If he drew black support away from Clark, he could potentially block the congressman from obtaining the party nomination. A letter from the Galveston correspondent for the *Houston Union* that appeared in the journal's April 7 edition suggested that dissatisfaction with Clark among blacks was widespread. He wrote that the "colored people do not favor the reelection of Clark, nor in fact the election of any white man now upon the carpet." Ruby even suggested that he might not give wholehearted support for Clark. Writing to James Newcomb, Ruby complained that Clark had not bothered to consult him about local affairs, that the "little general" had given him "but slight attention."[3]

Ruby's problem in assuring the renomination of Clark was exacerbated when a number of other politicians emerged to challenge the congressman, possibly hoping to take advantage of black disillusionment with him. Among the first to make his intention to run for Congress known was Louis W. Stevenson, the white former Loyal League organizer who had been so critical of George Ruby when Ruby returned from the Regular Session of the Legislature. At roughly the same time that Stevenson made it known that he would run, B. Rush Plumly, representative for Galveston in the Twelfth Legislature, indicated that he intended putting his name forward in the Houston convention. Newspaper items later reported that in addition to Clark, Stevenson, and Plumly, Richard Allen had announced his own plan to seek the nomination. Allen, a long-time associate of Ruby in the Loyal League and the black representative from Harris and Montgomery Counties in the Twelfth Legislature, could have attracted considerable support from within the black community. Others spoken of as potential candidates included Richard Nelson, another black associate of Ruby and a justice of the peace in Galveston. Some news reports even suggested Matt Gaines as a candidate. Ruby's name also came up, even though he repeatedly avowed that he was content with serving in the state senate and did not want his name put forward. Which of these candidates they should support generated considerable discussion among black voters. A reporter who had stopped at Barney's and Jake Hamilton's saloons, two establishments associated with Republican operatives in Galveston, wrote that the questions of who would run and who would receive the nomination were on everyone's lips. He found local blacks even supporting the almost unknown Wright Cuney, perhaps Ruby's closest associate in the Republican Association and Loyal League. Cuney, the reporter wrote, had "more talent than any colored man in the district except Senator Ruby." When the editor of the *Houston Union* talked with three visitors to his office he found no agreement among them. The uncertainty concerning the nomination was reflected particularly by the fact that one of the *Union*'s undecided visitors was Horatio Ruby, George's brother, who had just moved to Galveston.[4]

Ruby's ability to control the convention for Clark became more difficult when Louis Stevenson began an open campaign to get the nomination. His move began after he received an endorsement from the *Calvert Tribune* in Robertson County in mid-March. He followed this by getting up mass meetings to elect delegates to the congressional district convention who favored him. The legitimacy of these meetings, however, was unclear. None of them had followed the rules set up by Tracy and been called by a county Republican executive committee. The first of these met on April 7 in Millican, Brazos County, and the procedure clearly was irregular. Local party officials did not call it, and the attendees chose delegates to go to the congressional district convention rather than to a senate district convention as required by Tracy and the party's state executive committee. The Millican delegates received no instructions about whom they should vote for, but observers believed all were Stevenson men. At a similar meeting held on April 15 in Huntsville, Walker County, Louis W. Stevenson was present with a number of supporters and managed to have delegates who supported his candidacy chosen. On April 17 Stevenson received the endorsement of another mass meeting in Grimes County. The resolutions passed at that meeting were pro-Stevenson and showed that Stevenson was taking advantage of Clark's unpopularity among black voters to gain support for himself. The resolutions stated, "In order to secure the advancement of the cause and the welfare of the people we must select a man who walks in the full light of the fifteenth amendment, without shrinking, and one who is emphatically a man of the people," with the assumption that Stevenson was such a man. Seven days after the meeting in Grimes County, Stevenson attended another mass meeting in Hempstead, Austin County, where he also sought delegates. By this time, however, opponents to Stevenson had begun to organize. When Stevenson attempted to get the Hempstead meeting to instruct their delegates for him, his opponents managed to block him. Instead the meeting voted to send an uninstructed delegation, although many of the men chosen backed Stevenson. Despite the setback in Hempstead, Stevenson had emerged as the front-runner among the challengers to Clark by mid-April.[5]

Ruby was in Austin attending the legislative session when the Stevenson movement got underway. Initially he said nothing about Stevenson, who actually may still have been a friend despite his previous criticism of the senator. He could not stand by, however, when it became clear that in order to secure the nomination Stevenson was promising that if elected he would remove several important supporters of the Davis administration from patronage positions and replace them with men who supported him. A newspaper article published in late April reported that "one of the prominent white candidates," undoubtedly Stevenson, was confident of his election and that he had already prepared a slate of men to fill key patronage jobs. The same listed the men he hoped to have removed, pointing to Nathan Patten as head of the Galveston custom house; Postmaster James A. McKee, who at the time was also mayor of Galveston; and US Marshal William E. Parker. In mid-April Ruby acted.[6]

On April 11 Ruby met with James Tracy and other legislators from the

Third District to discuss how to proceed. Initial reports indicated that they had decided to postpone the convention until July, thus allowing Clark time to counter Stevenson. A later report said that it would not be held until September. Initially, the administration press attempted to avoid attacking Stevenson outright. An item in the *Houston Union* that congratulated an informal meeting in Galveston that had not chosen delegates to the convention provided an insight into the administration's initial justification. The article insisted that uninstructed delegates were desirable because when in convention they should be "free to consult with their fellow delegates from the other parts of the districts, and to harmonize upon the best candidates." This was a clear attack on the decision of previous meetings to endorse Stevenson. The article went on, insisting, "We must have no stocked Conventions in behalf of any man, and it had better not be attempted." This could only have been directed against Stevenson since he was the only man at this point who had pledged delegates. Any candidate, to be successful in the general election, had to "command the strength of the whole Republican party in his district," the author argued. The article inferred that this was not Stevenson but Clark, a man who possessed "talents, culture and fidelity," but it offered no direct criticism of Stevenson.[7]

Ruby and party secretary Tracy began a more aggressive move against Stevenson after another meeting held in Austin on April 21. At this gathering Ruby, as head of the executive committee for the congressional district, caucused with Congressman Clark, Collector of the Customs Patten, Edward Quick of the *Union*, and Tracy. Clark's presence suggested that the Davis administration and its supporters finally had agreed to back Clark wholeheartedly, even though Ruby and the others still insisted in public that they were open to supporting whomever the convention nominated. Three days after the meeting, Tracy sent a letter to the *Union* describing the decisions made in the meeting, decisions that represented a decisive strike against the Stevenson campaign. Tracy said that the convention definitely would be delayed. More importantly, however, he charged that in some cases the so-called conventions that had been held up to this point had not been regular and had not been fair. Party leaders in Austin had heard numerous complaints from some legislators who wanted to run but were in Austin with the legislature and unable to campaign while those with no official position were busy stacking the cards in their favor. Of course the only one in the latter category was Stevenson. Tracy further insisted that the nomination must be made according to party rules and through authorized conventions. "A disregard of it, as in several cases occurring recently in the Third Congressional District, inevitably leads to confusion and disorder," he charged. Taking aim at Stevenson, he wrote that it was "a very easy matter to get a small handful of people together and secure the endorsement of an individual." If others did the same thing, however, it would only lead to confusion and internal party strife. "We must all abide our party machinery," he insisted.[8]

Tracy's demand that meetings abide by party rules gave Ruby the pretext for action. He called a formal meeting of the Congressional District Executive Committee for the evening of April 25 to act on Tracy's instructions. The committee immediately delayed the convention, deciding that it should not be held until the first Wednesday in August. The Austin correspondent for the *Houston Union*, probably Tracy, welcomed the delay, observing that the field had already become crowded and that postponing the election would "keep down political excitement, for the present, at least." Tracy, if he was the correspondent, still appeared willing to accept anyone the convention would nominate, although by this time both he and Ruby had concluded that Clark was their candidate. Tracy also recognized Stevenson as a formidable candidate, but observed that Congressman Clark had some "warm and influential friends working for him."[9]

Ruby made a further announcement regarding preparations for the convention on May 26. This time he let it be known that the Executive Committee had met again and decided on a new basis of apportioning delegates to the convention. The May 26 message, unlike the original one, indicated that the process earlier outlined by Tracy should be followed explicitly. County executive committees were to be formed to call county conventions, announcing the dates at least fifteen days prior to the actual meeting. The county conventions would then select delegates to the state senate districts, where delegates would be chosen for the congressional district convention. His announcement made it clear that none of the delegates for Stevenson chosen in the irregular conventions would be admitted to the district convention, although they could attend if a formal county convention ratified their nomination. In effect, Ruby's announcement negated the work of all of the earlier mass meetings, effectively erasing Stevenson's early advantage.[10]

Heads of the senate district executive committees immediately implemented Ruby's new instructions. The effort by Senator William A. Saylor, head of the committee in the Seventeenth Senatorial District, was a typical example. Saylor's district consisted of Brazos, Burleson, and Milam Counties. Brazos was the only county that had held a mass meeting in the district, and Saylor suggested that it had been knowingly done to subvert the party's established procedures for the benefit of Stevenson, since he received its endorsement. Saylor expressed regret that men in his district had called a convention that was "contrary to all usages and customs governing political parties." Only the district's Executive Committee could call a convention. Now, acting as chairman of that committee, he announced that no conventions would be held at least until some later time in May and that "due notice . . . will be given and time and place designated." More importantly, he indicated that "*no delegates will be recognized except those elected under a call from the Executive Committee of the District.*" Saylor, in effect, ensured that the men chosen in Brazos County to represent Stevenson at the district convention would not be seated.[11]

Ruby's moves signaled to Stevenson that he now faced serious opposition from Republican leaders connected to the Davis administration. Stevenson found himself forced to defend himself against charges that he was proceeding outside the organizational structure of the Republican Party. In a letter to the editor of the *Calvert Tribune,* Stevenson wrote that he believed that the charges made that someone was stocking conventions were directed at himself, and he denied that he had done so, even saying, falsely, that he had been present at none of the conventions when they voted for delegates. Further, he understood that some of his enemies circulated reports that he had no intention of supporting the nominee of the Republican convention if he was not the choice and that he intended remaining in the field regardless of the nomination, refusing to back Clark if he was nominated. That charge, he said, was not true. The editor of the *Union* responded with an article that disingenuously denied that he had ever charged Stevenson with stocking conventions, even though Stevenson was the only man who had acquired any delegates in the conventions held up to that point. Further, writing that he had not personally made any charge against Stevenson, the editor contended that "charge has been made, and it is easily sustained, that unauthorized meetings were gotten up by irresponsible persons, for the purpose of stocking the nominating Convention."[12]

Ruby in the past had used the Loyal League to assure control of the convention. The league would have made sure that county conventions sent delegates to the senate and congressional district conventions favorable to the administration's candidate. An attempt by Republicans opposed to Secretary Newcomb and Chairman Tracy to take over the state league organization made this more difficult and challenged Ruby's ability to control the convention. This splinter group had developed in the last days of the legislative session. It consisted of a coalition of legislators and other officials who believed that in a variety of ways Newcomb and Tracy had acted against their interests. Treasury Secretary George W. Honey, who had broken with Davis over issuing railroad bonds, typified the group. Critics like William B. Moore and James B. Cassidy had been earlier supporters of Jack Hamilton. Representative George H. Slaughter from Smith County hated Newcomb because of his interference in local politics in that county. Senator Phidello W. Hall from Robertson County believed that Newcomb wanted to undermine his position in his district. United States Senator Morgan Hamilton, long a critic of the administration's police and frontier legislation, joined them. Hamilton's presence allowed them to claim that they represented a reform movement, while in fact their revolt amounted to little more than a struggle for power. That spring, Moore and Cassidy launched *The Reformer* in Austin, a Republican newspaper that openly criticized Newcomb and Tracy. In May, Slaughter and Hall moved to wrest control of the Loyal League from Newcomb. Ruby feared that if they succeeded they might then move to gain control over the league councils in his congressional district. Recognizing the danger, Ruby encouraged Newcomb to ensure that the national organization understood these men did not represent the official organization of the league in Texas. Ruby, in turn, worked to make sure that the local councils continued to recognize Newcomb as the president of the state league.[13]

The attack on league leadership began when Slaughter, the vice president of the state council, called for a meeting of the state league's executive committee to discuss Newcomb's leadership. Newcomb had been pressured earlier to call the committee together, but he refused to act when he became aware that Slaughter wanted the meeting to depose him. It is unclear how many actual officers of the league appeared at the meeting, but the ones who did voted to oust Newcomb. Governor Davis and the national organization ultimately intervened, confirmed their support of Newcomb, and repudiated the Slaughter-led league. Slaughter refused to back down, however, and for a time two rival leagues existed. This created serious problems for Ruby. In Galveston two rival league councils organized, undermining Republican unity. Ruby finally brought the two rivals together in a single council, then worked to suppress the dissidents elsewhere in the Third District. Ruby began circulating a letter written by Newcomb and endorsed by Governor Davis that assured local councils that Newcomb was the only Grand President of the Texas Union League and that the national organization recognized Newcomb as such. The letter helped Ruby shut down the revolt and at least brought the league behind the administration's candidates, although Slaughter's effort may have demoralized Republican voters in some counties by making it unclear who the real regular Republican candidate was.[14]

In the midst of the Stevenson challenge to Clark and the threatened takeover of the Loyal League, Ruby faced an even greater threat to his control over black voters when Matt Gaines came out against Clark. Gaines's discontent with Clark developed into a full-scale attack by Gaines against the congressman and, at the same time, Ruby. The black coalition that provided the backbone of the Republican Party appeared to be fragmenting. On June 14 Gaines held a meeting in Brenham, where according to one account he raked "Gen. Clark & Stephenson [sic] from top to toe" and also turned on Ruby. C. J. Stockbridge, the local representative from Gaines's district in Washington County, also came in for abuse for his votes on the Pacific Railroad and the School Bill. These men, in Gaines's view, were carpetbaggers who had done nothing for the real Republican Party, the "black men of Texas." In a speech much publicized in the Democratic press, Gaines pointed to Congressman Clark and complained, "He has worn his tight pants and switched his gold-headed cane long enough at our expense. Where are the school houses he promised us? Not here." For the first time in his career Ruby faced a potential revolt from among the former slaves who had been core of his power up to this time.[15]

Gaines's speech advanced a different sort of radicalism than Ruby's. When Gaines talked about equal rights in his speech, he was not talking about the same things Ruby wanted. Instead, Gaines spoke as a hardcore progressive who now demanded that the rich be taxed to provide the services necessary for blacks to secure a place in postwar Texas. The Democrats said that they groaned under taxation; Gaines said, "Glad of it. Let them groan." Their old masters had not given blacks anything when slavery ended, and now they refused to sell them land. Even the Republicans discriminated, providing separate schools when all men should have the right to go to whatever school they wished. "If a white man has a right to crawl into a colored woman's cabin at night, and have children by her, that child has a right at the school to sit by the side of her black child and her white child." Gaines clearly had taken enough. "They call me an extreme Radical," he said, "but we are not so extreme as the Democrats were when they were in power." All he had to do then was to make "ten bales of cotton and got a pair of red shoes, a pair of white breeches and a promise of a whipping at Christmas to make me a good negro the next year." Gaines suggested, in the end, that he wanted to go to Congress to protect the interests of his fellow former slaves. "I am ready; and I am more capable of doing it than Clark." "The white man is prejudiced," he said. "Justice demands that we send a black man."[16]

Black unrest ran beyond Gaines. In late June, Richard Nelson, the black justice of the peace in Galveston, announced that he planned on running, further threatening Ruby's leadership. Nelson's hostility to both Clark and Stevenson encouraged his decision to run, and in announcing his intention he played particularly on the idea that as white men the two potential candidates had failed to represent their black constituents. Nelson referred to the two as "[s]ome persons" who "presume they have claims upon the colored man which can only be adjusted by the latter abandoning all rights and privileges in their keeping, conceding to us (the colored citizens) only the right to vote for them." Nelson asked whether or not blacks were still slaves, no longer sold on the market, but nonetheless handed over "shackled and fettered" from one ambitious political scheme to another. Blacks were free, and that did not just mean they were free to "work and drudge." As a free man, Nelson stated that he would resist political debasement and not submit to "the dicta of a junta or the pronunciamento of a conclave." Focusing further on the white politicians, Nelson asked if it was any more dishonorable to vote for a black man than to accept a black man's vote. If whites would not accept them as candidates, blacks should repudiate the white man's ambitions. With Nelson joining Gaines in insisting on a black candidate, Ruby confronted an even greater problem in securing Clark's nomination.[17]

The situation worsened for Ruby when several key white Republicans in the district shifted their support from Clark. Most of these men were like the "reformers" Honey, Moore, and Cassidy in Austin, men with frustrated ambitions who saw Stevenson as opening up new opportunities for patronage positions. These men included Chauncey B. Sabin, district judge in Galveston, who wanted to be named United State district judge, and James A. McKee, the Galveston mayor and postmaster, whom state Republican leaders had repeatedly wanted to remove from office. In mid-June, Sabin, McKee, and Stevenson began to work to have men favorable to their interests put into office when they began lobbying Houston police chief E. M. McCormick to fill the vacant United States marshal position, as opposed to Ruby's candidate, Captain William H. Griffin, the deputy city marshal of Galveston. Ruby recognized this new upheaval for what it was, a struggle for federal offices. In mid-June he informed Newcomb of the problem in Galveston and warned that he feared that Sabin had become "too much influenced" by Stevenson. He also believed that Samuel Dodge, a Galveston Republican and district judge for Harris County, also had fallen under the influence of Stevenson. Ruby thought that Dodge had been manipulated by the Galveston County criminal clerk, former deputy United States marshal George P. Douglass. He recognized that Stevenson had gained important allies in these men and was convinced that Stevenson had become a major problem for Clark's renomination. In his letter to Newcomb he characterized Stevenson as a "bad and turbulent demagogue."[18]

The fact that the Democratic Party had reestablished itself more firmly than at any time since the Civil War made all of this internal turmoil within the Republican Party even more challenging. On January 23, 1871, Democrats had held their state convention in Austin and declared war on the state's Republican administration. Its platform "arraigned" the Davis administration for its declarations of martial law and its efforts at protecting the ballot box, seen by Democrats as throwing difficulties in the way of the people voting. It attacked the Republican majorities in the house and senate for expelling Conservative members, subsidizing a "corrupt" press, and attempting to remove Senator Morgan Hamilton. Characterizing Republican actions as "high crimes and political misdemeanors," the Democratic platform invited "all good men" to cooperate with them to "release the people of oppression, ruinous and unequal taxation" and restore honesty to government. They promised a return to a government that restricted the power of the federal government and returned regulation of suffrage and election to the states. The reorganized Democratic Party ultimately held its own congressional district convention and nominated Dewitt C. Giddings, a former Confederate officer and a member of the Constitutional Convention of 1866, to run against Clark. Republican division in the face of this resurgent Democratic Party threatened a course that would be political suicide.[19]

In the midst of new Democratic militancy, a black revolt, and a white-led schism within the Republican Party, Ruby shared his fears with Newcomb. In public, however, he tried to remain above the fray. Like Tracy, Ruby did not appear to be actively engaged in lining up delegates to the convention, even though behind the scenes he worked to bring blacks back in line behind the administration. On the surface he attended to the usual public activities expected of political leaders, but these actions did make a public demonstration that he retained his leadership role. He dutifully appeared at the celebration of June 19 in Galveston, the day known then as Freedom Day. Frank Webb, a black newspaper publisher, read the Emancipation Proclamation and then Ruby delivered a "long address" that emphasized the progress that blacks had made since securing their freedom. He had used the same themes to inform his talks in the North the previous fall, and in focusing on progress he steered clear of any explicitly political statements. He told his listeners that emancipation had not guaranteed them the rights assured to whites, and he warned that they must not relax on their path to full freedom, urging them to acquire the "culture only derivable from education and self-respect." Success would be achieved only by self-help. While not overtly political, his statements nonetheless differed markedly from Gaines's views in their contention that only with black self-improvement could progress be made. On June 26 he joined other prominent local black politicians and religious leaders in examining the students at the Barnes Institute, a school created for blacks in Galveston by Sarah M. Barnes of the American Missionary Association and at this time part of the new public school system. Even an event such as this, while not explicitly political, had political overtones for Ruby. Congressman Clark also attended and furnished the prizes for the students excelling in their studies. Ruby again spoke at this meeting, emphasizing the theme of self-help and the promise of achievement that it would bring. He closed by praising the school and its students for the progress they were making.[20]

Ruby also became involved in the Laborer's Union Association of Galveston's efforts to become part of the Colored National Labor Union, again avoiding any apparent interest in the congressional race while also asserting his place as a Republican leader. The Laborer's Union Association had been formed in Galveston in September 1870, while Ruby was in the legislature. The group began to expand its activities following a convention in Houston in June 1871. Ruby did not attend the Houston convention, possibly prevented by the hurricane that hit Galveston at this time or the near tragedy for his family when his brother Horatio, working as a customs inspector in Galveston, nearly drowned when the bark *Virginia Dare* grounded and sank in the midst of the storm. Even though he was not present, the goals of the LUA and the CNLU's goals connected him to the organizations. Both were similar to groups George's father Reuben had been associated with prior to the Civil War. They sought to make labor respectable, but also to devise means for laborers to help themselves morally, mentally, and physically. Although primarily a black organization, the CNLU encouraged whites to join and stated its intention to ignore the "sickly sentimentality which induces distinctions by reason of color." Ruby's support of the development became apparent later when he played a prominent role in a meeting the LUA held in Houston on August 3.[21]

The purpose of the August meeting was the selection of delegates to represent Texas in a "Convention of the Southern States" to be held in Columbia, South Carolina, on October 18. That convention had been called by Henry M. Turner, a prominent preacher with the African Methodist Episcopal Church, future bishop of that church, and the black postmaster of Macon, Georgia. Turner had concluded such a meeting was necessary after consulting with important black leaders across the South, and Ruby was among the men he consulted. The "Convention of Southern States" proposed to consider the "peculiar condition of the colored people in the Southern States" and to look into the "local causes" that produced these conditions. The efforts of the LUA and Turner's Columbia convention certainly meshed with Ruby's long-term work. Ruby actually presided at the Houston meeting, and he supported the efforts of these organizations. He did not go to Columbia, however, because he had to attend the legislative session that began in September.[22]

Ruby turned to an additional cause that summer, one he made known at the Houston meeting of the LUA. Abba Burton, an African American and the wife of Sheriff Walter Burton of Fort Bend County, had been put off a train of the Galveston, Houston and Henderson Railroad when she refused to leave the first class car and be put into a coach "among ruffians and blackguards." Ruby had his own experiences with being denied first-class passage on a common carrier in the past, and he stepped in to the situation and insisted that under the Civil Rights Act and the Fourteenth Amendment to the United States Constitution the railroad could not so discriminate. Ruby helped move a resolution through the convention asking all men who favored "equal rights, irrespective of race or color, or previous condition" to assist Sheriff Burton by contributing funds that would allow him to take the company to court.[23]

At the same time that Ruby engaged in these local activities, he also made sure that he remained connected with politicians and political issues outside of Texas, and he demonstrated continuing interest in broader national Republican politics. He remained in particular contact with politicians in Louisiana. One of those men was Pinckney Benton Stewart Pinchback, a free black from Georgia who had gone to New Orleans during the war where he served as an officer in the First Louisiana Native Guards. Pinchback had remained after the war and become involved first in the school system, then in Republican politics. In 1871 he was the president pro tempore of the Louisiana state senate and director of the New Orleans public schools. Ruby had met Pinchback when he lived in New Orleans, and Ruby recognized early in Pinchback's political rise in Louisiana that he should remain in contact with him. After receiving a copy of the *Louisianian*, which Pinchback owned and used to back his political career, Ruby took the time to write a note to the senator congratulating him on its publication. Ruby told him that he believed the paper supplied a "need long and seriously felt" among Louisianans. He also praised the newspaper for expressing the wants and wishes of blacks and advocating their interests. Ruby flattered Pinchback for doing "noble work."[24]

Ruby's apparent indifference to the congressional campaign through much of June, even though he had already begun to organize his district, may have been partly due to his own uncertainty as to who would best serve the district as congressman. He clearly did not believe Stevenson to be a viable candidate, but he also realized that Clark, as has been shown, had done a poor job of working with Ruby and other blacks in his district. Clark's failure had helped prompt the revolt of Gaines and Nelson. By the end of June, however, Clark recognized that not courting Ruby had added to his problems, and Clark attempted to resolve the differences that had developed with Ruby. Ruby informed Newcomb on June 29 that Clark had learned that he, Ruby, controlled matters, meaning the black vote not only in his senate district of Galveston, Brazoria, and Matagorda Counties but also in the entire Third District. Clark, as a result, asked Ruby if he would give him his open support. Ruby wrote that while "chagrined at Clark's impolitic action hitherto, I replied favorably to his request." Ruby believed that Clark would begin to gain ground in the contest but remained unimpressed with him. He wrote of the congressman to Newcomb, "Though by all odds the best of all candidates or aspirants in this district, Clark is certainly a poor politician."[25]

Ruby, following this rapprochement with Clark, became more active in the campaign. The editor of the *Houston Union* recognized the shift. He suggested that Ruby initially had refused to take sides because of his friendship with all of the potential candidates. The editor thought that in the end Ruby had come to see that he had to support the "long-tried and true party leadership." He also believed that Ruby had finally come to see Stevenson and Gaines as promoting some sort of "bastard Republicanism" that would destroy the party's chances in 1872. Ruby certainly saw them as much more radical candidates and demonstrated his middle-class perspective on problems that had been typical of his entire career. In a letter to Newcomb, Ruby referred to Stevenson and Gaines as "Reds," associating them with the leftist radicals who had been part of the Paris Commune, radicals usually referred to as Reds. In another letter Ruby described Clark's opponents as "communists." Once Ruby reached the conclusion that either Stevenson or Gaines would destroy the Republican Party by their radical policies, the editor of the *Union* observed, Ruby began doing all that he could to assure the victory of Clark, the administration's choice. That meant lining up black Republicans for Clark and diverting them from any support for Stevenson or Gaines. Aroused, Ruby brought behind him "the serried cohorts of colored Republicans, who are as true to the gleam of his glittering blade as Clan-Alpine's warriors were to the bugle-call of Rhoderick Dhu," referring to a character from Walter Scott's *Lady of the Lake* who led the highland clans in a war against King James V of Scotland.[26]

Ruby had made earlier efforts at reorganizing the league, but he turned aggressively at this point to bringing them in line behind Clark and dealing with Clark's rivals. As early as June 23 he had complained to Newcomb that the league in Galveston remained unorganized and that he regretted that he had not received permission to reorganize it himself. By July 6, still not having received word from Austin, he had decided to act on his own. He informed Newcomb that he intended putting the league on "so secure, substantial and united a footing that success for the future shall come on every effort." In the same letter he informed Newcomb that George Lawrence, an organizer who carried the blessings of the national league organization, had arrived in Galveston, and that he hoped soon to make a favorable report on the local league council. Within two weeks Ruby reported that the Galveston Republicans had managed to create an excellent league council that he believed would prove efficient in the campaign. Wright Cuney, by this time Ruby's closest political associate in Galveston, headed the new council.[27]

While working to reorganize the league, Ruby also proceeded to bring the officials of the new public school system to Clark's support. When Governor Davis appointed the former Galveston police chief and Ruby's candidate for United States marshal, William Griffin, to be the district's supervisor of education, Ruby welcomed the action. He immediately informed Newcomb that he believed Griffin would make a good school officer, but he also thought he would be useful in the upcoming campaign. Griffin could appoint local school directors. These positions had only small salaries associated with them, but considerable prestige, and the right men as directors could use their status to influence local voters. Their control over the examination, certification, and appointment of teachers also represented a potential tool for influencing the politics of the system's teachers. For Galveston, Griffin immediately appointed Ruby, Collector Nathan Patten, Wright Cuney, league organizer George Lawrence, and Galveston city alderman F. C. Mosebach to the public school system's board of directors. Ruby ultimately resigned the position after being informed by the governor that holding it was incompatible with his office as a state senator, but the others remained. Whether or not the administration actually used the schools other than in Galveston for political purposes is unknown, although their political opponents believed that they had. The editor at *Flake's Bulletin* complained that "not a school supervisor or director has been appointed in this district who was not pledged beforehand to use his influence for Clark."[28]

Under Ruby's second call for nominating conventions, the first county convention met in Navasota, Grimes County. The convention elected delegates to the district convention committed to Stevenson, just as had the earlier irregular meeting held there. The result showed that the Stevenson threat remained real despite efforts to sidetrack him. Ruby set the nominating process underway in his own senate district on June 23. As chairman of the Senate Executive Committee, he called for the county committees in Galveston, Brazoria, and Matagorda to provide for county meetings to elect delegates to Houston. The convention in Matagorda indicated that Stevenson remained a serious threat when it instructed the delegates to support Stevenson. By the middle of July, however, enough county conventions had been held that despite the number of delegates chosen for Stevenson, the *Houston Union* predicted Clark would have an unquestioned majority. To further ensure this result, in counties where "irregular" conventions had been held and the delegations asserted that they represented those counties, regular Republicans held new conventions that elected rival delegations to go to Houston and contest the Stevenson delegates. Under the rules, the delegates chosen in the first conventions and generally committed to Stevenson probably would not be seated. The election of competing delegations from these counties raised the possibility of a serious floor fight that Ruby would have to control.[29]

Ruby responded to the Matagorda convention by beginning a more active campaign for Clark in Brazoria and Galveston Counties. On July 22 he attended the county convention in Brazoria. He found Stevenson there as well, working to secure the delegates. Stevenson spoke first and responded to charges that he would not support the nominee of the congressional district convention by saying that he would support any nominee, but only if the nomination was made by a "*legitimate convention.*" Stevenson appeared on the verge of carrying the meeting when Ruby made his presence known and the crowd called on him to speak. Ruby tore into Stevenson, saying that in his opinion Stevenson did not possess the qualifications to serve as a representative of the district. The report from Brazoria indicated the convention responded to Ruby with loud cheers, and cries that "Ruby is our man!" One of Stevenson's supporters reportedly said that he believed "Ruby could make the people believe that black was white." Ruby's appearance disrupted the meeting that Stevenson had appeared on the verge of controlling. As a result, the convention elected delegates without instructing them for either Stevenson or Clark.[30]

On July 30, Ruby moved to take control of the Galveston County convention. Accounts of the convention were highly biased by the politics of the newspapers, with each candidate's newspapers providing different stories of what happened. Even before the convention began, signs of a physical confrontation between Stevenson and Clark supporters were in the air. The reporter from the pro-Stevenson newspaper in Austin, the *Reformer*, contended that Collector Patten had said several days before the delegates gathered that "blood would be shed, if necessary, to elect the Clark delegates." He also maintained that Ruby had telegraphed the governor asking him to send the state police into the city because he expected a serious disturbance. In fact, Ruby already had enlisted extra constables. The hostile writer for the *Reformer* characterized these men as "desperate and sanguinary strikers from New York," discharged police men, sixty blacks from the Morgan Steamship Company, all arrayed for Clark, paid from two to five dollars, and supplied with whiskey. One of the constables was Ruby's brother, Horatio. Of course there is no way of knowing the truthfulness of the article's charges. That Governor Davis accepted Ruby's assessment of the upcoming convention was apparent when Davis did send state police. Again, the Stevenson men charged that they would be used to defeat them in the convention. Subsequent events suggest that the Stevenson men did want to create a disturbance and that Ruby had little reason to bring the lawmen in to assure Clark's nomination.[31]

Galveston Republicans finally gathered in Sylvester's Hall on the morning of the thirtieth and the regular party organization controlled the proceedings. The temporary chairman, collector of the port Nathan Patten, called the meeting to order and proposed that Ruby be elected permanent chairman. When the body overwhelmingly elected Ruby, the regular organization's control of the convention was clear, virtually assuring Clark's nomination. At that point, according to the report of the Democratic *Galveston News*, Stevenson and his supporters tried to disrupt the meeting. The official account that appeared in the *Houston Union* agreed that the Stevenson men had caused an uproar. The correspondent for the *Reformer*, however, wrote that after Ruby took the chair, a mob of pro-Clark supporters broke into the convention brandishing "open razors and pistols." They occupied all of the seats and removed anyone from the floor who opposed Clark. The constables and state police, according to the *Reformer*'s man, sat by and "winked" at the assaults on Stevenson men, with the behavior of Horatio Ruby being the "most atrocious." While both the *Union*'s and

Reformer's correspondents had a clear bias in their account, the report of the *News* suggests that the story provided by the *Union* may have been more accurate.[32]

With order restored, Patten moved immediately that Ruby and Wright Cuney, Ruby's protégé, be named delegates to the Houston convention, with both men committed to Clark. When Richard Nelson, who intended running himself, attempted to speak, the crowd howled him down. The meeting then passed resolutions endorsing their choice of delegates to the Houston convention and stating their approval of the work of the state and national Republican administrations. The reporter for the *Galveston News* observed in assessing the convention that it was a "forced job" carried out by Patten. On the other hand, he complimented Ruby for presiding with dignity. "His deportment," he wrote, "forced approbation even from his enemies; he was cool, calm and self-possessed. He went there to do a piece of dirty work, and he did it as decently as such work could be done."[33]

Neither Stevenson nor Richard Nelson accepted the results of the meeting. Nelson charged that the meeting had been packed with Clark supporters, suggesting that these were there illegally. He contended he actually represented the majority of Republican voters. Nelson declared himself an independent candidate. Stevenson and his supporters, most of whom were not seated in the convention, moved on to the county courthouse where they held their own meeting. Many of the men who followed Stevenson were from Galveston and earlier had expressed their opposition to the leadership of James Tracy. They included Judge Dodge, Judge Sabin, Mayor McKee, and two prominent black ministers from the city, Rev. Elias Dibble of the AME Church and Rev. Israel S. Campbell of the Baptist Church. Johnson Reed, Galveston's black district clerk, also showed up. They quickly selected two pro-Stevenson men to go to Houston and adjourned.[34]

A day later, before the opening of the district convention in Houston, the two main candidates, Stevenson and Clark, were present and busily canvassing delegates for votes. On the evening of July 31, Stevenson's supporters met in a secret session at the Hutchins House to determine their strategy in the convention. Later reports concluded that they believed the only way to carry the convention was to contest the seating of the Clark delegates. At the same time as the Stevenson men caucused, Clark men busily buttonholed other delegates to ensure their support for the congressman. At least one report from the correspondent of the Democratic *Galveston News* indicated the Clark had been busy trying to buy Stevenson supporters. Richard Nelson remained in the field, although few people gave him a chance of securing the nomination by this time. The fact that Senator Gaines appeared to have backed off his challenge was a major plus for Clark. In late July, T. A. Wilmans, editor of the *Brenham Inquirer*, reported to Newcomb that Gaines had visited him and told him that while he opposed Clark, he promised to "listen to reason and may be brought around." A meeting between supporters of Stevenson and Clark at the Jockey Club Billiard Room at noon on August 1 sought to harmonize the candidates. The men attending, however, found no basis for a compromise.[35]

The convention to nominate the candidate for the Third District opened in Houston on August 2. Reacting to the disturbance that had happened at Galveston and possibly fearing something similar in Houston, Ruby asked for additional state police at the meeting. Whether or not the governor sent them, however, is not clear. They were not needed though, since Ruby maintained a firm hand on the proceedings. Prior to the convention's opening he announced that only authorized delegates, elected alternates, and newspaper reporters would be admitted to the main floor. Further, he informed the convention that only individuals with tickets would be admitted to sit in the gallery. He furnished these tickets to delegates to distribute to their friends, although the delegates had to apply to him for the tickets. Ruby was determined that no mob would disturb the proceedings, and he held to his plan.[36]

As chairman of the executive committee, Ruby called the convention to order. Tracy was on the floor, working for Clark, and he immediately nominated Ruby to serve as the permanent chairman of the convention. The delegates elected Ruby, an early indication that the majority of delegates supported Clark. Immediately after Ruby's election, a resolution was introduced from the floor clearly aimed at Stevenson. It required all candidates to recognize beforehand that they would accept the decision of the convention. The resolution passed, again indicating the strength of the pro-Clark delegates. That evening the convention turned to nominations. Tracy put Clark's name before the delegates. Jackson Lumpkins, a young black farm worker, nominated Richard Allen, and Thomas J. Powell placed Ruby's name in nomination. Ruby quickly declined. A voice vote followed, with Clark receiving thirty-four votes, Allen two, and Stevenson, who had not been officially nominated, one-half of a vote. Allen then moved that Clark's nomination be made unanimous. What had earlier appeared to be a potentially contentious convention moved quietly to a decisive choice. Clark's success may be attributed largely to Ruby, who had successfully managed to retain control over the league and the local party apparatus.[37]

The campaign platform adopted by the convention endorsed the national Republican Party, the Grant administration, and the Davis administration. It went on, however, to condemn the "bolters and disorganizers" and to state that they would not associate with anyone who attempted to disorganize either the party or the Loyal League. The latter was aimed specifically at Morgan Hamilton and the men who had attempted to wrest control of the league from Newcomb the previous May. The platform pledged the district's Republicans to support the legislature's acts to improve the state, maintain peace, and promote prosperity. The delegates praised the efforts by the legislature and the administration to provide protection and education. In the end, they passed resolutions committing themselves to defeat the "common enemy, the Democrats." The platform, engineered in part by Ruby, turned any Republicans who refused to support Clark out of the party.[38]

Events in Houston outraged the Stevenson faction, even though Ruby had held the convention to the party's rules. Stevenson's supporters, including eighteen of the irregular delegates who had not been seated in the regular convention, moved from the convention hall to Young America Hall.

Judge Dodge, who had left the regular convention intending to stick with Stevenson, called the convention to order. Senator Hall and Judge Sabin, two other whites who had refused to move back into the Clark camp, joined Dodge. Edward DuPish, one of the black delegates from Galveston, urged those present to remain firm and devoted to Stevenson, and J. H. Washington, who was one of the delegates from the irregular convention in Grimes County, nominated Stevenson as a candidate. The motion carried unanimously and the bolters adjourned. Stevenson had taken his revolt into the general election.[39]

Ruby actively campaigned for Clark for several weeks after the convention adjourned. The need to return to Austin when the session of the Twelfth Legislature reconvened in September, however, limited what he could do. One of his most important appearances came when he, United States Marshal Parker, Wright Cuney, and Richard Nelson, who by this time had given up his own campaign to favor Clark, travelled to Houston to meet Governor Davis when the governor went on the road to canvass for Clark. The party met Davis and escorted him to Galveston for a rally in that critical county. Ruby chaired what turned into a tumultuous meeting on Wednesday, August 16. Following Ruby's assumption of the chair, a group of Stevenson supporters attempted to break up the meeting. The correspondent of the *Houston Union* blamed Johnson Reed, P. W. Hall, Frank Webb of the *Galveston Republican*, Rev. Campbell of the black Baptist Church, and several employees of James McKee in the post office for the attack. Judges Sabin and Dodge watched on but apparently did not participate in the disturbance. The uproar forced Ruby to call in the city police to restore order. After the meeting returned to calm, in order to ensure things remained quiet Ruby named his closest associates as vice presidents, including Wright Cuney, Collector Nathan Patten, Richard Nelson, and school supervisor Griffin.[40]

When Governor Davis appeared, the Stevenson crowd renewed their efforts to disrupt the meeting. Ruby, however, kept a tight leash on the proceedings. In his speech Davis attacked the Democrats but ultimately turned to the election in the Third District and insisted that Republicans must come together. He pointed to the fact that General Clark had received a majority of the vote in Houston and insisted the supporters of other candidates must accept that fact. Stevenson, he said, was a good man, but a vote for him would give the election to D. C. Giddings, the Democratic candidate. The Democrats, he said, supported Stevenson just for the purpose of splintering the Republican Party. Democrats advised Republicans not to abandon Judge Sabin, Dodge, and Mayor McKee, who supported Stevenson, but the governor believed they should vote for Clark. At this point cries of "no" came from the crowd, and Ruby gaveled them down. When the governor said that Clark had been fairly nominated, Ruby again was forced to call for silence. When the turmoil continued Ruby asked the police to remove all the men disrupting the meeting. After the governor finished his speech, Ruby declared the meeting at an end and then accompanied the governor to Col. Patten's home, walking there in a torchlight procession.[41]

Ruby responded to the Davis speech optimistically. He informed Newcomb afterwards that Davis had "made a very fine impression" and, as a result, he believed that the Stevenson party, already a minority, was further reduced. That idea allowed him to conclude that continued pressure on the Stevenson supporters ultimately would lead them to abandon their candidate and that "all will be well in our Congressional District." Ruby proceeded to do his part in Galveston and the other counties. In Galveston he participated in the reorganization of the Republican Association in the city in preparation for the election. In the meeting on August 24, Ruby's associates secured all of the leadership positions. Ruby himself was named to the executive committee. Ruby's control of the association assured that at least the organized portion of the Republican Party in Galveston remained united behind Clark.[42]

During the campaign, Ruby advised Newcomb on matters in other counties in his district in addition to continuing to harden support for Clark in Galveston. In an effort to assure that Clark carried Brazoria County, he cautioned Newcomb to see that the chief of the state police keep an officer who had been transferred to Shelby County in Brazoria. Ruby believed that with the Clark campaign getting ready to canvass Brazoria, the policeman, a black man who had been in the United States Army, would be "very useful to us." Ruby had previously found the man useful politically, and he urged that the transfer, if necessary, be delayed until after the election. If it was critical to have a policeman in Shelby County, he advised Newcomb to have an Irish policeman transferred from Brazoria. Ruby believed that the Irishman lacked the "*suaviter in mod* [sic] as well as *fortier in re*, the ability to be pleasant in manner and strong in deed, requisite in Brazoria for our candidate Clark." Ruby thought the possibility of intimidation in Brazoria existed and required a police presence. The ability to be pleasant but act forcefully when necessary, however, was a requirement. For Ruby, the safety of the polls was at stake.[43]

Ruby travelled to Brazoria County with Clark in late August where the two held meetings throughout the county. The largest of these took place on August 28 in Brazoria. James Tracy accompanied the party and delivered the introductory address at the meeting. Clark followed. Ruby then addressed the crowd in what must have been an especially long speech, for the meeting adjourned for a short time in the middle of it. The correspondent for the *Houston Union* reported that Ruby spoke with his "usual strength and eloquence, [and] did not fail to draw the attention of the meeting." The crowd responded to his remarks with loud applause. Whether or not any of the speaking changed minds, the men at the rally clearly were for Clark. When the meeting adjourned the crowd sang "We'll rally round the flag, boys," the anthem of the Loyal League.[44]

During his time in Brazoria, Ruby showed that he had the ability to place strong pressure on Stevenson supporters. Johnson Reed, who had become one of Stevenson's most steadfast supporters in Galveston, later said that he had been present in Brazoria and had even been allowed to speak for Stevenson. After Reed's address, however, Ruby approached him and told him that he was a fool to pursue his course. At least according to Reed, the senator explained to him that he might jeopardize his position as district clerk in Galveston County if he persisted in supporting Stevenson. Reed perceived this as a direct threat, although Ruby may simply have meant that a Democratic victory would assure Reed's ultimate loss as well. It certainly was not beyond Ruby, however, to use his influence to control political offices. He also pressured Judge Samuel Dodge. During the campaign Dodge received warnings that his job might be in jeopardy if he did not switch to support Clark. Nothing happened during the election, but after Ruby returned to the legislature he introduced a bill in the senate to abolish Dodge's court. Also, Ruby attempted to get rid of the assistant engrossing clerks in the legislature, a move that Democratic observers believed aimed specifically at Frank Webb, one of the clerks who began publishing the *Galveston Republican* to support Stevenson. Throughout the campaign Ruby also worked to have Governor Davis remove certain city officials in Galveston who he believed did not support the Republican cause.[45]

Ruby's ability to continue active campaigning came to an end September. In part his early removal from the campaign trail may have been for personal reasons. In September, Lucy gave birth to the couple's first child, Mabel Virginia. In addition to being at home for her birth, the senator also had to prepare for his return to Austin when the legislature went back into session. Ruby left Galveston on September 9 to return to Austin. When he changed trains in Houston, he, along with other legislators returning to the capital city, visited Tracy and Quick at the *Union*. They then took a special train for Austin the next day. The campaign was over for Ruby. In Austin, he and other Republicans awaited the results.[46]

Ruby came back to Galveston just prior to the election to be present as its citizens went to the polls on October 3, and he remained in the city during the four days of voting. The results were a disaster for the Republican Party. Only in the Third District was the election close, and even there the Democrats won easily. Democrats turned out en masse and used the usual tactics of intimidation to prevent Republicans, especially black Republicans, from going to the polls. After the election, Clark wrote to Newcomb that nearly all blacks in Limestone and Freestone Counties had been prevented from voting. In most of the other counties the numbers of blacks who had been unable to vote ranged from one hundred in Bosque to nearly a thousand in Leon. A letter to Newcomb from Hill County indicated that Democrats there had used "direct and indirect" intimidation to limit black voting. In addition the ballots of black voters were marked so that they could be distinguished to ensure that they had not voted for Clark.[47]

Intimidation certainly took place, but the Republican Executive Committee provided a probably more realistic explanation for what had taken place in a published address to Texas Republicans after the results were in. In it, the committee attributed much of their defeat to the cost of the programs they had implemented. The school system, they argued, was heartily approved of by the people, but the Democrats had undermined it in the public eye by misrepresenting its provisions and misstating its purposes. Defending the frontier and inaugurating the new government were all expensive, but they were necessary. Still the Democrats had attacked the programs as too expensive, when the administration had, in fact, tried to minimize costs. Still, in everything that the administration had attempted, it had been "reviled and slandered." Even the levels of taxation had been grossly exaggerated. All in all the Democratic press had persistently abused and misrepresented the administration, effectively alienating men who either took no part in the election or cast their votes with the Democrats. The government's reforms had proven unpopular among men who should have sustained them. Still, the men on the Republican executive committee believed a Texas with Republican policies would bring the state into the modern era and onto the "high-road to prosperity." They urged all Republicans to redouble their efforts to ensure success in the 1872 elections.[48]

As to the election in the Third District, Giddings initially received a clear majority of votes. Governor Davis, however, certified Clark as the winner following the rejection of large numbers of pro-Giddings votes from Bosque, Brazos, Freestone, Harris, Limestone, and Washington Counties because of a variety of reasons. Some counties had sent in no official returns. In some instances ballots had been numbered contrary to the state's election laws. Some counties opened white men's voting places, another illegal practice. In some cases Democrats had voted non-citizens. Open violence and intimidation had disrupted the polling in Freestone and Limestone Counties. The revised returns gave 18,407 votes to 17,082 for Giddings and 409 for Stevenson. Giddings contested Clark's election in Congress, however, and ultimately won his challenge and took the seat when Clark apparently did nothing to support his claim.[49]

For Ruby, the particularly important result was in his own state senate district. In it, Clark carried both Brazoria and Matagorda Counties but lost badly in Galveston County. The results in those three counties, uncontested, was 2,189 votes for Giddings, 1,815 for Clark, and 332 for Stevenson. Even without Stevenson in the race, Giddings would have won. Significantly, the turnout for both Clark and Stevenson, the Republican vote, was twenty-nine fewer in number than Governor Davis had received in 1869. Giddings's vote was nearly seven hundred votes more than Hamilton received in the 1869 election. Ruby's district had become Democratic. Ruby had successfully managed the campaign in terms of controlling Republicans both in his congressional and senate districts. That was not enough, however, to overcome a tidal wave of Democratic voters who turned out in larger numbers in every county in the district. Ruby now faced the continued problem of trying to attract white support without losing black voters to more radical Republican opponents. In the wake of the congressional elections, however, Ruby began to look for new options for his career.

CHAPTER XI

LOOKING FOR NEW DIRECTIONS, 1872

Mindful of Right, We Dare to be True—Masthead of George Ruby's Galveston Standard, *June 3, 1872*

The 1871 congressional election signaled a major change in the course of Reconstruction in Texas, and also in the career of George Ruby. The voting pattern in his district gave a clear warning that he had little in the way of a political future in either Galveston or the state. He had retained support among black voters, but despite his efforts to gain support from the white business community, the vote suggested that he had made no inroads into that group as voters. The Galveston newspapers, the voice of the powerful commercial interests of the city, continued to attack the senator and frequently appealed to the racism of their readers to ensure their votes never shifted to him. In fact, businessmen found that they could choose Democratic candidates who would support their interests, particularly their railroad interests, as strongly as any Republican. Further, the Davis administration had often opposed these concerns and had shown little ability to gain support for them from the federal government. They did not need Republican legislators, congressmen, or governors, and they especially did not need a black senator. Ruby's actions in the wake of the 1871 election showed his awareness of the difficulty of his situation. He continued actively to represent the legislative agenda of prominent white Galveston businessmen. He remained a loyal Republican. He played a major role in the general election that occurred in the fall of 1872. Still, he began looking to other possibilities for his future. The year 1872 was a critical one for Ruby.

The 1871 congressional campaign was still going on when Ruby returned to Austin for the Twelfth Legislature after it returned from its adjournment. That session began on September 12, a month before the election, and legislators hesitated to begin any real business until they knew the election's outcome. Legislators did take care of the usual organizational business, electing legislative staff and naming men to committees. Ruby moved immediately to take advantage of the election of staff members to move against some of the Republicans who had remained supportive of Louis Stevenson after the nominating convention, signaling to them that their desertion of the regular party had placed their positions in jeopardy. Their failure to support Congressman Clark exacted a price. The most important of these men was Frank Webb, the Galveston newspaperman who was one of Stevenson's most prominent black supporters. Webb had worked as the assistant enrolling clerk in the previous session. Ruby had the position eliminated and Webb discharged. Ruby also tried to eliminate the criminal court of Galveston and Harris County, a post held by Judge Dodge. In this effort Ruby failed, but he still sent a clear message of the intention of the Republican leadership to punish men who did not maintain party loyalty. He also may have been responsible, although not through legislative action, in having Governor Davis remove Johnson Reed from the Galveston City Council. Ruby showed himself capable of playing political hardball when necessary.[1]

Contemporaries understood that Ruby intended to intimidate the men who had caused so much trouble for the party. The editor of the *Galveston News* contended that Ruby had violated state and federal laws prohibiting interference with citizens on account of their choice in voting, an ironic accusation considering Democratic intimidation of voters. In this case, the editor suggested that Webb and Reed in particular should prosecute the violators of the law. He noted that Governor Davis had said when he canvassed the Third District that "*cobwebs*" would be dashed from people's eyes. Clearly these "cobwebs" were men like Webb and Reed, and the editor suggested that Senator Ruby had construed the governor's statement to be taken literally when he had proceeded to dash Webb's name from the list of enrolling clerks. Was not the move to abolish the criminal court a similar threat intended to intimidate a citizen? None of the victims of Ruby's efforts, however, chose to take up the challenge of the *News* to make charges against the senator. In the end, Ruby simply played the game of contemporary politics. Support earned rewards. Failure led to punishment.[2]

When the senate took up its normal business, Ruby worked much as he had in the previous sessions even though his future in the senate looked dim. He retained his places on the Committee on Engrossed Bills and the important Judiciary Committee. He returned to the Committee on Private Land Claims, and for this session he assumed the position of chair. In this session he also continued to play a major role in forwarding Governor Davis's agenda by sponsoring major pieces of its legislation. Among these were bills that established a new code of criminal procedures for the state and changed the dates for holding district courts. Ruby also helped to shepherd another law through the legislature that provided penalties upon boat, railroad, or stage companies that discriminated against anyone on the basis of race. The law confirmed the state's commitment to the equality of all persons before the law. Common carriers were prohibited from making any distinctions in carrying passengers, and the new law provided that anyone convicted of making such distinctions could be punished with a $100 to $500 fine and imprisonment for thirty to ninety days. The Davis administration continued in this case to carry out an agenda designed to protect the black community, a program backed by Ruby.[3]

He also stood by the various officers of the administration, effectively limiting a Democratic attempt to defame Superintendent of Education Jacob DeGress. When Democrats with the support of some Republicans created a committee to investigate charges that DeGress had benefitted from school book purchases, Ruby added sections to the resolution creating the committee that restricted its mandated scope. He effectively blocked a Democrat-sponsored bill that would have exempted keepers of hotels and boarding houses from prosecution under the civil rights provisions of the state's constitution. When Senator Matt Gaines introduced a resolution to discontinue taking the fifteen copies of the *State Journal* provided for each member, a move to punish its publishers, James Tracy, and Secretary of State Newcomb for their role in the congressional campaign, Ruby moved a call of the house, a parliamentary maneuver that delayed consideration of the resolution and effectively blocked Gaines. In all of these actions Ruby remained an effective worker in the senate for Davis and his administration.[4]

As in the previous sessions of the legislature, members of the senate, both Republicans and Democrats, recognized Ruby's skills as a parliamentarian, despite the usual Democratic public attacks on him. As a result, he frequently took the chair as the senate's presiding officer in its sessions. The greatest recognition of his abilities from his peers came in the middle of the session when Don Campbell, president of the senate and senator from Marion County, died. The Galveston newspapers suggested that many senators from both parties considered Ruby to have a serious chance of succeeding Campbell. As a black man, his choice actually was unlikely, but the fact that his political enemies believed that Ruby was capable of directing the business of the senate suggested that even his Democratic opponents had a more positive view of Ruby than they ever admitted publicly. He was not elected, however.[5]

The final session of the Twelfth Legislature passed new laws on a wide variety of matters including civil rights, the courts, the penal code, minutemen on the frontier, and the school system, but its attention to special legislation was more extensive. Legislators introduced and passed a massive number of special laws that incorporated more railroads, bridge companies, insurance companies, banks, towns, clubs, and anything else that needed a state charter. By the end of the session the legislature had passed 166 special laws. Ruby contributed to this flood of bills, continuing to introduce legislation backed by prominent Galveston businessmen. He sponsored a bill creating the Island City Real Estate and Homestead Association, a savings bank backed by A. M. Hobby, M. V. McMahan, and others described by the *Galveston News* as the "best and safest business men of our city." He introduced legislation incorporating the Texas European Steamship and Land Company. This company included among its incorporators C. W. Hurley, owner of C. W. Hurley Shipping and Commission Merchants in Galveston, along with two of his associates in the shipping business, a former Galveston alderman, and an important wholesale grocer. Their charter authorized them to own, build, and operate steamships to carry immigrants from Western Europe to Texas. Ruby also supported the Harbor Trust Company, which proposed digging a channel four hundred feet wide and twenty-five feet deep from the eastern end of Galveston Island, where no channel previously existed, into the bay, thus allowing another entry into the harbor. Again, the incorporators were prominent Galvestonians, often former Confederates, and included the cotton merchant William L. Moody, Jesse Batts, C. W. Hurley, and others. The editor of the *Galveston News*, offering support for the company, called the group a "strong list." Ruby worked on the behalf of these important men, but, in the end, they gave him little in the way of political encouragement.[6]

The last session of the Twelfth Legislature finally adjourned on December 2, 1871. By that time the Republicans in the legislature had come face to face with the disastrous loss in the congressional election. Their conclusions concerning that loss and their response presaged a major shift in the direction taken by white Texas Republican leaders, portending changes that did not promise a favorable future in the party for Ruby or men of his race. Ruby attended a meeting of the Republican State Executive Committee, a group composed largely of legislators, in Austin on October 23. It offered the first official response to the election and blamed the loss primarily on Democratic intimidation. In its memorial to the people of Texas, the committee contended that one step to halting intimidation was the enactment of an efficient registration law that would protect every citizen in the exercise of the right of suffrage. It also sought a new apportionment of legislative districts prior to the upcoming election, contending that many districts had been gerrymandered in favor of the Democrats. Critically, however, the committee backed away from having the state protect voter rights directly. In fact, recognizing how the cost of government had helped bring about opposition to Republican programs, it supported the reduction of the number of district courts. Instead of having state officials enforce election laws, it insisted that it was the duty of the federal government to enforce the Fourteenth and Fifteenth Amendments and protect voters. The Enforcement Acts passed by Congress in 1870 and 1871 had broadened the powers of the president to intervene in local affairs to suppress racial disorders. The committee insisted that the president should use the United States commissioners, marshals, deputy marshals, and special district attorneys to do so. It effectively denied that the state had a role in carrying out these duties. In the end, the committee's statement had the practical effect of abandoning state protection of black voters and, consequently, black politicians.[7]

Ruby still had time to serve in the senate, but on his return to Galveston he faced renewed attacks by his opponents attempting to discredit him. The charges, even though never proven and usually at odds with what was known of Ruby's character, were repeated over and over, giving the sense that he was involved in corruption even if he was not. Indeed, by this time Democrats had embraced a strategy of charging all Republican officials with dishonesty and corruption to defeat them, a strategy that helped create the characterization of the Republicans that prevailed after the Democrats returned to power. This time the *Independent*, a Democratic newspaper in Jefferson, accused Ruby of associating with lobbyists, an accusation that suggested he was being paid for his votes. Ruby replied quickly to the allegation, publishing a rebuttal in the *Houston Union*. Ruby denied that he had ever accepted anything from a lobbyist. If his accusers did not believe him, he challenged them to look at how little property he actually possessed. Additionally, he declared that while in Austin he had never visited any of the places where the "lobby" assembled, obviously pointing to the fact that much of the lobbying done in Austin took place in saloons. Such places had no interest for him, a man firmly committed to temperance. Above all, he maintained that his own "[p]ersonal dignity of character, apart from any other considerations, forbade my frequenting bar-rooms, visiting gambling or other dens of iniquity, or doing ought unbecoming." Such a response, of course, never brought an end to the attacks on his character, even though the validity of his defense speaks well of Ruby's moral qualities.[8]

In the face of an unpromising future, Ruby still worked to maintain his control over the Republican Party in his senate district and especially in Galveston, but on his return to the city after the legislature adjourned, he turned to a new endeavor that suggested that he intended finding opportunities outside the legislature. He began publishing a newspaper. In mid-February 1872, Ruby went to New Orleans, where he was welcomed by the editor of the *New Orleans Republican*, who called the senator "one of the most influential and faithful Republicans of our sister State." Ruby's trip to the Crescent City was for the purpose of purchasing supplies and equipment to publish a newspaper. He named his paper the *Standard*. While he initially planned to publish the paper only twice a week, in the first edition he announced that he hoped that he could issue it daily. He also announced what he hoped to make of his newspaper. First of all, he let it be known that he intended the *Standard* to be a Republican paper and to use its pages to support the Davis administration and also to advocate the candidacy of President Ulysses S. Grant for the Republican nomination in the upcoming 1872 presidential election. In a letter to James Newcomb, Ruby admitted that his new paper included a political purpose and asked if the state government might lend it support, welcoming whatever financial backing that he could get. He understood that money might not be available, but if Newcomb could provide no funds he wanted at the very least "aid and sympathy." If nothing else, he urged the secretary to submit an occasional for the paper. The *Standard*'s first edition appeared early in April 1872, and, as Ruby had proposed, it showed itself to be a strong advocate for Grant and the current state government. On its masthead, Ruby had included a motto that reflected the new editor's character, "Mindful of Right, We Dare to be True." In creating a successful Republican newspaper in Galveston, however, Ruby faced an uphill battle. Not only was his paper a Republican one at a time his party's fortunes were bleak, he faced competition in news coverage from the powerful *Galveston News* and *Flake's Bulletin*. Both had been in business for years, had wide circulation throughout the state, and had become modern newspapers with national and international coverage.[9]

Ruby unquestionably meant his *Standard* to have a political agenda, but he also had broader ambitions for his newspaper and maybe even for himself as a publisher if his political future collapsed. Ruby had been an inveterate letter-writer for newspapers since his time in Haiti, and he proved to be a capable author. The editorials he published matched in skill those written by Ferdinand Flake at the *Bulletin* and Willard Richardson at the *News*. In the prospectus of the *Standard*, Ruby evidenced his larger ambition when he stated that he meant the paper to be much more than a political sheet. He advertised it as a "Family Paper" that would provide the latest news from "all parts," including telegraphic reports, market reports, commercial news, and all matters of local importance. He promised to provide his readers with information on political, religious, scientific, agricultural, and literary subjects. He also indicated that he would support all "moral reforms and public measures, having or [sic] their object the improvement of the condition of Texas and her Interests." For a subscription of five dollars per year, Ruby promised that the *Standard* would be devoted "chiefly to solid matter." On the other hand, he wrote that "light and entertaining topics will have a place" as well. Ruby pledged a paper that would be "second to no paper in the State."[10]

Ruby followed the first edition of his newspaper by actively promoting it, sending the paper to black journals elsewhere in the nation, and encouraging their editors to recommend that their subscribers pick up the *Standard*. He received some significant endorsements. The editor of Frederick Douglass's *New Era* in Washington, DC, welcomed Ruby's effort, praising it as reflecting the character of its editor. "For those who know Mr. Ruby," he wrote, "we need not state that it is conducted with tact and ability." Its columns, he went on, "display industry and good judgment." Ruby obviously hoped to take advantage of the upcoming presidential election to secure party support and give his paper a start, but the fact that the *Standard* continued publication for at least a half a year following the election suggests that Ruby hoped that it would have a life beyond the 1872 campaigns. Unfortunately for Ruby, he never received the Republican Party's financial support, and without it the paper did not survive beyond that time.[11]

During its run, the pages of the *Standard* not only testified to Ruby's ambitions as a publisher, but they also provided evidence of the other activities he used to support himself and his family. Ruby used the newspaper to advertise the various services he was equipped to provide as notary. In one advertisement he offered his services as a conveyancer. Exactly what that meant in Texas at the time is unclear, but Ruby's time spent in Haiti and Louisiana would have familiarized him with the role notaries played in property transactions there. In both places, conveyancers handled legal aspects of land transactions, and it may be assumed that Ruby, although not an attorney, offered the same sort help in Texas. In one edition of the *Standard,* he also offered French and Italian immigrants assistance in dealing with legal matters in the United States. He promised that he could notarize papers they might need either in the United States or in their native lands. His advertisement, suggesting that he possessed some fluency in both French and Italian, offered the help of "L'Honorable G. T. Ruby, Notaire Publique." He went on to note "avertit les citoyens Francaiset Italiens qu' ila pourraient avoir besoin soit ici ou dans leur pays natal [sic]," that he could provide services needed by French or Italians needed either in Texas or their native lands.[12]

Through its existence, Ruby used his newspaper to promote the basic idea of racial equality that he had long advocated. His editorial pages provide particular insight into his views on race problems and their solutions. The newspaper's history, however, also indicated his willingness to work practically to achieve that end. When he started the paper, he hired black workers whenever he could. This practice got him into trouble with white employees when he hired a black man to one of the skilled jobs, a compositor's position. No black man had held such a job in Galveston previously, and two of the white printers presented Ruby with an ultimatum. They refused to work with the black compositor and threatened to quit unless Ruby fired the man. Ruby believed that his Democratic opponents had encouraged the white workers to make their threats to destroy Ruby's business. Ruby, however, refused to give in to the blackmail and let the two white workers go. He hired two black printers to replace them. The action made clear that Ruby not only supported equal opportunities in theory but in practice. He also managed to keep printing the paper despite this effort to stop its publication.[13]

Ruby's search for other potential venues for his career and reform work also took him onto the national scene, where he became prominent in his support of efforts to get the passage of a new civil rights bill sponsored in the United States Senate by Senator Charles Sumner of Massachusetts. This particular bill had been introduced into the Senate in December 1871, and was similar to other proposed legislation introduced in May 1870, January 1871, and then again in March 1871. The new bill offered far-reaching protection, providing that the federal government would guarantee "equal and impartial enjoyment of all accommodation, advantage, facility, or privilege furnished by common carriers, whether on land or water; by inn-keepers; by licensed owners . . . of theatres or other places of public amusements; by trustees . . . teachers, or other officers of common schools and other public institutions of learning . . . [and] by officers of church organizations, [and] cemetery associations." It further barred discrimination on the basis of color in any "law, statute, ordinance, regulation, or custom." This time, Sumner attached it as an amendment to a bill granting amnesty to former Confederates, intending either to assure blacks of their civil rights or to block the amnesty bill. Sumner's bill got hung up in the Senate once again, and he encouraged both his white and black allies nationwide to offer support. For southern blacks like Ruby the backing away by state governments from the protection of basic civil rights made this bill essential.[14]

Ruby had supported such measures from the beginning of Reconstruction, and in 1872 he joined with other blacks around the nation to advocate Sumner's new bill. In Galveston the creation of the Galveston Civil Rights Association on January 15 was the first step towards providing that backing. Ruby was in New Orleans at the time, but his allies sponsored the meeting, indicating Ruby's support of the group. Forty men attended the Civil Rights Association's first meeting at the AME Church. Johnson Reed, who had been president of the previous year's labor convention, took the presidency of the association, having reconciled with Ruby by this point. The association elected John DeBruhl, an employee in the Custom House and part of the cadre of black treasury department appointees associated with Ruby, as secretary. Unquestionably representing George Ruby's interest, even though the senator was not there himself, his brother Horatio was elected assistant secretary.[15]

The following April, 1872, Ruby attended the Colored Men's National Convention in New Orleans, marking his certain connection with the Galveston Civil Rights Association. He, Wright Cuney, and Representative Richard Allen sailed to New Orleans on the Morgan Line's *Norfolk*, reaching the city on April 10 after a trip uneventful enough, given Ruby's previous experience with the Morgan Line, that the *State Journal* remarked on how kindly Ruby had been treated. The Colored Men's Convention was another of the gatherings of black leaders to voice their concerns with national issues that had begun prior to the Civil War, of the sort that had attracted George's father Reuben. The New Orleans convention had been called by Frederick Douglass, the prominent black abolitionist and advocate of equal rights, and was a continuation of a similar meeting in Charleston held the year before. Douglass set the agenda for the New Orleans meeting in a telegram that he sent to Congressman John Mercer Langston, who spoke for Douglass when Douglass was delayed in getting to New Orleans. "Let our demand be, first, legal equality; second the passage of the Civil Rights Bill." Douglass further urged the delegates to assure no rupture occurred in the Republican Party, an ironic position given his own candidacy for vice president on the Equal Rights Party ticket later that year. To allow the Republican Party to be disrupted, he wrote, would give power to the Democrats and not work for the well-being of blacks.[16]

Ruby's appearance at the convention associated him with some of the most prominent black leaders in the nation at that time. They included, of course, Frederick Douglass, the best-known African American social reformer of the age. Northerners present included Peter H. Clarke, a black abolitionist, publisher, and educator from Ohio, and George Lewis Ruffin, a black member of the Massachusetts legislature. Newspapers also noted the presence of many blacks who had risen to prominence in the South during Reconstruction. Lieutenant Governor Alonzo J. Ransier and Secretary of State Francis L. Cardoza represented South Carolina. John Mercer Langston, a black congressman and Douglass's personal representative until he arrived, was from Virginia. James T. Rapier was a candidate for Congress from Alabama, while Ruby's friend Lieutenant Governor P. B. S. Pinchback of Louisiana was the leader of the Louisiana delegation. Ruby's presence and his role in the convention signified that at least among black leaders he had achieved a considerable reputation of his own.[17]

The convention opened on April 11 and elected officers. Douglass had not yet arrived, but the delegates immediately elected him president of the convention. Ruby's friend James H. Ingraham from New Orleans was chosen first vice president. The convention elected Ruby as permanent secretary. Election to this post provided further evidence of the esteem in which Ruby's associates held him, for the secretary did more than simply take minutes; he also helped establish the convention agenda and handle the correspondence and publications related to the meeting. Countering any desertions from the Republican Party by black workers was the first business dealt with by the delegates. James Rapier moved towards that goal when he introduced a resolution that repudiated the Labor Reform Convention held at Columbus, Ohio, which had been sponsored by the National Labor Union, for nominating its own candidate for president. The resolution also condemned the Liberal Republican convention, held in Cincinnati, for its nomination of a candidate to run against President Grant. Lieutenant Governor Pinchback opposed the resolution, not because he supported their decisions to oppose the president but because it implicitly condemned Senator Charles Sumner, who supported the Liberals. At that point the convention bogged down and waited for Douglass's arrival.[18]

On April 13, with Frederick Douglass finally presiding, the convention's Committee on Civil Rights reported resolutions that aligned closely with Ruby's long-term goals. The resolutions essentially advocated the Sumner civil rights bill, asking politicians to support legislation that removed all disabilities from blacks, protected them, and secured redress against common carriers that discriminated on account of color. The delegates demanded equal access to education and instruction in the schools, the right of entrance and entertainment in hotels, places of amusement, and other places of public resort, and redress against those who refused access. It suggested that when the American people fully understood the wrongs done against blacks, justice would be done.[19]

They got around the problem that Rapier raised with his blanket condemnation of the Labor Reform and Liberal Republican conventions by adopting resolutions thanking President Grant for appointing black men to office. They threw their support to his and Vice President Schuyler Colfax's reelection. At the same time, they promised to work against all politicians who opposed Sumner's civil rights act and acknowledged their indebtedness to Charles Sumner. In a direct attack against Democrats, who frequently charged that blacks wanted the government to legislate social equality, they declared that there was a difference between what they considered civil and social rights. They equated social rights with social standing. The latter could be determined only by personal merit and individual achievement and not by law. Again, countering a frequent Democratic attack on black aspirations, they specifically denied that forced school integration was the dominant idea of the convention and, indeed, rejected the idea of racial amalgamation.[20]

On the last day of the convention the members gave Douglass authority to name delegates to attend another national convention, should one be needed. Douglass's appointments included the elite of black politicians in the South at the time: Pinchback of Louisiana; Ransier of South Carolina; Mifflin Gibbs of Arkansas; Rapier of Alabama; Henry McNeal Turner of Georgia; and John J. Spellman of Mississippi, editor of the *Jackson Colored Citizen.* The same was true of the men he selected from the North. These included George T. Downing of Rhode Island, an intimate of Senator Sumner; Lewis H. Douglass of New York, a former non-commissioned officer in the Fifty-Fourth Massachusetts Infantry and son of Frederick Douglass; and Charles Henry Langston, a Kansas educator. Douglass chose Ruby to represent Texas, providing further recognition of Ruby's significance among the nation's black leadership.[21]

Ruby had little further opportunity to support the Sumner bill, however, for when he returned to Texas he faced the urgent problem of organizing Republicans in Galveston and his district for the election to be held that October. The 1872 election would be the first general election held in the state since 1869 and would be critical for the future of the state's Republican Party and the Davis administration. There was of course the presidential election, but more critically for Texas Republicans there were important local contests. All of the seats in the Texas House of Representatives would be contested. A third of the seats would be open in the senate. Additionally, there would be a new election for the United States Congress. A reapportionment following the 1870 census had given Texas an additional seat. The four sitting congressman faced reelection, but in addition an at-large seat would be at stake. County and city offices would be part of the election. Two major amendments to the state constitution also would be on the ballots. One would permanently establish the seat of government in Texas, with Houston vying with Austin for that place. Another would repeal the constitutional restriction on land grants for internal improvements. Holding on to the house and senate were particularly important for the future of Republicanism in the state. Ruby's job was delivering his district for the party.

As in 1871, Ruby had to deal with an insurgency within the Republican Party itself. This time it was the emergence of the Liberal Republican movement. Liberal Republicanism had developed the previous year in Missouri. Senator Carl Schurz from that state was its initial leader, but it soon grew into a national movement. Its chief aims were to attack what it considered to be the corrupt wing of its own party, the wing connected to President Grant. By this time the Liberal Republican's supporters favored bringing an end to Reconstruction and also legislating civil service reform to bring an end to the patronage system that they considered to be a corrupting influence on both the party and the government. The Liberal Republicans had held their convention in Cincinnati on May 1–4, 1872. The Liberals nominated Horace Greeley to run on their ticket. This was the convention opposed by the Colored Men's Convention in New Orleans. Liberal leaders also thought that it might be possible to bring about a fusion with Democrats who had come to be known as "New Departure" Democrats, men who were willing to accept the results of the war and Reconstruction to gain control of the government. Ironically, given black opposition to the Liberals, Charles Sumner became associated with the reformers.

Liberal Republicans in Texas held their first organizational meeting in Austin at about the same time that Ruby was in New Orleans attending the Colored Men's Convention. While the meeting was in Austin, those who attended elected delegates to the Cincinnati Convention from other counties as well as from Travis County. The list of delegates indicated that the majority of these Liberal Republicans had been part of the Jack Hamilton campaign in 1869 and had never fully supported the Davis administration. The delegates included Judge Thomas Stribling, a prominent former Unionist, and Julius Berends, a bookseller and prominent German leader in the Republican Party, both from Bexar County. Ferdinand Flake of *Flake's Bulletin*, a long-time critic of the Davis administration, was selected to represent Galveston. Former governors Elisha M. Pease and A. J. Hamilton were also chosen. Both of these men had opposed Davis in 1869 and had been part of a taxpayer's movement in the fall of 1871 that had condemned the Republican administration's taxes. Albert Bledsoe, the state's comptroller, who had been a strong supporter of Governor Davis but believed that the International Railroad Company had secured its grant of bonds from the legislature by bribing legislators and that many Republican leaders were implicated in the scandal, also aligned with the Liberals.[22]

When the Texas Liberals arrived in Cincinnati, the character of the Texas Liberal Party could be seen even more readily as consisting for the most part of politicians who had broken with the regular party organization or who had never been a part of it. Pease, Hamilton, and Stribling were notably present. Senator Morgan C. Hamilton, whom the regular Republicans of Texas had attempted to remove from office, also appeared on that day. When the Texans voted for the party's nominees, they overwhelmingly supported Horace Greeley of the *New York Tribune* for the presidency, and he ultimately secured the nomination. They supported a Missourian, B. Gratz Brown, for vice president, and Brown received the nomination. The Texans aligned with the Liberal Republicans continued to pursue the same course in politics that they had the previous September in seeking some sort of middle course that would bring them together with Democrats willing to accept Reconstruction. Such a coalition posed a serious threat to regular Republicans in Texas and to Ruby, virtually guaranteeing a defeat unless the party could hold on to its base in the black community and attract more white voters. Ruby's ability to mobilize the black political base became even more critical in the circumstances.[23]

Ruby began his efforts to organize for the upcoming campaign in Galveston with a meeting of Republicans held on May 1. Ruby had by this time turned most of the day-to-day operations of the party in Galveston over to Wright Cuney. Cuney, as the chairman of the Galveston County Executive Committee, called the meeting to elect delegates to the upcoming state Republican convention in Houston. Reporters from the Republican and Democratic newspapers present at the event provided widely varying accounts of what followed, but it was clear that dissidents within the Galveston party, usually arguing that they wished to reform it and consisting of men who had been part of the Stevenson revolt the previous year, were ready to try to take over the party organization. The *Galveston News* indicated that Judge Samuel Dodge, whom Ruby had tried to get rid of the previous year, protested the meeting and printed a letter that indicated he considered Cuney's call to be irregular. He believed he was still chairman of the county executive committee. Contending the Cuney meeting was illegal, Dodge wrote that he would not attend the state convention if chosen by the Cuney gathering. As in 1871, however, Ruby maintained tight control over the convention. At the May 1 meeting Ruby was present, and he pushed forward the administration agenda. The delegates chose Collector Patten as temporary chairman, indicating that Ruby had the votes in the convention to place party regulars into position. Patten then nominated Judge D. J. Baldwin, a former supporter of A. J. Hamilton who then served as district attorney for the federal courts on the recommendation of the Davis administration, as permanent chair. Ruby also nominated other officers, including Henry Allen, the successful black candidate for secretary. The reporter for the *News* suggested that the meeting became fractious, with party leaders forced to use the police to suppress dissent. He wrote that when Patten moved to appoint a committee on resolutions, John DuPish, a former Stevenson supporter, complained that this appeared to be a one-man meeting run by the "Patten, Ruby, and Cuney" party, and objected to the proceedings. Another man in the audience then declared that this was just another "put up job." When R. F. Cordua, another reformer connected to the local temperance society, continued to complain, and refused to be silenced, the chair, according to the *News* reporter, called on the police to remove Cordua, who, in turn, fought the police as he was carried out. At this point another former Stevenson supporter, Justice Richard Nelson, allegedly complained that unless the people had a voice in selecting the committee he would withdraw from the meeting.[24]

The fact that the reporter for Richard Nelson's newspaper, the *Representative*, described a completely different meeting suggests that the reporter for the *News* may actually have been trying to stir up more trouble among Republicans. The account in the *Representative* suggested that the meeting had to a considerable degree focused on promoting harmony within the party in the face of the resurging Democrats and the Liberal Republicans. Following the naming of the Resolutions Committee, headed by Ruby, this reporter informed his readers that Benjamin F. Williams, the representative from Colorado County who had been another Stevenson man in 1871, delivered a speech calling for harmony within the party while the committee drafted its resolutions. The resolutions themselves indicated no continuing strife. Instead, they expressed loyalty to the national party and praised General Grant for his representation of the people. In the wake of the previous campaign season's difficulties, they deprecated all divisions within the party's ranks and pledged themselves to secure harmony in their conduct. The delegation included Judge D. J. Baldwin, Representative Plumley, Collector Patten, United States Marshal William E. Parker, Nelson from the *Representative*, Wright Cuney, and Ruby. The former Stevenson supporters, however, got only one position on the delegation, Frank Webb from the now-defunct *Galveston Republican*.[25]

On May 14, 1872, the Republican Party held its state convention in Houston. Ruby attended and once again played a major role in the operations of the convention when he was elected, along with James Newcomb, one of the secretaries. The election of Ruby and Newcomb, plus the selection of James Tracy to head the credentials committee, indicated that the administration controlled the convention, although the same sort of turmoil that had plagued the party since the previous year persisted. A floor fight broke out almost immediately over whether or not the convention would seat proxies, men considered to be Davis supporters who were chosen to represent counties from which delegates could not travel. Some black delegates complained that this was the effort of the convention managers to control the convention for their candidates. Ruby attempted to get the chair's recognition to move acceptance of the proxies, but amidst the turmoil the chair adjourned the convention. At the end of the first day the reporter for the *Galveston News* believed that despite the problems, James Tracy had the "inside track" for the administration's nominees. He also believed that a conflict had arisen between Tracy and Superintendent of Education De-

Gress, although he failed to elaborate on the character of their differences. In the end, however, the two reportedly harmonized, thus putting an end to another potential internal problem.[26]

On the second day of the convention the delegates finally moved to create a permanent organization, naming Richard H. Taylor of Fannin County, a supporter of Governor Davis, as president. Ruby again secured a position as one of the convention's secretaries. Taylor attempted to settle the disputes among the various factions, promising that he was "not the slave of any ring or clique" and that he came from the "plow-handle party, without the stain of official corruption." During the subsequent speeches Ruby and the other black delegates worked to ensure that the convention strongly endorsed efforts at securing full civil rights for blacks. Matt Gaines offered a resolution that proposed sending no delegates to the national convention unless they pledged themselves to vote for Grant and to support the civil rights bill. Richard Nelson, on behalf of the Galveston delegation, introduced a resolution endorsing the course of Senator Sumner, "believing the Civil Rights bill to be the natural outgrowth of the 15th Amendment." Ruby remained behind the scenes, not taking to the floor, although his hand could be seen in the resolutions of support for Sumner and the civil rights bill, resolutions which reflected the goals set in the New Orleans Colored Men's Convention.[27]

On the third day the convention finally settled on its platform, largely indicating its support for the National Republican Party and its basic tenet of sustaining the doctrine of equal rights, maintaining its commitment to Ruby and the party's black constituents. The convention also endorsed the Grant administration and the president's run for reelection. It attacked the Greeley candidacy, stating the party's contention that Greeley's run was essentially a Democratic one and not supported by any true Republican. The platform also endorsed the "personal integrity and the incorruptibility" of Governor Davis, then declared it the duty of the state to educate all children, to practice rigid economy, to condemn "official stealing," and to advocate frontier protection. A further resolution endorsed Governor Davis as a candidate for vice president. A fight then blew up again over who would go to the national convention. When the report of the committee assigned that task came before the convention, a motion was made to lay it on the table. The Tracy faction voted aye, while the DeGress faction voted no. In the vote the ayes won, forcing a reconsideration of how to name delegates. Ultimately, a decision was made to let the congressional delegations for each district recommend delegates to Philadelphia. Ruby was chosen to go to Philadelphia as the delegate at large for the Third Congressional District. Although the coverage of the *News* suggested considerable friction still remained at the end of the convention, the reporter for *Flake's Bulletin*, another hostile source but not as much as the *News*, described the convention as adjourning "amidst the best of seeming good feeling." [28]

Ruby returned to Galveston and immediately left for Philadelphia to attend the National Republican Convention. Wright Cuney and Representative Richard Nelson once again accompanied him, going as alternate delegates. They left Galveston on May 25, arriving at Brashear City where they took the train to New Orleans and arrived on May 27. On his arrival Ruby was welcomed as a visiting dignitary and a friend. The administrator of the police department took the three on a "*tour de la ville.*" Ruby also called on a large number of local public officials, learning what he could about local politics. As in most of his previous trips out of the state, he worked to secure connections with the local politicians. He paid a social call to the editor of the *New Orleans Republican*. He visited men with whom he had made connections during the days he spent in the state's public school system prior to his move to Texas and then during the Colored Men's Convention. These included James H. Ingraham, who was one of Ruby's earliest acquaintances in the city and who was now surveyor of the Port of New Orleans. Ruby saw in Ingraham a model of the African American success story, a man who "by earnest work and unselfish purpose" had benefitted the Reconstruction process in the state. Ruby also made contact with the most prominent federal officials in the city, including men who were part of what political opponents disparagingly called the Custom House Ring, including Collector of Customs James F. Casey and the United States marshal, Stephen B. Packard.[29]

In letters to his *Galveston Standard*, Ruby described in some detail the political situation in Louisiana, proving himself once again to be an acute observer of the local political scene. He found that the Republican Party in Louisiana faced the same sort of internal divisions being dealt with by the Texas party, a struggle between Republican officials at the state level and federal appointees. At the time, Louisiana Governor Henry C. Warmoth was considering a move to support the Liberal Republican movement, backed by then Lieutenant Governor Pinchback. Warmoth's alignment with the Liberals made some sense, since he had become exceedingly unpopular with Marshal Packard and Collector Casey, leaders of the Custom House Ring. To advance their cause, Warmoth and Pinchback had called a convention to meet in New Orleans while Ruby was present, and Ruby sent firsthand accounts back to his readers in Galveston. Warmoth and Pinchback, however, had come to a disagreement on how this convention should proceed, with Warmoth wanting it to endorse Greeley and make nominations for state offices. Pinchback simply wanted to select delegates to send to the Republican convention in Philadelphia. Ruby reported that it was unclear how Warmoth and Pinchback would resolve their differences, since Warmoth controlled many of the country delegates while Pinchback controlled the delegates from New Orleans. In the end, Warmoth secured control of the convention's offices but failed to secure the endorsement of Greeley and the nominations he desired. Later that June an effort at patching up the differences between the Warmoth–Pinchback faction and the Custom House Ring failed in a meeting in Baton Rouge, a breakup that led to disastrous results for the Republicans there in the future. Ruby's reporting was a clear warning of the dangers of internal party divisions. Events in Louisiana also had significance for his own future.[30]

Ruby's reporting from New Orleans took particular note of the fate of black Louisianans who had attended the Liberal Republican convention in

Cincinnati, sounding a warning to black Texans against supporting any party other than the Republican Party. It suggested negative results for blacks supporting Greeley and his party. In Cincinnati, Texas Liberals found that black people living in Cincinnati opposed the Liberals and objected to any blacks supporting the organization. As a result, the delegates could not find "decent" accommodations and were forced to room in "obscure quarters." Indeed, the locals subjected them to "insults." The group included Louis T. Delassize, the administrator of the New Orleans waterworks and one of the city's prominent creole leaders, whose white wife was born in France. Worse, the Liberals found themselves despised by white Democrats as well. The latter reportedly jeered at the presence of the blacks who were willing to "barter the dearest rights of their people by their presence there."[31]

Ruby and his party finally left for Philadelphia on May 29. The trip proved to be an eventful one. His train, filled with the Texas delegation riding in "one of Pullman's best," at a cost of $140 each way, and with numerous Louisiana delegates to the Philadelphia convention, left New Orleans to the music of a band and the "waving of handkerchiefs, the huzzas of the crowd and the benedictions of friends." Thirty miles out of the city the train stopped, prevented from moving forward by the wreck of a freight train. After waiting most of the day the train returned to New Orleans. The delegates started again on May 30. This time the train moved forward without delay, and Ruby and his fellow delegates arrived in Philadelphia on June 2. Their arrival in Philadelphia, however, was not auspicious and differed little from that of the black delegates who had gone to the Liberal convention. They arrived at the Continental Hotel, the convention hotel, and created what a reporter for the *Philadelphia Inquirer* called a "slight disturbance in the political atmosphere." They were told that all of the rooms in the hotel were engaged. After consulting with national committee members, the national leaders finally arranged for the black delegates to lodge elsewhere. They did take their meals at the Continental. "It is stated," the reporter wrote, "that this is the first colored party that ever took their meals at this restaurant." White delegates did find rooms at the Continental.[32]

Ruby and the black delegates also found the convention itself to be unwelcoming, reflecting an already changing attitude on the part of Northern Republicans to the situation in the South. A reporter for the *New York Herald* contended that the black delegates from Texas were the "noisiest and wildest" but that they were largely ignored. When the temporary president of the convention made initial assignments, he named numerous white Texans to the temporary committees, including Representative W. A. Saylor to the credentials committee, Judge W. A. Ellett to the permanent organization committee, Senator J. W. Talbot to the Resolutions Committee, and James Newcomb to the Committee on Rules and Regulations. Ruby, eventually, was named as a secretary of the convention. At a national convention, however, the position was largely honorific and had little real function.[33]

There actually proved little to do for the Texans, black or white, although Ruby did have at least one opportunity to make himself known to a wider audience. As to the outcome of the convention, Grant's nomination was assured from the beginning, as he possessed the almost unanimous support of delegates from the Northern states. Texans could do little other than add their own voices to that majority. When it came time for the Texas delegation to cast its vote for the presidential nomination, the chairman of the delegation, President pro tem of the State Senate Webster Flanagan, addressed the convention, saying, "Texas, unlike any other State, casts 16 votes, and would like to have the privilege of casting 32 votes, and would that it were 32,000, for U. S. Grant. (Applause)." Ruby had his opportunity to speak when nominations opened for the vice presidency. At that time the newspapers reported that "a colored delegate" from Texas rose to speak. The unnamed delegate surely was Ruby, who had the reputation as being the best speaker among the blacks in the delegation. Ruby nominated Governor Davis for vice president. Reporters could barely hear him because of confusion on the convention floor, but the delegate pushed ahead in putting Davis's name forward, praising Davis as a "'man within her own borders,' who was always 'in favor of right and justice.'" It was a singular moment for Ruby in the public eye, even though lost in the confusion of the convention and the lack of concern by white reporters for the lone black delegate to make a nomination. In the end the Texans cast all of their votes for Henry Wilson for vice president, going along with the decisions of the national party's leaders.[34]

Ruby returned to New Orleans following the convention and was in the city on June 21. An item in the *New Orleans Republican* noted that he intended going to Maine in order to visit his father in Portland, but he did not make the trip. By the end of June he was back in Texas, where he began working for Grant's reelection. He appeared first at a meeting of city Republicans held in Houston to ratify Grant's nomination by the national convention. The opposition press, as always, published articles intended to undermine Ruby's credibility and also to help disorganize the Republicans. An item in the *Houston Telegraph* reported that Ruby had actually admitted that Greeley, the Liberal candidate, had been an abolitionist before the war. The editor wished all Republicans would admit that Greeley supported emancipation and securing black rights. The *Telegraph* and *Flake's Bulletin* also reported that after hearing Ruby's speech the crowd had voted to endorse Greeley. Ruby's own paper, however, denied anything like that happened and instead indicated that the event had been a "great meeting." A correspondent of the *Houston Union* likewise reported no endorsement of Greeley and wrote that Ruby had given a "very good Grant and Wilson speech." The only complaint made by the *Union*'s correspondent was that the address had not gone over well with the crowd. He believed that Ruby's speech may have been "too elevated in sentiment and language for the audience," a comment that suggested Ruby may have become less connected to his constituents.[35]

In the midst of the presidential campaign, Ruby had to deal with the usual complications related to local party affairs. One of the most significant, because it suggested that the Grant administration might be shifting away from supporting local party organizations when filling patronage jobs, was word that former Congressman Clark had been named to the important position of postmaster in Galveston. By this time local Republicans considered Clark an outsider who had done little to hang onto his seat in Congress, providing little evidence in the congressional hearings concerning his contested election with Giddings. The appointment of someone out of favor among Texas Republicans denied the state party one of the choicest patronage positions in the state. Ruby's newspaper responded to this bad news with an expression of friendship for Clark but at the same time suggested that it would be better if someone from among the business interests of Galveston be named. If there was no such person, then any good local Republican would do. The editor of the *Galveston News* was struck by the change in feeling towards Clark on the part of Ruby. "'*Et tu Rube?*'" he wrote. "This is the most unkindest cut of all." His own party no longer revered Clark. The editor went on to suggest, however, that "it is not that Ruby loves Clark *less*, but the office of postmaster *more. Quin* [sic] *sabe.*" Later rumors suggested that Ruby had been appointed postmaster for Galveston, in the place of former Congressman Clark. This would have provided Ruby a future in Texas, given the unlikelihood of his maintaining his position in the senate. The rumor, however, proved false.[36]

Even with the disappointment that President Grant caused with his failure to appoint Ruby and his placing of Clark in the position instead, Ruby remained loyal and continued an active campaign through the summer. He chaired a meeting in Galveston on the evening of July 15 that ratified the Philadelphia nomination. On July 25 he participated in the organization of a Grant and Wilson Club in Galveston, an organization that attempted to appeal to German voters with the naming of F. C. Mosebach as president but with Ruby's associates named to all of the other offices. On August 5 he appeared at a meeting organized to elect delegates to the congressional district convention in Houston and read political tracts from his own newspaper. This meeting then chose Ruby, his brother Horatio, and other members of Ruby's Galveston faction to go to Houston. He helped resolve a dispute between members of the Galveston Grant and Wilson Club concerning whether or not to open their meetings at a gathering on September 18. Ruby opted for moving away from the secrecy local whites usually associated with the Loyal League. He was present, along with his brother Horatio, at a meeting in Galveston's Second Ward on October 3 that organized its own Grant and Wilson Club. By October, Ruby had the organization of Galveston at least well in hand.[37]

His efforts paid off on October 10, when Galveston County Republicans held their convention at Morian Hall to nominate candidates for sheriff, treasurer, surveyor, and hide inspector. The officers were in the Ruby camp, with Johnson Reed, still back in line in the regular party, calling the meeting to order and John DeBruhl elected president. The convention presented a new strategy for the county organization. Despite the domination of the meeting by blacks, all of the candidates selected to run for office were white. Not only Ruby, but party leaders too had realized by this time that black candidates had no chance of being elected in Galveston and that to nominate black candidates offered no hope of success. Ruby appeared to have agreed to this situation, even if reluctantly. The reporter for the *Galveston Bulletin* recognized the shift. Reporting on a talk he had had with a black delegate, he quoted the man as explaining that "de niggas couldn't 'spect to 'lect dar men, and didn't keer ef de white trash was bested!" While the quotation obviously was made up by the reporter, or at least the dialect was, further information on the convention suggested that finding candidates that could attract white Democratic support was at the center of Republican considerations at the time. In addition, Republicans had come to realize that their black constituents could not even help to bankroll the party. In an evening session, a collection was taken up to pay for the expenses of delegates to the senate district convention in Brazoria, but only $5.85 was realized. Ruby then proposed that the alternates be permitted to go to Brazoria, suggesting that they had the wherewithal to defray the half-fare rates being offered by the railroads. At Brazoria, the shift from black candidates was even more evident, with only John DeBruhl chosen to run for a seat in the legislature. The other two positions went to previous white unknowns—Christopher Olfson, a young attorney from Galveston, and Christopher Higgins, a school director in Brazoria County.[38]

Ruby moved on to campaign more widely after his districts selected their candidates. On October 20, at Bryan in Brazos County, he appeared with leading white Republicans. These included A. J. Evans, the Republican candidate for Congress in the Third District, who hoped to unseat D. C. Giddings, and was at the gathering speaking for his candidacy. United States Senator James W. Flanagan, long at odds with the Davis administration, also was there and spoke on behalf of President Grant. Flanagan urged his listeners to give their support to the president, arguing that they should feel indebted to him for their freedom and the privileges they held as citizens. After a barbecue dinner, Ruby spoke, although newspapers provided no coverage of what he said. On October 18, Ruby appeared in Calverton, the future town of Calvert in Robertson County, at a Republican barbecue along with Evans, Judge Anthony B. Norton, Governor Davis, Colonel Charles C. Gillespie, and other white speakers. Again, little note was paid to what Ruby said or how the crowd received him. The shift from reliance on black candidates and black support was even more apparent in these gatherings. Except for Ruby, all the speakers were white, and even Republican newspapers had begun to ignore Ruby.[39]

The returns in the congressional election had not been good, but those in the 1872 election proved even worse in Ruby's senate district. In every one of the counties the vote for Grant was less than that for Clark in 1871. In Galveston County, President Grant picked up 1,252 votes while Horace Greeley secured 2,413. More critically, in Matagorda County few voters turned out and the president received 365 votes to Greeley's 135. Only in Brazoria did the Republicans manage to get a good turnout, 1,019 to 244. Still, Ruby's district overall polled 2,636 votes for the Republican president and 2,792 for his challenger, although the relatively low vote for Greeley probably reflected the reluctance of many Democrats to vote for him. The legislative vote was even more disturbing. Three Democrats and three Republicans had run for the three seats to represent the Third Senatorial District in the House of Representatives in the Thirteenth Legislature. T. M. Joseph was the leading Democratic candidate, receiving 2,440 votes in

Galveston, 216 in Brazoria, and 136 in Matagorda. His fellow Democrats received roughly the same number of votes. They received a combined total of 2,792 votes, astonishingly the exact same number cast for Greeley in the district. John DeBruhl, the one black candidate in the race, ran slightly behind Grant, receiving 1,239 votes in Galveston, 1,004 in Brazoria, and 335 in Matagorda, for a total of 2,578 votes. While the Republican candidate actually carried Brazoria and Matagorda Counties, the Galveston vote overmatched those totals. In a presidential election, the turnout for both parties had increased. Republican candidates in the 1871 congressional race had received only 2147 votes. The results clearly indicated that Ruby's place in the state senate would not be safe in the next election, indeed not safe for any Republican candidate.[40]

The 1872 election results confirmed what had been apparent in 1871. A Republican candidate, and especially a black one, had little future in the Twelfth Senate District. No matter what Ruby had done to attract white voters and especially the business interests of his district, white business leaders in Galveston would not support him or any other Republicans. These elections forced Republicans to consider new tactics if they hoped to continue to play any role in state or even local politics. At the same time, the returns required George Ruby to think even more seriously about his own course in the future. In the immediate wake of the 1872 elections he gave no indication of what he considered that course to be. With still another term to serve in the state senate, he nonetheless looked for a new road that would allow him to achieve the goals he had pursued throughout his political career. Events in 1873 saw him continue to search for the path to his future and to consider whether or not that future would be in Texas.

CHAPTER XII

THE LAST POLITICAL FIGHT IN TEXAS, 1873–1874

"[A]s good a selection for that place as his party could have made. He is a man of considerable ability."—On Ruby's appointment as chairman of the State Republican Executive Committee, Galveston News, *August 22, 1873*

The results of the 1872 general election in George Ruby's senate district, marking the return to the polls of white Democratic voters, all but ensured the end of Ruby's career as an elected official in Texas. Because he had drawn the long term in 1870, he remained a member of the Thirteenth Legislature when its session began in January 1873, but the balance of power had shifted there, leaving him few options for exercising any real power. To ensure a future where he could continue to pursue his long-sought goal of obtaining equal rights for his race, or even to make a living, he was forced to look elsewhere than political office for such opportunities. Throughout that year he hoped to receive some sort of patronage appointment in the federal government. He may also have thought he could remain politically active in Galveston as the publisher of his newspaper, the *Standard*. The survival of his newspaper depended, however, on whether or not he could get contracts for federal printing since such subsidies were required by almost every successful newspaper at the time. He also began looking outside of Texas for prospects, something he had actually been considering all along. The year 1873 was a critical one for Ruby, as he focused on the next stage of his life.

His work in the state senate occupied much of Ruby's time in the spring of 1873. The Thirteenth Legislature began its session on January 14 of that year. The session was a particularly long one and did not adjourn until June 24. When Ruby arrived in Austin, the makeup of both houses of the legislature made clear the impact of the previous election on the Republican Party. Democrats had carried races not only in Ruby's district but also across the state. In the house of representatives, where every seat had been up for election, the Republican majority had disappeared. Just thirteen Republicans remained out of the eighty-eight representatives. In the senate, where only a third of the members were up for election, Republicans held only thirteen of the thirty seats. Democrats controlled both houses, although in the senate they did not have the two-thirds majority necessary to override a gubernatorial veto. In the session, Ruby continued to serve on numerous committees, including important ones such as the committees on constitutional amendments, judiciary, public debt, redistricting, and state affairs. He also remained as chair on the Committee on Engrossed Bills. Given the Democratic majority, however, Ruby had little ability to influence the course of events during the five and a half months of the legislative session.[1]

Ruby and the other Republican senators had to watch as the Democratic majority began dismantling the Davis administration's legislative legacy. Democrats moved almost immediately to abolish the State Police. They altered the State Militia to get rid of the State Guards that Davis had used as a force to respond rapidly to violence. They also shifted the power to declare martial law out of the hands of the governor. As to the public schools, the majority essentially moved control of schools to county school boards, effectively limiting the power of the state superintendent of schools, ending any sort of central administration. A new printing law shifted the public printing from the Republican *State Journal* and other party newspapers to Democratic journals. The majority also passed particularly critical legislation relative to black voting. They reapportioned legislative districts, gerrymandering them by placing majority black counties together with white majority counties in a way that created new districts with more white voters than black, thus minimizing the impact of black voting in elections. They shifted voting from the county seat, where order might be better maintained and fraud prevented, to precincts. They limited elections to one day, abandoning the four days required in the old law. Particularly relevant for Ruby's future, the legislature passed a law providing for a general election to be held on the first Tuesday in December, December 2, 1873. This measure, aimed by Democrats at purging the senate of even more Republicans, would bring an end to the long terms drawn by Ruby and other Republicans in 1870 and force new elections in their districts. Ruby attempted to block most of this legislation by sustaining the governor's vetoes, but enough Republicans abandoned the governor so that the Democrats succeeded in their efforts.[2]

Ruby also found himself unable to resist a flood of corporate giveaways considered by the now Democratic-controlled legislature. Ruby had not opposed state support for corporations, and he had backed the issue of state bonds for the International Railroad, despite the opposition of Governor Davis. Still, the gift of state bonds and tax breaks for corporations enacted by the Thirteenth Legislature was extravagant, and Ruby opposed much of what happened. Before the Thirteenth adjourned it passed 319 special laws, including the creation of thirty-eight railroads, four canal companies, and five bridge companies. To support these creations the legislature also passed some fifty-three special laws authorizing counties and towns to issue bonds or raise taxes to promote such developments, and gave away thousands of acres of state lands. The Democrats had accused the Republicans of extravagance, but their own legislation far surpassed the corporate giveaways dealt out by their Republican opponents. Ruby voted against most of these measures, but he was now with the minority. Again, Ruby saw enough Republicans vote with the Democrats that his vote to sustain the governor's vetoes was unsuccessful.[3]

Despite his relative inability to maintain the governor's militia, police, and schools or to prevent the massive giveaways, Ruby did continue to take care of the day-to-day business of his constituents. On January 30, for example, he introduced a bill amending the charter of the Galveston Medical College. Later he submitted a resolution that was sent to a special committee to consider the erection of monuments to Stephen F. Austin and Sam Houston. He provided support for a legislative resolution to Congress that encouraged the federal government to construct a ship channel across the Florida peninsula and into the Gulf of Mexico. In April he unsuccessfully attempted to keep the senate from trying James Tracy and removing him from his seat in the house of representatives for alleged fraud. He also made what the reporter for the *Galveston News* called an "eloquent and elaborate attempt" to defeat a Democratic-sponsored house resolution of sympathy for white paramilitaries arrested in the wake of the Colfax Massacre in Louisiana.[4]

On June 2, Ruby introduced one of the more significant pieces of legislation favoring his district when he put forward a bill to donate five thousand sections of land, 640 acres in each, for the improvement of Galveston Harbor. The measure had strong support in the Galveston business community. Ruby argued that such a gift was important to the welfare of all Texans since they were "vitally interested in the welfare of the metropolis." Galveston, he said, was the great ocean outlet for the state. He further believed that if Texas provided such funds, the federal government might do so as well. "The gods help them who help themselves," he said. Democratic legislators objected to the grant, however, arguing that it was the federal government's business to improve the harbor since it received all of the revenue from the port. Democratic opposition from two East Texas legislators, Senators Thomas J. Word from Palestine and Thomas Broughton from Sherman, effectively shelved this measure, which could have been extremely beneficial for Galveston.[5]

Even while the legislature remained in session, Ruby looked to strengthening his ties with Governor Davis in the hopes that Davis could obtain a patronage position for him. That meant he also had to ensure that Davis remained in control of the state's Republican Party. That control was not certain. Governor Davis had to run for office again in December 1873, but his reelection was unlikely, and Davis's opponents within the party stood a good chance of seizing control of the party. These men generally were disappointed office seekers within the party who had been left out of the patronage in the past and hoped to get such appointments by wresting control of the party from Davis. They were joined by some men holding patronage positions who had been put in place because of their connections with northern politicians and had never really supported the local Republican administration. Ruby's future, at least in part, depended on whether or not he could make sure that Davis maintained control over the party, and Ruby spent much of 1873 working to make sure of Davis's control.

A letter sent to President Grant on June 18, 1873, and leaked to the Democratic press the following August, made clear the extent of the opposition to Davis as head of his party and the character of his opponents. The men who signed the letter represented a varied group of Republican politicians, all of whom had some grievance with the governor. They included legislators such as Senators Albert J. Fountain of El Paso and William A. Saylor from Bryan, and Representative Rush Plumly from Galveston. The group also included former Liberal Republican Julius Schuetze, publisher of the German language *Vorwärts* in Austin, and Judge Chauncey Sabin, a supporter of Louis Stevenson in 1871. Edward H. Quick, former coeditor of the *Houston Union* and aggrieved at James Tracy for his dismissal, also signed the letter. Particularly noteworthy among the signers was Postmaster William Clark, whose appointment Davis had opposed. Subsequent reports in the *New York Times* suggested that United States District Attorney for the Eastern District of Texas D. J. Baldwin also supported this effort to push Davis from his position as party leader. The group came to be known by various names, although newspapers frequently referred to it as the Clark faction, after the former congressman.[6]

The June 18 letter blamed Governor Davis for the defeats the Republican Party had suffered in 1871 and 1872, and charged that Davis had pursued an "unwise and injudicious" course. The authors contended that the governor had alienated many "good" Republicans and also prevented many "conservative" men who had no sympathy with the Democrats from joining the party. They described the governor's policies as "rule or ruin," suggesting that he had blocked good Republicans, usually meaning themselves, from securing the nominations in party conventions or appointments to patronage jobs. As to what policies the party had pursued that turned off conservative interests, the group pointed to the creation of the state police, the militia, and the expensive public schools. As a result the party had failed to attract the businessmen they hoped to attract. Of course to get rid of these programs essentially amounted to an abandonment of the party's black constituents. The letter closed with the suggestion that the Republican Party make no nominations for the upcoming election but instead support independent candidates and even Democrats who would accept the results of Reconstruction. These charges hid what really motivated these men. The article that accompanied the letter when it appeared in the *New York Times* suggested that the federal officers who had joined the Clark faction had done so because they feared Governor Davis intended to have them removed from office. They had reason to be fearful, for Davis certainly believed that the men who constituted this faction had done little to help the state party. Of course others wanted federal jobs. The fact that this group was willing to abandon black officeholders and voters reflected the fact that at least some believed the party needed to abandon its biracial character and become more fully controlled by whites.[7]

The Clark faction did not, however, control the party's machinery in Texas, and Ruby's support of Davis was critical to his maintaining control. A test of that ability came with the Republican state convention planned for the summer in 1873. The success of Davis in the state convention depended on success in precinct, county, and district conventions. Control of those, in turn, depended on ensuring that black voters turned out for these conventions and backed Davis. Turning out the black vote was a job that fell to Ruby. If Ruby had any chance at getting a federal appointment, Davis had to remain in control of the party. Davis, in turn, needed Ruby. A *New York Times* report on Governor Davis's trip in late June to meet President Grant to negotiate whether or not to turn over to federal authorities Satanta and

Big Tree, two Indian chiefs in the hands of state authorities, suggested Davis had broached the topic of removing federal officeholders who opposed his renomination when he met with federal Washington officials. Washington wanted the chiefs. Davis wanted to control appointments. The same article suggested that Davis hoped to control the black vote in Texas by promising black leaders he would use his influence with the president. Allegedly, Davis had already assured Ruby that if the president removed Clark, Ruby would get the postmastership in Galveston.[8]

Whether Governor Davis promised Ruby anything cannot be known with certainty. No direct evidence indicates such a bargain, although Ruby's behavior suggests that the two may have reached some sort of understanding since Ruby devoted much of his time in the months before the election to bolstering the governor's support within the black community, both in Texas and nationally. Securing support from black leaders nationally particularly had the potential of providing a powerful lobby pressuring the Grant administration to maintain its support for Davis. In April a series of letters by "Think" and "Olympus," written from Galveston and Houston, began to be published in the *New National Era,* Frederick Douglass's newspaper in Washington, DC. These letters appeared to come from different correspondents, although both of the supposed writers used pseudonyms rather than their real names. In all probability Ruby actually wrote all of them, an assumption based on the fact that they provided inside information on local politics that Ruby would have known best and reflected Ruby's thinking at the time. In addition they addressed concerns that displayed his political interests. Ruby also was a friend of the publisher and had corresponded in the past with Douglass's son Lewis, then the editor of the *New Era.* The first of these letters, written by "Think" from Galveston on April 22, appeared on May 8, 1873. The author showed an acute awareness of the political situation for Republicans in Texas. He recognized the relative hopelessness that Republicans could hold on to statewide political power. The Democratic Party, he acknowledged, had a fifty-thousand-vote majority over Republicans in any statewide election. Still, he remained hopeful. Democrats in the legislature had "dug their own graves" by promising things they could not deliver and, as a result, Republicans could succeed if they approached the upcoming election with the "shrewdest political management." He advised his national audience that Texas Republicans were not fearful, even given the Democratic majority, but realized that in the new election Republican success required the "highest order of political knowledge."[9]

"Think" never made clear what he meant by shrewd management or political knowledge, but he was precise in identifying the mismanagement that stood in the way of success. The Grant administration had failed to help Texas Republicans with its appointment policies and even with the federal government's choice of the newspapers picked to print public documents such as congressional proceedings and statutes. He pointed to the Justice Department's recent replacement of William Parker as United States marshal by Thomas Ochiltree as symptomatic of the government's failure to support local Republicans. "Think" argued that Ochiltree was only a nominal Republican and had already moved to hurt the real party. Ochiltree had not only replaced a loyal Republican by taking his office but had shifted the publication of the official announcements of his office from real Republican newspapers to disloyal ones, including the *Galveston Times*, a paper partially owned by Ochiltree. He went on to charge that the *Times* not only was not a Republican journal but actually devoted itself to "the abuse of the negro and Republicans generally." Of course he had taken the printing patronage away from the only other Republican newspaper in Galveston after the closing of *Flake's Bulletin* the previous fall—Ruby's *Standard.* If "Think" was Ruby, he had reason to complain.[10]

The *New Era* published additional letters from Texas almost monthly after the first "Think" letter. The recurring theme of all of them was that the men who held important federal offices in Texas did little to help the Republican Party and actually were hostile to black party leaders, even though wanting black support in elections. A letter from "Olympus," Ruby again, written from Galveston on May 21, suggested that federal officials had organized a "white man's party inside the Republican party." Blacks, he advised, had to recognize this fact. Their manhood demanded that after understanding the purpose of this group they had to "break the 'Ring,' drop those who have organized it." "Olympus" pointed out how little blacks had received from the "Ring" when he indicated that only nine blacks held federal positions in Texas and five of them, perhaps, received $4.00 per diem and the others, porters, $2.50 per diem. Federal officials in Galveston, he complained, "always drop us until election times, and at election times find out we have dropped them." In the end, he argued, blacks would "never enter into the field of complete freedom and manhood until we cease to be the slaves of unscrupulous politicians. . . . The time has come to make new demands upon the leaders of the Republican party, and if they do not listen to us, to make new leaders." The letter had the very strong imprint of Ruby's lifelong demand that blacks receive equal treatment in such matters.[11]

By late June "Olympus" turned his attention to Galveston's Postmaster Clark. Again, that "Olympus" probably was Ruby may be assumed since both Ruby and Governor Davis had determined to get Clark removed. Clark's latest transgression, according to "Olympus," was that he had courted favor among whites and appealed to their prejudices by telling them they needed to support him as postmaster or they would have a black man appointed, probably Ruby. "Olympus" insisted that Clark was the "center of the white man's ring in Texas," and his appointment raised questions about the purpose of the president's appointments. "Olympus" concluded that men like Clark were "buying and selling the Federal offices as if they were merchandise." Such behavior brought contempt not only on the national administration but also on local Republicans, who feared that President Grant did not care any more about the success of their party. Again resonating with Ruby's own point of view, "Olympus" turned from his condemnation of Clark to an elaborate praise of Governor Davis, whom he called the "best and bravest Governor in the South." More men like Davis in the party, he believed, would attract hundreds of new supporters. Unfortunately, Davis was unique among white Republicans.[12]

Ruby may have been at work shoring up support for Governor Davis on the national scene, but an even more important task faced him in Texas. At home he confronted a potential revolution among black leaders against Davis and his administration in the form of a movement to have a convention of black Texans held in Brenham on July 3 to discuss political conditions in the state, a convention that the Democratic press believed would be the first step in abandoning Davis. On June 7, 1873, thirty black leaders issued the call for this convention of "colored citizens." Ruby was not one of the men on the list. The stated purpose of the meeting actually was somewhat ambiguous, calling for the men who attended to discuss and address the concerns for the "welfare of the colored people of this State," in particular the situation related to their "political, social, religious, educational and industrial condition." According to the men who signed the call, they wished to "consult as to what steps it will be best for us to pursue in the future to elevate our condition."[13]

The political significance of the proposed convention initially was unclear, but Ruby could not afford to be left out of it. The call immediately raised concerns with the editor of the administration's official newspaper. The editor of the *State Journal* found worrisome the possibility that these men hoped to "become a separate power to advance their peculiar interests." Such a course would leave them in danger, he warned, of being "left in an isolated position." He insisted that the interests of the state's black population were not separate from those of the rest of the community and that the good of the whole would be achieved through the Republican Party. He hoped that the meeting would assemble, then adjourn to come together within the Republican convention to be held in Dallas later in the summer. Democratic journals believed that it was possible that the convention intended forming a black man's party. In fact, they even encouraged such a course, hoping somehow to make political capital of such a development. The editor of the *Galveston News* contended that the "colored brother is tired of picking bones and munching crusts while the white Radicals enjoy the meat and the bread of the loaves and the fishes." The *Houston Telegraph* welcomed what it considered to be the "independent course" of black politicians, who, its editor believed, could no longer be fooled by white office seekers and who would make their own political decisions. "[C]uffee proposes to go it alone," he concluded.[14]

Davis and his white supporters had some reason for concern since many of the men who signed the call for the convention had been fractious in the past. Possibly the best known of the men who signed the call was Senator Matt Gaines. Gaines had almost bolted the state organization in 1871 when he opposed the nomination of Congressman Clark and considered running for the position himself. The name of Benjamin F. Williams, member of the constitutional convention, representative from Fort Bend County in the Twelfth Legislature, and not always a reliable supporter of the administration, was also on the letter. Williams had supported Jack Hamilton in 1869 and flirted with the Liberal Republicans in 1872. Justice Johnson Reed, who had become Ruby's political thorn in the side in Galveston once again, also signed. The list also included several new men, potential leaders in the black community. James H. Washington, a twenty-three-year old Oberlin graduate, principal of the black school in Navasota, and member of the Thirteenth Legislature, signed. Washington had openly called for new leadership in the party. Frank J. Webb, another name on the list, was the Stevenson supporter and editor of the *Galveston Republican*, whom Ruby had managed to get dismissed as a secretary in the legislature in 1871.[15]

The list, however, also included men who had been faithful to Davis and closely associated with Ruby in the past, raising questions as to the exact character of the call. Prominent among the Ruby loyalists was Wright Cuney, clearly established by this time as Ruby's protégé and the man who now controlled Galveston Republican politics when Ruby was in Austin for legislative sessions. Walter Burton, sheriff of Fort Bend County, past president of the Loyal League there, and recipient of Ruby's supporting efforts when his wife had been thrown off a train when she wouldn't leave her first-class coach, also signed the call. Representatives Richard Allen from Harris County, Henry Phelps from Fort Bend County, and Meshack Roberts and

Henry Moore of Harrison County, all of whom had been loyal supporters of Governor Davis and associates of Ruby, signed the call.[16]

The results of the convention turned out to be completely different from what Democratic newspapers had predicted and the administration's *State Journal* had feared. The convention opened on July 3. The eighty or ninety men who were present represented what was probably the largest gathering of the state's black leadership up to that point, and it included delegates from all of the factions within the state's Republican Party. George Ruby appeared in Brenham, despite not having been party to planning the meeting, and he made his presence felt on the first day. When the delegates elected officers for the convention, they chose some of the men who seemed unsatisfied with Davis's leadership to important positions. They elected Matt Gaines first vice president. Johnson Reed received the vote for third vice president, James H. Washington for assistant corresponding secretary, and Frank Webb, corresponding secretary. The key position of president, however, went to Wright Cuney and the second vice presidency to Richard Allen. While the convention recognized the legitimacy of the critics of the administration, the delegates ultimately placed Ruby's allies into the critical positions needed to control the proceedings.[17]

Cuney's election was particularly important for control of the convention. The president appointed key committees, including the committee on resolutions and the committee that determined who should be seated as official delegates. When Ruby presented himself as a representative from Brazoria, even though he apparently had not been selected in the Brazoria meeting to choose delegates, the committee on credentials allowed Ruby to be seated on the floor as a regular delegate. The correspondent for the *Galveston News* believed that this move provided Ruby the opportunity to oppose what it had thought was the purpose of the convention, developing opposition to the renomination of Davis as governor. If that had ever been the intention of the convention, and if Ruby was the primary lobbyist in favor of Davis, the results placed the strongest supporter of Davis on the convention floor.[18]

Following the election of the officers and the seating of Ruby, the delegates called on Ruby to speak. The senator began his address by saying that he had not expected to take part in the convention, and he thanked the delegates for allowing him to participate. Much of his speech restated themes that had become central to the addresses he had made previously, largely positive and congratulatory about the state's black community's progress since the war's end. He pointed in particular to the freedmen of Washington County. They had nothing in 1865. They now owned some $150,000 worth of property. "[P]ossession of that land," he said, "was the greatest stride towards freedom and perfect citizenship that the colored people had made." He emphasized the idea that blacks had shown their capacity to raise themselves up. Black people in Texas had proven the capacity of their race.[19]

From congratulating the delegates on the accomplishments of their race, Ruby turned to politics. His words indicated that his thoughts may have begun to take a new direction. First, he defended his race from accusations that they were incapable of participating in the democratic process. Hostile Democratic reporters on the floor had emphasized confusion in the convention during the morning, but he contended there was no more disorder in this meeting than there had been in the previous Democratic state convention or on the floor of the Thirteenth Legislature when it had adjourned. He thought that blacks not only could become equals to whites in their power of self-government, but that they had already shown themselves to be so. At this point he sent a warning to those white Republicans who threatened to abandon his race. If they did, blacks would refuse to support them. At the same time, however, he appeared desirous of mollifying whites. The demands of the state's black population were modest, he insisted. All they asked of whites was that they "help us forward and to improve, and not throw us back in the march of progression." In addition, he insisted, blacks wanted to be accepted as "equal in a political sense." White acceptance of these aspirations would lead to the betterment of the whole people of the state. It made no sense, his argument went, to reverse the gains that had been made in securing these very modest goals.[20]

Rather than being an outsider in the convention, Ruby's speech set the tone of subsequent orators. Justice Johnson Reed followed Ruby, and his speech, like Ruby's, began by congratulating blacks on the improvements they had made in their condition and prosperity. He also praised their advances in civilization, meaning their acquisition of education and property and the improvement in their society. Like Ruby, he elaborated on what blacks wanted from their white neighbors, adding specifics to Ruby's broader requests. The parallels between the two speakers suggest some coordination between them. If there had been disagreements before the convention, these looked to have been resolved. Reed told whites that all blacks wanted were the "rights guaranteed to us by the laws of the United States and the State of Texas." He desired that the difficulties between blacks and whites be resolved, and that peace exist between blacks and whites in all circumstances, and observed that "If old slaveholders would recognize in the colored race the good qualities they oftentimes possess, the effort to live in peace would not be hard." Reed went on to ask that whites give up their prejudice against the education of the race (the hostile correspondent reporting on the convention denying such prejudice existed). In addition, he asked that the bars to black landholding that existed (again denied by the correspondent) be loosened. The radicalism expected from the convention by white observers simply failed to materialize.[21]

Any idea that the convention intended to form a new party, especially one based on race, or that the convention was designed to oppose Governor Davis, died on the second day. When the speaking began, Senator Matt Gaines took the floor to give what white observers had believed would be the keynote of the meeting and a call to move away from Davis. Instead, Gaines, often a critic of Secretary of State Newcomb and of the role of the administration in the congressional elections in 1871, came to the support of the governor with a resolution that rejected any abandonment by blacks of the Republican Party. Instead, Gaines introduced a declaration, quickly adopted, that offered Governor Davis the heartfelt thanks of the convention. Davis had "faithfully discharged his duties, and has administered the laws of the state to all parties without regard to race or color." In addition, Davis, Gaines insisted, had "done all in his power to befriend the colored citizens of this state." The passage of this resolution made it clear that black Republicans intended to resist any effort to abandon the civil rights programs that had been embraced by Governor Davis. Gaines, like Reed, had come in line with Ruby's basic position. Following the adoption of Gaines's resolutions, Cuney and other convention officers asked Gaines to withdraw the resolution, stating that they wanted to avoid making the convention into a political one but rather one to advocate their civil rights. Gaines agreed. Democratic newspapers saw this as a refusal to endorse Davis, but in fact the delegates had shown him overwhelming support.[22]

Events in the convention suggested that Ruby was not yet done politically. If the men who called the convention actually had intended to abandon Davis, he had thwarted that effort and actually brought them to Davis's support. When appointed to the Committee on Resolutions, he further dominated the convention's outcome and ultimately became the primary author of the convention's address. He, surprisingly working with Frank Webb, integrated the ideas he had put forward in his speech into the convention's "Address to the People of Texas." The document reaffirmed resolutions earlier adopted in the convention that blacks had no intention of organizing a black man's party. Instead, they hoped to promote friendlier feelings between the races. Black desires were not radical: they wanted protection; they wanted education; they desired to be treated equally with access to places of public resort or on public conveyances, an equal chance in life. As to politics, they lectured Democrats on why they opposed that party. Democrats charged that black interests were such that they would always support increasing the tax burden on whites. The address responded that whites must remember the condition in which blacks found themselves and for which whites were responsible. In slavery, blacks had been kept in ignorance, shut out of the "knowledge of letters." That had to be corrected. In addition, when whites considered the tendency of blacks to support Republicans, they had to remember that from the first day of black freedom these men had "set their faces in steadfast opposition to our political, educational and social progress." Whites and especially Democrats had done all of this with "a blind spirit of malignant opposition." Whites should not be surprised when blacks gave their support to men who "declared themselves adhesive to those great principles embodied in the recent amendments to the constitution," even if those men might have abused that support to secure their selfish ends. Now, the address expressed a willingness to unite with those white Democrats willing to "abate their prejudices and to concede to us willingly all those rights and privileges that sweetens [sic] the enjoyment of civil life," and it issued a warning to Republicans willing to abandon these ideals. Ruby had exercised considerable ability in shifting the potential course of the convention. The editor of the *State Journal* congratulated the delegates for taking the high ground and observed that the Democrats who had predicted blacks would go out on their own must now be disappointed. The same must be said of those white Republicans who had looked for blacks to break with the Davis administration.[23]

Ruby moved along another avenue to reinforce black support for Governor Davis following the Colored Men's Convention. This effort was through the black Masonic Lodge. The first lodge of black Masons in Texas was organized in Austin on April 10, 1873, while the legislature was in session. Its founders probably included most of the black legislators, and Ruby was one of them. The new Mount Bonnell Lodge was established under the authority of King Solomon's Grand Lodge of the Free and Accepted Ancient York Masons, for the State of Kansas, and Jurisdiction, which included Kansas, Colorado, Wyoming, Nebraska, the Indian Territory, and Texas. The Kansas Grand Lodge, in turn, was created under the auspices of the National Compact Grand Lodge of North America, a branch of Prince Hall Masonry. The Grand Lodge listed the Mount Bonnell Lodge as Lodge No. 23. Three other lodges had come into being shortly after this, Galveston Lodge No. 25, the Houston Magnolia Lodge No. 24, and the San Antonio Lodge No. 22. The Texas lodges remained in operation long after Reconstruction, and black politicians remained associated with them.

When the local lodges created the Grand Lodge of Texas, Wright Cuney was elected the first Grand Master.[24]

The Masonic Lodge was a useful organization within which black leaders could continue their political work in Texas. Nothing is known of how the Mount Bonnell Lodge operated, or of the subsequent lodges created in Galveston, Houston, and San Antonio, but Freemasonry among northern blacks had traditionally provided an institutional framework for the development of black community. It played a particularly important role in the development and articulation of political viewpoints, providing a forum for the development of organizational expertise, fostering leadership, repairing schisms, and reconciling rivalries. In many ways these lodges had served the same role for blacks in the North that the Loyal League had served for blacks in the South. The league was gone in Texas in 1873, dropped by James Newcomb when he concluded that it played a role in keeping whites out of the Republican Party, but Freemasonry offered blacks a useful replacement. In addition, the secret character of Freemasonry allowed black leaders to cooperate and coordinate their actions free of white oversight or control. Ruby's public activity as a Mason indicates that he saw Freemasonry as such a tool. While whites might oppose the league, they could hardly be opposed to Masonic lodges since many white politicians were lodge members themselves.[25]

Only two weeks after the Colored Men's Convention, Ruby traveled along with Representative Richard Allen and Wright Cuney to Leavenworth, Kansas, to attend the annual meeting of the Kansas Grand Lodge. Ruby arrived on the morning of July 16 and visited with the editor of the *Leavenworth Times*, who found him to be a "man of culture and force and a representative of the progressive element of Texas." Scheduled to begin on July 17, the convention did not really get underway until the next day when it convened, examined the credentials of the delegates, and named committees. Ruby and Allen went onto the Committee on Grievances. On July 19, the representatives considered various resolutions. Of particular significance for Ruby, the body approved a resolution that addressed the communications problems inherent in a jurisdiction covering roughly five states. The committee recommended that newspapers in the jurisdiction be chosen to communicate Masonic news. They included Ruby's *Galveston Standard* on the list. The recommendation had the potential of spurring subscriptions to his paper, promising to give the *Standard* new life since with the Democrats in control he no longer could get any government printing contracts from the state.[26]

The convention did not meet on Sunday, but on July 21, the next day, voted to elect officers for the jurisdiction. They reelected William D. Mathews as Grand Master, a post he had held since the organization of the Kansas Lodge in 1868. They chose Richard Allen to the largely ceremonial post of Grand Junior Deacon. Ruby was chosen as Texas District Grand Master, a post that gave him authority over the local lodges in Texas and provided him with another means of influencing black voters. In addition, the Grand Master named Ruby as one of the Lodge's foreign correspondents. This position kept him in contact with lodges throughout the nation, giving him another way to influence black opinion nationally in favor of the Davis administration.[27]

On July 22 the Grand Lodge installed its officers on the Kansas Agricultural and Mechanical Fair Grounds. At ten o'clock the participants in the day's affairs began a procession from downtown Leavenworth to the fairgrounds, headed by the band of the Fifth Infantry and followed by the representatives of the visiting lodges. The Texas representatives marched first in line. On reaching the grounds the Grand Officers were installed, and after the installation those who attended adjourned for a picnic lunch. Then, speeches were made. Three of the Texans spoke that afternoon: Richard Allen, Wright Cuney, and Ruby. Among the speakers Ruby stood out, making what the reporter for the *Leavenworth Times* called the "political speech of the day." He began with a theme that he had used in the North before, praising Texas and Texans for the progress that had been made in ending the conflict that had developed between the races. He even believed that the day was not too far in the future when "civil rights would be accorded to all irrespective of color or condition." A correspondent for the *Atchison Champion* noted that Ruby also sounded another theme that had been recurring in his political speeches lately. Ruby demanded that the Republican Party pass Senator Sumner's civil rights bill, which had been introduced repeatedly. It was time, he suggested, to use the political clout of the black community to secure this end. He recommended that blacks not support Republicans who failed to endorse the civil rights bill and instead aid those willing to help. The reporter for the *Times* was impressed by the senator's speech and praised Ruby as a "fine scholar and a very effective speaker."[28]

After the speeches the crowd dispersed and the Masons marched back to their headquarters. Ruby spoke again that evening when the various women's groups associated with the Lodge joined the men in Laing's Hall for what the local newspaper described as a "social reunion" that lasted into the late hours. At the evening gathering Ruby joined two ministers on the stage to address the crowd. The choice of Ruby to speak was another instance that showed how widely he had come to be seen as a particularly inspiring speaker. Ruby and the others who talked avoided any political comments that evening but instead focused primarily on complimenting the "Ladies of the Court." They also congratulated the representatives of the visiting lodges for the unity that had been achieved among the various degrees present and congratulated the officers of the Grand Lodge for how they managed the gathering.[29]

After the Grand Lodge meeting ended, Ruby visited other towns in Kansas attempting to obtain subscribers to the *Standard*, but he was back in Galveston by August 6 to begin preparing for the state Republican convention. A mass meeting held in Galveston that evening to select delegates to the state Republican convention in Dallas presented Ruby with his first opportunity to ensure that pro-Davis delegates showed up at the state convention. Whether or not he could do that was not certain. Earlier, in March, while Ruby was still in Austin, Republicans in Galveston had met to nominate a candidate for a position in the state House of Representatives to fill the place left vacant by the death of Representative Alexander

Rossy, a Democrat. Johnson Reed, John DeBruhl, and other prominent black politicians met with some Germans who had been associated with the previous year's Liberal movement in what the press called the German Liberal Republican Convention. Reed and DeBruhl had both proven that they could not be counted on to support the regular party's candidates in previous campaigns, and this time they helped obtain the nomination for Judge Chauncey Sabin, one of the Stevenson party in 1871, and not the choice of the administration. Sabin's choice could be seen as a major shift in who controlled the black vote in Galveston. Ruby had to control the upcoming Galveston nominating meeting from being taken over by bolters like Reed and DeBruhl if he had any chance of remaining in favor with the party's state leadership.[30]

When the Galveston county convention opened on August 6, Ruby faced opposition. Democratic newspaper accounts of that meeting, with no Republican newspapers left to cover it, did not name the men who opposed Ruby, but later events indicated that they included Johnson Reed, who reversed the course he had taken in Brenham, and other blacks who had been prominent in the 1871 Stevenson movement. These included Henry Ballinger and Stephen Paschal. White supporters included Rush Plumly and Galveston Justice of the Peace Sanford Mason. What exactly happened in the meeting is uncertain given the biased coverage, but Ruby did manage to have a pro-Davis delegation elected to the state convention. The hostile reporter of the *Houston Daily Mercury* wrote that Ruby and what he called the Custom House Ring controlled the convention from the beginning. He charged that Ruby, who chaired the convention, abandoned a proper program and let the gathering dissolve into a "regular mob meeting" that suppressed all opposition. He also claimed that the entire process was filled with "fraud" and other forms of corruption. In the same vein, the *Galveston News* later printed a complaint allegedly written by a black man who also claimed the meeting was a complete fraud and that the tellers wrote down the names of the regular party's candidates no matter who the voter chose. Democratic reporters even failed to provide clear information on the delegates selected at the meeting. The *Mercury's* man reported that Wright Cuney had been elected a delegate but Ruby had not, when the reverse was the case. Then, the reporter claimed that despite not being elected, the tellers counted Ruby in. News like this, probably complete fabrications, served to undercut the legitimacy of the Republicans' selection process. Such false news also tarred Republicans with the charge of corruption, helping to undermine all efforts by the party at gaining broader support.[31]

Following the convention's adjournment, Ruby's opponents refused to accept the decision of the convention. In an effort to give themselves the semblance of legitimacy, these men held ward meetings on August 12 to elect delegates to what they called the genuine county convention. They held that convention the next night at the office of Justice Mason. The reporter for the *Houston Mercury* believed that the chief hostility these men felt was towards Ruby and Collector Nathan Patten, who they charged controlled the party to their exclusion. Johnson Reed attended the meeting at Mason's office, along with Ballinger, Paschal, and Plumly. The press took particular notice of the presence of Wright Cuney's brother, Joe, to suggest that the movement had a wide base. The correspondent of the *Houston Mercury* believed that his was a significant defection, one that administration leaders could not ignore. It represented an uprising of the "People" against the "tyranny and fraud" of the men who had dominated Galveston Republican politics. Again, such accusations served the purpose of white Democrats interested in breaking up the Republican organization. The group chose a "People's Delegation" to go to Dallas that included Reed and other dissidents.[32]

When Republicans gathered in Dallas on August 19 it was clear that despite the existence of opposition groups such as the one headed by Reed that Ruby and other supporters of Governor Davis had successfully managed to ensure a pro-Davis majority, with the black delegates unanimously behind the governor's renomination. Their success was evident from the beginning when the delegates chose Adam G. Malloy as temporary president. Malloy, a veteran brigadier general in the Union army, was close to

Davis. Davis had appointed Malloy a general in the State Guard and only the previous spring named him state inspector of the penitentiary. Malloy named a credentials committee that favored Davis, including Ruby's brother Horatio and Collector Patten's brother as well. The committee subsequently settled all disputes in favor of the Davis faction, quickly disposing of Johnson Reed's "People's Delegation." When choosing permanent officers, the delegates elected Mayor S. G. Newton of San Antonio, an appointee of Governor Davis and chairman of one of the regular organization's senate committees. They chose Ruby as one of the vice presidents and Wright Cuney as one of the secretaries.[33]

Once control of the convention was established, Ruby and the other Davis supporters moved to nominate the governor as the party's gubernatorial candidate. Democratic newspapers had speculated up to the day of the convention that the Republicans would adjourn without making nominations, as had been proposed earlier by the Clark faction of federal officeholders. That did not happen. Governor Davis spoke at the morning session and received an uproarious reception that showed he still remained popular among the party's rank and file. When the delegates proceeded to nominate candidates for governor, the only person nominated was Davis. After his nomination, the convention moved to close nominations and unanimously chose him as their candidate. After all of the speculation about the party's course, the nomination was anticlimactic. The account sent to the *State Journal* stated that the opposition "was ashamed to show itself." The reporter for the *Galveston News* concluded that the result was due largely to the Galveston delegation and particularly to Ruby and Cuney. Following the vote for Davis, the delegates turned to the other offices. Both Ruby and Cuney were put in nomination for lieutenant governor, although Ruby asked his name to be withdrawn. Ironically, given the demands of the Colored Men's Convention for blacks to be recognized more fully by the party, all of the nominees for other state offices were white. Ruby did, however, receive the unenviable appointment as chairman of the Republican State Executive Committee.[34]

Even though all of the Republican candidates for state offices were white, the convention did recommit itself to its advocacy of full civil rights for blacks. In fact, the platform closely paralleled that of the Colored Convention. Party leaders at least recognized the importance of their black constituency in this way. The platform began by condemning the Thirteenth Legislature's dismantling of the existing public school system and pledged that the party would create a viable system of free public schools, a goal long supported by the state's black leaders. In addition, the platform called for the passage of laws that would protect every citizen "in the enjoyment of all his rights as a citizen," clearly reacting to the Thirteenth Legislature's abolition of the state police system. The platform also opposed passage of any laws that applied unequally to people because of their race, place of birth, or belief. Shifting from these reassertions of traditional party goals, the platform further condemned the Thirteenth Legislature's passage of private legislation that favored speculators and "worthless corporations" or that was "in favor of the rich and against the poor." In particular, it condemned its attempts to take land intended for homesteads and sell it. The rest of the platform echoed plans adopted in previous conventions and approved the course of the National Republican Party and the Grant administration.[35]

Following the adjournment of the convention, Ruby returned to Galveston and began carrying out his role as the party chairman and also campaigning for Republican candidates. He did receive something of a compliment from a reporter from the *Galveston News*, a journal with few good words to say about Ruby, when he observed that Ruby's choice for that position was "as good a selection for that place as his party could have made. He is a man of considerable ability." The thankless job was to coordinate campaign activities as well as ensure the party was organized at the local level. It also exposed him to insult. Governor Davis left it up to Ruby to manage his campaign in the state, and on September 11 Ruby wrote to John Ireland, manager of Democratic candidate Richard Coke's campaign, to engage in debates at places Coke might consider convenient. Coke refused to reply to Ruby, saying that he would have no communication with him because "he was a nigger." Coke later denied that charge, contending that he simply would treat with no one other than Davis to set up the debates. In the end the two held no joint debates.[36]

In the past Ruby had accompanied Republican speakers in their campaigning, particularly when they appeared in the state's counties with large black populations. In this campaign Davis gave speeches at meetings in eastern Texas for the most part, but Ruby did not accompany him. Presumably he was trying to organize voters in the black majority counties closer to Galveston. Otherwise, Ruby may have written letters to local Republicans pushing them to prepare for the campaign, although if he did, none of the letters survived. He may also have worked through his Masonic connections to encourage and mobilize the black community, but the secrecy of that organization meant no public record of such efforts existed. In fact, following his work to secure Davis's nomination, his own activity in the campaign suggests that either he was a man who had little hope for a Republican victory in the upcoming election or that white Republican candidates had no desire to have a black man speak for them. He did attend the governor's speech in Galveston's Turner Hall on September 16 and served as the chairman of the meeting.[37]

His pessimism regarding the upcoming election was also apparent when the Republicans of the Twelfth Senate District turned to nominate a senatorial candidate. Pro-and anti-Ruby factions had existed in Galveston since 1871, with constantly changing personnel. On October 11 the two rival county executive committees created prior to the state convention met to discuss whether or not they could unify on legislative and local candidates, with the Johnson Reed group remaining hostile to Ruby. The Galveston correspondent of the Democratic *Houston Mercury* believed that they had agreed to work together but only on the basis that Ruby would not be forced on the party in the district convention in Brazoria. The writer believed that, of the thirteen delegates chosen for the convention, only one supported Ruby and the rest were openly against him. He believed that old wounds left over from past conventions would be reopened if Ruby managed to secure the nomination "by fraud or force." The reporter observed that the "opposition to Ruby is deep and nearly universal." Whether or not the *Mercury*'s account is true or not cannot be known. In the past Ruby had repeatedly shown his ability to bring his constituents to his support in the face of such opposition. Possibly this time he did not bother to argue his case.[38]

When the Twelfth Senate District held its convention in Brazoria on November 1, Ruby did not attend. He possibly could have secured the nomination for the senate seat from the Twelfth District if he had been there. In the past, even if he faced opposition within the Galveston delegation, he could count on delegates from Brazoria and Matagorda Counties to come to his support. That his renomination was possible was made even clearer when his supporters gained control of the convention. When the delegates elected a temporary chairman they chose a pro-Ruby man. Ruby's brother Horatio was named to the credentials committee, usually a sign that George had the votes to be nominated. Then, the delegates elected Johnson Reed permanent president. Ruby's name was placed in nomination, but John DeBruhl, who had been part of the Ruby machine, nominated the former Liberal Republican, Judge Chauncey Sabin. In what the *Galveston News* saw as a stunning defeat for Ruby, Sabin secured the nomination by a vote of nineteen to nine. It is not clear, however, that Ruby even wanted the nomination. Maybe he had concluded that it was time to test the idea that a white Republican could secure the white votes that Ruby had never found. Perhaps Ruby gave way to Sabin thinking that his future lay elsewhere. In his role as party chairman, Ruby had shown no real interest in campaigning. In that role and in his non-action in the senate convention Ruby appeared to have given up.[39]

Ruby did show up on November 11 at the Galveston County Republican meeting held to ratify the choices made in Brazoria and to choose nominees for county offices. While playing no role in the proceedings, he did give a speech. As the committee on credentials debated who officially represented the various wards, the delegates called on him to make a speech. They clearly still held him in high esteem and valued what he had to say. In many ways what he said sounded like a valedictory address. Ruby warned his audience that Republicans faced a "hard task" if they were to succeed in December. He indicated that he had accepted the fact that victory might require Republicans to nominate men who were not "true *bona fide* Republicans." He accepted that many in the party proposed to defeat the Democrats, even if that required them to use "Democratic material." While everyone said that the Democrats could not be beaten, in Galveston one had been beaten in an earlier municipal election when Republicans put forward a former Democrat. Perhaps the party could keep a Republican as the representative of the Twelfth in this way. He closed his speech urging the delegates to do their best to maintain the party. His ending sounded like he might not be there to help.[40]

Ruby's pessimism was well-founded. The election was another Republican disaster. The shift in tactics apparent in the senate nomination of a white candidate accomplished nothing. The day after the election the *Galveston News* predicted that Sabin had lost to his Democratic opponent based simply on the returns from Galveston County. Galveston had polled enough votes to counter any that might come in later from the countryside. When final returns were in Sabin had received 1,249 votes in Galveston to Democratic candidate Benjamin C. Franklin's 2,380. In Brazoria the vote for Sabin was 715 to 196 for Franklin. Matagorda County's votes were not published. The Brazoria County vote made clear that the idea that running whites rather than blacks might attract more votes did not work, with Sabin receiving over three hundred fewer votes than the Republican congressional candidate, the much-disliked Clark, did in 1872. In Galveston the Republican vote remained much as it had the year before, indicating that Sabin attracted no more votes than the Republican in 1872. Sabin not only had failed to attract more votes, he actually had failed to turn out the usual Republican base. Worse, Sabin had not managed to carry his district for the party's candidates for statewide office. In a major defeat, Governor Davis lost not only the Twelfth District but the overall election. Davis's opponent, Richard Coke, defeated the governor with over a hundred thousand votes to Davis's roughly fifty thousand.[41]

Even before the results of the election were fully known, Ruby turned to other matters. Shortly after the election he attended a mass meeting of blacks in Galveston that voiced support for the civil rights bill that Senator Sumner had reintroduced in Congress once again. The body passed resolutions encouraging Congress to pass the bill, then voted resolutions that endorsed Governor Davis, praising him as the "leader and father of the Republican party in this State." The delegates also urged the governor to contest the results of the just-completed gubernatorial election based on already-filed court challenges to the constitutionality of the election law passed by the Thirteenth Legislature. While Davis never personally challenged the results, a Houston election case sent to the state supreme court ended in a decision that declared the law under which the election had been held to be unconstitutional. The famed Semicolon Case nullified the election, but Democrats refused to accept the court's decision and ultimately used the threat of violence to force Governor Davis out of office before his term actually expired the following January. Ruby was not in Texas for this confrontation. The Galveston civil rights meeting voted to send him and Wright Cuney to Washington, DC, to attend the National Equal Rights Convention. The two left Austin on December 4.[42]

The National Equal Rights Convention assembled on December 11 in the hall of the House of Representatives. Cuney was named to the Committee on Permanent Organization on the first day. The Committee on Credentials recognized twenty delegates from Texas. This included many other prominent black politicians from Texas in addition to Cuney and Ruby, including Representative Richard Allen, Justice Johnson Reed, future state legislator William H. Holland, and John DeBruhl. It is unclear, however, how many of these men actually were in Washington or if Ruby and Cuney served as proxy for most of them. On the second day the Committee on Permanent Organization submitted its report on officers and recom-

Delegates to the National Civil Rights Convention, Washington, DC, December, 1873 (Library of Congress).

mended P. B. S. Pinchback as president, linking Ruby to that Louisiana politician once again. The delegates elected Pinchback unanimously, then chose vice presidents from each of the states that had sent delegates. Ruby represented Texas.[43]

In the following three days of the convention the delegates pushed forward resolutions that were increasingly demanding relative to civil rights. Few black politicians had ever urged social equality, but the resolutions passed by this convention demanded equal access to all institutions supported or licensed by government. "The citizen," the delegates affirmed, "is entitled to whatever belongs to him, and is not bound to accept an equivalent." They were particularly insistent that the rights guaranteed to them by the Fourteenth and Fifteenth Amendments not only be asserted, but be supported by action of the government. Ruby made no speeches in the convention, although he had long supported such action. Ruby was active, however, and chaired the Committee on Historical and Industrial Statistics and delivered a report that asked the members of the convention to gather for each state such "facts, historical and statistical, in relation to the negro race in America, for the reference of all who desire to know the true history of what our life-long opponents have conceded to be the most remarkable race, measured by their surroundings and advantages, our country has produced." He also went with all of the delegates to meet with the president at the White House on August 14.[44]

Ruby's trip to Washington may also have been one in search of a federal appointment. Democratic newspaper accounts suggested that he was there to have Clark removed from the Galveston post office and possibly have himself or Cuney put in the position. One account reported that he met with President Grant, Secretary of the Treasury William A. Richardson, and Attorney General George H. Williams, accompanied by state senator Webster Flanagan and United States Marshal Tom Ochiltree. Indeed, following the election, Galveston Republicans again blamed many of the federal office holders for the defeat, contending that the officers had not contributed funds to carry on the canvass nor supported Republican candidates. One letter that appeared in the *New National Era* in Washington attributed the defeat to the "unpopularity of our Federal officers," pointing particularly to the appointment of Congressman Clark as postmaster in Galveston. The writer insisted that Clark would "sink any party to which he is attached." The author considered Tom Ochiltree a man who would "drive any decent, respectable man from our ranks." The only federal officer in the state he considered decent was Collector Patten. Given this critique of the federal officials, the fact that Ruby accompanied Flanagan and Ochiltree was surprising. It is not known what Grant told them, although the president reportedly assured them that the "Union interests of Texas" would not be sacrificed. He did not, however, remove Postmaster Clark.[45]

Ruby returned to Galveston by December 28. For all practical purposes, his political career in Texas was over. In early April, 1874, rumors circulated that he might attempt one more try for office, a seat in the state house of representatives following the resignation of W. L. Moody, the man who held the district's "floater" position from Galveston, Brazoria, and Matagorda. Democrats warned that word had been received from Matagorda that the freedmen there intended to elect Ruby for the vacant seat. The editor of the *Galveston News* warned that apathy on the part of the Democrats and "a little management" on the part of the Radicals might allow Ruby to succeed. It is unclear, however, that Ruby ever intended to run. His name was on the ballot, but when the vote was counted after the April 17, 1874, election, he had received few votes. When early returns showed a very small turnout in Galveston, the editor of the *Galveston News* still worried that with such a small vote Ruby would be successful if he had managed to mobilize the black vote in Brazoria and Matagorda Counties. Even in those counties, however, there was little evidence that Ruby had campaigned. The official returns for Galveston gave Ruby only 70 while the Democratic candidate received 701. In Brazoria and Matagorda Counties Ruby carried the election, but the turnout was small. In Brazoria he received 353 votes, half that of Sabin the previous year, to 138 for his opponent. In Matagorda the vote was 118 to 67. Black voting either was demoralized or Ruby had never really intended to run.[46]

If he had any serious intention of remaining in Texas, and if he had actually sought the nomination for the April election, that vote would have convinced him to look elsewhere for a new future. In addition, the Grant administration showed no signs of removing the federal officials whose removal might have opened the way for a federal appointment in Texas. In late May, Ruby still played a small role in the Republican Party, calling for a consultation of Republican leaders to meet in Austin, but he did not attend. At roughly the same time he and his wife sold their home and property in Galveston, lots 4, 5, and half of lot 6 in block 553 for $4,500. This transaction signaled Ruby's intention to leave Texas. The end of Ruby's career in Texas was received quietly by the contemporary press. No Republican newspapers remained by this time. Democratic editors were only too happy to see him go. He had passed nearly eight eventful years in Texas working to create a government that recognized the equal rights of its black citizens and protect them in those rights. Those goals were never acceptable to the majority of whites in the state, however, and, as these white men reasserted their own political majority through the Democratic Party, Ruby had no chance to further the goals for which he had fought. Having sold his Galveston property, Ruby and his family moved on. New Orleans, Louisiana, became the next stop as he continued his efforts to secure equality for his race.[47]

CHAPTER XIII

THE CONTINUED FIGHT FOR EQUALITY, LOUISIANA, 1874–1882

[A] faithful fearless advocate of the rights of our people.—Observation of P. B. S. Pinchback on George Ruby, Weekly Louisianian, *August 15, 1874*

Ruby moved to New Orleans in the spring of 1874, not a surprising move given his longtime connections with that city and its black elite. In Louisiana, however, he could not assume the same role that he had in Texas. Here he found himself a newcomer, much welcomed, but having to compete with an already-established black political leadership created from among the state's antebellum free black community and added to since 1867 by rising freedmen. Ruby ultimately became a part of the black leadership, but he never held another elected office during his life in Louisiana. Still, he found new opportunities to pursue his vision of equality and justice. Working as a newspaperman and tying himself to both black and white Republican officeholders and candidates for office, Ruby ultimately continued to influence political opinion and decisions in his new home.

Initially Ruby considered returning to teaching. In May 1874, he applied for a teaching position in the New Orleans schools. William G. Brown, the Louisiana superintendent of education, reported that Ruby had demonstrated his qualifications and received a certificate to be a teacher of the first grade, probably the highest level in the schools. Brown's recommendation indicated that Ruby was already in New Orleans by May.

Even though he applied to teach, Ruby never went back into the city school system. Instead, on August 15, the owner of the *New Orleans Louisianian*, Ruby's longtime acquaintance P. B. S. Pinchback, announced that Ruby was taking over the editorial management of his newspaper. The statement welcomed Ruby as an "educated, thorough gentleman with a large experience not only in public life but in politics and journalism." He assured his readers that Ruby would maintain the newspaper's outspoken Republicanism and that it would continue to be a "faithful fearless advocate of the rights of our people." He promised, in addition, that its contents would be more varied and that the paper's readers would find it "more attractive." Ruby had found a home where he could continue to pursue his broader social and political goals and, with luck, also support his family.[1]

Ruby had met Pinchback at many of the national black conventions that he attended, and for a man with Ruby's ambitions Pinchback was a logical man with whom to connect. Pinchback may have been the most powerful black politician in Louisiana at the time. The biracial son of a white Georgia planter, he had come to Louisiana in 1862, served for a time in the Union army, and then opened a commission business in New Orleans with C. C. Antoine, a future lieutenant governor of the state. Subsequently, Pinchback was on the state's board of education, served as acting lieutenant governor from 1871 to 1872, and briefly filled the job of governor in 1872. In 1873 he had been elected to the United States by the Republican legislature, one of two seats, the other controlled by Democrats, that existed in 1873 as a result of a disputed election in 1872. Congress seated neither Pinchback nor the Democratic-elected candidate, however, in a contest that lasted until 1876 and ended without Pinchback getting the office. In 1874, when Ruby arrived in New Orleans, Pinchback controlled black voting and had taken a position within the local Republican Party opposing what was known as the Custom House Ring in New Orleans, although forming alliances at that time with individual leaders of the ring such as former United States senator and disputed state governor William Pitt Kellogg and United States Marshal Stephen B. Packard. At one point, Pinchback even considered an alliance with white Democrats if they would guarantee that they would respect black civil rights. His political position was similar to that of Ruby, and the two established what seemed to be an easy rapport.[2]

The August 22, 1874, edition of the *Louisianian* was the first published under Ruby's editorship. In the prospectus published in that edition he announced that he had assumed the editorship of the paper and addressed how he intended to run it. Ruby returned to many of the themes that had characterized his political efforts in Texas. He noted that the paper had been initially founded to "furnish to our people the information—guidance—encouragement and counsel which they so much needed in the transition from their former unfortunate condition into the new and better estate of American citizenship," a task that he always assumed the black leadership must exercise for the race. He then pointed to the two major components of the job he had set for the paper and himself. The paper, he wrote, would advocate "the security and enjoyment of broad civil liberty, the absolute equality of all men before the law, and an impartial distribution of honor and patronage to all who merit them." He pointed particularly to education in this matter. At the same time, he insisted that he would work to "allay animosities" and obliterate the memory of the "bitter past." The paper would work to promote harmony and union "among all classes and between all interests." Promotion of harmony meant even advocating the removal of political disabilities still applying to former Confederates. All of this, he proposed, would lead to an elevation of Louisiana to an "enviable position among her sister States." His words reflected his still optimistic belief that blacks could somehow reach some sort of accommodation in the exercise of power.[3]

Ruby's assumption of the editorship of the *Louisianian* and his hopeful opening words came at almost the same time as one of the state's most violent Reconstruction episodes. In Louisiana the results of the 1872 state election remained unsettled in 1874. As seen, two legislatures existed, and two men also claimed to be governor. One was John McEnery, a Democrat who had been supported by former Republican governor Henry C. Warmoth and a number of the Liberal Republicans in 1872. The other was William Kellogg, elected as a regular Republican. Kellogg managed to take over the actual offices of the governor, but he and other Republican officeholders whose claims to office were disputed faced repeated efforts, often violent, by white Democrats to remove them. In 1873, for example, Grant Parish was the site of the Colfax Massacre, a confrontation between a white militia and blacks who attempted to defend Republican officeholders. The pitched battle that took place resulted in the death of as many as 150 blacks. Tension remained, and Ruby's move to New Orleans came at the time when supporters of McEnery, backed by the Crescent City White League, an army of the Democratic Party, attempted to take control of the state government and drive Kellogg out. On September 14, 1874, an estimated five thousand members of the league seized control of the statehouse, the armory, and the city's downtown. Governor Kellogg called up the city's police force and militia units and attempted to disperse the mob, but in what came to be called the Battle of Liberty Place or the Battle of Canal Street, the mob attacked the police and militia, inflicting heavy casualties and driving them away. Kellogg ultimately called for the support of federal troops from the United States Army's local garrison. After three days of fighting the United States troops finally moved into the city and put down the violence.[4]

Ruby was in the city during the riot, and in the wake of the events of September 14 he published editorials that provided some of the clearest statements of his views on race relations, opinions that probably also reflected Pinchback's. In a column entitled "Review of the Situation," Ruby surprisingly blamed events on the Kellogg administration. Kellogg and his associates had failed to sustain the Republican Party and instead abused power. Kellogg had temporized with "blatherskites" and appointed men with "no doctrine, principle, or party" to important positions. This had provoked opposition among whites in the South that had "culminated in riot, outrage, and murder." Ruby charged that if Governor Kellogg had appointed capable men and removed dishonest ones, the Battle of Canal Street would not have happened. Further, he contended that Kellogg had injured

Republican interests by removing Republicans from office and appointing Democrats under the guise of compromise with political opponents. That policy, he pointed out, had effected no reconciliation with white Democrats. In all of his activities, Kellogg had "deepened and broadened the chasm between our people and for the time, made it appear to the unthoughtful that there is no hope for better things." His analysis differed little from his views of what had taken place in Texas.[5]

In the same edition Ruby published another column entitled "Our Difficulties and Their Solution." He again condemned the Kellogg administration for its appointment policies, but in this column he also went after the Democratic opposition that he said cursed the state with an "impolitic and violent class, who, casting to the winds all the appliances of peace for the redress of the grievances they announce seem bent 'to unloose the dogs of war' and run riot." The result was that they undermined the agricultural and business prosperity of the state. Despite his experiences in Texas, Ruby remained remarkably optimistic as to the solution. "Our remedy," he wrote, "lies in a simple expedient . . . which consists in an agreement to toleration." It was time for Louisianans of all of the state's political faiths not only to tolerate each other but also to observe the "due privileges and immunities of all." He went on to write that the "absolute rights of all citizens before the law should be conceded." Members of the White League, who were fellow citizens, had to understand that blacks possessed not only a common claim to rights but also a common interest. If concessions were made, blacks were "anxious and willing upon the basis we have indicated to exert all the strength of a generous nature and a noble purpose to rebuild our waste places. But toleration, recognition of manhood and an agreement to harmonize differences must be the rule. This is the solution to our difficulties."[6]

Responding to the Canal Street confrontation in the same edition, under a column entitled "Caution," Ruby counseled the city's black population that they had a role to play in achieving peace. He recognized that anti-Republican journals were publishing "sensational articles" calculated to arouse the "base passions" of whites and "perpetuate the fear and suspicions of the colored people." Ruby asked that blacks consider, given this situation, that people "cannot be too careful in regard to the treatment of their neighbors, as mutual confidence and respect for each other are the things needful for our redemption." While their political enemies slandered them, blacks must not respond in kind. He urged the black community to be "discreet, respectful and law-abiding." They must act with caution at a time when every offence would be "magnified and heralded to the country." The self-improvement, self-control aspect of Ruby's worldview had come through again, as well as his continuing belief that some sort of racial peace could be achieved if whites would only accept blacks as having equal rights.[7]

Despite the unsettled state of political matters, Ruby quickly embraced a lifestyle in New Orleans that he had not enjoyed in Texas. The city's black politicians and black elites welcomed him into the rich social life of New Orleans. By January, 1875, he was elected a member of the Louisiana Club, a private club that included Pinchback, Louisiana Secretary of State Peter G. Deslonde, and James H. Ingraham, Ruby's acquaintance from earlier trips to New Orleans. A contemporary report in a Democratic newspaper indicated that most of the members, although not all, were black. Membership did include Oscar F. Hunsacker, a white official with the Internal Revenue Service whom Ruby had known in Galveston. Probably the majority were Republican politicians, labeled in the article as "office-holders or stipendiaries." In addition, the item in the *Picayune* thought most of the members were associates of Governor Kellogg, although that is questionable since neither Pinchback nor Ruby approved of his course. In a typical attack on the character of Republicans by a Democratic journal, the article also charged that the club consisted largely of drunkards. The club's secretary later published a denial of this allegation in the *Louisianian*. The presence of Ruby, by this time a member of the club's executive committee, gave the lie to the charge, for he remained a confirmed teetotaler and certainly was not a drunk.[8]

Ruby's political associations also involved him in a large number of social activities. On March 22, 1875, Pinchback returned from Washington, where Congress still had not made a decision as to whether or not to seat him, and a select group welcomed Pinchback home with a private dinner party. The hosts of the dinner party included Ruby. On the evening of the twenty-fifth of that month Ruby helped to organize a public reception for Pinchback. At that reception Ruby served as one of the vice presidents of the evening's proceedings. In April, he participated in a gathering at the home of the state superintendent of education to honor William G. Brown, the superintendent of schools for the state, and Ruby was one of the men who made speeches that evening. Later, in August, he attended a reception given by Superintendent Brown for Mrs. P. B. S. Pinchback, who had just returned from Washington. A description of the affair appeared in the *New Orleans Republican* and reported, "here were present the *elite* and beauty of our city" in an evening of music and dancing. Ruby attended along with many of the other party members connected to Senator Pinchback.[9]

A particularly important event took place on December 27. On that date Ruby attended a reception for Mexican General Porfirio Díaz at the home of Lieutenant Governor Caesar Antoine. The guests included many of the usual associates of Pinchback, including Superintendent Brown, State Senator J. Henri Burch, Congressman Charles E. Nash, and Ruby. Toasts were made in beakers of "Krug," a French champagne, and speeches followed. The speakers dwelled on the urgent need to improve trade relations between the United States and Mexico and also on possibilities of liberating Cuba from Spanish control. Ruby demonstrated the breadth of his achievements that evening when he, along with two others in attendance, "utilized their talents as linguists in aid of those who did not comprehend the language of the speakers." Ruby probably had acquired a bit of Spanish while in Texas to add to his knowledge of French that he had gained in Haiti, although exactly when he acquired these languages is unknown.[10]

In addition to his political associations, Ruby also established contacts within the nonpolitical social groups in the community. Among these was the New Orleans Athenaeum Literary Club. On January 15, 1875, he attended the weekly gathering of that club at the home of Lieutenant Governor

Antoine. Members, including both men and women, "recited some choice pieces in prose and verse" from the best English and American authors. Although little is known of his family life, this was the type of event that his wife might have attended. On January 28, 1875, he was one of the members of a committee of that club that published resolutions of condolence on the death of William Weeks, who had been the state's secretary of state. In February, Ruby appeared at a service in the Common Street Baptist Church sponsored by the Athenaeum Society to commemorate the "valuable services" rendered by the "great patriot and champion of abolition," Gerritt Smith, who had died recently. Ruby was named one of the vice presidents of the meeting. J. Sella Martin, president of the Society, and Bishop John M. Brown of the AME Church made the opening remarks. Ruby made the principal address, closing the meeting with what the *New Orleans Republican* called "appropriate eulogistic remarks."[11]

Ruby also became an active member of the Central Congregational Church, an opportunity for religious association he apparently didn't have in Texas. He attended a meeting of the congregation on November 17 to consider the resignation of C. H. Thompson, its pastor, who had accepted the position of president of Alcorn University in Mississippi. The meeting appointed Ruby to the committee to draft resolutions expressing the feelings of the congregation about Thompson's departure. Called on to speak, Ruby made what a correspondent from the church called "interesting remarks" on the interests of the church and the services lost by Thompson's departure. Thompson's leaving, he told the congregation, placed an obligation on the church's members to continue the ways that the minister had taught in order that good might be produced. Education, which Thompson had encouraged, presented a high claim upon all. Ruby "eloquently presented" his remarks, the correspondent observed.[12]

Such activity continued through his days in New Orleans. Several years after his arrival he became a charter member of the Americus Club. This club drew its membership from among young black men in the city and sponsored events such as public lectures designed to improve the health and intellectual life of the community. In October 1879, the club opened its doors on Rampart Street with a parlor, reading room and library, billiard room, and refreshment room. Ruby also maintained his connections with the Masonic Lodge. In New Orleans he moved into a new order of the Freemasons, the Knights Templar. In 1879 he appeared at a reception for the Grand Master of the District of Columbia Commandery where he, listed as Sir George Ruby, toasted the press. Whether or not his toast was with wine or water was not stated. After several years in New Orleans he may no longer have been an advocate of complete abstinence.[13]

Ruby indulged in the social life of New Orleans, but his overarching interest remained politics, and through his position as editor of the *Louisianian* he became almost immediately involved in the city and state's politics. As editor of Pinchback's paper, his primary task was to provide coverage of his employer's activity and support his political positions, but he did not restrict that support to writing editorials. Ruby also helped to organize campaign events and appeared at them as a featured speaker. His first publicized foray into this area was supposed to take place when he was invited to speak at a "grand mass meeting" of Republicans in the Sixth District of New Orleans on October 30, 1874, a rally held prior to the state's congressional, legislative, and municipal elections to be held on November 2. He was scheduled to appear with United States Marshal Packard and Pinchback, but for some unknown reason none of the three appeared. Obviously, Ruby did not give his address.[14]

Ruby did get to speak when he accompanied Pinchback to Terrebonne and Lafourche parishes on November 1 to hold rallies to get Republicans out for the next day's election. At Houma, Pinchback attacked what he called the "compromise scheme of the Democratic White League," the so-called "Terrebonne Plan," that proposed to offer blacks a share of public offices in parishes where whites were in the minority as long as they also elected whites. Pinchback commended what he called the "compromise spirit," but the plan in black majority parishes, he believed, was an effort to accomplish a Democratic triumph by getting Democrats elected in places where only Republicans should have been elected. The article Ruby wrote about the speech was unstinting in his praise of Pinchback, describing how well received his speech had been. He noted that each illustration of his logic with a witty saying or clinching of his argument by a humorous anecdote was received with rounds of applause. It was, Ruby wrote, one of the best speeches Pinchback had ever delivered. Ruby also spoke following the lieutenant governor, describing his own effort as a "few appropriate remarks." At Thibodeaux, three thousand listeners heard Pinchback with "rapturous attention." Again, Ruby followed Pinchback's speech with "concluding remarks."[15]

The result of the 1874 election was as uncertain as the Louisiana contest in 1872. One historian has written that there was "no way short of black magic to determine who won the election." Ruby did not remain in New Orleans following the contest. Shortly after the canvass, Ruby made a short journey to visit Lucy's family in Washington, DC. Possibly Lucy and the children were already there, for Lucy was pregnant at the time. Given the potential dangers of the election, he may have sent the family to safety with Lucy's mother and father, especially given Lucy's pregnancy. While in Washington he may also have sought some sort of patronage position in the federal government. Such a job was essential for any newspaper editor or would-be politician. The income of a newspaper editor seldom amounted to enough to support a family. A government job would not only have provided the money needed for his family but also would have made it possible for him to engage in the travel necessary for political campaigning. That this may have been part of the reason for his trip was indicated by the fact that shortly after he returned, he received a job in the New Orleans custom house. While still in Washington, he and Lucy also became parents again. On December 2, 1874, Lucy gave birth to their second child, their son George Nalle.[16]

The appointment at the custom house was as a clerk. His political connections in Washington and New Orleans had paid off. By May 1875, he was on the rolls of employees at the custom house, having been promoted to the position of special deputy surveyor. Quickly integrated into the staff, he joined with the others in his office in signing a letter of best wishes to J. M. Parker, who had been the surveyor but had left after receiving an appointment as the city's postmaster. As in Galveston, Ruby's job offered him a considerable amount of security and probably involved little enough work that he could spend most of his time editing the *Louisianian.* The position provided him with a salary of $1,400 per year, roughly equivalent to $32,000 in 2019, plus with the moiety system still in place a share of the revenue generated by his office may have doubled that amount. The salary and other income would have provided a good supplement to the money he made as an editor. With some exceptions, Ruby held various posts in the Custom House through the rest of his life in New Orleans.[17]

In addition to his local work, Ruby continued to participate in efforts by blacks to effect broader national political ends. He attended the Colored Editors Convention in Cincinnati, Ohio, in August 1875, although that was done as much in Pinchback's interests as his own. Pinchback hoped to create an organization of black newspapers in the hopes that he could unite the black press "in sentiment and idea." Ruby traveled to the convention with Superintendent William G. Brown, Morris Chester, and J. Sella Martin, editor of the Carrollton *True Republican.* Pinchback gave the keynote address and encouraged those attending to pursue the unification of the black press. He considered black newspapers to have a political mission. "We recognize," Pinchback said, "that our futures are in our own hands; the philanthropist of the North has halted. We must chisel out our own fortune. Even now the colored man has it thrown in his teeth in the halls of Congress that too much had been done for the colored man." The response, Pinchback suggested, was that the eight hundred thousand black voters in the South had power and that it was time for them not to grovel before any people or party. Pinchback's ideas remained akin to those of Ruby, and Ruby worked in the convention to secure the success of Pinchback's plans for a black press organization. Ruby served on the committee on credentials and also was elected to be the convention's secretary.[18]

On December 11 Ruby appeared at another Pinchback-sponsored gathering, a mass meeting of "colored citizens" at New Orleans's Mechanics Institute. Its primary purpose was to urge the seating of Senator Pinchback in Washington, but it also provided a forum for consideration of ways that blacks in the South could be better protected and a discussion of the desirability of having a national "colored convention" to consider that problem. The meeting included virtually every prominent black leader in New Orleans. Chaired by Lieutenant Governor Antoine, the names of the vice presidents included virtually everyone involved in local politics, with George Ruby on the list. The meeting passed resolutions urging Congress to seat Pinchback, then went on to insist that the state government in Louisiana was unable to protect the lives and rights of blacks, and asked the federal government to intervene. The meeting's resolutions insisted that all efforts by blacks to participate in government met resistance from white Democrats. As in Texas, Ruby now encountered a resurrected white power structure that, in the words of those at the meeting, met all efforts by blacks with the declaration that "this is a white man's government, and none but white men shall govern it." Their resolutions called on white Republicans to provide unqualified support to the protection of the rights of blacks if they expected blacks to continue to support the party.[19]

By 1875 Ruby had established himself enough in the public eye that he began to attract attacks by the Democratic press. Responding to one of his editorials in the *Louisianian*, the editor of the *Mandeville Wave* picked up some of the same themes that had been used against Ruby in Texas. In this case the editor attacked Ruby for claiming to be black so that he could secure an office. Ruby was instead, according to this editor, a "Camanche [sic] Indian from Texas" and he was unable to secure office despite his claims to be black, a falsehood given Ruby's position in the custom house. "We all know him," the editor wrote. "We know that he disorganized and defeated the Republican party [sic] in Texas and that he toted his turbulent carpetbag across the line to inaugurate the same Comanche Indian proceedings here."[20]

Ruby, of course, dismissed the claims that he was not black and the charges that he had somehow defeated the Republican Party. He simply went on with his political activity. In 1876 he took part with Pinchback in the maneuvering that led up to the presidential election to be held that year. Republicans held their convention in New Orleans in late June, and on the first day of the meeting, June 27, it was clear that the Republicans were divided between supporters of Pinchback and a group known as the Custom House Ring. Collector of the Customs James F. Casey, husband of one of President Grant's sisters, headed this group, although whites who held other key federal posts, including United States Marshal Stephen Packard, linked themselves with Casey at times. The division potentially threatened Ruby's position in the custom house, although at this time his support of Pinchback did not work against him since Casey, Packard, and Pinchback reconciled by the end of the convention. The first test of the relative strength of the two factions came when the delegates selected the temporary chairman. Pinchback won, defeating his opponent by a vote of 127 to 119. On the third day, however, the convention nearly broke apart over the seating of delegates but ended with conciliatory addresses given by Pinchback and Marshal Packard, who spoke for the Custom House faction. It was not until the sixth day of the convention that, following continued maneuvering over delegates and proxies, the convention moved to a vote on the gubernatorial nominee. The two most significant nominees were Governor Henry C. Warmoth and Marshal Packard. No candidate received a majority on the first ballot, but on the second many of the minor candidates withdrew and threw their support to Packard, who won. Pinchback spoke following Packard's victory, indicating that while the two had been on bitterly different sides on political issues, their personal relationship had been friendly and he "rejoiced" in Packard's choice. At the end of the meeting, the party seemed to be in harmony, and Pinchback was named chairman of the Republican State Central Committee. Ruby had not been a delegate to the convention, but he attended, and at the first meeting of the Central Committee the members chose him to serve as corresponding secretary.[21]

In the months leading up to the 1876 election, Ruby campaigned in a variety of settings both for Packard and for the Republican presidential candidate, Rutherford B. Hayes. On Wednesday, October 4, he attended the meeting of the Ladies' Union Republican Circle of the Third Ward. That evening the women passed resolutions dealing with the economic life of women in the South. Accepting that "liberty and happiness of every people depended greatly upon the compensated employment of their industry," and that the women of the Third Ward were capable of carrying on different kinds of industry, they asked for assistance in establishing modes of employment in the ward that would "enable us to earn a livelihood and keep at home some of the money now sent out of the State to buy manufactures elsewhere." They wanted especially the creation of a cotton mill in the ward. Ruby was among those who spoke to the assembly, addressing not only the economic aspirations of the participants but also speaking about the election and the need of Republicans to support their candidate. A report indicated that "at the conclusion of Mr. Ruby's remarks the people present were so filled with enthusiasm that they sung the campaign battle song to the air of 'John Brown's Body'":

> Hurrah for Hayes and Wheeler, right noble men and true:
> Shake out the grand old ensign, the red, the white and blue,
> And where the demon drove the hogs send Tilden and his crew,
> As we go marching on![22]

Presumably Ruby expected the women of the circle, who could not vote, to encourage their husbands to go to the polls.

Ruby also campaigned outside of New Orleans on at least one occasion, a fact that indicated his reputation as a campaign speaker had spread beyond the city. On November 5 Republican leaders in Houma held a meeting to counter one convened by the Democrats. The local Republicans brought in a group of speakers from New Orleans, including Ruby and Superintendent of Education Brown. The visiting New Orleans politicians arrived on the train with "Mr. Alber's brass band" and a large crowd, estimated by the reporter for the *New Orleans Republican* to include two thousand voters, escorted them down the main street of town to the speaker's stand. Through the afternoon various politicians addressed the crowd with Ruby delivering an address in the middle of the afternoon. He addressed the crowd for almost two hours, with one reporter calling him the most forceful speaker of the day. Ruby talked about national and state affairs and, according to a reporter for the *Republican*, made his points "so conclusively that the immense assemblage grew wildly enthusiastic." On the day of the election, November 7, Ruby was back in New Orleans, where he served as chair of the election commission, another government job that offered him pay, at the Custom House polling place in the Fourth Ward.[23]

When the polls closed in the 1876 election in Louisiana, the results for both the presidential and gubernatorial contests were uncertain once again. Initially, the Democratic presidential candidate, Samuel J. Tilden, appeared to have bested the Republican, Rutherford B. Hayes, but the state Returning Board threw out enough votes in counties that had seen considerable violence prior to the election to give Hayes the victory. The same result occurred in the gubernatorial race where the Democratic candidate, Francis T. Nicholls, appeared to have won, only to have the Returning Board reject enough votes to declare Packard the winner. In the legislative elections, the board's count reversed what appeared to have been Democratic victories in both the Senate and the House of Representatives into Republican majorities. The result of this post-election maneuvering was that the electoral votes for Louisiana were contested and the result appealed to Congress. Locally, the board-approved legislature met in the state capitol and inaugurated Packard. The legislators considered legitimate by the Democrats met in another location and inaugurated Nicholls. Louisiana, in effect, had two governments once again.[24]

Ruby had supported Packard in the election, but the changing political situation put Ruby into another precarious situation. In February 1877, the outcome of the elections in Louisiana remained undetermined, although by that time a compromise was understood to have been reached that gave Rutherford Hayes the Louisiana vote and the presidency. In New Orleans, however, the two claimants of the governor's office remained at odds. The Packard government was "barricaded in the State House, protected directly by the Metropolitan Police and indirectly by federal troops." Nicholls, on the other hand, had secured the support of the White League and used it to take over the New Orleans police stations and to secure the chambers of the state supreme court. Not only two governors but two legislatures also existed. In this stalemate, Pinchback hoped that the Packard government would elect him to the United States Senate. The Packard legislature failed to do so, and Pinchback left the Packard legislature, to which he had been elected, and entered the Nicholls body, throwing his support to Nicholls's claim. Nicholls, in return for Pinchback's move, pledged to protect blacks in the civil and political rights they had secured in Reconstruction. Even though Ruby held a post in the custom house, Pinchback was his primary patron and he remained a supporter. In Pinchback's cause, Ruby stopped editing the *Louisianian* and became editor of the *State Register*, a newspaper published in New Orleans and Carrollton and backed by Pinchback.[25]

Ruby used the *State Register* to drum up support for Pinchback's shift to Nicholls. Completely reversing the position he had taken the previous autumn, Ruby now wrote that he could no longer support Packard because he represented a "political element" in the state that had "contributed nothing towards its welfare." Ruby believed that Nicholls, unlike Packard, would bring "peace to the State, and with peace will come prosperity and its consequent blessings." He believed that Nicholls, while he had been a political opponent, was nonetheless a "patriot" and would work for the good of the state. Pointing to the concessions regarding protection of blacks in their rights obtained by Pinchback, Ruby stated that he believed that Nicholls would "see that life and property are respected and the laws are honestly and fairly executed." This, he believed, was all that any Louisianan, black or white, could ask for. On the other hand, he concluded, "neither will they be satisfied with less." The editor of the *Richmond Beacon*, from Rayville, Louisiana, did not see Ruby's shift in position as prompted by recognition of the rightness of Nicholls's cause. He saw it rather as recognizing the inevitable and abandoning a sinking ship. A more likely explanation was that Ruby simply voiced the opinions of his patron Pinchback and that he agreed that Nicholls's concessions might be the best way to guarantee that the government would respect the rights of black Louisianans.[26]

On April 26 Nicholls took control of the Louisiana statehouse, and his subsequent actions helped push Ruby to the most radical views that he had ever held. With Nicholls in power, it remained to be seen whether or not he would honor any commitment to the protection of blacks in their rights. It soon became apparent that would not be the case. Ruby, as he had written, proved that he would be satisfied with nothing other than such protection. The attack on rights secured in Reconstruction came quickly and, in June 1877, the New Orleans school board moved to segregate the public schools. Ruby went with a delegation to meet with Governor Nicholls to protest the action. Ruby had always been a strident advocate of equal rights, and in the face of this effort at reversing the gains blacks had made he became increasingly radical. He demanded that a right he believed belonged to blacks constitutionally as well as by statutes be respected. He asked who was white and who was black in a "community like this—of doubtful ancestry" and insisted that if the school board pushed the matter further it would have the effect of "carrying the war into Africa." In effect, Ruby threatened to make the racial heritage of some of the white elite of New Orleans known if the board separated the schools. He claimed to "have those facts in our possession which it would be unpleasant to some in high circles were we to use them." He would do that "in the event of separate schools." In the end, however, his threat failed to stop the segregation of the schools. In his stance towards white politicians, Ruby had come to sound much more like his colleague Matt Gaines in 1872, abandoning the conciliatory approach that he had taken through much of his career and becoming more confrontational.[27]

Ruby's position on integrated schools also marked his movement away from Pinchback and the beginning of an effort to lay out a new course for himself. He resigned from the *State Register* and disappeared from public notice and publishing newspapers for a time. He may have been uncertain what he should do, given the political realities of the time. His home life may also have contributed to his lower political and social profile. Little is known of his relationship with his wife or his children, although he appears to have been a good husband and father. The public record, however, provided almost no information on either George's wife or the rest of the family. George appeared frequently on the society pages of the New Orleans papers, but these newspaper reports seldom mentioned wives. What is known is that the family continued to grow and George's responsibilities increased. By 1878 their daughter Mabel was seven years old and probably enrolled in the city's public schools. Their son George was five. Then, on August 8, 1878, the couple had a second son. In keeping with the Ruby family's tradition of naming children after figures who were significant to the history of the race, Lucy and George named this new son Victor with a middle name of Tecumseh, probably in honor of General William Tecumseh Sherman.[28]

Ruby as a public figure appeared again when he began publishing his own newspaper, the *New Orleans Observer*. Its first edition came out on May 30, 1879. This time he not only edited the paper but owned it too and no longer had to be the voice of Pinchback. The editor of the *Donaldsonville Chief*, a Republican newspaper, called the *Observer* "radically Republican, straight-out and clear through." In announcing the new journal, Ruby admitted that the *Observer* would be Republican, noting that he believed the "principles which underlie and control that party are necessary to the welfare and continued prosperity of the country." He also made clear his particular intention of attacking the racism prevalent in Southern society. "Believing the spirit of caste and caste distinctions growing out of the monstrous evil of human bondage should be utterly abolished in Free America," he wrote, "the *Observer* will spare neither the keen weapons of ridicule nor sarcasm in holding the mirror up to nature and portraying the fallacy of such sentiments in American society." Intending his paper to be second to none in the state, however, he also announced that it would include topics of art, literature, science, religion, and society on its pages, as well as market reports and political and foreign information, the same sort of material he had included in the *Standard* in Galveston. The *Observer* remained his mouthpiece for the remainder of his career.[29]

In addition to his newspaper, Ruby became integrally involved in what came to be known as the Exoduster Movement, the emigration of thousands of blacks from Louisiana and the rest of the South to Kansas. A colonization movement had been created earlier in Caddo Parrish, Louisiana, in 1870, in response to the violence against tenant farmers there, and the movement continue to grow as violence increased. Ruby became a supporter of colonization, and on April 3 he published in the *Observer* a call for a convention to meet on April 17 in New Orleans to consider whether or not blacks should leave Louisiana. Ruby later denied that he had initiated the call, claiming instead that he had simply acted in response to the requests of numerous clergymen and teachers who were concerned with the plight of a large number of refugees from the northern parishes who had fled their homes and come to New Orleans. The meeting was held at the Free Mission Baptist Church in New Orleans, and hundreds of interested men were present. Ruby played an important role in the convention, even though not an officer. He chaired the committee on business that issued a scathing report that blamed the desire of blacks to leave the state solely on their treatment by whites. Ruby was the author of the report, indicating that the stories he heard from refugees from many of the rural parishes told of crime and lawlessness prevalent everywhere. Whites denied blacks their basic rights. They were unable to secure just recompense for their labor or to effect honorable dealings with planters. "Justice," was, in Ruby's words, "a mockery, and the law a cheat." Ruby contended that with government in the hands of the very men who backed the mob, blacks had no choice but to emigrate. Although he did not advise any individual to leave Louisiana, he recommended that all blacks support the movement. Rather than "stem the tide of this mighty movement," he believed that brotherhood and manliness, probably meaning self-respect, demanded that blacks "wisely and practically aid it."[30]

On the last day of the convention, Ruby spoke at the request of the delegates and elaborated on his thoughts about emigration. Ruby said that he favored emigration, but he urged blacks to give thorough consideration to when and where to go and counseled his listeners not to stampede. Pinchback also attended the meeting and openly opposed the course Ruby had taken. The April 17 convention marked a clear and permanent break between the two men. Ruby appeared now also to have determined no compromise with whites could be made, that without white concessions the races were at war. As the meeting adjourned he called on the men in the convention to sing the "Battle Hymn of the Republic," a song that had been the rallying cry of the Loyal League, and now remained a hymn of unity. Ruby had what one reporter called a "soft tenor voice," and with all of the delegates standing he began singing the first stanza by himself. No one joined in until the chorus when the band began to play and the "building rung with 'Glory, glory, Halleluja! Glory, glory, Halleluja!, Glory, glory, Halleluja! As we go marchin' on." The reporter found that Ruby's voice added "not a little" to the singing.[31]

Ruby appeared again on May 23 to talk about the Kansas migration, this time at a meeting of the Colored Independent Migration Association that was held in Lafayette Square. The group moved on to Taylor's Hall at the corner of Perdido and St. Jane Streets, where approximately two hundred people were gathered to hear speakers address them on the issues involved in emigrating. The reporter for the *Times-Picayune* wrote that Ruby "spoke in a quiet, thoughtful tone, advising the colored people to look well ahead before taking such an important step." Ruby went on to say, however, that he had given the matter much consideration. He had concluded that the change would be for the better. Kansas had fertile soil and mineral wealth and he believed that blacks "had the enterprise and perseverance necessary to develop its great resources." He admitted that it was cold, and that whites often asserted it was too cold for blacks. It was not that cold, he said, then went on, "[I]f the negro [sic] could stand the treatment received at the hands of the white people for the last fifteen years, he could stand a little cold weather."[32]

Shortly after the New Orleans meetings Ruby attended a convention in Vicksburg sponsored by white businessmen and planters from the Mississippi Valley concerned with the potential loss of laborers that the exodus might produce. Ruby spoke before the meeting, telling the men who had gathered that the exodus might in the short run produce a loss of productivity, but that in the long run he believed it would work to their advantage. He believed there were parts of Louisiana that would be better if all blacks left. He also warned the men at the convention that they should not pursue any "unwise course" and try to stop blacks from leaving because that would only increase the impetus behind the exodus. In the end, the convention promised to protect blacks in their rights, but when Ruby returned to New Orleans he warned the delegates to the convention that their resolutions concerning the protection of black rights were all well and good, but that ideas had to assume tangible shapes. "What the laboring masses of the Mississippi Valley demand," he wrote in the *Observer*, "are works and not words. Pledges innumerable, strong and weak, from Governors, legislators and civic functionaries, they have had in abundance—but words, words, mere words did not secure them any measure of their rights." Only if something was done to achieve those ends would blacks quit leaving the South. If not, they would leave to "go elsewhere, to freedom and security of citizenship."[33]

In his support of the exodus, Ruby found himself alone among Louisiana's principal black politicians. In later testimony before a congressional committee that investigated the movement to Kansas, Ruby indicated that Republicans in Louisiana not only "frowned upon this convention" but afterwards openly opposed the exodus. He believed that Republican politicians had taken this position because it took population away from counties where party leaders believed they could control the vote. Seen as a threat to their political power, even if only within the party, he believed that they would "do what they could to put a stop to it." Ruby's support of the exodus alienated him not only from the state's black leadership but from the Republican Party, at least for a time. Always present at party conventions in the past, he did not attend the state convention held in New Orleans on October 20–21, 1879. Ruby did, however, use his editorial columns to support the convention's gubernatorial nominee, Judge Taylor Beattie, an attorney and former Confederate officer who had become a Republican. During the campaign the editor of the *Abbeville Meridional* described Ruby's *Observer* as a "rabid little Republican sheet" that denounced the Democratic state ticket and hoped to "seduce wavering and disaffected Democrats to the support of its ticket" and Judge Beattie.[34]

At some point after the state election, and what had by then become the predictable Democratic victory, the falling out between Ruby and Pinchback became personal as well as political. Ruby's reprinting of an item concerning Pinchback published in the *Washington Star* (Washington, DC) provided the apparent cause. The article said that that Pinchback had been in Washington recently, suggesting that while there he pressured Secretary of the Treasury John Sherman to place him in one of the federal offices in New Orleans if Sherman won the election. Sherman, in turn, wanted to appoint Pinchback because he thought it would bring the Louisiana delegate to his support in the upcoming Republican nominating convention. The offensive part of the item came when it alleged that President Rutherford Hayes had opposed the appointment because he understood that Pinchback was the "owner of three-high-toned Negro faro banks in New Orleans." Ruby's publication of the article outraged Pinchback, who accused Ruby of printing the article knowing that its charges were false and that it would injure him politically. In an editorial in his *Louisianian* on February 21, 1880, Pinchback called Ruby an "impecunious vagabond who has managed to eke out a miserable existence in this community for the last year and a half by the publication of a cheap personal advertising sheet called the *Observer*." He then denounced Ruby as "a slanderer, falsifier sycophantic fraud and coward." A friendship that had appeared to survive the two men's political break now ended.[35]

The break between Ruby and Pinchback worsened over time. Several days after Pinchback printed his attack on Ruby, the two met in the New Orleans post office. Ruby reputedly greeted Pinchback and Pinchback refused to recognize Ruby. Instead, Pinchback struck Ruby with his cane. On March 6 Pinchback made a further printed attack on Ruby in the *Louisianian*. This time he called Ruby a "cowardly maligner" who was "tired of his miserable existence" and who through his "villification" [sic] was attempting to force Pinchback to "rid this community of his worthless presence." Pinchback appeared ready to fight a duel with Ruby. In the end, he said that he would not act only because Ruby was a "despicable wretch," and further, that "there are many good reasons why I cannot afford to do it just at this time." One of these good reasons, he suggested, was that fighting such a coward would be a disgrace, but by then it may have also been that such a confrontation with Ruby could have ended any chance that Pinchback would get a federal appointment.

Ruby, in fact, was on his way to Washington at the time of Pinchback's March 6 editorial. The congressional committee considering the exodus of blacks from the South had called him to the capitol to testify. On March 10, 1880, Ruby appeared before the Senate committee. Senator William Windom of Minnesota, who headed the committee, asked Ruby what he knew about the exodus of blacks to the north. Ruby explained that his role as an educator and journalist in Louisiana provided him the necessary background and then referred specifically to the information he had received at the April 17, 1879, convention called by his newspaper to discuss whether or not blacks should leave the state. He explained that the convention had made it very clear that interest in leaving the state was "rife." The movement, he observed, had not emerged from among the black religious, educational, or political leaders but from among the people, and he saw it as a grassroot movement. While he attributed it partly to the economic conditions faced by blacks, he saw the movement primarily as a response to "armed mobs and outrages practiced upon them because of their political sentiments." Ruby took much the same position he had taken in the previous meetings, when Democratic senators cross-examined him and asked him if he encouraged blacks to leave the state even though he personally did not intend to do so. Ruby answered yes. While it was safe for him to live in New Orleans, he believed his life would be in danger should he ever go into any of the bulldozed parishes.[36]

Much of what Ruby said during his Senate testimony was similar to his statements at the conventions in 1879, but as he finished his first day's testimony he ended with what may have been the most pessimistic statement he had ever made about race relations in the South, one that came to a large extent from his own experiences. In answering a question placed by one of the committee members as to what the election of a Democratic president would do relative to the exodus, Ruby suggested it would only hasten it. Up to that point he had been talking largely about rural workers, but citing another newspaper editor's writings, he turned to the experience of urban blacks. Even in the city, he said, it was difficult for a black man to have a measure of his rights as a free man. "[T]he better educated he is," Ruby said, "the better advantages he may have had elsewhere, the more culture he possesses, the more keenly, of course, he feels the outrages imposed upon him." Ruby's words appeared to reflect his personal despair, the despair of an educated, well-read, cosmopolitan man in a community where racism had triumphed.[37]

Ruby returned to party politics after he returned from Washington, a necessity given the fact that he still held a job in the custom house, and Treasury Secretary Sherman wanted the Republican nomination for the presidency in 1880. Ruby became an active advocate for the Sherman candidacy, possibly as a means of holding on to his job after his break with most of Louisiana's political leaders. As a part of the campaign for Sherman's nomination, Ruby went back to Texas to attend the Republican state convention in Austin on March 24, where he worked to see how many delegates he could pin down for Sherman. He also brought large quantities of the *Washington World*, Sherman's campaign paper, with him to distribute. He found, however, that getting delegates for Sherman was difficult. Most of the white federal appointees in Texas actually supported the candidacy of former president Ulysses S. Grant. Governor Davis, Ruby's longtime friend, backed Grant as well. Ruby's only success on the trip may have been with his former protégé, Wright Cuney. The *Galveston News*, when tallying the number of delegates who probably would vote for Grant, listed Cuney as doubtful.[38]

Back in Louisiana, Ruby attended the Republican state convention in New Orleans on May 24 to elect delegates to the national convention in Chicago. The convention was another contentious one in which Pinchback, Representative T. T. Allain, Senator Henry Demas, and Judge Beattie, supporters of the nomination of former president Grant, walked out when the Custom House Ring secured control over the seating of delegates. The delegates who remained in the convention included supporters of James G. Blaine and Secretary Sherman. In the end, the convention sent to Chicago a delegation not committed to any particular candidate, but rather composed of supporters of both of these candidates. Former governors Warmoth and W. P. Kellogg and former chief of police and current Collector of Customs Albert S. Badger led the delegation. Ruby, clearly a Sherman supporter, was present at the convention and once again became a delegate to the national convention, although this time as an alternate.[39]

Sherman did not get the Republican nomination in 1880, but he did return to the United States Senate. Nonetheless, a Republican, James A. Garfield, secured the White House, guaranteeing that Republicans would fill the federal patronage positions in New Orleans. As a result, Collector Badger retained his place at the New Orleans Custom House. Ruby, perhaps for his loyalty to the Warmoth faction in the state convention and for Sherman in the campaign, managed to get a new position in the Custom House. On December 2, Badger appointed Ruby as a clerk in the Weigher's Department, a newly created position that had been recommended by the Treasury's Special Agent, who had visited the Custom House earlier. Ruby received an annual salary of $1,200. Party loyalty got him his position. His political nonconformity, however, soon threatened that job.[40]

Ruby continued to publish the *Observer* and he remained involved in politics, but increasingly he was more of a political maverick. By 1882 the *Observer* had failed, but he began publishing another newspaper, the *Republican*. This new paper supported the election of Judge Taylor Beattie for Congress in Louisiana's Third District, marking Ruby's break with the Custom House Ring. Beattie had been nominated when his supporters bolted the regular district convention after the Custom House Ring gained control over seating the delegates. The Beattie faction contended that the Ring then stacked the vote for its candidate, former senator William Kellogg. Ruby, who had long been considered to be part of the Ring and survived changes in who held the federal appointments, now broke with it. Ruby vigorously attacked Kellogg, challenging Kellogg's claims that he had done more than anyone else to further the material interests of Louisianans. Ruby maintained that Kellogg had "been more active in the senate to further his own interests than anything else." Further, he charged the senator with being bribed by the Texas Pacific Railroad with a payment of over two hundred thousand dollars to secure his support for their bills. Pointing to Kellogg's absence at critical votes, Ruby concluded that "Louisiana would have been served better if Mr. Kellogg's seat had been vacant." Ruby's position amounted to virtual political and economic suicide and seems unexplainable. Ruby, however, appeared by this point to be tired of the established white officeholders and distributors of patronage, their promises, and their failures to look after the interests of blacks. Always hopeful that blacks could secure their basic rights, he no longer saw the Ring as the means to gain that end. Ruby's position came at an immediate cost, one he probably knew would happen once he broke with the Ring. An item in the *New Orleans Times-Democrat* only a month after his attack on Kellogg reported that Ruby had lost his post at the Custom House.[41]

The 1882 congressional campaign and his support of a reform candidate turned out to be Ruby's last contest. He had spent all of his adult life fighting for equality, but that struggle ended suddenly. On the morning of October 31, 1882, he died after suffering only a short illness. A report in the *New Orleans Picayune* described his death as having been caused by "congestion of the brain." The mortuary report for the city indicated he had died of malarial fever. Many contemporary newspapers considered his death to have been a significant enough event that they published obituaries. The *New Orleans Times-Democrat* noted his death and went so far as to describe Ruby as a man "of some attainments," something the paper would never have done while Ruby was still alive. The *Boston Globe* reported his death in obituary entitled, "Death of a Noted Colored Man" and recognized him as a "very eloquent speaker." The obituary was even picked up by the *London American Register*. His place of burial is unknown. While he left behind a legacy of work on behalf of his race, he appeared to have left little behind for his family in terms of property or wealth, contradicting all of the previous assertions that he had become wealthy by corruptly selling his votes while in Texas. Shortly after George's death, Lucy and the children moved back to Washington, DC, where she still had family and perhaps could take advantage of some of her husband's political connections. Lucy spent most of her adult years as a worker in the Government Printing Office and died in Washington on February 14, 1925. George Nalle Ruby, the oldest son, lived for a time with his mother in Washington, then moved to Boston, dying there on April 28, 1945. George and Lucy's daughter Mabel lived with her mother and also worked in the Printing Office and taught in the District's public schools. She died two years after her mother on November 7, 1927. Victor lived with his mother until 1900, then worked as a government messenger in the District, where he remained into the 1940s. The date of his death is unknown.[42]

George Thompson Ruby lived an extraordinary but unfortunately short life. He, with certainty, did not fit the negative stereotype of black leaders created in the post-Civil War years and perpetrated by a later generation of historians. In this he was not unlike many of the other black leaders who emerged in the Reconstruction South and particularly those who had been free before the war. He had experienced opportunities that gave him the skills necessary for leadership. His public school education was something virtually unknown for the great mass of African Americans in antebellum

America. Through his family he had known of the struggle for black equality and the means used to further that goal. His time in Haiti and Louisiana, part of his journey to Texas, gave him to an even greater extent contact with men and women working for the betterment of his race. Perhaps his family's commitment to abolition and his own experiences with the free people of Haiti also gave him an empathy with the freedmen with whom he worked that made him acceptable to them as a leader, even though he had little in common with them other than race. Given all of those advantages, the leadership role he played in Texas was hardly surprising.[43]

What is different about Ruby is the breadth of his experiences and the readiness he demonstrated in shifting tactics to secure the greater goal of a community in which African Americans could control their own lives. Historian Eric Foner observed in an essay review that black leaders have often differed among themselves as to how to define themselves. Some have seen themselves primarily as representatives of the black community, while others identified more closely with predominantly white nonracial parties. Some were black nationalists, some believed in self-determination, while others sought political solutions through white alliances. Ruby embraced all of these positions, changing how he attempted to achieve his overarching goals to meet the conditions that he encountered. He went to Haiti believing that blacks could never be truly free in the United States and could prosper only in a community controlled by blacks. In Louisiana he took on the role of a teacher, appearing to re-embrace his family's ideas of self-improvement and the idea that if blacks somehow demonstrated to whites their capacities, whites would accept them as equal. In Texas he retained his belief in self-improvement, both as an educator and also by encouraging self-improvement through the recognition of black accomplishments, but he also came to believe that through political alliances with whites equality might be achieved through the law. Turning to a political career in Texas, Ruby helped wed the state's black population to the Republican Party and pressured that party to work to offer blacks lasting political and social equality. Within that party, Ruby served in the state's constitutional convention in 1868–1869, headed the Grand Council of the Loyal League, sat in the state senate, and even held the position of chairman of the Republican State Executive Committee. In the end, in Louisiana he returned to his original view, concluding that only an abandonment of the South for black communities in Kansas would make possible the kind of world he hoped to both create and live in.[44]

The changes Ruby made in his tactics contribute to the complexity of evaluating him. Still, throughout his career, men and women of his race saw him as an extraordinary spokesman for their interests. His white allies also respected him for his contributions to their political agenda. Even his political enemies, except in the heat of political contests, at times recognized his accomplishments. No matter the change in tactics, the struggle always was about creating that society where blacks could be truly free, safe to pursue their own interests, and to actually exercise some power. That remained the constant in Ruby's life. Sadly, in terms of the result, the fight was against an enemy of privilege and power that refused to recognize blacks either as equals or even as human. That same opponent willingly used violence to maintain the status quo in race relations, a status quo that assumed black inferiority. He could not match those men in brute strength. In the end, George Ruby was not the sort of man Texas history traditionally has seen as a hero. He was not a frontiersman or a cowboy. He did not fight in the Texas Revolution or the Civil War. He was not white. Still, there was something heroic about him. When considering him as a man who unflinchingly stood by his ideas of what was right, who spent his entire life attempting to create a Texas and an America that lived up to the promise of the Declaration of Independence—that all people are created equal and endowed with basic rights—he contributed much to the state's history, serving as a model for a future generation of black leaders such as Wright Cuney and also demonstrating the commitment of his race to securing their basic rights. It was that commitment that led him to the floor of the state senate on the afternoon of June 17, 1870, where he spoke of a revolution and urged Texans to take a new path to change the past.

NOTES

INTRODUCTION

1. *State Journal Appendix*, 91.

2. Charles W. Ramsdell, *Reconstruction in Texas* (New York: Columbia University Press, 1910), 317–18 (first three quotations), 201 (fourth quotation); W. C. Nunn, *Texas Under the Carpetbaggers* (Austin: University of Texas Press, 1960), 15.

3. Eric Foner, *Reconstruction: America's Unfinished Revolution, 1863–1877* (New York: Harper & Row, 1988), xxi; Howard N. Rabinowitz, "The Changing Image of Black Reconstructionists," in *Southern Black Leaders of the Reconstruction Era*, ed. Howard N. Rabinowitz (Urbana: University of Illinois Press, 1982), xv–xxiv, xvi (quotation); J. Mason Brewer, *Negro Legislators of Texas and Their Descendants: A History of the Negro in Texas Politics from Reconstruction to Disfranchisement* (Dallas: Mathis Publishing Co., 1935). See Eric Foner, *Freedom's Lawmakers: A Directory of Black Officeholders during Reconstruction* (Baton Rouge: Louisiana State University Press, 1993) for an overview of recent work on all known black lawmakers.

4. Randall B. Woods, "George T. Ruby: A Black Militant in the White Business Community," *Red River Valley Historical Review* 1 (Autumn 1974): 269; Carl H. Moneyhon, "George T. Ruby and the Politics of Expediency in Texas," in *Southern Black Leaders of the Reconstruction Era*, ed. Howard N. Rabinowitz (Urbana: University of Illinois Press, 1982), 363–389; James Smallwood, "G. T. Ruby: Galveston's Black Carpetbagger in Reconstruction Texas," *Houston Review* 5 (Winter 1983): 24–33, 33 (first and second quotations), 24 (third quotation).

5. Barry A. Crouch, "A Political Education: George T. Ruby and the Texas Freedmen's Bureau," *Houston Review* 18 (1996): 144–156; Barry A. Crouch, "Black Education in Civil War and Reconstruction Louisiana, George T. Ruby, the Army, and the Freedmen's Bureau," *Louisiana History* 3 (Summer 1997): 287–308, 308 (quotation).

6. Merline Pitre, "George T. Ruby: The Party Loyalist," in *Through Many Dangers, Toils and Snares: Black Leadership in Texas, 1870–1890* (Austin: Eakin Press, Revised Edition, 1997), 180–189.

7. "The Changing Image of Black Reconstructionists," in *Southern Black Leaders of the Reconstruction Era,* ed. Howard N. Rabinowitz (Urbana: University of Illinois Press, 1982), xv–xxiv.

CHAPTER I

1. Information from Horatio Ruby Bible (Horatio was the brother of George Ruby) provided by Bob Greene, Portland, Maine; Maine, Early Marriage Records,

Maine Early Death Records, accessed May 17, 2017, www.archives.com; "Praying Payson of Portland Maine," accessed June 1, 2017, http://enrichmentjournal.ag.org/200503/200503_116_Payson.cfm; *A Memoir of the Rev. Edward Payson, DD., late of Portland Maine,* accessed June 1, 2017, https://archive.org/details/memoirofrevedwar01cumm; *Emancipator*, June 3, 1841.

2. *Eastern Argus*, Sept. 19, 1826; Information from Horatio Ruby Bible provided by Bob Greene, Portland, Maine; Bob Greene, "Portland, On the Record: A Look at Early Portland and a First Family," in *Maine's Visible Black History: The First Chronicle of Its People,* H. H Price and Gerald E. Talbot, (Gardiner, Maine: Tilbury House Publishers, 2006), 43, 254, 271, 145–46, 160–64.

3. *Freedom's Journal*, Mar. 16, 1827; John W. Cromwell, *The Negro in American History: Men and Women Eminent in the Evolution of the American of African Descent* (Washington, DC: The American Negro Academy, 1914), 35; *Houston Daily Union*, July 30, 1870.

4. Horatio Ruby Bible; Maine, Early Marriage Records, Maine Early Death Records, www.archives.com consulted May 17, 2017; *The Portland Directory* (un.: un, 1831), 70; *City Advertiser, Annexed to the Portland Directory* (Portland: Arthur Shiley Printers, 1834), 20; *The Portland Directory* (un.; un: 1837), 65.

5. Walter M. Merrill, ed., *The Letters of William Lloyd Garrison* (Cambridge: Belknap Press of Harvard University Press, 1971), I, 162, 172–77, 175 (quotation); *Liberator*, Jan. 1, 1831; Russel B. Nye, *William Lloyd Garrison and the Humanitarian Reformers* (Boston: Little, Brown and Company, 1955), 55–57; Quaker Meeting House Plaque, accessed May 17, 2017, http://www.waymarking.com/waymarks/WM78W1_Friends_Quaker_Meeting_House_Portland_ME.

6. Merrill, *The Letters of William Lloyd Garrison*, 175.

7. *Liberator*, Nov. 1, 1834; "Fessenden, Samuel," in *Appleton's Cyclopaedia of American Biography*, eds. James G. Wilson and John Fisk (New York: D. Appleton, 1900), II.

8. George Thompson to William Lloyd Garrison, Oct. 28, 1834, in *Letters and Addresses by George Thompson During His Mission in the United States, From Oct. 1, 1834, to Nov. 27, 1835*, George Thompson (Boston: Isaac Knapp, 1837), 16.

9. *Catalogue of the Officers and Students of Bowdoin College and the Medical School of Maine, April, 1833* (Brunswick: Press of Joseph Griffin, 1833), 4; "Pomeroy, Swan Lyman, Dd," McClintock and Strong Biblical Cyclopedia, accessed May 19, 2017, http://www.biblicalcyclopedia.com/P/pomeroy-swan-lyman-dd.html; *First Annual Report of the American Anti-Slavery Society; with the Speeches Delivered at the Anniversary Meeting, Held in Chatham-Street Chapel, in the City of New York, ...* (np: np, 1834); *Third Annual Report of the American Anti-Slavery Society with the Speeches Delivered at the Anniversary Meeting Held in the City of New York on the 10th May, 1836, and the Minutes of the Meetings of the Society for Business* (New York: William S. Door, 1836).

10. *Constitution of the American Society of Free Persons of Color, for Improving Their Condition in the United States: For Purchasing Lands; And For the Establishment of a Settlement in Upper Canada, Also the Proceedings of the Convention with Their Address to Free Persons of Colour in the United States* (Philadelphia: Printed by J. W. Allen, 1831), 9; Leon Litwack, *North of Slavery* (Chicago: University of Chicago Press, 1961), 72;

Stephen Middleton, *The Black Laws: Race and the Legal Process in Early Ohio* (Athens: Ohio University Press, 2005), 42–72.

11. *Minutes and Proceedings of the First Annual Convention of the People of Colour, Held by Adjournments in the City of Philadelphia from the Sixth to the Eleventh of June, Inclusive,* 1831 (Philadelphia: Published by Order of the Committee of Arrangements, 1831), 15 (quotations).

12. *Liberator*, May 23, June 13, 1835; Price and Talbot, eds., *Maine's Visible Black History*, 43–44, 270; *The Portland Directory; Containing the Names of the Inhabitants, Their Occupations, Places of Business, and Dwelling Houses, and the City Register, with Lists of the Streets, Courts and Wharves, the City Officers, Public Offices, Banks, &c.* (Portland: A Shirley, Printer, 1837), 10.

13. *Minutes of the Fifth Annual Convention for the Improvement of the Free People of Colour in the United States, Held by Adjournments, in the Wesley Church, Philadelphia, from the First to the Fifth of June, Inclusive, 1835* (Philadelphia: Printed by William P. Gibbons, 1835), 24–25; John W. Cromwell, "The Early Negro Convention Movement," *Occasional Papers No. 9, The American Negro Academy* (Washington, DC: Published by the Academy, 1904), 10–11.

14. *Minutes of the Fifth Annual Convention for the Improvement of the Free People of Colour*, 31–32; *Liberator*, Aug. 8, 1835; *The Minutes and Proceedings of the First Annual Meeting of the American Moral Reform Society, Held at Philadelphia, in the Presbyterian Church in Seventh Street, below Shippen, from the 14th to the 19th of August, 1837* (Philadelphia: Printed by Merrihew and Gunn, 1837), 28.

15. *Liberator*, June 13, 1836.

16. *Liberator*, Sept. 29, 1837.

17. Horatio Ruby Family Bible.

18. Price and Talbot, *Maine's Visible Black History*, 271.

19. Price and Talbot, *Maine's Visible Black History*, 270–71.

20. *Emancipator*, June 3, 1841; Horatio Ruby Family Bible.

21. Leslie M. Harris, *In the Shadow of Slavery: African Americans in New York City, 1626–1863* (Chicago: University of Chicago Press, 2003), 217–218.

22. *Liberator*, July 10, 1840; Harris, *In the Shadow of Slavery*, 210–11; Eric Foner, *Gateway to Freedom: The Hidden History of the Underground Railroad* (New York: W. W. Norton & Company, 2015), 63–90.

23. *Liberator*, July 10, 1840 (quotation); *Colored American*, July 25, Aug. 15, 1840.

24. *Colored American*, Aug. 1, 1840; *Liberator*, Aug. 21, Sept. 25, and Oct. 2, 1840.

25. *National Anti-Slavery Standard*, September 24 (first and second quotations), Oct. 23, Nov. 5 (third and fourth quotations), 1840, Jan. 28, 1841, accessed May 24, 2017, http://americanabolitionist.liberalarts.iupui.edu/vanren.htm.

26. *Colored American*, Nov. 21, Dec. 5, 7 (quotations), 1840, Oct. 9, 1841; Phyllis F. Field, "Republicans and Black Suffrage in New York State: The Grass Roots Response," *Civil War History* 21 (June 1975): 136–47.

27. *National Anti-Slavery Standard*, Feb. 4, 1841 (quotations); *Liberator*, Apr. 9, 1841.

28. "From the New-York Mirror of Liberty," *Liberator*, July 30, 1841.

29. *Liberator*, Sept. 9, 24, Oct. 22 (quotations), 1841.

30. *Boston Evening Transcript*, Aug. 22, 1849 (quotation); *New Hampshire Patriot*

and State Gazette, Aug. 30, 1849; *Philadelphia Public Ledger*, Nov. 12, 1849; *Portland Argus*, Dec. 6, 1849.

31. *The Seventh Census of the United States: 1850, . . . An Appendix* (Washington, DC: Robert Armstrong, Public Printer, 1853), 4; S. B. Beckett, *The Portland Directory & Reference Book for 1852–53* (Portland: Printed by Brown Thurston, 1852), 178, 202, 203, 209.

32. "Reuben Ruby: Hackman, Activist," Maine History Online, accessed Aug. 14, 2016, https://www.mainememory.net/sitebuilder/site/875/page/1286/display; Bob Greene, "Portland: On the Record: A Look at Early Portland and a First Family," in *Maine's Visible Black History*, eds. Price and Talbott (Gardiner, ME: Tilbury House, 2006), 44; *U.S. City Directories, 1822–1995* [data base online], accessed May 25, 2017, Ancestry.com.

33. *Liberator*, Nov. 1, 1850.

34. Price and Talbott, *Maine's Visible Black History*, 164–165; At the time, Hall was twenty-six years old, the son of Daniel and Margaret Hall. His parents were farmers. 1850 and 1860. US Manuscript Census, Cumberland County, Maine.

35. Price and Talbott, *Maine's Visible Black History*, 164, 357; Rosella Adeline Loveitt, "The Social History of Portland Maine, from 1840 to 1860," MA Thesis, (University of Maine, 1940); *Memorial of Rev. William H. Shailer, D.C.* (Portland: B. Thurston and Co., Printers, 1883), 10–11; *Portland Press* (Portland, Maine) in *Galveston Republican*, Mar. 16, 1868 (quotation); *Portland Daily Press*, Oct. 8, 1870.

CHAPTER II

1. Floyd John Miller, *The Search for a Black Nationality: Black Emigration and Colonization, 1787–1863* (Urbana: University of Illinois Press, 1975), 54–55, 74–81, 232–35.

2. Miller, *The Search for a Black Nationality*, 235–37; James Redpath, ed., *A Guide to Hayti* (New York: G. Woolworth Colton, 1861), 9; John R. McKivigan, *Forgotten Firebrand: James Redpath and the Making of Nineteenth-Century America* (Ithaca, NY: Cornell University Press, 2008).

3. *Pine and Palm*, May 18, 1861; *Weekly Anglo-African*, Jan. 5, 1861, in William Seraille, "Afro-American Emigration to Haiti during the American Civil War," *The Americas* 35 (Oct. 1978), 186.

4. Redpath, *A Guide to Hayti* (Boston: Haytian Bureau of Immigration, 1861), 9–10 (quotations).

5. Redpath, *A Guide to Hayti*, 98 (quotation).

6. Willis D. Boyd, "Redpath and American Negro Colonization in Haiti, 1860–1862," *The Americas* 12 (Oct. 1955), 169–70, 172–73, 176, 181.

7. Report of James Redpath to M. Plésance, Feb. 9, 1861, (first quotation), accessed June 12, 2018, https://archive.org/stream/reportscorresponoohait#page/188; *Pine and Palm*, June 8, 1861.

8. *Pine and Palm*, May 25, 1861.

9. *Pine and Palm*, May 25, 1861 (quotations), Oct. 12, 1862.

10. *Pine and Palm,* May 25, 1861.

11. *Pine and Palm,* May 25, 1861.

12. *Pine and Palm*, May 25, June 22 (quotations), 1861.

13. *Pine and Palm*, June 22, 1861.

14. G. T. Ruby to the editors, July 18, 1861, in *Pine and Palm*, Sept. 28, 1861.

15. G. T. Ruby to the editors, July 14, 1861, in *Pine and Palm*, Sept. 7, 1861; G. T. Ruby to the editors, July 18, 1861 (quotations), in *Pine and Palm*, Sept. 28, 1861.

16. G. T. Ruby to the editors, Aug. 31, 1861, *Pine and Palm*, Nov. 9, 1861; see also March 6, 1862.

17. G. T. Ruby to the editors, Aug. 31, 1861, *Pine and Palm*, Nov. 9, 1861; Boyd, "James Redpath and American Negro Colonization in Haiti," 172.

18. Boyd, "James Redpath and American Negro Colonization in Haiti," 178–79.

19. G. T. Ruby to the editors, Aug. 31, 1861, *Pine and Palm*, Nov. 9, 1861; "Health Hints for Emigrants," *Pine and Palm*, June 15, 1861.

20. *Pine and Palm*, Mar. 6, 1862.

21. *Pine and Palm*, May 8, 1862.

22. *Pine and Palm*, May 15, 1862.

23. *Pine and Palm*, May 15, 1862.

24. *Pine and Palm*, May 15, 1862.

25. *Pine and Palm*, May 15, 1862.

26. Redpath quotation in Miller, *The Search for a Black Nationality*, 247. See also 245–47.

27. *Pine and Palm*, Aug. 28, 1862.

28. *Pine and Palm*, Sept. 4, 1862; *New York Tribune*, Aug. 15, 1862. See also *Daily National Intelligencer*, Aug. 6, 1862, *Douglass' Monthly*, Sept. 1862, for information on attacks on blacks in the Midwest.

29. "Emigration --G.T.R.," *Pine and Palm*, Sept. 4, 1862.

30. McKivigan, *Forgotten Firebrand*, 81–83.

31. *Pine and Palm*, May 15, 1862; *Consolidated Lists of Civil War Draft Registrations, 1863–1865*. NM-65, entry 172, 620 volumes. NAI: 4213514. Records of the Provost Marshal General's Bureau (Civil War), Record Group 110. National Archives at Washington DC; Ancestry.com. *U.S., Civil War Draft Registrations Records, 1863–1865* [database on-line]. Provo, UT, USA: Ancestry.com Operations, Inc., 2010.

CHAPTER III

1. *Portland Daily Press*, Apr. 14, 1864.

2. *Investigation of Causes of Migration of Negroes from Southern to Northern States, Testimony*, pts. 2 and 3, 46th Cong., 2d sess., *Senate Reports*, no.693, (ser. 1900), 55; "Letter from New Orleans," *Liberator*, Feb. 26, 1864.

3. "Letter from New Orleans," *Liberator*, Feb. 26, 1864,

4. "Letter from New Orleans," *Liberator*, Feb. 26, 1864.

5. "Letter from New Orleans," *Liberator*, Feb. 26, 1864.

6. *Second Annual Report of the New England Freedmen's Aid Society, (Educational Commission): Presented to the Society, April 21, 1864* (Boston: New England Freedmen's Aid Society, 1864), 48; William F. Messner, "Black Education in Louisiana, 1863–1865," *Civil War History* 22 (1976), 45–46.

7. "Letter from New Orleans," *Liberator*, Feb. 26, 1864; *Investigation of Causes of Migration of Negroes from Southern to Northern States, Testimony, pts. 2 and 3*, 46th Cong., 2d sess., *Senate Reports 693*, 38; *Boston Daily Advertiser*, Aug 30, 1866 (quotations). Ruby, in his testimony before Congress, remembered working for Rev. Hooker, a Baptist minister killed in the July 30, 1866, New Orleans Riot. The only minister killed in that affair was Rev. Horton, a Baptist minister who ran a school in

New Orleans at the time Ruby arrived. In probability Rev. Horton was the man who Ruby worked for and either his memory had failed him on the matter or the reporter failed to record Horton's name correctly in the transcript of the hearing.

8. "General Orders, No. 38, Mar. 22, 1864," in *Official Records of the War of the Rebellion* Ser. 3 (Washington: Government Printing Office, 1888–1901), vol. iv, 193–194, hereinafter cited as *OR*; William F. Messner, "Black Education in Louisiana, 1863–1865," *Civil War History* 22 (March 1976): 47.

9. *Report of the Board of Education for Freedmen, Department of the Gulf, for the Year 1864* (New Orleans: Office of the True Delta, 1865), 8–9.

10. *Report of the Board of Education . . . for the Year 1864*, 14; B. F. Burnham to H. R. Pease, Jan. 20, 1866, "Reports and Other Records," Records of the Superintendent of Education and of the Division of Education-Louisiana, Bureau of Refugees, Freedmen and Abandoned Lands, National Archives, Record Group 105, Microfilm 1026, Roll 3; 8–9 (quotations), hereinafter RSE-Louisiana, BRFAL, NA, RG105, M1026, Roll 3.

11. Howard A. White, *The Freedmen's Bureau in Louisiana* (Baton Rouge: Louisiana State University Press, 1970), 167–169; "Freedmen's Bureau," 39th Cong., 1st sess., *House Executive Documents*, no. 70, 8.

12. G. T. Ruby to M. A. Warren, Nov. 1, 1865, "Correspondence Received Relating to Employment Recommendations, Jan. 1864–Sept. 1868." RSE-Louisiana, BRFAL, NA, RG105, M1026, Roll 9; *New Era* in the *National Anti-Slavery Standard*, Feb. 17, 1866.

13. W. H. Pearse and Robert G. Seymour to H. R. Pease, Dec. 1, 1865, "Reports and Other Records," RSE-Louisiana, BRFAL, NA, RG105, M1026, Roll 3.

14. W. H. Pearse to H. R. Pease, Dec. 28, 1865, "Reports and Other Records," RSE-Louisiana, BRFAL, NA, RG105, M1026, Roll 3.

15. Mortimer A. Warren to H. R. Pease, Jan. 31, 1866, "Reports and Other Records," RSE-Louisiana, BRFAL, NA, RG105, M1026, Roll 3.

16. J. W. Alvord, *Second Semi-Annual Report on Schools and Finances of Freedmen, July 1, 1866* (Washington: Government Printing Office, 1868), 8, 9 (quotations); "Circular No 27," in "Freedmen's Bureau," 39th Cong, 1st sess, *House Executive Documents*, 70, 30; White, *The Freedmen's Bureau in Louisiana*, 173–177.

17. *Houston Daily Union*, July 30, 1870.

18. G. T. Ruby to Capt. A. G. Studer, Apr. 12, 1866, "Reports and Other Records," Received by the Board of Education from School Agents, Apr. 1864–Mar. 1865, RSEL, BRFAL, NA M1026, Roll. 3.

19. G. T. Ruby to Capt. A. G. Studer, Apr. 12, 1866, "Reports and Other Records," Received by the Board of Education from School Agents, Apr. 1864–Mar. 1865, RSEL, BRFAL, NA M1026, Roll. 3.

20. G. T. Ruby to Capt. A. G. Studer, Apr. 12, 1866, "Reports and Other Records," Received by the Board of Education from School Agents, Apr. 1864–Mar. 1865, RSEL, BRFAL, NA M1026, Roll. 3.

21. G. T. Ruby to Capt. A. G. Studer, May 1, 1866, "Reports and Other Records," Received by the Board of Education from School Agents, Apr. 1864–Mar. 1865, RSEL, BRFAL, NA M1026, Roll. 3.

22. G. T. Ruby to Capt. A. G. Studer, May 1, 1866, "Reports and Other Records,"

Received by the Board of Education from School Agents, Apr. 1864–Mar. 1865, RSEL, BRFAL, NA M1026, Roll. 3.

23. G. T. Ruby to Capt. A. G. Studer, May 16, 1866 (quotations), G. T. Ruby to Lt. Wadsworth, May 14, 1866, "Reports and Other Records," Received by the Board of Education from School Agents, Apr. 1864–Mar. 1865, RSEL, BRFAL, NA M1026, Roll. 3.

24. G. T. Ruby to Capt. A. G. Studer, May 16, 1866, "Reports and Other Records," Received by the Board of Education from School Agents, Apr. 1864–Mar. 1865, RSEL, BRFAL, NA M1026, Roll. 3.

25. G. T. Ruby to Capt. A. G. Studer, May 18, 1866. See also Ruby to Lt. C. P. McTaggart, May 17, 1866, "Reports and Other Records," Received by the Board of Education from School Agents, Apr. 1864–Mar. 1865, RSEL, BRFAL, NA M1026, Roll. 3.

26. *National Anti-Slavery Standard*, Sept. 22, 1866; *New Orleans Times-Picayune*, July 19, 1866 (quotation); "Investigation of Causes of Migration of Negroes from Southern to Northern States, Testimony, pts. 2 and 3," 46th Cong., 2d sess., *Senate Reports*, no. 693, 53.

27. *National Anti-Slavery Standard*, Sept. 22, 1866; *New Orleans Times-Picayune*, July 19, 1866; "Investigation of Causes of Migration of Negroes from Southern to Northern States, Testimony, pts. 2 and 3," 46th Cong., 2d sess., *Senate Reports*, no. 693, 53; *New Orleans Daily Crescent*, July 19, 1866 (CA).

28. *An Act to protect all Persons in the United States in their Civil Rights, and furnish the Means of their Vindication*, 31, 39th Cong. 1st sess. (1866), 27–30.

29. *New Orleans Daily Crescent*, July 19, 1866; *National Anti-Slavery Standard*, Sept. 22, 1866; James DeGray to Assistant Commissioner, July 3, 5, 1866, Register of Letters Received, vol. 2, Records of the Assistant Commissioner for Louisiana, BR-FAL, NA, RG105, Roll 5; G. T. Ruby to A. G. Studer, July 5, 1866, referred to AAG Capt. A. F. Hayden, "Endorsements Sent," RSE-Louisiana, BRFAL, NA, RG105, M1026, Roll 2.

30. James K. Hogue, *Uncivil War: Five New Orleans Street Battles and the Rise and Fall of Radical Reconstruction* (Baton Rouge: Louisiana State University Press, 2011), 32–35.

31. Hogue, *Uncivil War*, 39–40; "New Orleans Riot," 39th Cong., 2d sess., 1867. *H.Ex.Docs*, no 68, 35 (quotation).

32. "New Orleans Riot," 39th Cong., 2d sess., 1867. *H.Ex.Docs.*no. 68, 6–7, 11, 35, 142–44.

33. John W. Alvord, *Fifth Semi-Annual Report on Schools for Freedmen, January 1, 1868* (Washington: Government Printing Office, 1868), 36; *New Orleans Times-Picayune*, Aug. 24, 1866; *New Orleans Times*, Sept. 2, 1866; *Daily True Delta*, Dec. 11, 1864.

CHAPTER IV

1. E. M. Wheelock to E. M. Gregory, Apr. 30, 1866, E. M. Wheelock to E. M. Gregory, Jan. 31, 1866, E. M. Gregory to J. B. Kiddoo, May 31, 1866, "State Superintendent Reports" in Records of the Superintendent of Schools-Texas, Bureau of Refugees, Freedmen and Abandoned Lands, National Archives, Record Group 105, Microfilm Series 821, Roll 16 (hereinafter RSE-Texas, BRFAL, RG105, M821, R16);

"Letter of the Secretary of War," 39th Cong., 2d sess., *Senate Executive Documents*, no. 6, p. 141, 147–49; J. W. Alvord, *Third Semi-Annual Report on Schools, January 1, 1867* (Washington: Government Printing Office, 1867), 27; *Houston Daily Union*, July 30, 1870.

2. Earl W. Fornell, *The Galveston Era: The Texas Crescent on the Eve of Secession* (Austin: University of Texas Press, 1961), 35.

3. US Bureau of the Census. *The Statistics of the Population of the United States . . . compiled from the Original Returns of the Ninth Census, (June 1, 1870)* (Washington: Government Printing Office, 1872), 64–67.

4. G. T. Ruby, October Report, Monthly Reports, 1865–1866, Jan.–Apr. 1867, RSE-Texas, BRFAL, NA, RG105, M822, Roll 12.

5. October, November, December, and January Reports, Monthly Reports from Teachers 1865-1866 and Jan.–Apr. 1867, RSE-Texas, BRFAL, NA, RG105, M822, R12; *Flake's Daily Bulletin*, Dec. 26, 1866 (quotation).

6. *New Orleans Tribune*, Dec. 20, 1866; P H. Sheridan to U. S. Grant, Oct. 20, 1866, in "Removal of Hon. E. M. Stanton and Others," 40th Cong., 2d sess, *House Executive Documents*, no. 57, 45,

7. *New Orleans Tribune*, Dec. 20, 1866.

8. Chap. CLIII – An Act to provide the more efficient Government of the Rebel States [Passed over President Johnson's veto March 2, 1867]; George P. Sanger, ed., *The Statutes at Large, Treaties and Proclamations of the United States of America from December, 1865, to March 1867....*, Vol. XIV (Boston: Little, Brown, and Company, 1868), 428–29.

9. January, February, April, May, Reports, Monthly Reports from Teachers 1865–1866 and Jan.–Apr. 1867, RSE-Texas, BRFAL, NA, RG105, M822, R12); Lists of Houses Rented and Teachers Employed (20) May 1869–June. 1870, Records of Schools, Jan. 1866–Sept. 1869. RSE-Texas, BRFAL, NA, RG105, M822, R18); *Flake's Daily Bulletin*, May 14, 1867 (quotation).

10. G. T. Ruby to C. Griffin, Apr. 10, 1867, "Letters Received," Records of the Assistant Commissioner-Texas, Bureau of Refugees, Freedmen and Abandoned Lands, National Archives, Record Group 105, Microfilm Series 821, Roll 7 (hereinafter cited as RAC-Texas, BRFAL, NA, RG105, M821, Roll 7; *Galveston Daily News*, May 1, 1869; Carl H. Moneyhon, "Union League," *Handbook of Texas Online*, accessed July 8, 2017, http://www.tshaonline.org/handbook/online/articles/wau01.

11. G. T. Ruby to C. Griffin, Apr. 10, 1867, "Letters Received," RAC-Texas, BRFAL, NA, RG105, M821, Roll 7.

12. *Flake's Daily Bulletin*, July 2, 1867.

13. *Flake's Daily Bulletin*, May 16, 1867; *Galveston Daily News*, May 16, 1867.

14. *Flake's Daily Bulletin*, May 16, 1867; *Galveston Daily News*, May 16, 1867.

15. "May Report, Monthly Reports from Teachers, 1865–1866 and Jan.–Apr. 1867," RSE-Texas, BRFAL, NA, RG105, M822, R12; J. W. Alvord, *Fourth Semi-Annual Report on Schools, July 1, 1867* (Washington: Government Printing Office, 1868), 55; US Bureau of the Census, *The Statistics of the Population of the United States . . . from the Original Returns of the Ninth Census, (June 1, 1870)* (Washington, Government Printing Office, 1872), 619.

16. Chas. C. Griffin to O. O. Howard, May 24, 1867, "Letters Sent," RAC-

Texas, BRFAL, RG105, M821, R; William L. Richter, *Over Reached on All Sides: The Freedmen's Bureau Administrators in Texas, 1865–1868* (College Station: Texas A&M University Press, 1991), 144–46.

17. Chas. C. Griffin to George T. Ruby, June 7, 1867, "Letters Sent," RAC-Texas, BRFAL, NA105, M821, Rl; G. T. Ruby to J. T. Kirkman, July 26, 1867, "Letters Received," RAC-Texas, BRFAL, NA, RG105, M821, R7; G. T Ruby to J. T. Kirkman, Aug. 12, 1867, "Letter Received," RSE-Texas, BRFAL, RG105, M822, R 4.

18. *Galveston Daily News*, Oct. 1, 1867.

19. G. T. Ruby to J. T. Kirkman, July 26, 1867, "Letters Received," RAC, BRFAL, NA, RG105, M821, R7; G. T. Ruby to J. T. Kirkman, Aug. 12, 1867, Letters Received, RSE-Texas, BRFAL, NA, RG105, M 822, Roll 4.

20. G. T. Ruby to J. T. Kirkman, Aug. 12, 1867 (first quotation), "Letters Received," RSE-Texas, BRFAL, NA, RG105, M822, R4; G. T. Ruby to J. T. Kirkman, July 26, 1867 (second quotation), "Letters Received," RAC-Texas, BRFAL, NA, RG105, M821, R7.

21. James L. Hailey, "Sterling, TX," *Handbook of Texas Online* (first quotation), , accessed July 12, 2019, http://www.tshaonline.org/handbook/online/articles/hts20; G. T. Ruby to J. T. Kirkman, July 26, 1867 (second quotation); "Letters Received," RAC-Texas, BRFAL, NA, RG105, M821, R7; G. T. Ruby to J. T. Kirkman, Aug. 12, 1867 (third and fourth quotations); "Letters Received," RSE-Texas, BRFAL, NA, RG105, M822, R4.

22. G. T. Ruby to J. T. Kirkman, July 27, 1867, Letters Received, RAC-Texas, BRFAL, NA, RG105, M821, R7.

23. G. T. Ruby to J. T. Kirkman, July 27, 1867, Letters Received, RAC-Texas, BRFAL, NA, RG105, M821, R7.

24. G. T. Ruby to J. T. Kirkman, July 26, 27, 1867, Letters Received, RAC-Texas, BRFAL, NA, RG105, M821, R7.

25. G. T. Ruby to J. T. Kirkman, Aug. 12, 1867 (quotation), "Letters Received," RSE-Texas, BRFAL, NA, RG105, M822, R4.

26. G. T. Ruby to J. T. Kirkman, Aug. 12, 1867 (quotation), "Letters Received," RSE-Texas, BRFAL, NA, RG105, M822, R4.

27. G. T. Ruby to J. T. Kirkman, Aug. 12, 1867 (quotation), "Letters Received," RSE-Texas, BRFAL, NA, RG105, M822, R4. (first quotation); G. T. Ruby to J. T. Kirkman, Aug.17, 1867 (second quotation), "Letters Received," RSE-Texas, BRFAL, NA, RG105, M822, R4.

28. G. T. Ruby to J. T. Kirkman, Aug. 12, 1867, "Letters Received," RSE-Texas, BRFAL, NA, RG105, M822, R4.

29. William L. Richter, *The Army in Texas During Reconstruction, 1865–1870* (College Station: Texas A&M University Press, 1987), 111–115.

30. *Flake's Semi-Weekly News*, Oct. 2, 1867; *San Antonio Express*, Sept. 13, 1867; G. T. Ruby to E. M. Pease, Aug. 16, 1867, Governor Elisha Marshal Pease Papers, Texas State Library and Archives; H. P. N. Gammel, comp. *The Laws of Texas, 1822–1897* (Austin: The Gammel Book Company, 1898), 863.

31. Chas. Garretson to O. O. Howard, Oct. 1, 1867, "Letters Sent," RAC, BRFAL, NA, RG105, M821, R1; G. T. Ruby to Chas. Garretson, Oct. 24, 1867, RAC, Texas, "Letters Received," BRFAL, NA, RG105, M821,, R14.

CHAPTER V

1. *Galveston Daily News,* July 5, 6, 1867.

2. *Flake's Daily Bulletin*, July 6, 1867.

3. G. T. Ruby to E. M. Pease, Oct [nd], 1867, Texas Governor Elisha Marshal Pease Papers, Texas State Library and Archives; G. T. Ruby to E. M. Pease, Oct. 12, 1867, Pease, Graham, and Niles Families Papers, Austin History Center, Austin Public Library.

4. *Galveston Daily News*, Oct. 12, 1867.

5. *Galveston Daily News*, Oct. 12, 1867.

6. *Galveston Daily News*, Oct. 12, 1867.

7. *Flake's Daily Bulletin*, Oct. 17, 1867.

8. *Flake's Daily Bulletin*, Oct. 17, 1867, Aug. 4, 11, 13, 17, 18, 20, Oct. 22, Nov. 11, 1867; *Galveston Daily News*, Oct. 4, 1867.

9. *Flake's Daily Bulletin*, Oct. 22, 23 (quotation), 24, 25, 1867.

10. *Flake's Semi-Weekly Bulletin*, Oct. 30, 1867.

11. *Flake's Daily Bulletin*, Dec. 8, 1867.

12. *Flake's Daily Bulletin*, Dec. 19, 1867.

13. *Flake's Daily Bulletin*, Dec. 22, 1867.

14. *Flake's Daily Bulletin*, Dec. 24, 31, 1867; Howard Cavener to Editor *Flake's Bulletin*, Dec. 25, 1867; *Flake's Bulletin*, Dec. 26, 1867.

15. *Flake's Daily Bulletin*, Dec. 25, 1867, Jan. 25, Feb. 8 (quotation), 1868; *Galveston Daily News*, Feb. 16, 1868.

16. *Flake's Daily Bulletin*, Feb. 2, 1868.

17. *Tabular Statement of Voters (white and colored) Registered in Texas . . . . and Tabular Statement of Votes (white and colored) cast at Election . . .* (Austin: US Army, Fifth Military District, 1870), 3; *Flake's Daily Bulletin*, June 28, 1866.

18. *Galveston Daily News*, Feb. 11, 12 (first and second quotation), 13, 1868; *Flake's Daily Bulletin*, Feb. 14 (third quotation), 1868.

19. *Galveston Daily News*, Feb. 11 (quotation), 12, 13, 14 (second quotation), 1868; *Flake's Daily Bulletin*, Feb. 11, 12, 1868.

20. *Galveston Daily News*, Feb. 16, 1868.

21. "Local Intelligence" *Flake's Daily Bulletin*, Feb. 16, 1868.

22. *Flake's Daily Bulletin*, Feb. 16 (first quotation), 18 (second quotation), 1868.

23. *Flake's Daily Bulletin*, Feb. 16, 19 (quotation), 1868.

24. *Flake's Daily Bulletin*, Feb. 18, 1868.

25. *State Gazette* quoted in *Flake's Daily Bulletin*, Mar. 3, 1868.

26. *State Gazette* in *Flake's Daily Bulletin*, May 8, 1868.

27. *Flake's Daily Bulletin*, Apr. 23, May 7, 1868.

28. *Flake's Daily Bulletin*, May 5, 7 (quotation), 1868; *Tri-Weekly Austin Republican*, May 18, 1868; *Austin Republican*, in *Flake's Daily Bulletin*, June 2, 1868.

29. *Galveston Republican* (quotations) in *National Anti-Slavery Standard*, May 16, 1868; *Flake's Daily Bulletin*, May 2, 1868.

30. *Flake's Daily Bulletin*, May 2 (first and second quotations), April 22 (third quotation, 1868.

31. *Galveston Daily News*, May 31, 1868 (first quotation), "An Old Texan" to *Galveston Daily News*, Apr. 11, 1862. See also *Galveston Daily News*, Mar. 21, Sept. 19, 1868,

and *Flake's Daily Bulletin*, Jan. 11, Mar. 13, 1868, and *Flake's Semi-Weekly Bulletin*, Jan. 11, 29, May 27, 1868, for examples of the conservative view of social equality.

32. *New Orleans Picayune* in *Flake's Daily Bulletin*, May 2 (quotations), 1868; *New Orleans Republican*, June 19, 1868, in *Flake's Daily Bulletin*, June 23, 1868; *New Orleans Picayune* in *Daily Austin Republican*, June 27, 1868; *Galveston Daily News*, June 23, 1868.

33. *Chicago Republican*, quotation in *Galveston Republican*, June 1, 1868; *Chicago Tribune*, May 19, 20, 21, 22, 1868.

34. *Flake's Daily News*, May 30, 1868; *Flake's Semi-Weekly Bulletin*, June 3, 1868.

35. *Flake's Daily Bulletin*, June 7, 1868.

36. *Flake's Daily Bulletin*, June 20, 1868; *Galveston Daily News*, June 23, 1868.

37. *Flake's Daily Bulletin*, June 20, 1868; *Galveston Daily News*, June 23, 1868; *Houston Weekly Telegraph*, June 25, 1868.

CHAPTER VI

1. *Galveston Daily News*, July 7, 1867; Carl H. Moneyhon, *Texas after the Civil War: The Struggle of Reconstruction* (College Station: Texas A&M University Press, 2004), 45–46, 91–92, 97.

2. *Daily Austin Republican*, June 15, 1868.

3. *Daily Austin Republican*, June 3, 4, 5, 6, 10, 1868.

4. *Dallas Weekly Herald*, June 13, 20, 1868.

5. *Galveston Daily News*, June 12, 20, 1868.

6. *Journal of the Reconstruction Convention which met at Austin, Texas, June 1, A.D., 1868. First Session* (Austin: A. Siemering & Co., Printers, 1870), 174; Betty Jeffus Sandlin, *The Texas Reconstruction Constitutional Convention of 1868*–1869 (Unpublished PhD Diss: Texas Tech University, 1970), 52–53, 55–61.

7. "Proclamation of Governor Pease," *Galveston Daily News*, Nov. 3, 1867; "Resignation of Attorney General Alexander," *Galveston Daily News*, Nov. 8, 1867; Constitution of 1866, III, sec. 1; "Black Codes," accessed Oct. 16, 2017, http://www.tshaonline.org/handbook/online/articles/jsb01.

8. *Daily Austin Republican*, July 29, 1868; *Journal of the Reconstruction Convention*, I, 270–79.

9. *Galveston Daily News*, June 30, 1868 (quotations); *Flake's Daily Bulletin*, June 30, July 3, 1868.

10. *Galveston Daily News*, July 3, 1868.

12. *Journal of the Reconstruction Convention, . . . First Session*, 174; Carl H. Moneyhon, *Republicanism in Reconstruction Texas* (Austin: University of Texas Press, 1980), 251.

12. E. J. Davis to E. M. Pease, July 14, 1866, Pease, Graham and Niles Families Papers, Austin History Center, Austin Public Library; Ernest Wallace, *The Howling of the Coyotes: Reconstruction Efforts to Divide Texas* (College Station: Texas A&M University Press, 1979), 3–45.

13. *Flake's Daily Bulletin*, June 30, 1868; Wallace, *Howling of the Coyotes*, 47; *Galveston Daily News*, June 30, 1868; *Daily Austin Republican*, June 25, 1868; Bills and Resolutions, 40th Cong., 2d Sess. House of Representatives, no. 1203.

14. *Journal of the Reconstruction Convention . . . . First Session*, 409–411; Wallace, *The Howling of the Coyotes*, 61–63.

15. *Journal of the Reconstruction Convention . . . . First Session,* 14, 195 (quotation); Carl H. Moneyhon, "The Democratic Party, the Ku Klux Klan, and the Politics of Fear," in *Still the Arena of Civil War: Violence and Turmoil in Reconstruction Texas, 1865–1874,* ed. by Kenneth W. Howell (Denton: University of North Texas Press, 2012), 243–66.

16. "Our Austin Letter," *Flake's Daily Bulletin,* July 10, 1868.

17. "Our Austin Letter," *Flake's Daily Bulletin,* July 10, 1868.

18. *Flake's Daily Bulletin,* July 21, 23, 26, 28, 30, 31, 1868; *Daily Austin Republican,* July 20, 22, 24, 26, 29, Aug. 1, 1868; William L. Richter, *The Army in Texas During Reconstruction* (College Station: Texas A&M University Press, 1987), 137–139.

19. *Flake's Daily Bulletin,* July 7, 1868.

20. *Daily Austin Republican,* July 21, 1868.

21. *Flake's Daily Bulletin,* July 7, 1868.

22. *Daily Austin Republican,* Aug. 12, 13, 14, 15, 16, 17, 1868; *The Freeman's Press,* Aug. 15, 1868; *Flake's Daily Bulletin,* Aug. 19, 1868; *Daily San Antonio Express,* Aug. 19, 1868.

23. *The Freeman's Press,* Aug. 15, 1868; *Galveston Daily News,* Aug. 20, 22, 1868; *Flake's Daily Bulletin,* Aug. 19, 1868.

24. *Daily Austin Republican,* Aug. 31, 1868. Wallace, *Howling of the Coyotes,* 66–67; Charles Ramsdell concluded that the convention adjourned because General Joseph Reynolds had refused to appropriate additional funds rather than for political reasons. Charles W. Ramsdell, *Reconstruction in Texas* (New York: Columbia University Press, 1910), 228–229.

25. *Flake's Daily Bulletin,* Aug. 21 (first quotation), 23 (second quotation), Sept. 4, 1868; *State Gazette* in *Flake's Daily Bulletin,* Aug. 28, 1868.

26. *Galveston Daily News,* Sept. 4, 1868.

27. *Flake's Daily Bulletin,* Aug. 6, September 4, 6, 10, 1868; *Galveston Daily News,* Aug. 6, 1868.

28. *Flake's Daily Bulletin,* Sept. 6, 1868.

29. *Flake's Daily Bulletin,* Sept. 6, 1868.

30. *Flake's Daily Bulletin,* Sept. 9, 1868.

31. *Flake's Daily Bulletin,* Sept. 10 (quotation), 11, 1868.

32. *Flake's Daily Bulletin,* Sept. 10, 1868

33. *Flake's Daily Bulletin,* Sept. 11, 1868; *Dallas Herald,* Sept. 26, 1868.

34. *Flake's Daily Bulletin,* Sept. 10, 1868.

35. *Austin Daily Republican,* Nov. 16, 1868.

36. *Journal of the Reconstruction Convention,* which met at Austin, Texas, Dec.7, A.D. 1868. Second Session (Austin: Tracy, Siemering & Co., 1870), 267–278, 330–31 (division vote, see also 521–524, 482–486 (suffrage vote), 509–510, 517–520 (election votes), 510–511 (election crime declaration); Ramsdell, *Reconstruction in Texas,* 242–258.

37. *Journal of the Reconstruction Convention . . . Second Session,* 378–80 (McKee affair), 458–59 (Protest), 519–520 (February 2 vote), 528 (resignation letter); *Austin Republican,* February 6, 8, 10, 1869; Ramsdell, *Reconstruction in Texas,* 242–252, 257 (quotation).

38. H. P. N. Gammel, *The Laws of Texas, 1822–1897* (Austin: The Gammel Book Company, 1898), vol. 7, 430; Ramsdell, *Reconstuction in Texas,* 258–260.

CHAPTER VII

1. *New Orleans Republican*, in *Houston Daily Union*, Feb. 26, 1869; *National Republican* (Washington, DC), Mar. 3, 1869.

2. *San Antonio Express*, Aug. 17, 1869; *Flake's Daily Bulletin*, Mar. 11, 1869; *Galveston Daily News*, Mar. 4, 11, 1869; B. Rush Plumly to Nathaniel P. Banks, Feb. 16, 1869, Nathaniel Banks Papers, Library of Congress.

3. *New Orleans Republican*, in *Flake's Daily Bulletin*, Apr. 3, 1869; *Flake's Daily Bulletin*, Apr. 9, 1869; *Galveston Daily News*, Apr. 4, 6, 7, 9, 1869; *New York Times*, Apr. 10, 1869; *New York Herald*, Apr. 1, 4, 9, 1869; (Washington, DC) *Daily National Intelligencer*, Apr. 12, 1869.

4. *National Republican* (Washington, DC), Apr. 2, 1869; *Flake's Daily Bulletin*, May 4, 1869 (quotation).

5. (New York) *National Anti-Slavery Standard*, May 1, 1869; *Houston Union*, May 5, 1869.

6. (New York) *National Anti-Slavery Standard*, May 1, 1869.

7. (New York) *National Anti-Slavery Standard*, May 1, 1869.

8. *Flake's Daily Bulletin*, May 4, 1869; (New York) *National Anti-Slavery Standard*, May 1, 1869.

9. *Flake's Daily Bulletin*, May 4, 1869; (New York) *National Anti-Slavery Standard*, May 1, 1869.

10. *Flake's Daily Bulletin*, May 4, 1869.

11. *Austin Republican* in *Flake's Daily Bulletin*, Apr. 14, 1869.

12. *Flake's Daily Bulletin*, May 4, 1869; *Houston Daily Union*, May 5, 1869.

1.3 *Houston Union* in *Galveston Daily News*, May 4, 1869; *Houston Telegraph* in *Flake's Daily Bulletin*, May 7, 1869.

14. *Houston Union*, March 29, 1869; G. T. Ruby to J. P. Newcomb, May 6, 1869, James P. Newcomb Papers, Briscoe Center for American History, University of Texas at Austin (hereinafter cited as Newcomb Papers, BCAH, UTA); Moneyhon, *Republicanism in Reconstruction Texas*, 107–108.

15. *Houston Union*, March 29 (first quotation), April 30, May 7 (second quotation), 1869; *Austin Republican* in *Houston Union*, April 26, 1869.

1.6 *Flake's Daily Bulletin*, May 9, 1869; *Houston Union*, May 5, 1869.

17. *Flake's Daily Bulletin*, May 12, 1869.

19. G. T. Ruby to J. P. Newcomb, May 16, 1869, Newcomb Papers, BCAH, UTA.

19. *Houston Daily Union*, May 19, 26 (quotations), 28, 1869; *San Antonio Express*, June 6, 1869; G. T. Ruby to J. P. Newcomb, May 27, 1869, Newcomb Papers, BCAH, UTA.

20. G. T. Ruby to J. P. Newcomb, May 6, 1869, Newcomb Papers, BCA, UTA.

21. *Houston Union*, June 18, 1869.

22. *Houston Union*, May 28, 1869; *Galveston Daily News*, May 25, 1869 (Gonzales quotation).

23. *Houston Daily Union*, June 9, 1869; *Galveston Tri-Weekly News*, June 11, 1869; *San Antonio Express*, June 11, 1869; *San Antonio Express*, June 11, 1869 (quotation).

24. *San Antonio Express*, June 18, 1869.

25. *Houston Union*, June 9, 14, 23, 1869.

26. *Houston Union*, June 21, 1869; *Galveston Tri-Weekly News*, June 18, 1869.

27. *Houston Union*, June 28, 1869.

28. "Circular Letter No. 2," *Daily Austin Republican*, Aug. 28, 1869; G. T. Ruby to J. P. Newcomb, May 27, 1869, E. J. Davis to J. P. Newcomb, July 4, 1869, Newcomb Papers, BCAH, UTA.

29. G. T. Ruby to T. G. Baker, July 15, 1869, T. G. Baker to W. E. Chandler, July 24, 1869, William E. Chandler Papers, Library of Congress; G. T. Ruby to J. P. Newcomb, Newcomb Papers, BCAH, UTA; *Galveston Daily News*, July 13, 1869.

30. *Houston Union*, July 31, 1869.

31. *Tri-Weekly Galveston News*, Aug. 2, 1869; *Houston Weekly Telegraph*, Aug. 5, 1869.

32. *Houston Union*, August 5, 7, 10, 1869; *Tri-Weekly Galveston News*, Aug. 4, 1869.

33. *Houston Union*, August 5, 12, 17, 1869.

34. *Houston Union*, August 5, 12, 17, 28, 1869; *Tri-Weekly Galveston News*, Aug. 4, 1869.

35. *Tri-Weekly Galveston Daily News*, Aug. 27, 1869, Aug. 20 (quotation four), 1869.

36. *Tri-Weekly Galveston Daily News*, Aug. 27, 30, 1869; *Flake's Daily Bulletin*, Aug. 29, 1869.

37. *Galveston News*, September 5, 1869.

38. G. T. Ruby to J. P. Newcomb, Sept. 12, 1869, Newcomb Papers, BCAH, UTA.

39. *National Republican* (Washington, DC, Aug. 20, 1869); "Associated Press Dispatches," *Galveston Daily News*, Aug. 22, 1869; *Galveston Tri-Weekly News*, Oct. 29, 1869 (quotation).

40. *Houston Union*, Oct. 21, 1869 (first quotation); *Galveston Tri-Weekly News* October 20, 1869 (second quotation).

41. *Houston Union*, Aug. 18, Oct. 25, 26, 28 (first and second quotations), Nov. 3 (third quotation), 1869.

42. *Houston Union*, Nov. 24, 1869.

43. *Flake's Daily Bulletin* in *Daily Austin Republican*, Aug. 26, 28, 29, 1869.

44. *Galveston Tri-Weekly News*, Aug. 16, 1869; *Tri-Weekly Texas State Gazette*, Aug. 11, 1869; *Weekly Houston Telegraph*, Sept. 2, 1869.

45. *San Antonio Express*, Aug. 17, 1869; *Weekly Houston Union*, Aug. 31, 1869; *Weekly Houston Telegraph*, Sept. 2, 1869.

46. *Houston Union*, Dec. 5, 1869; *Galveston News*, Dec. 7, 9, 1869.

47. William Anderson to the editor, Apr. 4, 1870, *New Era*, Apr. 28, 1870.

CHAPTER VIII

1. *Journal of the Senate of the State of Texas, Provisional Session of 1870* (Austin: Printed by Tracy, Siemering & Co., 1870), 4, 8, 11.

2. *Journal of the Senate of the State of Texas*, 17, 20–22, 25, 28–29.

3. *Journal of the Senate of the State of Texas*, 37–38, 41, 42.

4. *Galveston Daily News*, Mar, 31, 1870.

5. *New Era*, May 26, 1870.

6. *New Era*, Mar, 31, 1870; *Galveston Tri-Weekly News*, Apr. 1, 1870; *New Era*, May 26 (quotation), 1870.

7. Richard Nelson to the editor, Apr. 18, 1870, *The New Era*, Apr. 28, 1870; *Daily Houston Union*, Apr. 13, 1870. For more on Cuney, see Maud Cuney Hare, Robert C.

Cotner, intro., *Norris Wright Cuney: A Tribune of the Black People* (Austin: Steck-Vaughn Company Publishers, 1968).

8. *Flake's Daily Bulletin*, Apr. 16, 1870; *Houston Daily Union*, Apr. 17, 1870.

9. *Houston Daily Union*, Sept. 2, 1870; *Tri-Weekly Galveston News*, Aug. 22 (quotation), 1870; *Flake's Daily Bulletin*, Apr. 28, 1870; *Dallas Herald*, May 7, 1870.

10. *Senate Journal of the Twelfth Legislature, State of Texas. First Session* (Austin: Tracy, Siemering & Co., State Journal Office, 1870), Index.

11. Gammel, *The Laws of Texas, 1822–1897*, vol. 6, 591–602, 727–29, 835–837.

12. *Flake's Daily Bulletin*, May 26, 1870; *Galveston Daily News*, May 24, 1870.

13. *Flake's Daily Bulletin*, May 11, 1870; *Houston Union*, May 25, 26, June 8, 9, July 21 (ship channel quotations), 1870; *San Antonio Daily Express*, May 29, 1870; H. P. N. Gammel, *The Laws of Texas, 1822–1897*, vol. 6, 556–562.

14. *Flake's Daily Bulletin*, May 18 (first and second quotations), June 16 (second quotation) 1870.

15. *Senate Journal of the Twelfth Legislature, State of Texas. First Session* (Austin: Tracy, Siemering & Co., State Journal Office, 1870), 13–14.

16. *State Journal of the Twelfth Legislature*, 14.

17. *State Journal of the Twelfth Legislature*, 14–15.

18. *State Journal of the Twelfth Legislature*, 17–18.

19. *State Journal of the Twelfth Legislature*, 18–19.

20. *Flake's Daily Bulletin*, May 12, 1870; Moneyhon, *Republicanism in Reconstruction Texas*, 138.

21. *Flake's Daily Bulletin*, June 7, 1870.

22. *State Journal Appendix, Containing Official Report of the Debates and Proceedings of the Twelfth Legislature of the State of Texas*, Vol. I (Austin: Tracy, Siemering & Co., Publishers, 1870), 45; *San Antonio Daily Express*, June 8, 10, 1870.

23. Thomas J. Powell to the U.L. of A., June 9, 1870, in *Flake's Daily Bulletin*, June 29, 1870; Moneyhon, *Republicanism in Reconstruction Texas*, 139–41.

24. *Flake's Daily Bulletin*, June 18, 24 (quotations), 1870.

25. *State Journal Appendix*, 91.

26. *Flake's Daily Bulletin*, June 26, 1870; *Dallas Weekly Herald*, July 2, 1870.

27. *Senate Journal of the Twelfth Legislature, . . . First Session*, 278–279; *Flake's Daily Bulletin*, June 26, 29, 1870; *Tri-Weekly Galveston News*, June 29, July 4, 1870.

28. *Flake's Daily Bulletin*, May 24, June 24, 30, July 2, 3, 1870; *Galveston Daily News*, May 7, 287, June 16, 23, 24, 1870; *State Journal*, May 4, 6, 1870; Morgan C. Hamilton to J. P. Newcomb, June 26, 1870, Newcomb Papers, BCAH, UTA; Moneyhon, *Republicanism in Reconstruction Texas*, 140–141.

29. "Four Months in the Capitol," *Daily Houston Union*, Sept. 14, 1870; *Senate Journal of the Twelfth Legislature*, 195, 472.

30. "Four Months in the Capitol," *Daily Houston Union*, Sept. 14, 1870; *Senate Journal of the Twelfth Legislature*, 698.

31. S. G. Reed, "INTERNATIONAL RAILROAD,"*Handbook of Texas Online*, accessed July 21, 2018, http://www.tshaonline.org/handbook/online/articles/eqi03. Uploaded on June 15, 2010. Published by the Texas State Historical Association; Nunn, *Texas Under the Carpetbaggers*, 34–35; *Senate Journal of the Twelfth Legislature*, 562.

32. *Galveston Daily News*, June 28 (first quotation), July 1, 1870; *Flake's Daily Bulletin*, July 1, 10, 1870.

33. *Galveston Daily News*, June 28 (first quotation), July 1, 2 (second quotation), 6, 1870; *Flake's Daily Bulletin*, July 1, 3, 5, 10, 27 (third quotation), 1870.

34. *Houston Daily Union*, July 24, 1870; *Tri-Weekly Galveston News*, Aug. 5, 15, 1870; *Flake's Daily Bulletin*, Aug. 17, 1870.

35. *Flake's Daily Bulletin*, Oct. 20, 1870.

36. Chas. W. Winn to G. T. Ruby, June, 1870, Thomas G. Baker to J. P. Newcomb, June 20, 1870, Richard Nelson to J. P. Newcomb, July 13, 1870, J. P. Newcomb to Thomas G. Baker, Nov. 5, 1870, Newcomb Papers, BCAH, UTA.

37. Cook Jenkins and Henry Bouden to George T. Ruby, July 30, 1870, George T. Ruby to Cook Jenkins and Henry Bouden, Aug. 8, 1870, *Houston Daily Union*, Aug. 16, 1870.

38. *Tri-Weekly Galveston News*, Aug. 22, 1870.

39. *State Journal* in *Houston Daily Union*, July 30, 1870.

40. *State Journal*, Aug. 17, 1870 (see also Aug. 20); *Houston Daily Union*, Sept. 24, 1870; *New Orleans Republican*, Sept. 1, 1870.

41. *Houston Daily Union*, Aug. 21, 1870.

42. *Flake's Daily Bulletin*, Aug. 27, 1870; Louis W. Stevenson to J. P. Newcomb, Newcomb Papers, BCAH, UTA; Louis W. Stevenson to Frederick Douglass, Sept. 15, 1870, in *Flake's Daily Bulletin*, Oct. 4, 1871.

43. Louis W. Stevenson to J. P. Newcomb, Aug. 28, 1870, Newcomb Papers, BCAH, UTA.

44. *Flake's Bulletin* quotation in *Tri-Weekly State Gazette*, Sept. 21, 1870.

45. *Galveston City Directory, 1871* (Galveston: John H. Heller, 1872), p. 12; *Texas Almanac for 1871* (Galveston: Richardson and Company, 1871), p. 112; see as one basis of calculating his wealth https://www.measuringworth.com/calculators/uscompare/relativevalue.php (accessed Jan. 1, 2019); for a discussion of the moiety system see Richard White, *The Republic for Which It Stands: The United States during Reconstruction and the Gilded Age, 1865–1896* (New York: Oxford University Press, 2017), pp. 354–357.

CHAPTER IX

1. *Houston Daily Union*, Aug. 31, 1870; *Galveston Tri-Weekly News*, Oct. 24, 1870; *Tri-Weekly Galveston News*, Apr. 29, Dec. 12, 1870.

2. "District of Columbia Marriages, 1811–1950," database with images, *FamilySearch* (https://familysearch.org/ark:/61903/1:1:XL94-NQL : 1 June 2015), G T Ruby and Lucy V Nalle, 1870; Ruby Family Tree, thanks to Bob Greene, Portland, Maine; *Houston Daily Union*, Nov. 18, 1870; *Constitution* (Middletown, Connecticut), Oct. 12, 1870; *Galveston Daily News*, Aug. 4, 1875; *Troy Whig* in *Janesville Gazette* (Janesville, Wisconsin), Oct. 13, 1870; *Troy Whig* in *New Orleans Republican*, Oct. 16, 1870.

3. *Houston Union News Bulletin*, Oct. 7, Nov. 18, 1870; *Constitution* (Middletown, Connecticut), Oct. 12, 1870; *Troy Whig* in *Janesville Gazette* (Janesville, Wisconsin), Oct. 13, 1870; *Troy Whig* in *New Orleans Republican*, Oct. 16, 1870.

4. *New York World*, Sept. 23, 1870, in *Chicago Tribune*, Sept. 26, 1870; *Galveston Daily News*, Oct. 8, 1870; *Daily Phoenix* (Columbia, South Carolina), Oct. 5, 1870; *Fairfield Herald* (Winnsboro, South Carolina), Oct. 12, 1870; *Southern Home* (Char-

lotte, North Carolina), Oct. 18, 1870; *Clarion-Ledger* (Jackson, Mississippi), Oct. 28, 1870.

5. *New York World*, Sept. 23, 1870, in *Chicago Tribune*, Sept. 26, 1870; *Boston Post* in *Galveston Daily News*, Oct. 6, 1870; *Portland Daily Press*, Oct. 8, 1870; *New Orleans Republican*, Nov. 6, 1870.

6. *New York World*, Sept. 23, 1870, in *Chicago Tribune*, Sept. 26, 1870; *New National Era*, Oct. 6, 1870; *New York Times*, Sept. 23, 1870; *Boston Post* in *Galveston Daily News*, Oct. 6, 1870; *Boston Post*, Oct. 12, 1870.

7. *New National Era*, Oct. 6, 1870 (first quotation); *New York World*, Sept. 23, 1870 (second quotation), in *Chicago Tribune*, Sept. 26, 1870; *New York Times*, Sept. 23, 1870; *Boston Post* in *Galveston Daily News*, Oct. 6, 1870; *Boston Post*, Oct. 12, 1870.

8. *New York World*, Sept. 23, 1870, in *Chicago Tribune*, Sept. 26, 1870.

9. *Portland Press*, Oct. 8, 1870; *Portland Advertiser* in *National Standard*, Oct. 20, 1870.

10. *National Standard*, Oct. 1 (quotation), 22, 1870 (quotation); *Tri-Weekly Galveston News*, Oct. 21, 1870; *New York Times*, Oct. 11, 1870.

11. *Houston Daily Union*, Nov. 16, 1870.

12. *New York Times*, October 11, 1870.

13. *Houston Daily Union*, Nov. 17 (first quotation), 22 (second quotation), 1870; *Tri-Weekly Galveston News*, Nov. 16, 1870.

14. *Flake's Daily Bulletin*, Oct. 7, 1870; *Galveston Daily News*, Oct 6 (quotation), 7, 1870; *Daily Journal*, Oct. 13, 1870.

15. *Galveston Tri-Weekly News*, Nov. 18, 1870.

16. *Houston Daily Union*, Dec. 7 (first quotation), 2 (second quotation), 1870.

17. *Houston Daily Union*, Sept. 29, Jan. 30, 1871; *Galveston Daily News*, Jan. 10, 1871; *Tri-Weekly Galveston News*, Jan. 18, 1871.

18. *Journal of the Senate of the State of Texas* [Regular Session] (J. G. Tracy. State Printer, 1871), 3, 43, 56, 48, 88, 110, 165, 225, 256, 284, 335.

19. *Journal of the Senate of the State of Texas* [Regular Session], 475, 638, 777, 1007, 1066, 1067, 1074, 1244, 1250–1251; Gammel, *Laws of Texas*, vi, 1429–1430, 1639–1641, 1640 (quotation).

20. *Journal of the Senate of the State of Texas* [Regular Session], 43, 63, 284, 391, 658, 838; Gammel, *Laws of Texas*, vi, 1158–1159, 1467–1468; *Tri-Weekly Galveston News*, Apr. 12, 14, 1871.

21. *Journal of the Senate* . . . . [Regular Session], 23–42.

22. *Journal of the Senate* . . . . [Regular Session], 6, 10, 14, 18, 19, 21; Patsy McDonald Spaw, *The Texas Senate: Civil War to the Eve of Reform, 1861–1889*, vol. I (College Station: Texas A&M University Press, 1999), 97–99.

23. *Journal of the Senate* . . . [Regular Session], 56, 61, 65, 68, 70–71; W. C. Nunn, *Texas Under the Carpetbaggers* (Austin: University of Texas Press, 1962), 40–42.

24. Barry A. Crouch and Donaley E. Brice, *The Governor's Hounds: The Texas State Police, 1870–1873* (Austin: University of Texas Press, 2011), 51–73, 74–92; Nunn, *Texas Under the Carpetbaggers*, 76–86.

25. *Journal of the Senate*. . . . [Regular Session], 187–211, 270–271 (quotation), 282–283; Crouch and Brice, *The Governor's Hounds*, 51–92; *Waco Examiner* in *Tri-Weekly State Gazette*, in Nunn, *Texas Under the Carpetbaggers*, 79–80.

26. *Journal of the Senate*. . . . [Regular Session], 79, 83; *Tabular Statement of Voters*

(white and colored) Registered in Texas at Registration in 1867 . . . ., 3.

27. *State Gazette* and *State Journal* in *Houston Daily Union*, Apr. 21, 1871; *Journal of the Senate. . . .* [Regular Session], 562–568, 674–679.

28. *State Gazette* and *State Journal* in *Houston Daily Union*, Apr. 21, 1871.

29. *Houston Daily Union*, Apr. 14, 1871; *Journal of the Senate. . . .* [Regular Session], 674–691, 696, 706.

30. *Houston Daily Union*, Apr. 14, 1871; Gammel, *Laws of Texas*, vi, 1029–1030; *Tri-Weekly State Gazette*, Apr. 24, 1871.

31. *Houston Daily Union*, Apr. 15, 1871.

32. *Galveston Republican* in *Houston Daily Union*, Apr. 24, 1871; "African Immigration," *Tri-Weekly Galveston News*, Apr. 19, 21, 26, 1871.

33. *Journal of the Senate . . . .* [Regular Session], 802–803, 1135–1137, 11481; *Houston Daily Union*, Feb. 3, 1871.

34. *Journal of the Senate . . . .* [Regular Session], 353; *Constitution of the State of Texas, 1869*, Article I, Sec. 21.

35. *Tri-Weekly State Gazette*, Apr. 26, 1871.

36. *Journal of the Senate . . .* [Regular Session], 1009, 1092, 1093, 1102–1121; Gammel, *Laws of Texas*, vi, 992, 993.

37. *Journal of the Senate . . .* [Regular Session], 935, 1071–1076, 1144, 1147–1148, 1211, 1217–1222, 1151.

38. *Journal of the Senate . . .* [Regular Session], 1217–1222.

39. *Houston Daily Union*, June 5, 1871.

CHAPTER X

1. *State Journal* in *Houston Daily Union*, Apr. 22, 1871 (quotations); see also *State Journal* in *Houston Daily Union*, Mar. 8, 20, Apr. 7, 1871.

2. Thomas W. Cutrer, "Clark, William Thomas," *Handbook of Texas Online*, accessed January 29, 2018, http://www.tshaonlineorg/handbook/online/articles/fcl17; G. T. Ruby to Republicans of the Third Congressional District" May 26, 1871, in *Houston Daily Union*, May 31, 1871.

3. Matthew Gaines to Republicans of the U. L. and A, Mar. 30, 1861 [sic], in *Tri-Weekly State Gazette*, Apr. 5, 1871; "Galveston News," *Houston Union*, Apr. 7, 1871 (first quotation); G. T. Ruby to J. P. Newcomb, June 29, 1871, Newcomb Papers, BCA, UTA.

4. *Houston Daily Union*, March 23, 27, Apr. 7, 11, 27 (quotation), 29, 1871.

5. *Houston Daily Union*, Apr. 2, 17, 19, 27, 1871; *Calvert Tribune* in *Houston Union*, Mar. 23, 1871.

6. *Houston Union*, Apr. 29, 1871.

7. *Houston Daily Union*, Apr.12, 17, 20 (quotations), 1871; *Galveston Tri-Weekly News*, Apr. 19, 1871; *Galveston Daily News*, Apr. 23, 1871.

8. *Houston Daily Union*, Apr. 27, 1871; *San Antonio Daily Express*, Apr. 28, 1871.

9. *Houston Daily Union*, May 1, 8, 1871.

10. *Houston Daily Union*, Apr. 22, May 6, "To the Republicans of the Third Congressional District, May 26, 1871," May 31, 1871.

11. *Houston Daily Union*, Apr. 29, 1871.

12. Letter from Hon. L. W. Stevenson, *Houston Daily Union*, May 23, 1871.

13. *Flake's Daily Bulletin*, May 27, June 1, 23, 1871; G. T. Ruby to J. P. Newcomb,

June 13, 1871, J. G. Tracy to J. P. Newcomb, July 6, 1871, Newcomb Papers, BCAH, UTA; *Reformer*, June 17, July 6, 1871; *Galveston Daily News*, May 21, 26, 1871.

14. G. T. Ruby to J. P. Newcomb, July 13, 1871, Newcomb Papers, BCAH, UTA; *Flake's Daily Bulletin*, July 14, 27, 1871; J. P. Newcomb to "Brethren," July, 1871, *Galveston Daily News*, July 25, 26, 1871; *The Reformer*, July 8, 15, 1871.

15. Ed. T. Randle to J. P Newcomb, June 21, 1871 (first quotation), Newcomb Papers, BCAH, UTA; *Handbook of Texas History; Houston Age* in *San Francisco Bulletin*, July 21, 1871 (second quotation) and in *Jamestown* (New York) *Bulletin*, July 28 1871.

16. *Houston Age*, June 22, 1871 in *San Francisco Bulletin*, July 21, 1871 and (Jamestown, New York), *Journal*, July 28, 1871.

17. *Houston Daily Union*, July 27, 1871.

18. G. T. Ruby to J. P. Newcomb, June 13, 1871, Newcomb Papers, BCAH, UTA.

19. *Galveston Daily News*, Jan 27, 1871; Moneyhon, *Republicanism in Reconstruction Texas*, 153.

20. *Representative* (Galveston), June 26, 1871 (quotation); *Houston Daily Union*, July 14, Aug. 4, 1871; *Galveston Representative* in *Houston Daily Union*, July 14, 1871.

21. "National Labor Union," in *Houston Daily Union*, Mar. 15, 1871 (quotation), *Houston Daily Union*, Sept. 16, 1870; *Tri-Weekly Galveston News*, June 7, 1871; *New Orleans Republican*, June 8, 1871.

22. *Galveston Representative*, July 15, 1871; *New Era*, Aug. 17, 1871; *Houston Daily Union*, Aug. 4, 1871.

23. *Houston Daily Union*, Aug. 4, 1871.

24. *Weekly Louisianian* (New Orleans), June 25, 1871.

25. G. T. Ruby to J. P. Newcomb, June 29, 1871, Newcomb Papers, BCAH, UTA.

26. *Houston Daily Union*, July 20, 1871; G. T. Ruby to J. P. Newcomb, June 13 ("reds"), July 7 ("communists"), 1871, Newcomb Papers, BCAH, UTA.

27. G. T. Ruby to J. P. Newcomb, June 23, July 6 (quotation), 13, 1871, Newcomb Papers, BCAH, UTA; George Lawrence to J. P. Newcomb, July 11, 1871 Newcomb Papers, BCAH, UTA.

28. G. T. Ruby to J. P. Newcomb, July 6, 1871, Newcomb Papers, BCAH, UTA; *Flake's Daily Bulletin*, July 19, Aug. 11 (quotation), 1871.

29. *Houston Daily Union*, June 26, July 8, 10–12, 14–15, 18–21, 24–26, 29, 1871.

30. *Houston Daily Union*, July 26, 1871.

31. *Austin Reformer*, Aug. 5, 1871.

32. *Houston Union*, July 31, 1871; *Tri-Weekly Galveston News*, July 31, 1871; *Reformer*, Aug. 5, 1871.

33. *Reformer*.

34. *Tri-Weekly Galveston News*, July 31, 1871.

35. *Galveston Daily News*, Aug. 2, 1871; T. A. Wilmans to J. P. Newcomb, July 27, 1871, J. P. Newcomb Papers, BCAH, UTA.

36. *Houston Daily Union*, Aug. 2, 1871.

37. *Houston Daily Union*, Aug. 1, 3, 1871.

38. *Flake's Daily Bulletin*, Aug. 4, 1871.

39. *Flake's Daily Bulletin*, Aug. 3, 1871; *Galveston Daily News*, Aug. 3, 1871.

40. *Houston Daily Union*, Aug. 17, 18, 1871; *Tri-Weekly Galveston News*, Aug. 18, 1871.

41. *Tri-Weekly Galveston News*, Aug. 18, 1871.

42. G. T. Ruby to J. P. Newcomb, Aug. 18, 1871, Newcomb Papers, BCAH, UTA; *Galveston Tri-Weekly News*, Aug. 25, 1871.

43. G. T. Ruby to J. P. Newcomb, Aug. 24, 1871, Newcomb Papers, BCAH, UTA.

44. *Houston Daily Union*, Aug. 31, 1871.

45. "Giddings vs. Clark," *House Misc. Docs.*, 42nd Cong., 2d sess., no. 163, 233, 235; G. T. Ruby to J. P. Newcomb, Aug. 18, 1871, James P. Newcomb Papers, BCAH, UTA; *Tri-Weekly Galveston News*, Sept. 15, 1871.

46. *Houston Daily Union*, Sept. 11, 1871.

47. W. T. Clark to J. P. Newcomb, Oct. 13, 1871, F. T. Wood to J. P. Newcomb, Oct. 18, 1871, Newcomb Papers, BCAH, UTA; *Weekly Democratic Statesman*, Oct. 5, 1871.

48. *Houston Daily Union*, Nov. 4, 1871.

49. "D. C. Giddings vs. W. T. Clark," *House Misc. Docs.* 42nd Congress, 2d sessions, no. 163, 7.

CHAPTER XI

1. *Journal of the Senate of the Twelfth Legislature of the State of Texas: Adjourned Session* (Austin: J. G. Tracy, State Printer, 1871), 4, 57.

2. *Flake's Daily Bulletin*, Sept. 15, 1871.

3. *Journal of the Senate of the Twelfth Legislature . . . . Adjourned Session*, 6, 57; H. P. N. Gammel, comp. *The Laws of Texas, 1822–1897* (Austin: The Gammel Book Company, 1898), vi, 18, 8–9, 15–21.

4. *Journal of the Senate of the Twelfth Legislature . . . . Adjourned Session*, 111, 168; *Flake's Daily Bulletin*, Oct. 22, 1871.

5. *Flake's Daily Bulletin*, Oct. 22, 1871.

6. *Journal of the Senate of the Twelfth Legislature . . . . Adjourned Session*, 36, 57; *Tri-Weekly Galveston News* (first quotation), Oct. 15, 1871 (second quotation); Gammel, *Laws of Texas*, vii, 91–92.

7. *Houston Daily Union*, Nov. 4, 1871.

8. *Tri-Weekly Galveston News*, Jan. 10, 1872.

9. *New Orleans Republican*, Feb. 11, 1872; G. T. Ruby to J. P. Newcomb, Mar. 12, 1872, A. W. Kempton to J. P. Newcomb, Mar. 17, 1872, Newcomb Papers, BCAH, UTA; *Galveston Standard*, June 3, 1872 (only three known editions of the *Standard* exist, and he reprinted his motto and purpose in each of them); *Daily State Journal*, Apr. 3, 1872; *Flake's Daily Bulletin*, Mar. 26, 1872; *Galveston Tri-Weekly News*, Mar. 29, 1872.

10. *Galveston Standard*, June 3, 1872.

11. *New Era*, Apr. 25, 1872.

12. *Galveston Standard*, June 3, October 31, 1872.

13. *New Era*, May 30, 1872; *Galveston Tri-Weekly News*, Mar. 29, Apr. 26, 1872.

14. David Donald, *Charles Sumner & The Rights of Man* (New York: Alfred A. Knopf, 1970), pp. 531–540, 531 (quotation); New York) *National Standard*, Apr. 1, 1871; *New York Herald*, Jan. 10, 1872, Mar. 18, 1871; *Philadelphia Inquirer*, Jan. 6, 1872.

15. *Flake's Daily Bulletin*, Jan. 16, 1872; see also *ibid*, Jan. 21, 1871.

16. *National Era* (New York), Apr. 18, 1872; *Daily State Journal*, Apr. 15, 1872; *Galveston Tri-Weekly News*, Apr. 26, 1872

17. *Boston Daily Journal*, Apr. 11, 1872; *Inter Ocean* (Chicago, Illinois), Apr. 11, 1872; *Flake's Daily Bulletin*, Apr. 11, 1872; *New Orleans Republican*, Apr. 10, 12, 1872.

18. *New National Era* (New York), Apr. 18, 1872.

19. *New National Era*, Apr. 18, 1872.

20. *New National Era*, April 18, 1872.

21. *New Orleans Republican*, Apr. 17, 1872; see also *Northern Ohio Journal*, Apr. 20, 1872 (CA).

22. *Galveston Daily News*, Apr. 13 1872; Brian Hart, "Bledsoe, Albert A.," *Handbook of Texas Online*, accessed March 02, 2018, *http://www.tshaonline.org/handbook/online/articles/fbl19*.

23. *Cincinnati Daily Gazette*, May 1, 3, 4, 1872.

24. *Galveston Daily News*, May 2, 4 (quotation), 1872; *Galveston Representative*, May 4, 1872.

25. *Galveston Daily News*, May 2, 1872; *Galveston Representative*, May 4, 1872.

26. *Galveston Daily News*, May 15, 16, 1872; *Flake's Daily Bulletin*, May 16, 1872.

27. *Galveston Daily News*, May 16 (first two quotations); *Flake's Daily Bulletin*, May 16 (third quotation), 17, 1872; *Galveston Representative*, May 25, 1872.

28. *Flake's Daily Bulletin*, May 17, 1872; *Galveston Daily News*, May 17, 1872.

29. *Galveston Standard*, June 3, 1872.

30. *Galveston Standard*, June 3, 1872; *New Orleans Daily Picayune*, June 12, 19, 20, 22, 1872.

31. *Galveston Standard*, June 3, 1872. In 1872 Reuben Ruby was the janitor in the Portland Customs House (*New Orleans Republican*, Apr. 16, 1872).

32. *Galveston Standard*, June 3, 1872 (first quotation); *Philadelphia Inquirer*, June 3, p. 8 (second quotation), 4, p. 3, 1872.

33. *New York Herald*, June 6, 1872 (p. 11); *Philadelphia Inquirer*, June 6, 1872.

34. *New York Herald*, June 6 (p. 11) (first quotation), 1872; *Philadelphia Inquirer*, June 6, 7 (p.2) (second, third, and fourth quotations), 1872; *Kingston (New York) Daily Freeman*, June 7, 1872.

35. *Houston Union* in *Galveston Tri-Weekly News*, July 3, 1872; *Houston Telegraph*, July 3, 1872; *Standard* in *Flake's Daily Bulletin*, July 4, 1872; *New Orleans Republican*, June 21, 1872.

36. *Galveston Daily News*, June 26, 1872 (quotation); *Tri-Weekly Galveston News*, Sept. 13, 1872.

37. *Flake's Daily Bulletin*, July 16, 23, Aug. 6, 1872; *Galveston Tri-Weekly News*, Sept. 20, Oct. 4, 1872.

38. *Flake's Daily Bulletin*, Oct. 11, 1872.

39. *Galveston Tri-Weekly News*, Oct. 16, 23, 1872.

40. *Galveston Tri-Weekly Civilian*, Nov. 13, 1872.

CHAPTER XII

1. W. J. Barker, comp., *Directory of the Members of the Thirteenth Legislature of the State of Texas* (Austin: State Journal Printing, 1873).

2. Gammel, *Laws of Texas*, vii, 456–61, 493, 467–468, 468–70, 482, 53, 46.

3. Gammel, *Laws of Texas*, vii, see index starting at p. 1510.

4. *Tri-Weekly Galveston News*, Jan. 31, Feb. 7, 12, Mar. 12, 1873; *Galveston Daily News*, Apr. 19, 1873; *Tri-Weekly Galveston Civilian*, Feb. 14, 19, 1873.

5. *Galveston Daily News*, June 3, 1873.

6. A. J. Fountain et al. to U. S. Grant, June 18, 1873, in *Galveston Daily News*, Aug. 9, 1873; Fountain et al. to U. S. Grant, in John Y. Simon, ed., *The Papers of Ulysses*

S. Grant (Carbondale and Edwardsville, Illinois: Southern Illinois University Press, 2000), vol. 24; *New York Times*, July 7, 1873.

7. Fountain et al. to U. S. Grant, June 18, 1873.

8. *New York Times*, July 7, 1873. For information on Davis's mission see: Brian C. Hosmer, "SATANTA," *Handbook of Texas Online*, accessed July 22, 2018, http://www.tshaonline.org/handbook/online/articles/fsa33. Uploaded on June 15, 2010. Modified on October 6, 2017.

9. "Think" to the editors, Galveston, April 22, 1873, in *New National Era and Citizen*, May 8, 1873.

10. "Think" to the editors, Galveston, April 22, 1873, in *New National Era and Citizen*, May 8, 1873.

11. "Olympus" to the editors, May 21, 1873, *New National Era and Citizen*, June 5, 1873. These salaries were the equivalent of $1,040 and $780 per year compared with the Galveston collector's annual salary of $4,500.

12. "Olympus" to the editor, June 28, 1873, in *New National Era and Citizen*, July 10, 1873.

13. "Call for a Convention of Colored Men," *Daily State Journal*, June 14, 1873; "Call for a Convention," *Galveston Daily News*, June 12, 1873.

14. "Call for a Convention of Colored Men," *Daily State Journal*, June 14, 1873; "The Colored Men's Convention," *Daily State Journal*, July 5 1873; *Galveston Daily News*, June 12, 1873; *Houston Weekly Telegraph*, June 12, 1873.

15. "Call for a Convention of Colored Men," *Daily State Journal*, June 14, 1873; "Call for a Convention," *Galveston Daily News*, June 12, 1873; Paul M. Lucko, "Webb, Frank J.," *Handbook of Texas Online*, accessed April 19, 2018, http://www.tshaonline.org/handbook/online/articles/fwekv.

16. "Call for a Convention of Colored Men," *Daily State Journal*, June 14, 1873; "Call for a Convention," *Galveston Daily News*, June 12, 1873.

17. "From Brenham," *Galveston Daily News*, July 4, 1873. The delegates represented, for the most part, the black belt counties—Walker, Washington, Caldwell, Waller, Montgomery, Colorado, Harris, Brazoria, Bastrop, Grimes, Travis, Fort Bend, McLennan, Galveston, Guadalupe, and Rusk Counties.

18. "The Colored Convention," *Galveston Daily News*, July 5, 1873.

19. Proceedings of the Colored Men's . . . Convention," *Daily State Journal*, July 5, 1873; "The Colored Convention," *Galveston Daily News*, July 5, 1873.

20. "Proceedings of the Colored Men's . . . Convention," *Daily State Journal*, July 5, 1873; "The Colored Convention," *Galveston Daily News*, July 5, 1873.

21. "Proceedings of the Colored Men's . . . Convention," *Daily State Journal*, July 5, 1873; "The Colored Convention," *Galveston Daily News*, July 5, 1873.

22. "Proceedings of the Colored Men's . . . Convention," *Daily State Journal*, July 7, 1873; "From Brenham," *Galveston Daily News*, July 5, 1873.

23. "Proceedings of the Colored Men's State Convention," *Daily State Journal*, July 7, 1873; "The Colored Convention," *Galveston Daily News*, July 6, 1873.

24. Charles L. Mitchel, *The Early Introduction of Bogus Freemasonry in the United States of America and Texas among Colored Masons* (San Antonio, Texas: Charles L. Mitchell, 1909), 17–22; *Leavenworth Times*, July 9, 1873; *Weekly Commonwealth* (Topeka, Kansas), July 22, 1873. It should be noted that white Masons considered the

National Grand Lodge, the Kansas Grand Lodge, and the subsequent Texas Grand Lodge to be illegitimate.

25. Stephen Kantrowitz, "'Intended for the Better Government of Man': The Political History of African American Freemasonry in the Era of Emancipation," *Journal of American History*, 96 (March 2010), pp. 1001–1026, 1002.

26. *Leavenworth Times*, July 17 (quotation), 18, 19, 20, 1873.

27. *Leavenworth Times*, July 25, 1873.

28. *Leavenworth Times*, July 9, 23 (quotations), 1873; *Atchison Daily Champion*, July 23, 1873.

29. *Leavenworth Times*, July 23, 1873.

30. *Tri-Weekly Galveston Civilian*, Mar. 5, 10, 1873.

31. *Houston Daily Mercury*, Aug. 13, 1873; *Galveston Daily News*, Aug. 6, 7, 1873.

32. *Galveston Daily News*, Aug. 13, 14, 1873; *Houston Daily Mercury*, Aug. 16, 1873.

33. *Galveston Daily News*, Aug. 20, 21, 1873; *Daily State Journal*, Aug. 20, 21, 1873.

34. *Galveston Daily News*, Aug. 18, 19, 21, 22, 1873; *Daily State Journal*, Aug. 20, 1873.

35. "Platform of the Republican Convention, Adopted at Dallas," *Galveston Daily News*, Aug. 21, 1873; "Platform of the Republican Convention," *Daily State Journal*, Aug. 20, 1873.

36. *Galveston Daily News*, Aug. 22 (quotation), Oct. 24, 1873; G. T. Ruby to John Ireland, Sept. 11, 1873, in *Galveston Daily News*, Sept. 14, 1873.

37. *Galveston Daily News*, Sept. 17, 1873.

38. *Houston Daily Mercury*, Oct. 19, 1873.

39. *Tri-Weekly Galveston News*, Nov. 7, 1873; *Galveston Daily News*, Nov. 5, 1873.

40. *Galveston Daily News*, Nov. 12, 1873.

41. *Galveston Daily News*, Dec. 4, 1873

42. Modus to the editor, Dec. 3, 1873, in *National Era and Citizen*, Dec. 11, 1873. See Carl Moneyhon, "Edmund J. Davis in the Coke-Davis Election Dispute of 1874: A Reassessment of Character," *Southwestern Historical Quarterly*, C (October 1996), 131–51, for a discussion of the election crisis.

43. *New National Era and Citizen*, Dec. 11, 18, 1873.

44. *New National Era and Citizen*, Dec. 18, 1873.

45. *Galveston Tri-Weekly News*, Dec. 19, 1873; *Houston Daily Mercury*, Dec. 16, 1873; Modus to the editor, Dec. 3, 1873, in *National Era and Citizen*, Dec. 11, 1873 (quotations).

46. *Galveston Daily News*, Dec. 28, Apr. 9, 17, May 7, 1874.

47. *Weekly Democratic Statesman*, June 4, 1874; *Galveston Daily News*, May 24, 1874. Whether or not the transaction was ever complete is not clear. Five years later the same property was listed for sale by the county for a failure to pay $49.50 in back taxes from 1874. *Galveston Daily News*, June 7, 1879.

CHAPTER XIII

1. *New Orleans Weekly Louisianian*, Aug. 15, 1874; *New Orleans Republican*, May 8, 1874.

2. Joe Gray Taylor, *Louisiana Reconstructed, 1863–1877* (Baton Rouge: Louisiana State University Press, 1974), 233–35, 256–57.

3. *Weekly Louisianian*, Aug. 22, 1874.

4. Ted Tunnell, *Crucible of Reconstruction, War, Radicalism, and Race in Louisiana, 1862–1877* (Baton Rouge: Louisiana State University Press, 1984), 202–203.

5. *Weekly Louisianian*, Sept. 26, 1874.

6. *Weekly Louisianian*.

7. *Weekly Louisianian*.

8. *Daily Picayune* (New Orleans), Jan. 29, 1875; *New Orleans Republican*, Jan. 28, 1875; *Weekly Louisianian*, Jan. 30, 1875.

9. *New Orleans Republican*, Mar. 23, 26, Apr. 18, Aug. 21 (quotation), 1875; *Weekly Louisianian*, Mar 27, Apr. 24, 1875.

10. *New Orleans Republican*, Dec. 28, 1875.

11. *New Orleans Republican*, Jan. 15 (quotation), Feb. 24, 1875; *Weekly Louisianian*, Jan. 30, Feb. 27, 1875.

12. *Weekly Louisianian*, Nov. 21, 1874.

13. *Weekly Louisianian*, May 31, Oct. 11, 1879.

14. *New Orleans Republican*, Oct. 30, Nov. 1, 1874.

15. *Weekly Louisianian*, Nov. 7, 1874.

16. Taylor, *Louisiana Reconstructed*, 302.

17. *Official Register of the United States, Containing a List of Officers and Employees in the Civil, Military and Naval Service on the First July, 1881*, vol. I (Washington, DC: Government Printing Office, 1881), p. 103; *Official Register. . . . 1877*, p. 88; *Official Register of the United States, Containing a List of Officers and Employees in the Civil, Military, and Naval Service on the First July, 1875* (Washington, DC: Government Printing Office, 1875), vol. 1, p. 145; *New Orleans Republican*, May 11, 1875; see https://www.measuringworth.com.

18. *Cincinnati Daily Star*, Aug. 4, 1875; *New Orleans Republican*, July 29 (quotation), Aug. 8, 1875.

19. *New Orleans Republican*, Dec. 12, 1875.

20. *Mandeville Wave*, in *New Orleans Times*, Sept. 27, 1875.

21. *New Orleans Republican*, June 28, 30, July 4 (quotation), 6, 1876.

22. *New Orleans Republican*, Oct. 8, 1876.

23. *New Orleans Republican*, Nov. 7, 1876.

24. Taylor, *Louisiana Reconstructed*, 491–93.

25. Taylor, *Louisiana Reconstructed*, 503–504.

26. *State Register* in *Galveston Daily News*, Apr. 28, 1877 (quotation); "Investigation of Causes of Migration of Negroes from Southern to Northern States, Testimony, pts. 2 and 3," United States Congress, *Senate Reports*, 46th Cong., 2d sess., no. 693 (ser. 1900), p. 38, 39; (Rayville, Louisiana) *Richmond Beacon*, Apr. 21, 1877.

27. *Galveston Daily News*, July 1, 1877.

28. "Investigation of Causes of Migration of Negroes from Southern to Northern States, Testimony, pt. 2," United States Congress, *Senate Reports*, 46th Cong., 2d sess., no. 693 (ser. 1900), p. 40; Family information provided by Bob Greene, Portland, Maine; United States Census. Manuscript Census of Population, 1930, District of Columbia, Enumeration District 214, Sheet 6B.

29. *Donaldsonville Chief*, July 6, 1878 (quotation); *New Orleans Observer*, May 10, 1879.

30. *Observer*, April 26, 1879, quoted in "Investigation of Causes of Migration of

Negroes from Southern to Northern States, Testimony, pts. 2," United States Congress, *Senate Reports*, 46th Cong., 2d sess., no. 693 (ser. 1900), p.38, 39 (quotations), 63, 66; (New Orleans) *Daily Picayune*, Apr. 18, 20, 22 (p. 2) 1879.

31. *New Orleans Times*, Apr. 22, 1879; Nell Irvin Painter, *Exodusters: Black Migration to Kansas after Reconstruction* (New York: W. W. Norton & Company, 1976), 213.

32. *Daily Picayune*, May 23, 1879.

33. "Investigation of Causes of Migration of Negroes from Southern to Northern States, Testimony, pts. 2 and 3," United States Congress, *Senate Reports*, 46th Cong., 2d sess., no. 693 (ser. 1900), p.51; *Baltimore Sun*, May 7, 1879 (first quotation); *New Orleans Observer*, May 10, 1879.

34. "Investigation of Causes of Migration of Negroes from Southern to Northern States, Testimony, pts. 2 and 3," United States Congress, *Senate Reports*, 46th Cong., 2nd sess., no. 693 (ser. 1900), p.54 (first quotation); *Daily Picayune*, Oct. 21, 22, 1879; *Meridional* (Abbeville, Louisiana), Oct. 18, 1879 (second quotation).

35. *Weekly Louisianian*, Feb. 21, 1880.

36. *Dallas Daily Herald*, Mar. 6, 1880; *Daily Picayune*, Feb. 24, 1880; "Investigation of Causes of Migration of Negroes from Southern to Northern States, Testimony, pts. 2 and 3," United States Congress, *Senate Reports*, 46th Cong., 2d sess., no. 693 (ser. 1900), p. 38, 58, 75; *New Orleans Daily Democrat*, Mar. 11, 1880.

37. "Investigation of Causes of Migration of Negroes from Southern to Northern States, Testimony, pts. 2 and 3," United States Congress, *Senate Reports*, 46th Cong., 2d sess., no. 693 (ser. 1900), 95.

38. *Austin Statesman*, Mar. 27, 1880; *Galveston Daily News*, Mar. 24, 25, 26, 27, 1880; (Chicago) *Inter Ocean*, Mar. 25 (quotation), 1880.

39. *Shreveport Daily Standard*, May 25, 1880; *Daily Picayune*, May 25, 1880; *Galveston Daily News*, May 25, 1880.

40. *Daily Picayune*, Dec. 3, 1880; *Official Register of the United States, Containing a List of Officers and Employees in the Civil, Military and Naval Service on the First July, 1881*, vol. I (Washington, DC. Government Printing Office, 1881), p. 103; *Official Register. . . . 1877*, p. 88; *Official Register. . . 1875*, p. 88.

41. "Two Candidates," *New Orleans Times-Democrat*, Aug. 23, Nov. 1, 1882; *New Orleans Republic* quoted in "Exit Senator Kellogg," *New Orleans Picayune*, Sept. 4, 1882; *Galveston Daily News*, Nov. 1, 1882.

42. *New Orleans Times-Democrat*, Nov. 1, 1882; *Boston Globe*, Nov. 1, 1882; *London American Register*, Nov 25, 1882; *Daily Picayune*, October 31, 1882; Family information from Bob Greene, Portland, Maine.

43. For an extensive discussion of black leadership in Reconstruction see Eric Foner, *Freedom's Lawmakers: A Directory of Black Officeholders during Reconstruction* (Baton Rouge: Louisiana University Press, 1993), particularly pp. xi–xxxii.

44. Eric Foner, "Rooted in Reconstruction: The First Wave of Black Congressmen," https://thenation.com/issue/February–11-18-2019-issue. (Accessed Feb. 4, 2019).

BIBLIOGRAPHY

PRIMARY SOURCES

MANUSCRIPT SOURCES

Austin History Center, Austin Public Library
Pease, Graham, and Niles Family Papers.

Briscoe Center for American History, University of Texas at Austin
James P. Newcomb Papers.

Library of Congress
Nathaniel Banks Papers.

National Archives
Records of the Assistant Commissioner, Texas, Bureau of Refugees, Freedmen and Abandoned Lands, RG 105 (M821).
Records of the Superintendent of Schools, Texas, Bureau of Refugees, Freedmen and Abandoned Lands, RG 105 (Microfilm 822).

Texas State Library and Archives
Texas Governor Elisha Marshal Pease Papers.

GOVERNMENT DOCUMENTS

Alvord, J. W. *Second Semi-Annual Report on Schools and Finances of Freedmen, July 1, 1866.* Washington: Government Printing Office, 1868.

_____. *Third Semi-Annual Report on Schools, January 1, 1867.* Washington: Government Printing Office, 1867.

_____. *Fourth Semi-Annual Report on Schools, July 1, 1867.* Washington: Government Printing Office, 1868.

Barker, W. J. comp. *Directory of the Members of the Thirteenth Legislature of the State of Texas.* Austin: State Journal Printing, 1873.

Gammel H. P. N. *The Laws of Texas, 1822–1897.* Austin: The Gammel Book Company, 1898.

Journal of the Reconstruction Convention which met at Austin, Texas, June 1, A.D., 1868. First Session. Austin: A Siemering & Co., Printers, 1870.

Journal of the Reconstruction Convention which met at Austin, Texas, Dec. 7, A.D. 1868. Second Session. Austin: Tracy, Siemering I& Co., 1870.

Journal of the Senate of the State of Texas, Provisional Session of 1870. Austin: Printed by Tracy, Siemering & Co., 1870.

Journal of the Twelfth Legislature, State of Texas. First Session. Austin: Tracy, Siemering & Co, State Journal Office, 1870.

Journal of the Senate of the State of Texas [Regular Session]. Austin: J. G. Tracy, State Printer, 1871.

Journal of the Senate . . . Adjourned Session.

Report of the Board of Education for Freedmen, Department of the Gulf, for the Year 1864. New Orleans: Office of the True Delta, 1865.

Sanger, George P., ed. *The Statutes at Large, Treaties and Proclamations of the United States of American from December, 1865, to March, 1867. . . .* Vol. XIV. Boston: Little, Brown, and Company, 1868.

State Journal Appendix, Containing Official Report of the Debates and Proceedings of the Twelfth Legislature of the State of Texas. Austin: Tracy, Siemering & Co., Publishers, 1870. vol. I.

Tabular Statement of Voters (white and colored) Registered in Texas . . . and Tabular Statement of Votes (white and colored) cast at Election. . . . Austin: U.S. Army, Fifth Military District, 1870.

US Bureau of the Census. *The Statistics of the Population of the United States, . . . compiled from the Original Returns of the Ninth Census, (June 1, 1870).* Washington: Government Printing Office, 1872.

United States Congress

39th Cong., 1st sess. *House Executive Documents*, no 70. *Freedmen's Bureau.*

39th Cong., 2nd sess. *Senate Executive Documents*, no. 6. *Letter of the Secretary of War.*

39th Cong., 2nd sess. *House Executive Documents*, no. 68. *New Orleans Riot.*

40th Cong., 2nd sess. *House Executive Documents*, no. 57. *Removal of Hon. E. M. Stanton and Others.*

42nd Cong., 2nd sess. *House Miscellaneous Documents*, no. 163. *Giddings v. Clark.*

46th Cong., 2nd sess. *Senate Reports*, no. 693. *Investigation of the Causes of Migration of Negroes from Southern to Northern States, Testimony.*

NEWSPAPERS

Atchison (KS) Daily Champion
Austin Republican
Austin Statesman
Boston Daily Advertiser
Boston Globe
Chicago Tribune
Cincinnati Star
Commonwealth (Topeka, Kansas)
Constitution (Middletown, Connecticut)
Daily Picayune (New Orleans, Louisiana)
Dallas Herald
Democratic Statesman (Austin, Texas)
Flake's Daily and *Semi-Weekly Bulletin* (Galveston, Texas)
Freeman's Press (Galveston, Texas)
Galveston Civilian
Galveston Daily and *Tri-Weekly News*
Galveston Republican
Houston Daily Mercury
Houston Union
Inter Ocean (Chicago, Illinois)
Janesville (WI) Gazette
Leavenworth (KS) Times
Liberator (Boston, Massachusetts)
Louisianian (New Orleans, Louisiana)
Meridional (Abbeville, Louisiana)
National Anti-Slavery Standard (New York)
National Intelligencer (Washington, DC)
National Republican (Washington, DC)
New Era and *New Era and Citizen* (Washington, DC)
New Orleans Crescent
New Orleans Republican
New Orleans Times
New Orleans Times-Democrat
New Orleans Tribune

New Orleans True Delta
New York Herald
New York World
New York Times
Observer (New Orleans, Louisiana)
Philadelphia Inquirer
Pine and Palm (Boston, Massachusetts)
Portland (ME) Daily Press
Reformer (Austin, Texas)
Representative (Galveston, Texas)
San Antonio Express
San Francisco Bulletin
Shreveport (LA) Standard
State Gazette (Austin, Texas)
State Journal (Austin, Texas)
Standard (Galveston, Texas)
Weekly Telegraph (Houston, Texas)

PRINTED PRIMARY SOURCES

Copies of correspondence from James Redpath, Haitian government General Agent of Emigration to Hayti, of persons of African and Indian origin from the U.S. and the Canadas; as well as reports to M. Plésance, Secretary of State of Exterior Relations of the Republic of Hayti; and various other items relating to the work of Redpath. From the Collection d'archives historique reunis par me Eugene L. Maximilien, Miami 1964-1972. https://archive.org/details/reportscorresponoohait. Accessed June 12, 2017.

New England Freedmen's Aid Society. *Second Annual Report of the New England Freedmen's Aid Society (Educational Commission): Presented to the Society, April 21, 1864*. Boston: New England Freedmen's Aid Society, 1864.

Redpath, James, ed., *A Guide to Hayti*. New York: G. Woolworth Colton, 1861.

Simon, John Y. *The Papers of Ulysses S. Grant*. Carbondale and Edwardsville, Illinois: Southern Illinois University Press, 2000.

SECONDARY SOURCES

Monographs

Crouch, Barry A., and Donaly Brice. *The Governor's Hounds: The Texas State Police, 1870-1873*. Austin: University of Texas Press, 2011.

Fornell, Earl W. *The Galveston Era: The Texas Crescent on the Eve of Secession*. Austin: University of Texas Press, 1961.

Foner, Eric. *Freedom's Lawmakers: A Director of Black Officeholders during Reconstruction*. Baton Rouge: Louisiana State University Press, 1993.

__________. *Gateway to Freedom: The Hidden History of the Underground Railroad*. New York: W. W. Norton & Company, 2015.

Hogue, James K. *Uncivil War: Five New Orleans Street Battles and the Rise and Fall of Radical Reconstruction*. Baton Rouge: Louisiana State University Press, 2011.

McComb, David G. *Galveston: A History*. Austin: University of Texas Press, 1986.

McKivigan, John R. *Forgotten Firebrand: James Redpath and the Making of Nineteenth Century America*. Ithaca: Cornell University Press, 2008.

Miller, Floyd John. *The Search for a Black Nationality: Black Emigration and Colonization, 1787-1863*. Urbana: University of Illinois Press, 1975.

Mitchell, Charles L. *The Early Introduction of Bogus Freemasonry in the United States of America and Texas among Colored Masons*. San Antonio: Charles L. Mitchell, 1909.

Moneyhon, Carl H. *Republicanism in Reconstruction Texas*. Austin: University of Texas Press, 1980.

_________. *Texas after the Civil War: The Struggle of Reconstruction*. College Station: Texas A&M University Press, 2004.

_________. *Edmund J. Davis: Civil War General, Republican Leader, Reconstruction Governor*. Fort Worth: TCU Press, 2010.

Nunn, W. C. *Texas Under the Carpetbaggers*. Austin: University of Texas Press, 1960.

Painter, Nell Irvin. *Exodusters: Black Migration to Kansas after Reconstruction*. New Orleans: W. W. Norton & Company, 1976.

Price, and Talbot, eds. *Maine's Visible Black History*.

Ramsdell, Charles W. *Reconstruction in Texas*. New York: Columbia University Press, 1910.

Richter, William L. *The Army in Texas During Reconstruction, 1865–1870*. College Station: Texas A&M University Press, 1987.

_________. *Over Reached on All Sides: the Freedmen's Bureau Administrators in Texas, 1865–1868*. College Station: Texas A&M University Press, 1991.

Spaw, Patsy Donald. *The Texas Senate: Civil War to the Eve of Reform, 1861–1889*. Vol. I. College Station: Texas A&M University Press, 1999.

Taylor, Joe Gray. *Louisiana Reconstructed, 1863–1877*. Baton Rouge: Louisiana State University Press, 1974.

Tunnell, Ted. *Crucible of Reconstruction: War, Radicalism, and Race in Louisiana, 1862-1877*. Baton Rouge: Louisiana State University Press, 1984.

Wallace, Ernest. *The Howling of the Coyotes: Reconstruction Efforts to Divide Texas*. College Station: Texas A&M University Press, 1979.

White, Howard A. *The Freedmen's Bureau in Louisiana*. Baton Rouge: Louisiana State University Press, 1970.

ARTICLES AND BOOK CHAPTERS

Barr, Alwyn. "Black Legislators of Reconstruction Texas." *Civil War History* 32 (December 1986): 340–352.

Boyd, Willis D. "Redpath and American Negro Colonization in Haiti, 1860-1862." *The Americas* 12 (October 1955): 169–82.

_________. "Negro Nationalism: A Factor in Emigration Projects, 1858-1861." *Journal of Negro History* 47 (January 1962): 42–53.

Kantrowitz, Stephen. "'Intended for the Better Government of Man': The Political History of African American Freemasonry in the Era of Emancipation." *Journal of American History* 96 (March 2010): 1001–26.

Messner, William F. "Black Education in Louisiana, 1863–1865." *Civil War History* 22 (1976).

Moneyhon, Carl H. "George T. Ruby and the Politics of Expediency in Texas." In *Southern Black Leaders of the Reconstruction Era*, edited by Howard N. Rabinowitz, 363-392. Chicago: University of Illinois Press, 1982.

_______. "The Democratic Party, the Ku Klux Klan, and the Politics of Fear." In *Still the Arena of Civil War: Violence and Turmoil in Reconstruction Texas, 1865–1874*, edited by Kenneth W. Howell, 243-66. Denton: University of North Texas Press, 2012.

Seraille, William. "Afro-American Emigration to Haiti during the American Civil War." *The Americas* 35 (October 1978): 185–200.

Smallwood, James, "G. T. Ruby: Galveston's Black Carpetbagger in Reconstruction Texas." *Houston Review* 5 (Winter 1983): 24–33.

Streifford, David M. "The American Colonization Society: An Application of Republican Ideology to Early Antebellum Reform." *Journal of Southern History* 45 (May 1979): 201–20.

Woods, Randall B. "George T. Ruby: A Black Militant in the White Business Community." *Red River Valley Historical Review* 1 (Autumn 1974): 269–80.

THESES AND DISSERTATIONS

Sandlin, Betty Jeffus. "The Reconstruction Constitutional Convention of 1868–1869." Unpublished PhD diss., Texas Tech University, 1970.

INDEX

GR = George Ruby